To

BEN ZEVIN

Whose help and encouragement made a great deal possible

EDITOR'S NOTE

The editor would like to express his deep indebtedness to the following persons who helped make this book possible: Jay Garon, H. Robert Gasker, Molly Strachan, John Culver, the late Joseph I. Greene, Russell F. W. Smith, Paul Jensen, and Charlotte Seitlin for editorial advice and suggestions; Arline Colgrove, Miriam Leikind, Elizabeth Elliott, and Gayle Clark of the libraries of Cleveland for their generous co-operation; Ruth Doman for editorial assistance. And to mv wife, who encouraged and assisted.

CONTENTS

INTRODUCTION

GUERRILLA: *one who carries on or assists in an irregular war or engages in irregular, though often legitimate, warfare in connection with a regular war; esp. a member of an independent band engaged in predatory excursions in wartime.*

PARTISAN: *a commander or member of a party of detached light troops engaged in making forays and harassing an enemy.*

IRREGULAR: *not belonging to the regular army organization but raised for a specific purpose.*

—Webster's New International Dictionary

THE IRREGULAR *has worn every uniform and frequently no uniform. He has fought in every country from ancient Rome to modern Burma and in every climate from the frozen wastes of Scandinavia to the tropic jungles of Malaya.*

He is a deceiver, a dissembler, a killer—ruthless and predatory. He usually stands outside the law of nations and may be legally branded a pirate, bandit, traitor or brigand.

He may be enlisted in the formal forces of a constituted government or he may have resorted to arms on his own decision. He is usually an amateur with nothing to gain but his freedom and nothing to save but his honour.

He fights a war that is not taught in schools and has no formal patterns— no traditions of line and logistics. His aim is to destroy, harass, and confuse. For the guerrilla survival is victory.

II

THE FORMS OF IRREGULAR WARFARE *are many. Amphibious guerrillas raid land areas from the sea. Air-borne guerrillas land behind the enemy lines by parachute or glider. World War II also saw the long-range penetration unit which drove far behind the enemy lines and there operated with air support. Camel and mule-borne guerrillas have invaded enemy-occupied areas. Traditionally, however, guerrilla warfare has taken the form of small units of men raiding the supply lines and bases of an invading enemy. Some of these groups grew larger and took the field as an army ready to fight for and hold ground as Tito did in Yugoslavia and Mao in China.*

III

THE HISTORY OF GUERRILLA WARFARE *is long and colourful. Irregular warfare has existed from the time the earliest primitive took an enemy village by surprise, ravaged it, and moved on. Gideon smote the enemy hip and thigh, the Maccabees fought a partisan campaign against the Syrian armies, and the Romans under Fabius Maximus harassed rather than faced Hannibal. In the centuries that followed, the Germanic tribes harried the outposts of the Roman Empire, and upon the dissolution of that empire, the Vikings raided the coasts of Europe. With the invasion of England by the Normans, the Saxons withdrew to the hills and fens from which such leaders as Hereward the Wake attempted to evict the invader. The border wars between England and the other nations of the British Isles usually took the form of irregular operations even as late as the Sinn Fein Rebellion in Ireland after World War I.*

On the Continent the Russian expansion to the east was frequently slowed down by guerrilla resistance. The Russians themselves used guerrilla warfare against Napoleon, as had the Spanish. Spain again resorted to guerrilla tactics over a century later in its civil war.

European armies seeking empires beyond the seas struggled with such native irregulars as the Zulus, the Moros, the Haitians, the American Indians, and the Afghan tribes.

In the Americas, where the terrain provided cover and space to move about, the regular soldier was incapable of coping with the frontier-trained irregular. Tactics learned from the Indians by such Revolutionary War guerrillas as Thomas Sumter, Francis Marion, and George Rogers Clark defeated the formal armies of Europe.

In the American Civil War such leaders as John Henry Morgan, Bedford Forrest, and John Singleton Mosby fused the cavalry tactics of the Europeans with the irregular tactics of the American Indians and created raiding forces which slashed at the very heart of the Union.

At the same time throughout South America, the natives under Bolivar were treating the Spaniards and their own tyrants in the same fashion.

In more recent times the irregular liaison officer who works with the native partisan has become an important element in the military forces of every country.

IV

THE TACTICS OF GUERRILLA WARFARE *are primitive, and they require cunning and imagination. The guerrilla lacks sufficient men to meet an enemy openly. He must compensate for his weakness with surprise. This becomes a weapon of incalculable strength when well used. Unable to meet the enemy in any prolonged battles into which the enemy can bring reserves—which the guerrilla never has—the guerrilla must be mobile, ready to disappear into the brush or the darkness. In case he is surprised, he must be able to move out of any position or camp that he may have taken. But this same mobility clearly limits the size of his weapons and the amount of his equipment.*

Because of his limitations of numbers and equipment, he must depend upon exact knowledge of the enemy. His intelligence, gathered from friendly civilians and his own forces, must be better than that of an army which can afford losses. A guerrilla leader usually counts his units as individuals and not as companies or regiments. So even small losses can be disastrous to a group. And as small losses come from small blunders or errors in calculation, the guerrilla leader must know the terrain over which he is operating and the enemy against whom he is fighting better than that enemy knows the terrain and himself.

With mobility, good intelligence, and surprise, the basic tactics of guerrilla warfare are the destruction of communications, the raid, and the ambush. These tactics, well and suddenly sprung on an enemy, keep him off balance and confused. At this point the guerrilla has won much of his battle.

V

THE STRATEGY OF GUERRILLA WARFARE is more complex because there can be several aims. When the guerrilla rises up in support of an outside force, as in Europe in World War II, he has achieved much if he prevents supplies from reaching the regular battle line, but he has achieved even more if he has forced the enemy to withdraw troops from that battle line to protect his supplies and fight the guerrillas.

When the guerrilla fights wholly on his own and not in support of an outside force, as happened in China and is now happening in Malaya, the strategy is very different. The aim is not to draw the enemy back toward the guerrilla unless he comes in small enough groups to eliminate him, but rather to restrict the enemy to what he considers safe areas and lines of communication. If this is the general strategy, eventually a successful guerrilla operation controls most of a country with the exception of the main highways and major cities. Such was the case in Greece, Albania, and even France before the invasion took place. Once an invader is confined to an area he considers safe, the guerrilla must select the moment in which he believes himself strong enough to strike at the enemy in those supposedly safe areas and either whittle him down or attack with the intention of holding the areas. This decision to convert from mobile and guerrilla warfare to positional and formal warfare can be fatal if made too soon.

VI

GUERRILLA WARFARE TODAY *has been revolutionized by three new developments: the radio, the aeroplane, and efficient weapons. The radio has given the guerrilla contact with his own scattered forces, as well as with the outside world. It has co-ordinated his actions with others and has made possible the relaying of intelligence which he on the spot is better able to gather than anyone else. It has enabled him to order his supplies from outside forces and to strike at targets indicated by a higher head-quarters, giving his actions greater and more specific value.*

The aeroplane has given the guerrilla a means of transportation into and out of an occupied area. It has freed him to range where he wants and meet his supplies at the point where he needs them. It has taken from him the burden of living off the land and acquiring his weapons from the enemy as he has had to do in the past. It has given him a means of evacuating his wounded and withdrawing when he is no longer able to fight.

The introduction of such automatic hand weapons as the tommy-gun has given the guerrilla a fire power which compensates for the size of his units. He can bring more to bear on a raiding point than ever before, and with the introduction of compact high explosives, he is able to attack and destroy larger targets.

VII

THE CONTEMPORARY IMPLICATIONS OF GUERRILLA WARFARE *are tremendous. The Communists have long recognized its value. Marx, Engels, Lenin, and Stalin all studied and wrote about it. The clandestine mind, the small cell structure, the absolute discipline, and Russia as a base for supplies and haven in the event of defeat have made the Communist guerrilla a dangerous force in the world. Ruthless in his disregard of reprisals against civilian populations and having nothing in the way of property to lose, he has not hesitated to take the field when assured of a sympathetic, neutral, or vacillating civilian population. By the close of World War II arms in great quantity had been dropped into Europe. Less than twenty per cent of these have been turned over to the Governments where Communist partisans operated. Thus an armed and organized guerrilla force of large size is prepared to fight in any European war.*

In the Far East the Chinese have emigrated in great numbers into almost every country of Asia, taking with them their own secret societies, of which the Communist is the largest and best organized. And no group in history has utilized guerrilla warfare as effectively as Mao Tse-tung's Chinese Communists.

However, in the past, guerrilla warfare has been an instrument in the fight for freedom against tyranny and occupation. The people of the satellite countries of Europe and Asia, if given intelligent guidance and adequate arms, may turn in guerrilla action against the Communists.

The stories in this collection are generally first-hand accounts by irregulars. The principles of selection were simple: Were they good stories—interesting, exciting and honest? And did they show fresh and different phases of guerrilla warfare? The weightier writings on irregular strategy and the politics of modern partisan warfare were omitted except for T. E. Lawrence's classic chapter on the former and Julian Amery's brilliant and brief analysis of the latter.

I have tried briefly to set these stories in time and circumstance. As editor I have tried not to draw the fine lines between resistance which takes place in urban communities and guerrilla warfare which requires space for movement. I have tried not to belabour the differences between regulars as irregulars and the native guerrilla in the field. I have avoided the fine lines drawn between a guerrilla who attempts sabotage and the saboteur, the guerrilla who collects intelligence and the spy. In short, if too rigid a definition is observed, a fascinating and vital subject could be reduced to a dull and academic one. The irregular's objective is simply to destroy the enemy. This book attempts to tell of the many ways in which he has tried to do so.

I. R. B.

MORGAN'S MARCH ON PANAMA

BY JOHN ESQUEMELING

COLD AND UNDECLARED WARS *have long been fought along the fringes of empire, but none was longer or bloodier than that between England and Spain in the sixteenth and seventeenth centuries. Intermittently, for over a century, the ships and colonies of both countries were targets for the irregulars authorized to plunder by their governments.*

Protests and apologies became commonplace formalities. Neither country gave or expected mercy. Though religious differences were frequently cited as a cause, for England the prizes were money and territory. Gold plate flowed from the Spanish colonies, and the English adventurers diverted as much of it as possible towards the British Isles. That the running fight was two-sided is clearly shown by the challenge dated July 5, 1669 which was posted on a tree at Point Negril in the West Indies:

> *I, Captain Manuel Rivera Pardal, to the chief of the squadron of privateers in Jamaica. I am he who this year have done that which follows. I went on shore at Caimonos and burnt 20 houses and fought with Captain Ary and took from him a catch laden with provisions and a canoa. And I am he who took Captain Baines and did carry the prize to Cartegena and now am arrived to this coast and have burnt it. And I am come to seek Admiral Morgan, with two ships of war of 20 guns, and having seen this, I crave he would come out upon the coast and seek me, that he might see the valour of the Spaniards. And because I had no time I did not come to the mouth of Port Royal to speak by word of mouth in the name of my King whom God preserve.*

The message reached Morgan at Jamaica, as did a commission of the Queen of Spain, to one of her Captains authorizing him to 'execute all the hostilities which are permitted in war, by taking possession of the ships, islands, places and ports which the English have . . .' in the West Indies. The challenge was accepted, but on English terms, and the war was fought in places of Morgan's choosing. He assembled his fleet and the men who, privateers, have been remembered in popular history as pirates. He chose Spanish ground, and with a fleet attacked the Island of Old Providence, moved on and took the Spanish fort at Chagres on the Isthmus of Panama, and then set out on one of the strangest and most courageous expeditions in history.

1

The story is told by a Dutch doctor, Henry Smeeks, who wrote The History of the Buccaniers *under the pen name of John Esquemeling. It has been modernized in part by the editor.*

CAPTAIN MORGAN left the castle at Chagres for Panama City with 1,200 men, 5 boats, and 32 canoes. On the first day they sailed only six leagues to a place called De los Bracos. The men were so cramped in the crowded boats that a small party went ashore here to stretch their limbs and sleep for a few hours. After they had rested a while, they scoured the neighbouring plantations looking for food. However, the Spaniards had carried all their provisions with them when they fled, and though this was only the first day of the journey, Morgan's men were already so short of food most of them had to satisfy themselves with a pipe of tobacco.

Very early the next morning, they continued their journey and came at evening to a place called Cruz de Juan Gallego. Here, they had to leave their boats because the river had gone dry and trees had fallen into it blocking the way.

The guides told them that about two leagues further on the country would be very good to continue the journey by land. Morgan planned to leave 160 men with the boats, intending to use the boats as a place of refuge in case of necessity. He gave these men strict orders not to leave the boats under any pretext. He feared they might be surprised and cut off in an ambush by the Spaniards who could easily be hiding in the surrounding woods.

The next morning, the third day of their journey, the rest of the men went ashore and began their march. They found the way so difficult that Morgan decided to transport some of the men in canoes to a place farther up the river called Cedro Bueno. They made their way up river with great difficulty and then sent the canoes back for those who were left behind. However, by evening the whole party was reunited. They were anxious to meet any Spaniards or Indians in hopes of taking some food for they were almost starving.

On the fourth day most of the pirates marched across country led by one of the guides. The rest went by water in the canoes. During the day two of the canoes kept ahead of this party searching out both sides of the river for ambushes. The Spaniards had spies who were clever and could at any time give warning to any place six hours before the pirates arrived there. About noon they found themselves near a place called Torna Cavallos, and the guide of the canoes began to shout that he saw a camp site. His shouts encouraged the pirates who were more interested in finding food than anything else. However, when they reached the place, they found nobody there. The Spaniards had fled and had left behind them only a few empty leather bags and a few crumbs scattered on the ground where they had eaten. The pirates were furious and tore down the few huts the Spaniards had built. Then, looking for anything to satisfy the gnawing in their stomachs, they began to eat the leather bags. They made a huge banquet of those, and even fought over the size of the pieces each one got. By the size of the camp site, they estimated about five hundred Spaniards had been there, whom, if they had been able to take them, the pirates would have certainly roasted or broiled to satisfy their hunger.

After they finished their leather lunch, the pirates marched on until they came to a place called Torma Munni. Here they found another camp site as barren as the first. They searched the neighbouring woods and found nothing to eat. Those who had saved some of their lunch made supper of it. First they took the leather and sliced it into small pieces and then beat it between two stones and rubbed it, dipping it often into the river to make it soft and tender. Then they scraped off the hair and roasted or broiled it on the fire. When it was cooked, they cut it into small pieces and drank it down with large quantities of water.

They continued their march the fifth day and about noon came to a place the guide called Barbacoa. Here they found traces of another camp, but the place was as barren of food as the others had been. A short distance away they found several small plantations but there was nothing to eat in any of them. Finally, after a careful search, they found a grotto which seemed to have been recently cut out of the rocks. Here they found two sacks of meal and wheat, two large jars of wine, and some fruit. Morgan distributed the food to those in the worst condition, and they continued their march. Those who were unable to continue on foot changed places with some of the men in the canoes, and they travelled until late that night and rested at an abandoned plantation.

On the sixth day they continued their march as before, some by land through the woods and the rest in the canoes. However, the going was slower now as the terrain was more rugged and the men were extremely weak from hunger. They tried, without success, to satisfy their stomachs with leaves and green herbs and grass. They arrived shortly at a plantation where they found a barn full of maize. They beat down the doors and began to eat it dry. Then they distributed the remainder and continued their march. After about an hour they found an Indian camp. They no sooner discovered this than they threw away the maize they were carrying, as they believed they would find food in abundance. However, they were wrong. They could see on the other side of the river about one hundred Indians who fled. Some of the pirates leaped into the river in hopes of taking some prisoners. But the Indians were much more nimble, and after killing two or three of the pirates with their arrows, they stood at a distance shooting at them.

They went no farther that day as they had to cross the river and continue their march on the other side, and so they camped where they were. That night there was little sleep. Around the fires could be heard complaints about Morgan and the way he was conducting the campaign. Many of the men were already eager to turn back. Some few swore they would not go on. A third group laughed at all of the grumblings, and one of the guides comforted them with the prospects of the riches of Panama.

On the morning of the seventh day they all cleaned their arms, and everyone discharged his pistol or musket without bullets to test their firelocks. When they finished, they crossed the river in canoes and continued their journey until noon when they sighted a village called Cruz. Being a good distance from the place, they were elated at what they believed to be fire from the chimneys. They rushed forward anticipating food only to arrive, sweating and panting, in an empty village where every building with the exception of the king's property had been put to the torch. The only things left behind were a few cats and dogs, which the pirates immediately killed and cooked. After a search, they found fifteen or sixteen jars of Peruvian wine and a leather sack of bread. As soon as they drank the wine, all of them fell ill. At first they thought the wine was poisoned, which frightened them into believing they were dying. It turned out, however, that they had eaten so much trash in the preceding days that their stomachs had rebelled. They were so ill during the rest of the day that they spent the night where they were.

They were now twenty-six Spanish leagues from Chagres and eight from Panama. This was the last point to which they could travel by boats, a fact which explained the large warehouses of the king. From this point on all supplies for Panama had travelled overland.

Morgan was forced to put all his men ashore and leave his canoes even though the men were in the worst physical condition. However, as he did not want to lose the canoes, he decided to send them all back except one which he might need to carry intelligence.

Assuming that many of the Spaniards and Indians belonging to this village had fled to neighbouring plantations, he warned his men against travelling in groups of less than one hundred. He feared surprise attacks and rightly, as one small group, foraging against orders, was attacked and fell back to join the main body. They had been assaulted with great fury, and one of their number had been kidnapped by the Spaniards. Even the restless vigilance of Morgan could not prevent such occurrences with undisciplined men.

On the morning of the eighth day Morgan sent two hundred men ahead of the main body to find a way to Panama, and search out any ambushes. The place where Morgan had to pass was especially suited to ambush as the defiles were only wide enough to hold ten or twelve men in a file and sometimes even fewer. They had marched about ten hours when they came to a place called Quebrada Obscura. Suddenly, and apparently from nowhere, several thousand arrows fell on them. It was presumed they were shot from a high, rocky mountain through which a narrow tunnel had been excavated. The arrows completely confused the pirates who were unable to locate their source. However, as the first barrage was not followed up, Morgan moved a little further on and entered a wood. As they did so, they could see Indians fleeing before them to another observation post. One group attempted to make a determined stand against the advance party and were holding their ground until the chief was wounded. His valour proved greater than his strength as he tried to raise himself and strike at one of the pirates with his javelin. Before he could strike a second time, he was shot to death with a pistol. Many of his followers were shot down defending their country.

The rest of the Indians escaped, leaving eight pirates dead and ten wounded. The pirates moved on and in a little while they came to a large open field where they could make out a small group of Indians on a distant hill. Morgan sent fifty men to see if he could capture any of them. He needed information and food, but the swift and well-fed Indians were not to be caught. While the attempt at pursuit was made, the wounded pirates were cared for.

The pirates found themselves in a wood with a mountain on each side. The Indians were situated on one of the mountains and the pirates took possession of the mountain opposite. Morgan was convinced that the Spaniards had set an ambush in the woods, which seemed convenient for that purpose. He sent two hundred men down to spring the trap and search the woods. The Spaniards and Indians on their side, seeing the pirates come down the mountain and head for the woods, seemed ready to fight as they did the same thing. But once they got into the woods and out of sight of the pirates, they disappeared, leaving the way open for Morgan to move his men through.

About nightfall a great rain fell, and the pirates marched faster hoping to find some cover for themselves and their arms, but the Indians had set fire to every house in the area. They had stripped the area of food and cattle, hoping to force Morgan's withdrawal. Eventually the pirates found a few small shepherds' huts into which they piled their arms, but the men remained outside in the rain, which continued to fall all night.

The next morning, the ninth, Morgan continued his march at daybreak while the fresh air of morning lasted. The overhanging clouds of the morning were some protection against the scorching sun. After about two hours they discovered a troop of twenty Spaniards observing them. Again they tried to capture them, but the Spaniards disappeared into the rocks and the hills leaving no trace behind. Finally, the pirates came to a high mountain; they scaled it, and in the distance they could see the South Sea.

This happy sight seemed to the pirates like the end of their labours. From where they stood, they could see one ship and six boats moving from Panama towards the islands of Tavogo and Tavogilla. When they came down from the mountain, they entered a valley where they found a large number of cattle and burden animals which they killed in quantity. While some were employed in the slaughter and cleaning of the cows, horses, bulls, and asses, others busied themselves gathering wood and building fires. After they cut the meat into convenient pieces they roasted and ate it with incredible haste and appetite. Their hunger was such that they resembled cannibals more than Europeans at the banquet as the blood ran down their beards onto their bellies.

When they had satisfied their hunger, Morgan ordered them to continue the march. Here again he sent before the main body some fifty men hoping to take some prisoners. He was very concerned that in the nine days he had found no one who could tell him the condition and forces of the Spaniards. At evening they came on two hundred Spaniards who shouted at the pirates and fled. A short time later they came within sight of the highest steeple of Panama. Once they sighted the steeple, they were incredibly happy, shouted and threw their hats in the air as if they had already won the battle and captured the city. They sounded their trumpets and beat their drums in a pre-victory celebration. Then they camped for the night, impatient for morning when they planned to attack the city.

Later on about fifty horsemen came out of the city to see what Morgan was up to. They came almost within musket shot of the pirate camp. They yelled for a time and threatened the pirates, and after making a great deal of noise, they withdrew to the city, leaving seven or eight of their number behind to watch the pirates. Immediately afterwards the big guns of the city started shelling Morgan's camp without causing any damage as the balls fell far short. The firing continued all through the night. About this time the two hundred Spaniards who had been seen earlier in the day appeared, seemingly with intent to block any attempt of Morgan's to withdraw. But the pirates, who were now in a sense trapped, instead of being frightened, placed their sentries and finished eating the remains of the slaughter they had made earlier in the day. After they were finished, they went to sleep on the grass with complete assurance and a great deal of satisfaction. They were confident of the results of the next day and were impatient for it.

On the morning of the tenth day, Morgan placed all of his men in order and with trumpets and drums sounding, the pirates continued their march directly towards the city. However, one of the guides pleaded with Morgan not to take the main highway leading into the city because of the increased chance of meeting heavy resistance and ambush. Morgan finally took his advice and cut through the woods even though the way was more difficult. When the Spaniards saw them approach over a route in which they were unprepared, they left their posts and large guns and came out to meet them.

The Governor of Panama assembled forces, which consisted of two cavalry units and four infantry regiments, and a large number of wild bulls which were driven by the Indians with some Negroes and others to help them.

The pirates came to the top of a small hill where they could see the city and the surrounding countryside. Here they saw the people of Panama extended in battle order. There were so many of them that for the first time the pirates began to doubt their chances of winning the battle. Most of them wished they were elsewhere or at least freed of the obligation to enter a fight which seemed so clearly against them. They thought about their position for some time, for they expected no quarter from an enemy against whom they had committed so many cruelties on all occasions. However, they encouraged each other and decided to fight. Morgan divided his men into three groups and sent forward about two hundred who were best able to handle guns. In this way they marched down the hill to meet the Spaniards who were waiting for them. As soon as they drew near, the Spaniards began to shout 'God save the King'. The cavalry immediately charged, but the field was so broken and soft that they were unable to turn and whirl as they desired. The pirates dropped to one knee and fired into the charging cavalry, and the battle was on. The Spaniards put up a good fight, but they were unable to split up the pirate ranks, and when the Spanish infantry tried to follow the cavalry, the pirates laid down enough fire to separate them. Seeing that this tactic would not work, the Spaniards tried to set the wild bulls against the pirates at their back in a desperate attempt to disorganize them. But most of the cattle ran away frightened by the noise of the battle. Some few broke through the pirate ranks; they were quickly shot after doing no more harm than tearing up the colour standards.

The battle lasted almost two hours during which time most of the Spanish horses were killed. The rest fled. And the infantry, seeing that they could not win, fired their last shots, dropped their guns, and ran their separate ways. The pirates were too tired from their long march and the fight to follow them. Many of the Spaniards hid themselves near by in the shrubbery, and most of these were caught and killed without quarter. Some religious men were brought as prisoners, but Morgan was deaf to their pleas and ordered all of them pistolled.

Shortly afterward a captain was brought before Morgan who interrogated him in detail about the strength of the city and found out that there had been four hundred horsemen, twenty-four companies of infantrymen each complete with one hundred men and about two thousand of the wild bulls. He also found out that the city had been fortified, trenches had been dug, and that at the highway entrance a fort had been built which housed eight large guns and was defended by about fifty men.

Once Morgan had this information he ordered an immediate march to approach the city from another direction. But before setting out, he inspected his men and found out that he had lost more than he had originally believed. Of the Spaniards he counted over six hundred dead in addition to the wounded and prisoners. Instead of being discouraged, however, his men were proud of their victory when they learned the total numbers of the Spanish, and once they were rested they moved directly toward the city.

It was a difficult march because the Spaniards had moved their larger guns to fire at the pirates as they approached. Morgan lost men with every step, but he did not break his advance and entered the city under fire. Within three hours it was his.

MORGAN FIRED THE CITY—*perhaps by accident*—*but he gained his rewards, not the least of them being a prize of over 400,000 gold pieces of eight, large quantities of jewels, silks, linens, plate, and gold and silver lace. Morgan returned to Jamaica a hero and a rich man. Eventually, after making his peace with the King for having overstepped his authority, he was knighted.*

But Morgan did not forget the Dutchman who wrote The History of the Buccaniers. *One third of that little book was about the capture and burning of Panama, and the barber-adventurer had libelled the man who was now a knight. The references in lurid detail to Morgan's 'tyrannical cruelty' which had 'blotted out all the splendour of his glory' were more than the now respectable privateer could take. He sued the English publishers for £10,000 damages and received two hundred pounds and twenty shillings costs along with an apology.*

But the Dutchman really won, for as the years have gone on, it is Smeeks' book that has been the basis for Morgan's reputation.

MORGAN'S MARCH ON PANAMA

men with every step, but he did not break his advance and entered
the city under fire. Within three hours it was his.

PARTISANS AGAINST NAPOLEON

BY DENIS DAVYDOV

MORGAN HIRED THE CITY—perhaps by accident—but he gained his
rewards, not the least of which was the 400,000 gold pieces of
eight, large quantities of jewels, silks, linens, plate, and gold and silver lace.

shilling cost along until in a hostage.

FEW GENERALS IN HISTORY *were as capable as Napoleon in dealing with
regular enemy troops and as incapable of coping with determined irregulars.*

*Cutting through Spain in 1808, he easily overran the militia hurriedly
brought against him, but the Spanish were only briefly beaten. They gave
up fighting Napoleon his way, dissolved their army into small units and,
with the support of British regulars, began to fight so successful an irregular
war that the very word guerrilla stems from this campaign. Guerrilla
chiefs José Martin Días and the Minas achieved such control over the areas
in which they operated that they were able to levy custom dues on all French
goods entering into Spain, excepting military supplies, which they did not
permit to pass without a fight.*

*In the summer of 1812, Napoleon turned his attentions east, crossed the
Niemen River, and invaded Russia. Driving over the scorched earth on
the greatest military adventure up to that time, he reached Moscow in
September. He was exhausted. His army collapsed from fatigue, and his
expanded supply lines broke down. He faced a Russian winter without
food, and after a month's looting he started the long march out of Russia.
But before he left an event took place which was to make a great deal of
difference in Napoleon's retreat.*

*A young soldier-poet by the name of Denis Davydov, remembering the
Spanish, requested permission to form a guerrilla unit to fight Napoleon.
A reluctant and not-too-imaginative field-marshal gave Davydov one
hundred and eighty men, and with this diminutive force the Russians
began the guerrilla campaign that played such an important part in their
war of liberation.*

*Davydov's journal was so descriptive of guerrilla warfare in Russia that
the Soviet Government reprinted it in 1941 in the midst of the war against
Hitler. The Davydov methods were so similar to those used against the
invading Nazis that his journal could readily be an account of World
War II. This portion of that journal was selected and translated for this
volume by F. E. Sommer.*

OUR road became more dangerous as we went farther away
from our army. The general and voluntary arming of the

population barred our way. In every village the gates were closed and guarded by old and young people with forks, stakes, hammers, and even some firearms. At every settlement one of us had to get close and tell the inhabitants that we were Russians, that we were coming to their aid and to the defence of the Orthodox Church. Their reply frequently was a shot or a hammer thrown at us, but fate protected us. We could have avoided the villages but I wanted to spread the rumour that our forces were coming back; I wanted to strengthen the will of the peasants to defend themselves and to induce them to inform us at once of the approach of the enemy. Thus we had to negotiate at each settlement before they let us in. But once they were convinced that we were Russians, they offered the soldiers bread, beer, and cake. Whenever I asked the inhabitants later on why they took us for French, they always pointed to my hussar mantilla and said: 'You see, sir, this is similar to their uniforms.'—'But don't I talk to you in Russian?'—'Well, they have all kinds of people in their army.' From then on I dressed in a peasant's coat, I let my beard grow and I substituted an image of Saint Nicholas for my order of Saint Anna; I also began to talk to them in their own dialect.

But these dangers were insignificant compared to those which awaited us in the territory occupied by the enemy troops and transports. The small number of people in our group in comparison with those escorting the enemy's transports or even with the bands of marauders, the strong detachments looking for us as soon as it became known that we were near Vyazma, the danger that unarmed people afraid of the French might give us away—all this threatened us with ruin. In order to avoid it, we passed the day on the heights near Skugorev, hiding and watchful. Before night we distributed fires at a short distance from the village and then, going much farther away from the place where we intended to spend the night, we lit other fires. Finally, retiring into the woods, we spent the night without fires. If we happened to meet any passer-by, we kept him until we were ready to move on. But if he succeeded in escaping, we had to change our place again. Depending upon the distance of the object on which we wanted to make an attack, we got up one, two, or three hours before dawn and broke into the transport of the enemy. If possible, we struck still another blow and then we returned by devious roads to the protection of the woods through which we gradually reached Skugorev. Thus we fought and wandered around from August 29 to September 8. I had been in savage battles before and I was afterwards, but I never shall forget that difficult time when I passed my nights leaning against the saddle of my horse and standing with my hands on the reins.

Having found out that a band of marauders had come to the village of Tokarevo, we attacked at dawn and captured ninety men who were covering a baggage train with household goods stolen from the population. The Cossacks and peasants had hardly begun to divide the booty when our outposts, concealed around the village, warned us that another gang of marauders was nearing Tokarevo. We got on our horses and hid behind the huts. A few yards from the end of the village we attacked from all sides with shouts and shooting. We tore into the middle of the train and took another seventy prisoners.

I distributed among the peasants the rifles and cartridges taken from the enemy and urged them to defend their property. I also gave them instructions how to deal with bands of marauders outnumbering them.

'Receive them with friendliness, offer them whatever you have to eat and, especially, to drink with a deep bow, because they do not know Russian and will understand gestures better than words. Put those who are intoxicated to sleep and when you are sure that they really are sleeping, rush for their arms and carry out what God has commanded you to do to the enemies of the Christian Church and of your native land. After exterminating them, bury the bodies in some inaccessible place. Be sure that no freshly turned ground marks the burial place. Cover it with stones, wood, ashes, or anything else. Burn all the booty or bury it in the same way as the bodies of the French. These precautions are necessary because another band of marauders surely would dig up the patch of fresh earth in the hope of finding money or other belongings of yours. If they should find, instead, the bodies of their comrades and things which had belonged to them, they would slay all of you and burn your village.'

Turning to the village elder, I continued: 'Now you watch, brother, that my orders are carried out. Always have three or four lads ready to jump on horses and gallop away in different directions to find me whenever they see a very large number of Frenchmen and I will come to your aid. Now you go and tell your neighbours what I just have told you.'

I did not want to give these instructions in writing because I was afraid that they might fall into the hands of the enemy and give away the methods which I had explained to the inhabitants for the extermination of the marauders. Then I had the prisoners tied up, and I sent them with ten Cossacks and twenty peasants to Yukhnov where they were to be delivered to the city administration against receipt.

As it was not my duty to defeat vagrants but to destroy transports of provisions and war material for the French army, I turned toward Tsarev-Zaimishch on the Smolensk highway. It was a clear and cold evening. A heavy rain had fallen the day before and had beaten down the dust on the path which we were following. Six versts from the village we ran into a horse patrol of the enemy but they did not see us and continued unaware. If it had not been necessary for me to get accurate information whether Tsarev-Zaimishch was occupied by troops and about their strength, I could have let these scouts pass without attacking them. But under the circumstances I sent a sergeant and ten Cossacks with good horses to intercept them and I ordered another ten Cossacks to attack the patrol directly. When the scouts saw themselves surrounded, they stopped and surrendered without a fight. There were ten privates and one junior officer. Through them we found out that a transport with ammunition was staying for the day in Tsarev-Zaimishch and that it was guarded by two hundred and fifty cavalrymen.

In order to take them completely by surprise, we turned off the road and went across the fields, taking cover under the edge of the forest. But when we came out on a clearing three versts from the village, we met a foraging party of the enemy, about forty men. When they saw us, they galloped at a headlong pace back to their detachment. There was no time for tactical formations. I left with our prisoners thirty hussars who could serve as a reserve in case of necessity and rushed with the remaining twenty hussars and seventy Cossacks in pursuit of those who had fled before us; we entered Tsarev-Zaimishch almost simultaneously with them. Terror magnifies things and is inseparable from panic. When we appeared, all soldiers scattered. Some we took prisoners not only without arms but even without clothes, others we pulled out of sheds. Only one group of thirty men tried to defend themselves, but they were mown down.

This raid netted us one hundred and nineteen privates, two officers, ten provision wagons, and one wagon with cartridges. The rest of the convoy fled. We surrounded our booty and quickly took it to Skugorevo. As my group had been in action or on the move uninterruptedly for thirty hours, we needed rest and therefore we remained there until the evening of the following day.

To make it easier for the horses, I used a method which I had observed several years before. Having designated four Cossacks for the outposts and twenty for a reserve, I divided the remaining ninety-six men into two groups and gave orders to unsaddle two horses in each group for one hour while their saddle gall was washed and powdered. After an hour these horses were saddled again while new ones were unsaddled. In this manner ninety-six horses were refreshed in twenty-four hours. Upon request, I gave permission to the reserve, too, to unsaddle one horse at a time.

On September 6 we turned toward Fedorovskoye, on the Smolensk highway, spreading everywhere the instructions which I had given to the peasants in Tokarevo. On the road we met a private who had escaped from a transport of prisoners taken from the Moscow Infantry Regiment. He told us that their transport of two hundred privates had stopped for the night in Fedorovskoye and that the convoy consisted of fifty men. We doubled our pace and as soon as we appeared near the village, everything in the transport assumed a different character, even without our help. The prisoners became the convoy and the convoy became the prisoners.

Soon afterwards I heard of the arrival in Yukhnov of administrative and judicial officials and also of two weak Cossack regiments wandering in the district of Yukhnov without any common purpose. This caused me to head at once for Yukhnov where I arrived on the 8th. I went immediately after the two objectives which were of interest to me, firstly the general arming of the population and, secondly, the joining of the Cossack regiments to my force. The former was accomplished without obstacles, thanks to the full co-operation of the local authorities. One hundred and twenty rifles which had been captured by my men and one large wagon with cartridges were made available for use by the first armed people, to whom I assigned a concentration point in the village of Znamenskoye.

The second objective required some diplomacy on my part. Although the commander of the Cossack regiments in question, Lieutenant-General Shepelev, had been known to me as a kind and noble character, I also was aware of the fact that a military command is very flattering to the personal pride. I was sure that as long as my force remained independent, my request for the incorporation of these regiments could not have any success. Therefore I pretended to place myself voluntarily under Shepelev's command. I sent him a report in which I said: 'Having chosen for reconnoitring a district adjacent to the government which is under the direction of Your Excellency for the military operations, I consider it an honour to

serve under your command and a duty to report all happenings.'
My good Shepelev melted away with rapture!

On the 9th I sent another courier with a vivid description of the
advantages of unity in action. I concluded the report with the
humble request to reinforce me with the Cossack regiments which,
like my own force, were under his command. While our diplomatic
correspondence was going on, I busied myself sending out through
the rural government instructions for the general arming. On the
10th I received orders in the evening to take under my command the
Cossack regiments which I had requested.

On September 12 I undertook reconnoitring in Vyazma. At
dawn we attacked within sight of the city an enemy detachment
covering a transport with provisions and artillery shells. The resistance was not equal to the impetuousness of the attack and the success
exceeded my expectations. Two hundred and seventy privates and
six officers laid down their arms and about one hundred men were
left on the battlefield. Twenty carts with provisions and twelve
artillery caissons with shells fell into our hands. Immediately two
wagons with cartridges and three hundred and forty rifles were
placed at the disposal of the commander in charge of the general
arming, and thus from the first few days on I already had in
Znamenskoye equipment ready for almost five hundred men.

On the 15th, about 8 a.m., the sentries discovered a large number
of wagons covered with white linen. We galloped a few steps and
saw them moving along like a fleet under sail. Three officers with
hussars and the Cossack regiments hurried to cut them off. The
vanguard struck at the convoy, which fled after a few pistol shots,
but as they were surrounded, they dropped their weapons. Two
hundred and sixty privates from different regiments, with their
horses, two officers, and twenty wagons full of bread and oats,
together with all horse trappings, were captured by us.

The success of my raids stirred the French governor to action. He
assembled all mounted troops which passed through and formed a
strong detachment of two thousand privates, eight officers, and one
staff officer, whom he ordered to clean out the whole stretch between Vyazma and Gzhat, to stop my raids, to smash my force by
all means, and to bring me to Vyazma alive or dead. I heard about
this 'discourtesy' on September 13 and on the 15th I was informed
that this detachment already was approaching Fedorovskoye. As
far as possible, I did not want any chances to interfere with my
actions and my moves. Therefore my entire force left Teplukha at
once. When we were out of sight, we made a sharp turn to the

right, crossed the highway, and retreated to Andreyevskoye. There, we spent the night using extreme caution and then proceeded at a fast pace to the village of Pokrovskoye.

My movements were based on three assumptions; either the detachment sent against me, after losing my track, would return to its original destination, that means continue on the road to Moscow, or, by chasing me from one place to another, would exhaust its horses and thereby offer me an opportunity to defeat them with less difficulty; or they could split up to catch me and this might expose them to defeat by individual groups.

On the evening of the 18th, after our arrival in Pokrovskoye, an escaped Russian war prisoner was brought before me who told me that exactly one thousand of our prisoners had stopped in Yurenev, guarded by a total of three hundred men. Avoiding Nikolskoye, we stopped about a quarter of a verst from Yurenev; there was still an hour left before dawn. Unfortunately, while our group was on the move, the transport of prisoners started moving again and thus made it possible for three battalions of Polish infantry to take up quarters in the village or camp nearby. When day broke, I looked over the terrain. Then I ordered sixty infantrymen to penetrate to the centre of the village, to yell 'Hurrah! Our people come over here!' and to attack the enemy with bayonets. At the same time the Bug cavalry regiment was to ride around the village and cut off the road of retreat. I kept my original group and the Teptyar regiment in reserve.

My orders were carried out to the letter, but the success was not what I had expected. When the infantry advanced into the village, my men found themselves in the midst of a strong enemy battalion. Shots resounded from the windows and in the streets. Standing shoulder to shoulder like brothers, my heroic soldiers opened for themselves with their bayonets a path to the Bug regiment which stood ready to extend a helping hand. In five minutes of battle thirty-five of my sixty men had fallen or were mortally wounded. The cavalry had cut off completely the battalion under attack, which intended to hold out awaiting the arrival of expected reinforcements. The besieged intensified their fire upon us from huts and gardens. Eager for vengeance, I called for volunteers to set fire to the huts where the enemy was hiding. More than two hundred men were caught in the flames. Realizing their inescapable ruin, the men ran out of the village in all directions. The Bug regiment captured one hundred and nineteen privates and one captain. The remnants retreated towards the other two battalions which were coming to their assistance. As we could not do anything with them, I ordered a gradual retreat. Their fire did little damage to us and we soon withdrew out of range.

At that time, one of the patrols reported that there was an artillery park about three versts from the battlefield. After I had sent the wounded under the protection of the Teptyar regiment to Pokrovskoye, I galloped with the remaining soldiers to the park and seized it without the slightest resistance. Returning from our partly successful expedition, I had at least the consolation that I had won over the field-marshal to my idea, and that light detachments had been assigned to harass the communications of the enemy.

We hardly had settled down in Pokrovskoye when I received reports that a transport of our prisoners numbering four hundred men had stopped not far from us. I ordered seven selected men to go to the village, shoot off their pistols, and disappear quickly. I wanted to alarm the convoy and make them look for a quieter place to stay. My plan turned out to be a complete success. As soon as the shots were heard in the village, the whole transport began to file out of the village. We attacked, and with the aid of the prisoners, the convoy of one hundred and sixty-six men and four officers was disarmed in an instant.

I was now burdened with too much booty, and I retired to the village of Gorodishche to give my men a rest. I distributed among the peasants what we did not need.

DAVYDOV *learned that to be a successful partisan he had to assume the role of a simple Russian peasant. It was as such a leader that Tolstoy immortalized him in* War and Peace *as Vasili Denisov. It was also as such a leader that he fought with higher headquarters to gain recognition for his men. However, when his men were finally decorated and he was forgotten, Davydov was indignant. He told headquarters what medals he felt he deserved. He received them at once.*

RANGER MOSBY

BY VIRGIL C. JONES

RANGER JOHN S. MOSBY, *who formed his partisan cavalry unit under Confederate General Jeb Stuart's direction, was one of the few men of his time aware of the basic concepts of good guerrilla warfare. The Virginian, ex-lawyer turned scout and then partisan chief, led his men for over two years across his native state. He harassed the Union supply wagons, destroyed their rail communications, kidnapped their generals, raided their camps, and gathered the intelligence reports that became the basis of several major campaigns.*

Mosby's genius was such that General Lee said, 'I wish I had a hundred more like him.' And General Grant, who in the years after the war was to become his friend at the expense of Mosby's reputation in the South, wrote, 'There were probably but few men in the South who could have commanded successfully a separate detachment, in the rear of the opposing army and so near the border of hostilities, as long as Mosby did without losing his entire command.'

Believing his safety lay in doing those things the enemy considered impossible, the slim little sandy-haired guerrilla colonel made his head-quarters near Washington. It was from this headquarters that he went to join his men that cold Saturday of January 9, 1864, near Upperville, Virginia. He believed that surprise was his best offensive weapon and that only guerrillas would be out in such weather.

His biographer, Virgil Carrington Jones, relates this story of the raider.

THEY rode up out of the horizon in all directions and approached slowly, alone or in small groups, cutting their own paths across the unbroken expanse. Some had been through massive drifts, as attested by the snow still clinging to the horses' sleek coats. It had been a terrific blizzard. Even now the skies were grey and fore-boding, and some of the younger men predicted there would be more snow before night. But the older members shook their heads. Too cold, they said.

By noon, one hundred and six men, made up of about an equal representation from each of the three companies, had arrived. The size of the force seemed to satisfy Mosby and he took the lead as they moved off, striking north. At dusk the cavalcade, bearing anything but a military appearance with its wide assortment of heavy coats, mufflers and boots, stopped at the home of Henry Heaton, well up in Loudoun County. This Ranger had forged ahead to notify his family of the approach of the horde of hungry fighters. When they arrived, fires blazed in every room of the spacious mansion, and downstairs in the large dining-room awaited the kind of food best suited to the cold ride ahead.

One, two, three hours passed in quick succession. At last a courier appeared from Stringfellow. The scout, this messenger said, had been over the entire area again and had found everything favourable to attack. He was waiting up near Harper's Ferry with ten men.

Mosby ordered his command into the saddle. It was 9 p.m. The clouds of the morning and afternoon had disappeared, and in their stead had come a clear stillness and a bluish-black canopy dotted by shivering stars.

For hours through the bitter cold the Rangers rode. Each man bore his own troubles; there was no talking. As they trotted along, many held the reins in their teeth and slid their hands under the saddle blankets next to the warm skin of their mounts. Quite a few cut holes for their heads in the centre of blankets and draped them like tents over their shoulders. Now and then some of them, to get their blood in circulation, dropped stiffly from the saddle and trotted along in the spray of fine snow kicked up by the horses' muffled hoofs.

Some time in the aching hours of early morning, Mosby halted and ordered fires built. John Underwood and others accustomed to the forest scattered through the trees, feeling for sticks and under-brush. In a few seconds, the wood was crackling and sizzling. Raiders pushed up to the flames in relays. Smith and William Chap-man found themselves side by side. Smith brought out a beautiful gold watch, snapped open its case and peeped at the dial. A birthday gift from his wife, he announced proudly to Chapman.

After another ride that seemed interminable, the courier who had come in at Heaton's led them to a sheltered spot on the Potomac River, a mile and a half below Harper's Ferry, where Stringfellow and his party waited. Thus reinforced, the Partisans travelled north-westward along the bank of the stream toward the Ferry. It was nearing the dead hour of morning and the cold had reached its severest stage. Clear and white stretched the frozen river. At one point along the way, sentries could be seen passing back and forth against fires blazing on the opposite shore. Mosby had made no announcement of his plans, and some of his raiders thought this camp across the river was the object of their expedition. But shortly afterward, when a locomotive whistle came in a long, lonesome blast, they supposed it was the train they were after.

Harper's Ferry had received rough treatment during the war. It had passed back and forth, from one army to the other, and its arsenal had been destroyed. Now in the hands of the Federals, it had been fortified to a high degree and was garrisoned by both cavalry and infantry. Rising high above it on the north was Maryland Heights, a bluff covered with trees and undergrowth, and on the Virginia side, where the Shenandoah empties into the Potomac, another spur of the Blue Ridge, Loudoun Heights, jutting up equally as towering. Stringfellow steered the Rangers toward these mountain bulwarks visible against the stars. Near a bridge across a small stream where he knew pickets were stationed, he turned off to the left, then led the way into a dense pine thicket for about two hundred yards to the bridge across the Shenandoah River. Stringfellow said it was Cole's headquarters they could see on the left of the road—a tall, bulky frame building—and that the camp was beyond it.

The party moved out of the thicket, advanced farther to the left and halted at the base of a wooded cliff, which they must scale to reach the camp. Men were allowed to close up and then, one by one, leading their horses, they began to climb. Often they floundered in the snow and clung desperately to bushes and other objects that gave them a handhold. There was no noise beyond the snorts of the animals and the heavy breathing of the men.

Mosby was among the first to make the climb. At the crest he found just enough room for his raiders to wedge in between the first row of tents and the cliff. Leaving Smith to hurry the remainder of the force up the hazardous route, he set off at a half run to scout the camp, moving stealthily and silently. In a few minutes he was back. Over the entire camp he had found nothing but sleeping men. Except for the snores of the snugly wrapped Federals, the entire plateau was as quiet as a tomb.

All the raiders were up by this time, ready for action, and Mosby was confident capture of the camp was a certainty. Up to dark, Stringfellow had been able to determine that between one hundred and seventy-five and two hundred men were on duty there. This would be a victory worth all the torture they had suffered to bring it about.

From back along the mountain side, the wind came in a low moan, kicking up runners of snow and sending them scurrying in and out like field mice along the rows of tents. A canvas flap near the waiting men broke loose and slapped futilely in the dying gust, then fitted back into the deathly stillness.

The wiry leader glanced once more through the camp, white and ghostly in the darkness. He turned to his lieutenants. One by one they moved off to execute his orders—Stringfellow and ten men to surround the house on the point of the hill and to capture Major Cole and his staff; Captain Smith and party to secure the horses and mules; Montjoy, with six men, to capture the picket they had avoided at the bridge on the way in, while the leader attacked the camp with the remainder of the men.

The blankets with holes in their centres were lifted from the shoulders of the men and strapped behind saddles. Mufflers and overcoats were loosened. Tingling fingers, partly paralysed with cold, were drawn reluctantly from gloves and fitted against the steel chill of revolvers. The torture seemed less severe to the Rangers in their excitement.

While he waited for the various parties to reach their destinations, Mosby dismounted a number of the men left with him and scattered them through the camp, ready to grab the surprised Yankees when they darted, sleepy-eyed, out of their cots. In a few minutes his entire force was stationed, revolvers ready, their eyes on the line of tents. The other parties must be almost in place.

Then, suddenly, like a clap of thunder, a shot sounded, startlingly loud, sharp and cutting. It came from the direction Stringfellow had taken.

Cause of the blast was never established definitely. In front of the stable where the officers' horses were quartered were several army wagons to which had been tied a number of mules. Perhaps the raiders who went after this prize spoke too loud. Perhaps there was someone awake at headquarters. Perhaps Stringfellow's men deserted him after they entered Cole's quarters. Perhaps a numbed finger pressed too tightly on a sensitive trigger. Perhaps someone in the tents was awake. The real answer, more likely, was snuffed out with the lives of men who fell during the furious fighting of the next few minutes.

Immediately following the shot, Mosby and the men with him waited in breathless suspense. Then over the hill from headquarters came horsemen, charging wildly. They were from Stringfellow's party, but their identity was blacked out by the darkness. The

Rangers poured a deadly fire at them, wounding and killing six before the mistake was discovered.

Like a flash now the camp came to life. Gun barrels appeared out of tent flaps and fired their death loads in the dark. Along the tent rows the furore was picked up and increased. 'Fire at every man on horseback!' 'Men, do not take to your horses!' 'Fire the tents and shoot 'em by the light!'

Frightened Federals, seeking the explanation of this sudden interruption to their sleep, dashed out into the snow and were shot at, or found their comrades and formed behind some barrier to blaze away with their carbines at the unidentified attackers. Some ran into the bushes on the mountain side and from there poured a deadly fire into the camp.

The voices of Mosby, Smith, Turner, Chapman, and others could be heard in the confusion, shouting for their men to charge. The fire became hotter. Tents were riddled with bullets. Figures, in grey and in blue, lay about, some in pools of blood; others tried to crawl to safety, Turner among them. Someone found him, got help, dragged him away.

Federal fire was coming now from the headquarters buildings and the barns. Captain Vernon of Cole's battalion rallied the Yankee cavalry at one side of the camp and set up a stiff resistance. Mosby felt it, felt the disadvantage under which his men were fighting, saw them firing at each other in the confusion.

The signal gun on the heights sounded. In a few minutes, reinforcements from the thousands of infantry troops at Harper's Ferry would be on them. Mosby realized that longer resistance was useless. In a shrill voice he called for a retreat toward Hillsboro.

But his cry did not reach all the Rangers. Some of them could hear only the pleas of their wounded comrades. Fount Beattie was down, crawling on the ground, with the second wound of his Partisan career. So were Charlie Paxson and William E. Colston, both just back from sick leave, both fatally wounded. So were others. John Robinson, Scot and ex-captain in the English army, was dead. Near by, dying, lay Joseph W. Owens.

Chapman rushed back into the camp. He had the idea Mosby was in there wounded. He spied Captain Smith on horseback, carrying away Henry Edmonds. 'Come on!' shouted Chapman. 'Mosby's in there—let's get him!'

Edmonds was left with another Ranger, and the two rode back. They recognized Lieutenant Gray and three others, including John Tyler Grayson, at one corner of the camp. Grayson joined them.

The firing had shifted to the rear of the camp, next to the mountain, where the Federals were making a stand in the bushes, up where Captain Vernon of Cole's cavalry lay helpless with a serious wound in the head. Charlie Paxson spied the trio. 'You're not going to leave me here!' he called. Grayson turned back to get an extra horse. Just then, from a near-by tent, a shot was fired. Smith and Chapman returned it. A Yankee sergeant gripped his carbine. He dropped to his knees, raised his piece, pushed aside the tent flap and pulled the trigger without aim. Smith leaped suddenly up from his saddle and fell from the right side. Both feet were caught in the stirrups and his head dangled in the snow in a pool of blood.

Chapman sprang from his horse and called to his comrade, but there was no answer. He endeavoured to lift Smith into the saddle: the wounded man was too heavy. Then he thought of the birthday watch and fumbled in the overcoat for the pocket where it was kept. His numb fingers could not loosen a single button. He knocked Smith's feet from the stirrups and led his horse out of the camp. He found Gray and asked him to help recover Smith's body and look for Mosby. Gray said Mosby had ordered a retreat and that they were the only men left. The pair galloped after the retreating Rangers.

Federals quickly formed pursuit. As dawn broke, they easily picked up the trail of Rebel horses in the snow and rode at a gallop. Up along the Shenandoah River, miles above where it empties into the Potomac at Harper's Ferry, the maze of tracks led. Union riders presumed they were getting nearer their quarry. But suddenly the hoof prints swung down the bank to the edge of the water, at a point directly across from a high cliff. There the pursuit ended. Search along each side of the stream failed to reveal the spot where the Loudoun Heights raiders had emerged.

THE RAID ON *Loudoun Heights was a failure. But failure was rare for Mosby, and as the war went on Grant placed a price on his head. Because of this he had trouble surrendering at the close of the war.*

When Lincoln was assassinated there was further trouble for the raider. In conjunction with Booth's attack on Lincoln, a certain Lewis Thornton Powell attempted to kill Secretary Seward. A hurried investigation showed that Powell had been one of Mosby's Rangers, and Colonel Mosby was sought as an outlaw. Subsequent investigation showed that Powell, who was eventually hanged, had deserted the Rangers a full year before the assassination.

Mosby was finally granted his parole as a Southern officer, and he returned to a law practice. From President Hayes he accepted a consulship in Hong Kong and served there from 1878 to 1885. While he was still in the Far East, the Chinese offered him a command in a war against France, but Mosby would not fight against a country that had helped the United States in the Revolution. When his tour of duty was over, he returned home to write and lecture.

Mosby lived until 1916, a poor, irascible, intolerant old man, scribbling defences of his hero, Jeb Stuart. He seemed to feel himself that he had lived beyond his time of glory, and just before he died, he said, 'I wish that life's descending shadows had fallen upon me in the midst of friends and the scenes that I loved.'

WAR CHIEF VICTORIO

BY PAUL I. WELLMAN

BACK IN THE FOG *of unrecorded history, the American Indian developed the techniques of battle which were to become his trade-mark. To counter these techniques the white invaders were forced to copy.*

The great Indian warriors, King Phillip, Joseph Brant, Pontiac, Black Hawk, War Chief Joseph, and others were brilliant tacticians, and when one realizes with how little they fought, their achievements are magnified.

Belittled as barbarians and accused of treachery, they fought the only way they knew with the only means they had to defend themselves against a relentless invasion by superior numbers.

Frequently the American Indian went to war to defend his lands, but often he was the instrument of the great powers of Europe. As the Allies furnished advisers and equipment to the occupied countries of World War II, so did the French, English, and Spanish to the Indians in the century-long battle for North America. Such men as Sir William Johnson and Captains Bird and Simcoe made careers of Indian warfare. They were the scalp-buyers, the calculating firebrands behind the raids on unprotected farms and villages. Reprisals generally fell upon the Indians.

When the white men made their treaties dividing the continent between them, the Indian stood alone and friendless. Pushed into a smaller and smaller area, he went to war for survival. Led by such men as War Chief Joseph, Sitting Bull, and Magnus Colorado, the Indians ravaged the Western Plains and then slowly drew back to the desert and mountains. In 1863, after more than thirty years of intermittent fighting, Magnus Colorado, the great Apache chief, accepted an invitation to discuss a treaty. He was captured and treacherously killed in his sleep, and the Apaches were dealt with ruthlessly.

Facing extermination or stagnation on a government reservation, the Mimbreno Apache chief, Victorio, finally settled down with his people at Ojo Caliente, New Mexico, in 1877. But within two years the government decided to uproot them and move them to San Carlos Reservation. In April, 1879, Victorio disappeared with thirty of his braves. The description of what followed is told by Paul Wellman, the novelist-historian.

WITH the troops hot on his trail, Victorio fled for Mexico, swinging around south of El Paso, and crossing the Rio Grande into the Big Bend Country of Texas, south of Fort Quitman. There he received reinforcements. Caballero, the aged chief of the Mescaleros, inspired by Victorio's bold move for freedom, also left the reservation with two or three hundred of his people and joined the Mimbrenos.

Victorio now had more than a hundred warriors. He began at once a series of the most baffling movements the United States army ever had to combat in Indian campaigns. The Mimbreno leader was a perfect master at deception. He pursued a settled policy with the Mexican sheep herders and small ranchers in the country over which he ranged. They were permitted to live on sufferance. So long as they furnished him with arms, food, and ammunition, just so long he allowed them to exist. All of them knew this. Their lives were pitiable; they were in constant terror. When the grim brown warriors with their steel-trap mouths rode up to the little adobe *casas*, the owners came forth with anything they demanded and were glad to get off with their lives. Replenishing his supplies in this manner and knowing every foot of the country, Victorio matched his wits against the best in the United States and Mexican armies and won for many months.

As soon as he entered Texas, the chief learned through his scouts —who probably never had superiors in the history of any warfare— that Captain Nicholas Nolan, with a detachment of the 10th (Coloured) Cavalry, was headed toward him. Too weak to fight any such body of troops, the Mimbreno retreated. He turned and twisted, trying to shake off the soldiers, but finally was forced to cross to the south side of the Rio Grande when Colonel George W. Baylor and a company of Texas Rangers pressed him too closely.

But it was only for a short time. In September, 1879, the Apaches appeared again—this time in New Mexico. Victorio never moved more secretly than he did that time. The first hint anybody had that he was north of the border was a message of blood. Captain Ambrose E. Hooker's company of the 9th Cavalry was camped near Ojo Caliente. Victorio passed that way, headed north to give some of the Mescaleros and Mimbrenos still on the reservation a chance to join him. But he needed horses and, when he saw the troop herd grazing under a guard on the night of September 4, he turned aside from his direct line of march. Victorio's shadowy skirmishers stole through the gloom. Orange flashes spurted out in the darkness as the rifles chattered angrily. With yells which sounded sharp and clear above the thunder of the stampeding horses, the Apaches were gone in a smother of dust.

Eight troopers were killed in the brief, bloody little battle, and forty-six of Uncle Sam's cavalry horses found themselves between the knees of Indian riders. Victorio did not lose a man.

The troops groped frantically through the desert for the Apaches but Victorio's people were gone almost as if they had disappeared into the air. Ten days later they struck again, suddenly, savagely.

It was near Hillsboro, New Mexico, this time. A posse of citizens, ranchers and miners had taken the trail. Victorio turned on them with a snarling fury which caught them unprepared. Ten of them were killed and all their horses were captured by the raiders.

All this time warriors were flocking to join Victorio, slipping away from their reservations and meeting him in the wilderness. He now had about one hundred and forty braves, including the Mescaleros under fierce old Caballero.

Lieutenant-Colonel N. A. M. Dudley, with two troops of the 9th Cavalry, rode hard to cut the Indians off following the Hillsboro fight, and found them on September 18, in the canyons at the head of Las Animas Creek. Dudley attacked at once. But Victorio's desert wolves were posted in almost impregnable positions among the rocks.

The rattle of rifles had scarcely started when Captain Charles D. Beyer galloped up with two more troops of the 9th, making a total of four companies in action. The Apaches were now badly outnumbered, but in spite of this the soldiers could not drive the Indians out of their position. Throughout the day the constant roar of the battle echoed through the hills and canyons. When night fell, Dudley discovered that in the day's fighting, from rock to rock and bush to bush, he had lost five enlisted men, two Navajo scouts and one civilian white scout killed, a number wounded, and thirty-eight horses killed or crippled. The troops did not know of a single Indian they had killed. It was clear to Dudley that Victorio was too strong for him in his present position. In the darkness the soldiers withdrew from the field, carrying their dead and wounded. Victorio had won a convincing victory.

The chief's purpose was now fulfilled. He had fought and beaten the white men three times, had killed twenty-six of them, captured a large number of horses, and picked up much booty. More important, he had been joined by a good many warriors from the reservations. He therefore began a retreat towards the border.

2*

But the troops were still in the field. With one hundred and ninety-eight officers and men of the 9th Cavalry, Major Albert P. Morrow struck Victorio near Ojo Caliente, and in a two days' running fight killed three Indians and captured sixty horses and mules, among them twelve of the animals taken from the hapless Hooker.

Four nights later prowling Apaches crept close enough to his picket lines to kill a sentry walking post. But Morrow kept on the trail. With the aid of a captured squaw he found and captured Victorio's camp. But the victory was an empty one. The cunning chief had vacated the camp before the troops arrived. That was on October 1, 1879. Morrow followed the Indians across the border into Mexico and fought another skirmish on October 27, near the Corralitos River, a night fight in which he lost one scout killed and two men wounded.

But the troops were at the limit of their endurance. They had been without water for three days and nights and their ammunition was nearly exhausted. If Victorio had counter-attacked he might have wiped Morrow's forces out. The troops were glad to retreat back to the border, reaching Fort Bayard on November 3, completely worn out.

Over in Texas the settlers and soldiers were congratulating themselves on having, for the time at least, rid themselves of the Indians. News came of the fighting in New Mexico, and at last word was received that Major Morrow had driven Victorio down into Old Mexico. The frontier breathed freely again.

But late one afternoon the stage coach from Fort Davis dashed into Fort Quitman with the driver and one passenger dead and arrows still quivering in the woodwork of its sides. Next came a report that the telegraph wires were cut and the poles chopped down between Fort Davis and Eagle Springs. The truth dawned on Texas: Victorio had in some manner eluded the troops who literally plastered the border those days, and was back in the Big Bend.

Colonel Grierson, at Eagle Springs, believed the Indians were headed for Fresno Springs and, knowing that this was an isolated watering place, he made a forced march by a short cut to get there first. He succeeded. When he reached the springs there was no sign of recent Indian visitation there. Grierson wasted no time. Soldiers were carefully posted around the springs in such a way that when the Indians came they could be permitted to reach the water, then surrounded and killed or captured. There were nearly a thousand troops concealed about the springs, and Grierson did not think that

Victorio had more than one hundred and fifty. It looked as if the old wolf was reaching his finish at last.

Shortly before eleven o'clock next morning, the first cautious scouts of the Apache advance were seen. Grierson's men were nearly suffocating with excitement, but he held them in check while the Indians came slowly toward the springs.

Suddenly out of nowhere a wagon train appeared, also crawling toward the springs. The Indians took to cover at the first hint of this unexpected arrival. Helplessly the concealed soldiers watched the unfolding of an ambush within an ambush as the Apaches, wholly unconscious of Grierson's proximity, prepared to overwhelm the train. As the minutes passed it became increasingly apparent that unless Grierson rescued them the teamsters who had thus blundered into the situation would be massacred to a man.

Angry and disappointed, the colonel gave the order which sent his men to avert the attack on the wagons. The appearance of the troops, riding over the rise toward them, was a complete surprise to the Apaches. But now they saw the trap into which they had almost fallen and began to retreat in earnest towards the Rio Grande. Grierson, before he took up the pursuit, probably used some warm language on the wagon master of that blundering train. In spite of his best efforts he could not overtake the Apaches, although he was so close behind them that his advance could see the Indians on the other side of the river when it arrived at the bank. There the soldiers were forced to turn back.

Victorio moved slowly down into Chihuahua. As they went south the Indians swept the country clean as far as the large ranches and prospectors were concerned, although they continued to observe the policy of sparing the sheep-herders and small farmers. The first stop was at the Santa Maria River, where there was an abundance of rich grama grass, together with plentiful wood and water—the three essentials of an ideal camping place. The location, however, did not satisfy the nervous Indians. It was too open and Victorio knew that Mexican troops might be expected at any time. In his present position he could easily be reached by them, and would be in a poor place for defence.

So Victorio ordered his people to break camp and moved them over into the wild and rugged Candelaria Mountains. There he took up a position which once more proved his genius as a leader. The new camp was not only perfectly located with regard to range for his horses and water and wood, but was beautifully strategic.

It was situated among almost inaccessible steeps, which would have been extremely difficult to attack successfully without serious loss to the enemy. Equally important, it afforded two or three towering peaks from which Victorio and his hawk-eyed scouts could see for twenty or thirty miles in every direction. Added to these advantages was the fact that it was near to the public road which ran between the city of Chihuahua and the Presidio del Norte—the Juarez of today—and all traffic could be observed.

Word of Indian depredations among the neighbouring ranches soon reached Carrizal, the nearest settlement. Cattle and horses had been stolen and atrocities reported. The Mexicans at Carrizal deduced correctly that there was a band of Indians operating from some *rancheria* in the Candelaria Mountains. But they failed to grasp the idea of how powerful a band it was, or that it was led by the redoubtable Victorio himself. Had Carrizal realized this, the tragedy which followed might have been averted.

The general notion was that there was only a handful of Indians to deal with—possibly a dozen or even fewer, of the 'broncho' savages who were always wandering through the desert country. ('Broncho' Apaches were outlaws who held no allegiance either to the United States or to the Mexican government, or to any of the recognized chiefs among their own people. There were always a few of these bands on the prowl during this period.) Early in November, Don José Rodriguez, one of the principal citizens of Carrizal and a member of one of the large land-owning families, organized a posse to scout for the Indians and if possible exterminate them. The expedition set forth on November 6, gay, confident, absolutely failing to comprehend the peril of its mission. Most of its fifteen members were from the better families of the district. It was a sort of a lark—dangerous but good hunting.

From his lofty watch tower in the Candelaria peaks, Victorio saw the small party of Carrizalistas while it was nothing but a tiny dust cloud, a score of miles away. That was November 7. The Mexicans were coming up an old beaten track which led from the Santa Maria River to a big 'tank' on the northern slope of the mountains in which the Apaches were camped. The possemen were riding along carelessly enough, but Victorio knew that if they continued that line of march, they would be certain to strike the main trail made by his band when he moved it into the Candelarias. As wily a strategist as ever the red race produced, he knew that once they saw the breadth of that trail, there was no chance of ever luring the Mexicans any further—and he wanted those rash Carrizalistas.

A delicate situation. But Victorio was equal to it. Calling forty or fifty of his warriors together, he laid a trap for the oncoming Don Rodriguez and his *compadres*. The trail led through a deep canyon which passed between two of the taller Candelaria peaks, both of which had done the Apaches good service as watch towers. In this gorge Victorio prepared as clever an ambush as ever an Indian devised; an ambush which was a psychological as well as a military masterpiece.

At the north side of the trail, among some large boulders, he posted some of his best marksmen—not many, but enough for his purpose. These would be the first to come into contact with the Mexicans, and Victorio counted on them to spring the real trap which was laid on the other side of the canyon, somewhat back from the trail itself.

On came the jaunty Mexicans, slouching with negligent grace in their saddles, chattering and smoking their corn-husk cigarettes, not dreaming of peril. A sudden spray of bullets from the boulders to the north greeted them. To the south of the trail lay some inviting rocks which would make excellent shelter. It was natural for them to seek the cover of these boulders—and that was exactly what Victorio had planned. Knowing human nature, he had not placed any braves among those particular rocks, but had posted his men *higher*, and back, so that the very friendly hospitality of the boulders should convert them into a death trap worthy even of his sinister intelligence.

As Don Rodriguez and his men threw themselves behind the shelter, preparing to fight the Indians on the north side of the canyon, beady-eyed warriors watched them from behind. They had the Mexicans at their mercy, and knew it. At the perfect moment the first rifle sounded from above—possibly Victorio's own—and the slaughter began. There was no escape and no protection from the terrific fire which broke from the higher cliffs.

One poor devil of a Mexican managed to squeeze into a crevice where his body was protected, but his legs protruded; there was no room for them inside. The Apaches turned their rifles in that direction and began deliberately, remorselessly to shoot those legs to pieces. How the helpless wretch must have writhed and screamed as his twitching limbs were struck again and again by the bullets of those pitiless marksmen. It was the sort of thing which appealed to the macabre Apache sense of humour. The twitching ceased after a time. The Mexican had bled to death. But the Indians kept on firing until they literally shot both legs off at the knees.

By that time every member of Don Rodriguez' party, including that elegant *hacendado* himself, was dead. As they vainly tried to find cover, they had been picked off coolly and deliberately from above. Their horses, plunging and rolling in their death struggles, added to the confusion by breaking their lariats and crashing down into the deep canyon to the east, in a smother of dust far below.

After a time the shooting ceased. Then the first of the furtive Indians stole forward from rock to rock. No rifle sounded to greet him. Others came down, one by one, until Victorio's warriors all stood among the slain, looting the bodies and making sure that there were none left living.

The failure of Don Rodriguez' party to return to Carrizal caused grave alarm. As the days passed, the fear grew into a conviction that the men had met some terrible fate. There was no proof of this, however, and at last a party of fourteen citizens of the town volunteered to try to find what had happened to their kinsmen. It was a dangerous thing to attempt, but they probably counted on the fact that the Indians seldom lingered long near the scene of a fight.

Following the trail left by Don Rodriguez, they too disappeared into the mountains. Days passed. They failed to return. When, after a reasonable time, the party had not made its reappearance, Carrizal went wild with excitement, rage and grief. It dawned upon the town that the Apache menace in the mountains was far more serious than had been supposed. A courier was sent to the Presidio del Norte, to beg for help. While he was making his report to Señor Ramos, in command at del Norte, Colonel Baylor of the Texas Rangers in El Paso, on the American side of the Rio Grande, heard of it and crossed the river to offer the services of his hard-riding, straight-shooting daredevils—an offer which was thankfully accepted.

With true Latin courtesy, Señor Ramos offered to Baylor the command of the united forces, but the Ranger declined because the campaign was to be on Mexican soil. Then Ramos placed Don Francisco Escajeda of Guadalupe, a seasoned and experienced soldier, at the head of the allied array, giving second command to Baylor. A force of one hundred well armed, well mounted men was soon on its way south toward the Candelarias.

Straight south rode the rescue party. It halted beyond Samalayucca where scouts were pushed forward to reconnoitre. There was going to be no blundering into ambush this time. Night fell, bitter cold. Deep in the canyon where they could not be seen by watchful eyes in the peaks ahead, some of the men kindled fires of greasewood and mesquite and there tried to warm themselves.

The scouts returned late in the night. Going to the bivouac of Don Escajeda and Baylor, they reported they had not seen a sign of Indians. The commander immediately ordered his men to mount. It was an all-night march this time, and the foot of the Candelarias was reached early the next morning.

Shortly after dawn, for the first time, they saw Indian signs. A great, broad trail it was, whose width and plainness indicated that it was made by a very large band. It looked fresh. The scouts examined it and pronounced it only two days old. It led toward Lake Santa Maria to the north. Evidently the Indians were gone. Still, no chances of a trap were taken. As the command entered the canyon between the two Candelaria peaks, a detachment was sent over the crest to the south while another took the northward steeps. The rest then proceeded down the gorge itself.

Not far had the beaters in front progressed when a shout brought the stragglers hurrying up. Scattered about in the rigid and awkward poses of death, lay the bodies of the unfortunates from Carrizal. The scouts looked here and there, then pieced together from the signs, the story of the battle.

And now the consummate cunning of Victorio revealed itself. The first ambuscade had been cleverly planned and executed. But when did it ever before occur to an Indian leader to use the victims of one victory as bait with which to trap a second party? This is exactly what Victorio had done. The manner in which the Apaches had destroyed the second Carrizal party, as deduced by the scouts, was as follows:

When the rescue expedition from Carrizal, looking for Don Rodriguez and his companions, arrived at the scene of the battle, there was not an Indian in sight. The Mexicans had every reason to believe the Apaches had been gone for several days. Therefore they relaxed their vigilance and began to gather the bodies of their kinsmen and place them together for burial.

The assumption that Victorio's warriors were gone was tragically wrong. All the time that the Mexicans were carrying the corpses of their friends to a central burying place, fierce eyes were fixed on them from above. Grieving, the Carrizalistas went about their sad work, oblivious of the fact that almost over their heads death awaited only the signal of the leader. Not until the bodies were all collected and the fourteen living Mexicans had gathered around their dead friends did the Apaches fire.

It was a repetition of the first fight. Nor is it likely that it lasted long. The Apaches were too numerous and too well situated.

Presently the Indians once more descended into the valley and bent over the dead. Carrizal would never again see the faces of her sons.

Escajeda and Baylor, reconstructing the events which took place in that bloody gorge, had only one thing to do—bury the dead. The bodies were collected and a disquieting thing was learned. The first Carrizal party had numbered fifteen. The second contained fourteen men, a total of twenty-nine in the two parties, which had ridden into the jaws of Victorio's trap. Only twenty-seven corpses were found. What had become of the other two Mexicans? No trace of the missing pair was ever discovered, but everyone knew what had happened to them. Too thorough, too sure was the Apache leader to have permitted them to escape. Somewhere along the trail, these two men, captured alive, suffered out their mortal hours, perhaps hanging head down over a slow fire . . . perhaps staked out, their mouths prised open with sharpened skewers, on some ant hill . . . perhaps twisting and writhing against the poisoned spikes of a tree cactus, lashed by green rawhide bands which, drying in the sun, bound them ever tighter and tighter against the torment . . . .

After his double *coup* in the Candelaria Mountains, Victorio pressed northward as fast as his horses could carry his people. Early in January he again crossed the border and stood on the soil of New Mexico. His old enemy, Major Morrow, took prompt and strenuous action. Every body of cavalry in the section was set in motion. Victorio found himself in a veritable hornets' nest. Even his matchless skill could not forever keep his people clear of the thronging multitudes of soldiers about him.

Near the head of the Puerco River, on January 9, he fought a stand-off engagement with Major Morrow and a battalion of the 9th Cavalry. Several of his warriors were hit and on the white side one enlisted man was killed and a scout wounded. Victorio drew off toward the San Mateo Mountains, where Morrow attacked him again on January 17. It was another inconclusive fight, but a brave young officer, Lieutenant J. Hansell French, was killed and two scouts wounded.

After that Victorio once more disappeared. The troops searched blindly for him through the barren mountains and across sun-smitten flats, but for nearly three months they never were near enough to see the dust cloud raised by his tireless marchers. Back and forth he swung, leaving a smoking wrack behind him. The chief seemed to grow more savage as the relentless pursuit continued. Some of the scenes the soldiers stumbled upon as they followed him endlessly, stirred black rage in their hearts. Women were found by their charred homes, torn limb from limb. Little children were discovered, looking as if wolves had worried them to death. And many men, prospectors, stage drivers, and cowboys, died horribly in the hills, leaving their mangled corpses as mute evidence of the bottomless cruelty of the Apaches into whose hands they had fallen. In that bloody raid Victorio killed upward of a hundred persons who are accounted for and enumerated. But there were dozens of others never heard from who met their end at the hands of his desert killers.

Not until April 8 did the soldiers find Victorio. Then it was the old story—an indecisive fight, with no results to show for it. Captain Henry Carroll, 9th Cavalry, and seven enlisted men were wounded during General Hatch's fruitless attempt to drive the Indians out of the strong position they had taken high up in the San Andreas Mountains. Three Indians were killed. Victorio drew off towards the east. Hatch, who took the trail the following day, decided that he was headed for the Mescalero reservation.

It was too disappointing, too disheartening. Something had to be done about it.

Those were sad days for the wretched Mescaleros who remained on the reservation near Fort Stanton and tried to keep the peace. They were caught between two fires. On one side were Victorio and their old chief Caballero, inciting them always to the war path, sometimes losing patience with their pacifistic ways, and doing spiteful deeds against them. On the other side were the soldiers who never believed them when they protested their innocence of trouble making, never gave them any rest if they as much as wandered outside of the confines of the agency.

Their one friend was their agent, S. A. Russell, who protected them all he could, advised them, and tried to stand between them and the military. Russell was hampered by the presence among the peaceful Indians of many malcontents who were always stealing supplies and smuggling them to the hostile bands. These supplies appeared frequently when camps of outlying raiding parties were captured, and gave rise to the charges that 'The Mescalero Agency . . . largely served as a base of supplies and recruits for the raiding parties of Victorio.'

Captain Thomas C. Lebo, on March 6, 1880, surprised and captured the *ranchería* of some 'broncho' Indians at Shakehand Spring, about forty miles south of Penasco, Texas. Lebo's men killed a chief of the band, captured four squaws and one child, and the livestock and supplies of the camp. Much material from the Mescalero Agency was found in this camp, in which, incidentally, a captive Mexican boy, Coyetano Garcia, was rescued and later restored to his parents near del Norte.

Because of this evidence, Generals Pope and Ord, commanding the departments of Missouri and Texas, ordered on March 24 that the Mescaleros remaining on the reservation should be disarmed and dismounted. General Hatch and Colonel Grierson were given the task. Hatch took four hundred men from the 9th Cavalry, sixty infantrymen, and seventy-five Indian scouts. Colonel Grierson had under him two hundred and eighty officers and men of the 10th Cavalry and the 25th Infantry, making a combined force of eight hundred and fifteen officers and men. The two commands were to meet at the agency.

In the meantime, a band of peaceful Mescaleros, not knowing of these plans, asked permission of Russell to leave the agency on a hunt. Russell granted the permission. He told the Indians they might camp on the Rio Tularosa, several miles west of the agency limits. This was a common procedure. Years before all the game had been killed off on the reservation and in view of the type of supplies issued by the government to the Mescaleros, the agent thought it no more than fair that they be allowed to eke out their larders with what game they could occasionally kill.

Camping, in accordance with the agent's instructions, near the head of the Tularosa, this band of Indians was 'discovered' by Grierson on April 12, when he appeared through the Sacramento Mountains. The colonel had found many Indian trails on his march. He assumed that these trails were made by 'marauding Indians'. Just why they should be 'marauders' is not clear, unless it was the officer's assumption that every Indian should be placed in that category. Without knowing anything about the band on the Tularosa or bothering himself to ascertain why they were camped there, he prepared at once to attack them.

It was early in the morning. Most of the Mescaleros were still asleep as Grierson surrounded the camp. All was ready for the charge which would be sure to kill many Indians when a messenger came spurring up with a message from Russell. The agent notified Grierson that these Indians were peaceful and were camping there by his special permission. He added that he had just ordered them back to the reservation and they had not yet had time to obey.

There is not much doubt that the Mescaleros in this camp were saved from a dreadful experience by the timely arrival of that courier. Another Camp Grant affair was averted.

Grierson, more or less grudgingly, marched on to the reservation as soon as he saw that the Indians were actually moving. General Hatch had already arrived. The Indians were quiet. Hatch decided he did not need all the troops he had brought. He began to send some of them west, leaving three hundred and fifty or so with Grierson. Russell summoned the chief Nautzilla and told him the purpose of the troops.

The disarming was scheduled to take place on April 16. Rifle firing was heard south of the agency at about ten o'clock that morning. The Indians were thrown into a minor panic. Word came in shortly that Lieutenant Charles B. Gatewood had come upon some braves 'driving off stock', had killed two of them, and was now bringing the livestock back to the agency. Russell was indignant. It appears that the stock in question had strayed away from the agency and the Indians had been sent by him to bring it back. While they were carrying out this errand, Gatewood had attacked them, with two fatalities resulting. Small wonder that the whole tribe seemed to have a bad case of nerves as Grierson began to disarm them.

It had been agreed between Grierson and Hatch that if more troops were needed than were then at the agency, three signal shots should be fired. Grierson saw that the Mescaleros were sullen and frightened. Some of them even began to slink away. He decided he needed the other troops. The signal shots rang out on the clear air.

Those shots crystallized the panic. In every direction the Indians rushed to escape. The confusion was enhanced by the sudden arrival of Hatch's troops, who tried to halt the Apaches and speedily found themselves fighting. Ten Indians were killed. Two hundred and fifty surrendered. But scores got away and made a bee-line for Victorio's camp, where they became among his most vindictive fighters.

With these reinforcements, Victorio began a southerly retreat. He fought a couple of sharp engagements, but was back in Mexico by early June. There he was temporarily safe. The Mexican government refused to permit United States troops to cross its borders.

A breathing spell was all the Mimbreno wanted. On July 31, Captain Coldwell of the Texas Rangers, on an inspection trip to Ysleta, Texas, began a journey to Fort Davis. Riding in the mail stage coach, of the type called a 'jerky' on the frontier, he passed through Quitman Canyon, where he discovered that Indians had cut off the stage coach from the other direction, killing its driver, E. C. Baker, and a passenger, Frank Wyant. In this manner Texas learned that Victorio was back within her borders.

And now began one of the biggest man-hunts in the history of the frontier. An agreement was made between General Ord, commanding the Department of Texas, and General Trevino, commanding the Mexican troops in northern Chihuahua, whereby the two nations were to co-operate in a campaign to run down Victorio. Trevino notified Grierson that about six hundred Mexican soldiers were ready to pursue the Indians south of the border, with additional troops coming. Grierson threw every soldier he could get into the campaign. Within the next few weeks, Victorio, whose forces never exceeded one hundred and seventy-five or eighty warriors, had to fight or dodge at least two thousand United States soldiers, and an equal number of Mexican troops, not to mention the hundreds of cowboys, miners and ranchers who hung about him in a cloud.

With only six men Grierson was at the spring of Tanajas de las Palmas, on the day Victorio's invasion was discovered. His young son, out west on a summer vacation from college, was with him 'looking for excitement', which he was to find, speedily.

Learning that the Apache camp was within ten miles of him, the colonel sent to Eagle Springs and to Fort Quitman for reinforcements for his small escort, and daringly remained with his half dozen men to watch the movements of the hostile Indians. His order was misunderstood at Fort Quitman where nothing was known of Victorio's proximity. The commanding officer there thought Grierson merely wanted an escort to bring him back to the fort. Lieutenant Leighton Finley was sent with fifteen men—a woefully inadequate force. At once another courier was dispatched by Grierson with peremptory orders for more troops and an explanation of the situation.

Grierson, occupying his exposed position far out in the desert, saw Victorio's advance guard approaching him at about nine o'clock on the morning of July 31. His twenty men were in a position as strong as they could find. The Indians observed this and instead of charging, they scattered about the place, ignorant of the fact that a courier had gone for help. Victorio planned to wipe out the whole force, in the Apache manner, with the least possible loss to himself.

Lieutenant Finley was ordered by Grierson to take ten men and prevent this enveloping movement if possible. The carbines began to crackle as the young officer attacked a vastly superior force of the

Indians and for more than an hour held them in check. This was probably not so much due to the Apache fear of him, as to the fact that they thought they had all the time in the world and were prepared to carry out their battle plans at leisure.

That hour proved the saving of Grierson. As the men lay among the rocks with the bullets whining overhead, or smacking among the stones and kicking up spiteful jets of sand and dust, blue uniforms appeared over the rise from the direction of Fort Quitman. It was Captain Charles D. Viele, with a troop of cavalry.

The Apache fire slackened. But Viele's troops, coming up, mistook Finley's advance detachment for Indians and opened fire on it. Nobody was hit although the bullets skipped most disconcertingly among the men. To avoid being riddled by his own friends, Finley ordered a retreat to Grierson's main position. The Apaches sprang in hot pursuit as he withdrew, hoping to prevent Viele from joining Grierson. But Viele now saw his mistake. He deployed his men and sent them forward among the rocks so fast that the Indians, in their own immediate danger, forgot all about Finley.

All up and down the field, heated like a blast furnace under the brazen sun of late July, the fight became general. Although there were now about a hundred troopers against him, Victorio pressed them hard. He might have punished them severely, were it not that Captain Nicholas Nolan arrived with another company of cavalry from Fort Quitman.

Outnumbered and half surrounded, Victorio at last retreated. The engagement had lasted four hours. Seven warriors had been killed and others wounded and carried back to the rear by the Apaches. The Mimbreno chief's force was too scanty to permit of such losses. On the white side, Lieutenant S. R. Calladay was wounded and one enlisted man killed.

Victorio rapidly fell back to the Rio Grande and recrossed into Mexico. But within four days the tireless raider was across the border into the United States again, heading with his warriors for the Van Horn Mountains. Brushing off one detachment of soldiers, he eluded Grierson's main command, which tried to pin him at Bass's Canyon, and on the evening of August 4 was in the passes of the Van Horns.

Grierson guessed that Victorio was heading for Rattlesnake Springs. He made a forced march to that important point, riding sixty-five miles during the next twenty-four hours, a terrific march considering the heat. The soldiers reached the springs well ahead of the Indians. Captain Viele had two troops in ambush. The Indians arrived at about two o'clock the next morning. They were greeted by a surprise volley and as the rest of Grierson's force came up, they were driven from the springs, losing several warriors.

Undaunted, Victorio fell back towards Bown's Springs in the Guadalupe Mountains. But again his arch-foe, Grierson, anticipated his movements. The chief found Captain William B. Kennedy's force waiting there. In the brush which followed, two Indians and one soldier were killed. The Apaches now retreated towards the Sacramento Mountains. There they came into contact with another of the swarming detachments, this time under Captain Lebo.

The border was crowded with soldiers as never before. Every way Victorio turned, he met troops. At last, about August 18, he gave up the attempt to remain in the United States, and once more led his people into Mexico.

Hunted like a mad wolf from mountain range to mountain range and from desert tank to alkali spring, Victorio and his faithful followers pushed southward from the Texas border and took refuge in the Tres Castillos Mountains of northern Chihuahua. September and October passed. The chief, now about sixty years old, was tired. But his young men were not. As the month of November opened, a large party of the younger braves went north again, while a second, somewhat smaller band, led by old Nana, Victorio's chief lieutenant, raided through Mexico. The older warriors and all the women and children remained with Victorio in the mountains.

News that the Indians were in the Tres Castillos district quickly reached Colonel Joaquin Terrazas at Chihuahua. He planned immediately a major operation against them. The colonel had spent some time in organizing a body of irregular troops, made up of men from such towns as Ascension, Janos and Casas Grandes, which were called the *Seguridad Publicos*, or, more familiarly, the 'S. P.s'. In their duties and semi-military nature, they were patterned after the Texas Rangers. For scouts, Terrazas enlisted a company of Tarahumari Indians from the mountains of that name. These Indians, while lacking the extreme deadly vindictiveness of the Apaches, were little their inferiors in most respects, and in one respect they were the superiors, not only of the Apaches, but probably of every living race of mankind. They were, and still are, peerless foot racers. Their name signifies that and their warriors were able to boast with truth that they could outstrip any horse in a race sufficiently long. It was nothing for them to cover as much as one hundred miles in a day, and they could jog along, kicking a small ball before them, at a speed which carried them forty miles in six or eight hours with the greatest ease.

Terrazas sent a message to Ysleta, Texas, asking Colonel Baylor of the Texas Rangers to co-operate with him, and marched north with his S. P.s and Tarahumari scouts.

Meantime Grierson's men were on the trail of the young warriors who were raiding into Texas without Victorio as a leader. Captain Theodore A. Baldwin had a short fight with them near Ojo Caliente, Texas. Four of his men were killed, but the action prevented the Apaches' immediate return to the main band which awaited them in the Tres Castillos. That delay was fatal. It is hard to believe that Victorio would have remained in one place for the length of time he did, had he not promised his young men to keep a rendezvous with them there. The great chance had come for Terrazas.

The Mexican leader had been joined by several bodies of fighting men from the United States. Colonel Baylor brought twenty of his Rangers. Lieutenant James A. Manney appeared with twenty Negro troopers. And Captain Charles Parker came to Terrazas' camp with sixty-eight Chiricahua Apache scouts. The combined expedition found Victorio's trail and followed it until all doubt that it led to the Tres Castillos was gone. Then Terrazas made a surprise announcement.

He blandly requested his American allies to return to their own side of the border, giving as his excuse his belief that Captain Parker's scouts were too wild and too nearly related to Victorio's people for safety. To the Americans it looked simply as if the Mexican, having made sure of his quarry, jealously wished to take all the glory to himself for the victory which had been made possible, in large part, by the scouting of the very Chiricahuas to whom Terrazas objected. There was nothing they could do about it, however, except to return. Reluctantly and thoroughly angry, the American detachments marched north and crossed the border.

At one place the Tres Castillos Mountains form a deep basin, which can be entered only through a box canyon. This spot had long been a favourite camping ground for the Indians and thither Terrazas led his command. When he arrived no Apaches were there, and he camped for the night.

Frantic signalling from his pickets posted on the peaks of the mountains overlooking the plain, warned him that something important was afoot. Soon a soldier came running to say that a large dust cloud could be seen coming towards the canyon. Terrazas himself climbed a lookout peak and with his powerful field-glasses made out definitely that the dust was raised by a large band of marching Apaches.

Here was unlooked-for good fortune. The Mexican commander hastily deployed his men to places of advantage. All traces of his campfires were concealed. In the cliffs around the basin, the soldiers and the fierce Tarahumari scouts lay, with every foot of the interior covered by their rifles.

For once Victorio was caught napping. The chief had no idea that troops were in the vicinity. Without fear or hesitation, he led his band, consisting largely of non-combatants, through the gullet of the box canyon and into the inviting valley beyond.

Then, when the Apaches were all inside, the rocks echoed to the reports of the rifles of Terrazas' men until the uproar was deafening, the canyon walls grew hanging curtains of drifting smoke, and the Indians died in a blight of lead and fire.

As has been said, Victorio's best warriors were away on a raid. He was greatly outnumbered. But the Apache was always dangerous, never more so than when he was cornered. Ringed completely around with rifles, and with the bullets cutting his people down about him, the chief summoned the survivors to make their going memorable. The Mexicans paid for their victory.

Darkness fell. Throughout the night the continued crashing of rifles echoed through the basin and spurts of fire lit the crags with lurid flashes. At early dawn the few remaining Apache warriors were still fighting, but their ammunition was almost all gone. About an hour after sun-up their guns were silent at last. Now the Mexicans charged forward, brave in the knowledge that their enemies were out of cartridges.

Victorio had been wounded more than once during the battle, but still he rallied his braves. Creeping forward with Terrazas' scouts was a Tarahumari Indian named Mauricio, famed for his uncanny skill with the rifle. Some time during the battle, he caught a glimpse of Victorio directing his few defenders. The black eye of the Tara-humari gleamed down the barrel; for an instant the sight picked out the bronze figure of the Apache chief; then the trigger finger pressed.

And so Victorio died—instantly, in the heat of battle, as he would have wished. His was a character difficult for the white mind to comprehend. He was an implacable enemy and his cruelty was notorious. But his long fight against the white man, carried on for years in spite of the heart-breaking odds against him, was inspired by something akin to what we call patriotism.

Most of Victorio's band died in the basin of the Tres Castillos with him. The few who escaped were harried wildly through the mountains. They were without leaders; surely Apache resistance was at an end.

MOST OF VICTORIO'S MEN *were killed with him. The governor of Sonora was so pleased with the news of Victorio's death that the killer was awarded a nickel-plated rifle.*

But the Indian Wars were not over. In the decade following Victorio's death Old Nana disrupted the south-west with no more than forty warriors, and Geronimo terrorized the United States-Mexican border area for three years.

The Indian Wars ended with the defeat of the Apaches, but the United States will always be indebted to this enemy for having taught it some uniquely American concepts of fighting.

JAGUNÇO REBELLION

BY EUCLIDES DA CUNHA

EARLY IN OCTOBER, 1896, *the magistrate of a small Brazilian community in the backlands sent a wire to the governor of Baia: the jagunços, or bandits, were coming. A hundred soldiers were dispatched to protect the small community. They were defeated and put to flight. The Brazilian military authorities were furious. Five hundred more troops were rushed into the backlands to punish the jagunços. They marched through the caatinga, or scrub forest, to Canudos, centre of the rebellion. The sun was so hot and the land so dry that a fallen body could dehydrate and hold its shape for years. On January 19, the column reached the town. The battle was brief and vicious. Again the soldiers were defeated and put to flight.*

When the news reached the capital, the government knew it had a war on its hands—one of the strangest wars in history. Hurried conferences were held. Everyone wanted to know what was happening in the backlands. What was the rebellion all about, and who were these jagunços?

Quickly the facts were collected. The African Kafirs, the Mestizos, descendants of the Europeans, the native Indians—all the hodge-podge of the interior—had been brought together at the once nearly deserted village of Canudos by Antonio Machiel, a religious fanatic who was also known as Antonio Conselheiro, The Counsellor. His interpretations of Christian doctrine seemed to suit the wild, uneducated dwellers in the fringe areas of the Brazilian backlands where life at its easiest was a vicious struggle for survival with the land and the climate. From all the areas where this strange prophet had preached, followers—the simple sertanejos, *or backland natives—had gathered at Canudos. The community had swelled to a city of over five thousand buildings. Professional bandits and murderers had joined the group which maintained itself by living off the surrounding villages. When the unbalanced Antonio preached open defiance of the Republic, the jagunços were willing to follow him.*

The Brazilian government prepared another expedition under its most ruthless commander, chunky, epileptic Moreira Cesar. With thirteen hundred men, Cesar set out for Canudos.

This account of the Moreira Cesar expedition was selected from Rebellion in the Backlands *by Euclides da Cunha. As a story and a military account it is considered by many the peer of* War and Peace.

Cunha draws a picture of guerrilla warfare in the caatingas, describes the approach of the regulars, and then writes of the guerrilla-like defence of Canudos.

THE caatingas are an incorruptible ally of the sertanejo in revolt, and they do in a certain way enter into the conflict. They arm themselves for the combat, take the offensive. For the invader they are an impenetrable wilderness; but they have numerous paths by which they are accessible to the backwoodsman, who was born and grew up there. And so, the jagunço turns warrior-thug, hard to lay hands on.

The caatingas do not so much hide him as extend him their protection. Upon catching sight of them in the summertime, a column of soldiers is not alarmed but continues to make its way, painfully, along the winding paths. Being able to see over the top of the leafless undergrowth, the men do not think of an enemy's being near. Reacting to the heat and with that relaxed air which is natural on long marches, they go along with a confused babble of conversation all down the line, punctuated by the clinking of their weapons and their jovial, half-repressed laughter. There is nothing, so it seems, that should alarm them. Certainly, should the enemy be so imprudent as to confront them here, they would make short work of him. These shoots of foliage could be slashed to bits by a few strokes of the sword, and it is not credible that this fine underbrush could impede the execution of prompt manœuvres. And so they go marching along, heroically unconcerned.

Suddenly, from the side, close at hand, a shot rings out.

The bullet whizzes past them, or perhaps one of their number lies stretched on the ground, dead. This is followed, after a while, by another, and another, whining over the heads of the troop. A hundred, two hundred, a thousand anxious eyes scan the foliage round about them, but can see nothing. This is the first surprise, and a shudder of fear runs from one end of the ranks to the other. The shots continue, not many of them, but there is no let-up; they keep on coming at measured intervals, from the left, from the right, from in front of them, with the entire band now under a constant and a deadly fire.

It is then that a strange anxiety lays hold of even the bravest ones whose courage has many times been put to the test, in the presence of this antagonist who sees them, but whom they cannot see. A company of sharpshooters is quickly formed, being with difficulty separated from the main mass of the battalions caught in the narrow path. These men now spread out around the edge of the caatinga, whereupon a voice can be heard giving a command, and there is a resounding hail of bullets through the branches of the stunted undergrowth.

But constantly, always at long intervals, the missiles from those other sharpshooters, the invisible ones, keep humming, all up and down the line. The situation rapidly grows worse, calling for energetic action. Other combat units are now detached and are detailed along the entire stretch of road, ready to act at the first word of command. The commanding officer resolves to launch an assault on the hidden enemy but soon finds that he is assaulting a phantom foe. With their bayonets, his men impetuously beat down the undergrowth, amid a widening range of bullets. They go forward rapidly, and the enemy appears to fall back somewhat. And then it is, at this moment, that the caatinga shows what a formidable antagonist it can be. The details rush on to the points from where the gunfire had been heard and are brought up short by the yielding but impenetrable barrier of a jurema thicket. They become entangled in a liana bed, which trips them up, snatches their weapons from their hands, and will not let them pass; and so they are compelled to turn aside and make their way around it. There may now be seen what looks like a running flame, a row of bayonets along the dried brushwood. It glitters for a few moments in the rays of the sun, filtered down through the leafless boughs, and then is gone, to be seen, gleaming, here and there farther on, beating against the dense rows of cactus, bunched together in the close squares of an immovable phalanx, bristling with thorns.

In great bewilderment the soldiers make a wide detour. Spreading out, on the run, they plunge headlong into the labyrinth of boughs and branches. Tripped by the slipknot lassos of the creeping quipá vines, they fall, or else are brought to a standstill, their legs held motionless by the powerful tentacles. They struggle desperately, until their uniforms are in tatters, in the feline claws of the macambiras with their crooked thorns.

They stand there cursing impotently, in rage and disappointment, as they struggle furiously but without avail to free themselves. Finally, the tumult dies away as the men spread out more and more, firing at random, without aim, with an utter lack of discipline, their bullets likely as not hitting their own comrades. Reinforcements come up, and the anguished struggle with the underbrush is repeated all over again, on a yet larger scale, as the confusion and the disorder increase—and meanwhile, round about them, steadily, rhythmically, fall the deadly well-aimed missiles of the terrible enemy, safe in his hiding-place.

Of a sudden, the firing ceases. The enemy is gone, and no one has had so much as a glimpse of him. The detachments with their numbers depleted now return to the column after all this futile beating of the brush. It is as if they were coming back from a hand-to-hand encounter with savages; their weapons are lost or hopelessly battered; there are deep gashes on their hands and faces; they are limping, crippled, and it is all they can do to keep from crying out with the infernal pain inflicted upon them by the prickly leaves of the caatinga, the thorn wounds that they bear.

The troop is then reorganized and the march is resumed. Two abreast, it goes on down the paths, the blue uniforms of the soldiers with their vermilion stripes and the brightly gleaming, swaying bayonets giving a strong dash of colour to the ashen-grey of the landscape. And so they march on until they are lost to sight in the distance.

Some minutes pass, and then, at the scene of the struggle, from the scattered thickets, five, ten, twenty men at the most rise up, and swiftly, silently, slip away among the parched shrubbery.

They meet on the highway and stand there for a moment or so gazing after the troop which is now barely visible on the horizon. And brandishing their muskets, still hot from firing, they hastily make for the trails that lead to their unknown dwellings.

As for the members of the expeditionary force, they will be more cautious after this. As they march along in silence, the soldiers cannot help thinking anxiously of this intangible enemy and are haunted by visions of sudden assaults. The commanding officer surrounds them with every possible precaution; detached companies skirt their flanks, and up ahead, a couple of hundred yards in advance of the column, is a squadron of picked men. Upon descending a rugged slope, however, they come to a ravine which has to be crossed. Fortunately, its sides have been swept clean by floods, leaving only a little grass stubble, a few slender cacti standing out here and there among the stone heaps and the dead and white-peeling boughs of the umbú trees, victims of the drought.

The advance guard goes down the side of the ravine, followed by the first of the battalions, slowly straggling after. One can see them now, down below, the entire vanguard of the column, following the twists and turns of the narrow valley, their weapons gleaming in the sun like some dark torrent shot with rays of light.

Then they suddenly haul up short with a convulsive shudder which they cannot control. A bullet has just whistled past them. This time the shots, fired at intervals as usual, appear to come from above and from a solitary marksman. Only discipline preserves order in the ranks now and restrains a panic which is on the verge of breaking out. As before, a detachment is told off and goes up the slope in the direction of the shots; but, owing to the bedlam of echoes, it is hard for the men to keep their bearings: and in this over-heated atmosphere the sharpshooter's hiding-place is not revealed by the smoke from his weapon, owing to the absence of condensation; and so he continues firing, leisurely but with terrifying effect, assured meanwhile of his own safety.

At last the firing ceases, and it is in vain that the soldiers, roaming over the slopes, seek for their vanished assailants. They return exhausted, the bugles sound, and the band is on its way once more, with a few men less. And when the last of them are out of sight, beyond the roll of the hill, there rises up from among the stone heaps—like a sinister caryatid amid these cyclopic ruins—a hard and sunburned face, followed by the rude and leather-clad torso of an athlete. Running swiftly up the steep sides of the ravine, this dreadful hunter of armed men is gone in a few moments' time.

The troops continue on their way, completely demoralized. From now on, these hardened veterans are as timid as a child. A shiver runs up and down their spines at each bend of the road, at every dead leaf that crackles in the brush. The army has come to feel that its very strength is its weakness. Without any manœuvrability, in a state of continual exhaustion, it must make its way through these desert regions under the constant threat of ambuscades and be slowly sacrificed to a dreaded enemy who does not stand and fight but flees. The conflict is an unequal one, and a military force is compelled to descend to a lower plane of combat; it has to contend not merely with man but with the earth itself; and, when the backlands are boiling in the dry summer heat, it is not difficult to foresee which side will have the victory. While the mighty Minotaur, helpless in spite of his steel armour and bayonet claws, feels his throat drying up with thirst and, at the first symptoms of hunger, turns back to the rear, fleeing the inhospitable and menacing desert, the aggressive flora of this region, on the other hand, takes the sertanejo to its friendly, caressing bosom.

The news that was brought the troops was very definite in character. In three weeks' time Canudos had grown in extraordinary fashion. Word of the victory over the earlier expedition—a victory that was made to appear a good deal more important than it was—had spread and was being embroidered with numerous romantic episodes. This ended the last hesitation on the part of those of the faithful who up to then had been afraid to join Antonio Consel-heiro's phalanstery. As in the early days of the settlement, groups of pilgrims in quest of the legendary haven were now to be seen at any moment of the day, coming over the tops of the hills with all their earthly possessions. Many of them bore in hammocks their relatives who were ailing—dying ones who sighed for a last resting-place in this holy ground; the blind, the paralysed, the leprous, looking for a miraculous and immediate cure at a mere gesture of the venerated miracle-worker. There were, as always, people of all sorts: small-scale cattle-breeders; credulous cowboys of athletic build, along with the various types of backlands vagabond; simple-minded mothers of families, sisters now to the most incorrigible and artful hussies. And invariably bringing up the rear of the processions, without joining in the litanies, walking along in solitude and aloof, as if contemptuous of it all, were the desperadoes, the bandits and professional assassins, now seeking a more extended theatre of operations in which to display their impulsive bravery and satisfy their longing for adventure.

At daybreak in the settlement tasks were assigned to all, and there were plenty of hands—enough and more than enough—to carry them out. Sentry forces of twenty men each, under the command of trusted leaders, were stationed, relieving those who had kept watch there during the night. Some of those who the day before had paid tribute and become members of the community now went out to work in the small plantations along the banks of the river on either side, while others became building labourers at the church. Others still—the more crafty and active ones—scattered out on delicate missions. Their task was to pick up what information they could concerning the new expedition, by talking with the faithful, who in these localities defied the vigilance of the authorities by acquiring contraband weapons, which, after all, was easy enough to do, and storing them away in hidden places. The function of the scouts was to keep an eye on all that was going on and to learn all they could through cautious inquiries.

And they all were happy as they set out for their various tasks. Small but noisy groups went down the roads, bearing weapons or implements of labour, and singing as they went. They had for-gotten the previous massacres, and deep in the soul of many lay the hope that now at last, perhaps, they would be left alone to live out their simple, uneventful lives here in the backlands.

Their leaders, however, had no illusions on this score. They were taking no chances but were bending all their efforts to the urgent task of defence; and throughout the long hot day the sertanejos could be seen, on the hilltops or along the edge of the roads, rolling, carrying, or piling up stones, digging up the earth with picks and hoes, and labouring incessantly. They were engaged in building trenches.

This method of hastily throwing up temporary fortifications was an ideal one. It consisted of making a circular or elliptical cavity in the earth in which the marksman could conceal himself and move about at will; around the edge of this cavity breastworks consisting of stones laid alongside one another were erected, with openings for the musket barrels. The work of building these epaulements was facilitated by the character of the talc-schist formations, which afforded stones of whatever shape and size might be desired. This goes to explain the extraordinary number of those holes in the ground which are to be seen in all directions round about Canudos, at regular intervals, and which look like the embrasures of a monster fortress without walls. Located in a cross-line of fire commanding the approaches, they were so distributed, especially in those long stretches where they took advantage of the dry bed of the creeks, as to render it extremely difficult for even the best and lightest of troops to effect a passage. And inasmuch as the defenders foresaw that their enemy, wishing to avoid such a passage, would turn aside and assault the border trenches, they constructed secondary ones on top of the slopes, close at hand, and other more distant ones arranged in the very same manner, in order that the marksmen driven back from the front line might be able to make a stand here and continue the fight. Thus, whether he kept to the highway or abandoned it, the enemy would find himself trapped in a network of rifle fire.

In making these preparations, the rebels stood in need of no tutoring. The earth itself was an admirable model: jagged saw-teeth spurs rising up like redoubts; rivers carving out their beds in the form of fosses and covered passageways; and on all sides the caatingas plaited into naturally formed tree fortifications. The jagunços would select the tallest shrubs and those with the greatest amount of foliage and would skilfully interweave the inner boughs without disturbing the outer branches in such a manner as to form, a couple of yards above the ground, a small hammock or platform capable of supporting comfortably one or two invisible sharpshooters, con-

cealed in the leaves. These singular turrets represented an old
ancestral custom, a stratagem long employed in ambush warfare
with the fierce panther and his kind. These native *mutans* (a platform
on which the hunter waits for his game), constructed in the manner
described and scattered here and there, served to complete the line of
trenches. Occasionally, the sertanejos would undertake fortifications
of a more imposing sort. They would discover a hill with great
round blocks of stone piled on its summit; they would clear out the
spaces between the rocks, wide openings filled with a rank growth
of thistles and bromelias, thus forming narrow windows concealed
by a dense growth of silk grass; after this, they would clear the spaces
within, until finally they were able to move about freely in a huge
blockhouse overlooking the trails and highways and from which
they might without risk to themselves command the most remote
points.

Their preparations, however, did not stop here. They also put
their weapons in order. The village was now filled with the sounds
of a strident orchestra, hammers clanging on anvils as they beat their
crooked scythes into shape, as they sharpened and steeled their
polished cattle prongs, as they tempered the broad blades of their
'scraping-knives', long as swords, as they braced their bows (which
were by way of being a compromise between the weapon of the
savage and the ancient crossbow), and as they adjusted the locks of
their antique muskets and double-barrelled shotguns. From all
these glowing forges there arose a great metallic din, the resounding
clang of a busy arsenal.

The supply of gunpowder acquired in the neighbouring towns
not being sufficient, they proceeded to manufacture their own. They
had the charcoal; the saltpetre was to be found along the surface of
the earth, farther north, near the São Francisco; and they had laid
in a supply of brimstone some while before. They were accordingly able to turn out an accurately compounded product which
rivalled the brand commonly used by hunters.

There was no lack of bullets, or at least of projectiles; the broad
mouths of the blunderbusses took everything: round pebbles, nail-
heads, horntips, broken glass, rock splinters, etc.

And, last of all, there was no lack of 'famous' fighters whose
amazing adventures were the talk of the entire region. Religious
sentiment is all-embracing in character, and, along with the instinct
to disorder, it had here brought together not Baians alone but individuals from all the border states. In addition to the jagunço of the
São Francisco and the cangaceiro of the Carirys, there were all sorts

of traditional 'bad men', heroes of former backlands conflicts and petty uprisings barely to be distinguished from one another even in the names they bore—that of the 'lizards', that of the 'hampers', that of the 'baskets', etc. A call to arms was being sent out over the countryside.

From day to day, strange-appearing newcomers arrived at the settlement, men who were absolutely unknown to anyone there. They came, their cartridge belts stuffed with bullets and their powder cases full; a double-barrelled shotgun slung across their sashes, from which dangled the inevitable parnahyba (sword-like knife); and on a bandoleer, the bell-mouthed blunderbuss. They simply appeared, that was all, and made their way to the public square without anyone's asking who they were or from where they came, as if they had been old acquaintances. The wily João Abbade received them there. He was their equal when it came to a turbulent past but was possessed of more astuteness and had, besides, the smattering of an education; he had been at one time a pupil in a public school in one of the provincial capitals of the North but had been forced to flee after he had murdered his sweetheart, which was the first crime he had committed. In any event, he was the man to hold these rowdies in check and discipline them. 'Commander of the Street' was the title he bore, an inexplicable one in that labyrinth of alleyways; but, without leaving the settlement, he exerted an absolute sway over the entire countryside for twelve miles around, being kept informed of what was going on by his swift-moving scouts who were constantly on the watch. All gave him unconditional obedience. In the assignment of numerous tasks of various sorts, in the performance of which the religious-minded countryman rubbed elbows with the hardened criminal, there was to be observed a rare co-ordination of forces; and the most perfect uniformity of views prevailed, with one purpose only in view, that of repelling the imminent invasion.

Nevertheless, as some of the prisoners afterward revealed, when the campaign was over, all these warlike preparations came near being brought to a sudden halt by one piece of news that was received, and the rebel community was so astounded and dismayed that it was on the point of immediately breaking up. This occurred when the scouts who had been sent out to various points to see what progress the invader was making came back and reported, as a matter of certain knowledge, not only the number and equipment of the troops, but the renown attaching to the name of the new commander. The feverish activity of the jagunços stopped short.

They were terror-stricken as they listened to the most exaggerated, the most extravagant and fanciful tales of the commanding officer's boldness and daring. He was the Anti-Christ, come to put the unhappy penitents to a last proof. They pictured him as the hero of many battles—fourteen, according to the account of one rude backlands poet, in a song which was later composed to celebrate the campaign. They could foresee the devastation of their homes, days of nameless torture, catastrophes of every sort. Canudos itself would be wiped out by fire, sword, and bullet. They had a gruesome name for him—'Head-chopper'.

Uninfluenced though they might be by the dread-inspiring rumours, the people nonetheless turned, at this juncture, to the solace of their religious faith; and not infrequently after that, their steeled weapons at their side, the entire population of the settlement would turn out in long penitential processions across the fields. The stream of incoming pilgrims had suddenly ceased. The feverish preparations for war were likewise at a standstill. The sentries as they left for their posts at daybreak no longer sang loud hymns of rejoicing as they went down the trails but scurried along cautiously in the thickets, remaining there, silent and watchful, for long hours at a time.

It was under these most distressing circumstances that the frail but numerous legion of the pious ones took the field to encourage the more apprehensive of the able-bodied fighting men. And at nightfall, to the glow of bonfires, the kneeling multitude would prolong their prayers beyond the appointed time, there in the arbour strewn with aromatic boughs from the caatingas. At the far end of the arbour, next the door to the 'Sanctuary', was a small pine table, covered with a snow-white cloth; and, when they had done saying their beads, a strange figure would come and approach this table. Clad in a long blue tunic without a girdle, which fell gracelessly over his emaciated limbs, with his back bent, his head down, his gaze lowered, Antonio Conselheiro would make his appearance. He would remain for a long time silent and motionless in the presence of this quiet, waiting multitude. Then slowly he would lift his wan face, suddenly illuminated by his flashing, piercing eyes, and he would pray.

Night then would fall, deep night, and the settlement ruled by this humblest of evangelists, who was yet so formidable, would go to its repose.

February 22 was the date set for the departure of the troops; and in accordance with military custom, on the afternoon of the preceding day they were drawn up in marching order for review and an inspection of arms and equipment. There were 1,281 men altogether, each with 220 cartridges in his belt and luggage, in addition to a reserve of 60,000 rounds in the general store.

The review took place; but, contrary to general expectation, in place of a command to stack arms and disband, the bugle sounded alongside the commander-in-chief, giving the signal, 'Column, march!' And Colonel Moreira Cesar, leaving the point where he had been stationed, galloped over and took his place at the head of the column.

It was almost dark when they set out on the march to Canudos. The whole thing was unexpected, but there was not the faintest murmuring in the ranks; the surprise reflected on all the faces did not interfere with the rigorous execution of manœuvres. The drums beat, up ahead; the various detachments fell in, marching two abreast as they entered the narrow highway; the artillery got under way, and the supply trains rumbled along.

The vanguard arrived at Cumbe within three days, the rest of the troops being detained for a few hours—with their commanding officer laid up in a near-by ranch house with another attack of epilepsy.

Before daybreak of the twenty-sixth, having reached the farm known as the 'Cajá Trees' the evening before, six miles distant from Cumbe, they struck out directly northward for the 'White Hills' more than eight miles farther on. It is at once less rugged and more arid. The steep-sloping hills are now few in number, and in their place is a vast expanse of highland plains. However, while the land here may be less rugged, it presents other obstacles which are perhaps even more formidable. The flat and sandy soil, with no depressions which in summer may provide life-giving water, is absolutely sterile. The rains are few and far between and do little more than wet the ground, being immediately sucked in by the sands.

In midsummer, from November to March, the desolation is complete. Whoever then ventures into this region has the impression of being in an enormous plantation of parched and interweaving boughs where the spark of a match would touch off a sudden conflagration, if indeed a conflagration did not occur by spontaneous combustion, in this season of drought, with the strong north-east wind rubbing the branches together in the blazing noonday sun.

It was at the most unsuitable time of the year that the expedition entered these parts, for a forced march, with the thermometer soaring; and in this dry, exhausting heat there was nothing to do but keep on marching until they came to the nearest place where they knew they would find a well, which would make it feasible for them to halt. They had a hard time of it indeed. The character of the soil made walking difficult, as the shifting sand slipped beneath their feet; and it was even more difficult for the wagon trains, as they sank up to their hubs. They would suddenly find their way barred with briar patches, which it was necessary to hack down with their knives. And all the while the intense dog-day heat was radiated by the burning sands. Small wonder, then, if by the time they arrived at 'White Hills', in the afternoon, the men were exhausted. Exhausted and very thirsty. They had marched for eight hours without a halt beneath that summer sun. But here, by way of quenching the unnatural thirst which came from the almost total depletion of their veins by perspiration, they found in the depths of a cave a few quarts of water.

Weakened as they were, the troops started off again, late in the afternoon; and, when night fell and the gleaming stars came out, they were still struggling along, doing their best to make their way through the tangled briar patches.

It may be imagined what this march was like, of twenty or twenty-five miles without a halt. A thousand and some thirst-ridden men fairly staggering beneath the weight of their equipment, in the heart of the enemy's territory. The dull thud of marching feet, the creaking of wagons and gun carriages, the clink of weapons in the desert stillness, an island of sound in a sea of silence—and all the while, in the tall weeds, there was an imperceptible crackling of boughs.

Accompanying the troops, creeping along the edge of the by-paths, were the spies sent out by the jagunços. No one paid any heed to them, however. Exhausted from their day's march, the expeditionaries had forgotten all about fighting; all that they could think of was the nearest wells, for which they were making, trusting implicitly, meanwhile, to the judgment and loyalty of their guides.

But at last they came to a halt in the middle of the road. Bringing up the rear, in the distance, a few crippled stragglers could be seen, while even the most able-bodied were limping along. The halt was a brief one, and such rest as they were able to snatch was an illusion. The officers slept—those who did sleep—with their horses' reins fastened to their hands. And the next morning, as they resumed their march before daybreak, they realized that they were in the danger zone. The remains of bonfires all along the way, some of them with the embers still glowing; the remains of excellent meals which had consisted of roast turtle and quarters of kid; fresh tracks in the sand, winding away, with many twists and turnings, into the caatingas— all these signs showed that the sertanejos had been there, and had even spent the night there, cautiously, invisibly keeping watch on the invaders. When the latter reached 'Old Wicket' ('Porteira Velha'), it looked as if they had actually come upon the enemy, and the vanguard broke ranks precipitately. There beside a bonfire was a two-barrelled pistol and a cowboy's cattle prong.

They arrived at 'Rosario' shortly before noon, just as a violent but passing shower was falling, a thing that is likely to happen in the backlands at this season of the year. It was here that the expedition pitched camp, in the enemy's own country; and it is not strange if now, for the first time, the men began to experience that feeling of apprehension which goes with war.

Colonel Moreira Cesar, meanwhile, had interned himself in the nearest caatinga, where he had ordered his tent set up. Receiving his staff officers there, he let them know that he was absolutely certain of victory. Various expedients were then suggested to him for rendering the attack safer. One of these called for first altering the order of march which had been followed up to then; it was suggested that the single column be divided in two, one portion to form a strong vanguard for reconnoitring and the first assault, while the other would come into action as a reserve force. In this way, should the enemy prove to be too strong for them, it would be possible to stage an orderly retreat to Monte Santo, where their forces could be reorganized and augmented. Contrary to what everyone expected, the commander-in-chief of the expedition did not turn down this proposal; and at dawn on the third the troops marched, in accordance with a clearly thought-out plan.

It was five o'clock in the morning when they began the march, and they were soon in the immediate vicinity of Canudos with its characteristic terrain: a hilly country, covered with a scraggly vegetation; with numerous tortuous-winding streams running through it, and with the land becoming all the while more rugged and hostile, save for those patches where the recent rains had left an ephemeral garment of green veiling the stone heaps and the mouths of caves. The evening showers, as usual in summer, had passed without leaving any trace, the parched earth, which had absorbed and repelled the moisture, remaining rough and dry. Round about for as far as the eye could reach, over the rolling hills and the elevated

plains, along the surrounding trails and on the eroded mountainsides
—everywhere were the same hues, the same monotonous yet impressive landscape; all Nature was motionless, gripped in the throes
of an enormous spasm, without a bloom on the naked boughs, no
beat of wings on the quiet and unruffled air.

The marching column, stretched out in a line almost two miles
long, was a dark and winding streak across this landscape. Ahead of
them to the north the troops could see, close at hand now, the final
circle of hills about Canudos, and they were not the least disturbed
in mind at thus drawing near their military objective.

They marched quietly, at their accustomed steady pace. All up
and down the line could be heard a vague, subdued murmur of
thousands of voices, suddenly punctuated here and there with bursts
of jovial laughter. In this singular alacrity with which they approached the enemy, our soldiers were displaying their most
prominent attribute. Men of all shades of colour and of diverse
races, they appeared on such occasions as this, involving dangerous
undertakings and calling forth strong emotions, to be governed by
some law of collective psychology; it was the instincts of the
primitive warrior that ruled their minds: the improvidence of the
savage, his unawareness of peril, his indifference to life and rashness
in the face of death. They went into battle as if bound for some
rowdy merrymaking. Intolerable creatures in times of peace, when
they grew soft and flabby and relaxed; nondescript on parade in
the street, without any kind of presence or aplomb, slouched beneath
their awkwardly handled rifles, they were different beings in time of
war. War, indeed, was their best training-ground and the enemy
their favourite drillmaster, one who within a few days made them
over into disciplined and hardened soldiers, giving them in a short
while, through long and wearing marches and actual combat, what
they never possessed in the flag-bedecked capitals—erectness of
bearing, firmness of step, precision of firing aim, swiftness in reload-
ing. They never give in to circumstances but will march for days at
a time over the most impossible of roads. In this they are inimitable.
There is never the least grumbling to be heard from them, no matter
what may happen; and none can equal them when it comes to going
without food and living for days 'on wind', as they say in their own
picturesque jargon. After the most trying of experiences, these wan-
faced heroes will still make light of misery and scoff at martyrdom.

In battle, to be sure, the Brazilian soldier is incapable of imitating
the Prussian, by going in and coming out with a pedometer on his
boot. He is disorderly, tumultuous, rowdy, a terrible but heroic

blackguard, attacking the enemy whether by bullet or sword thrust with an ironic jest on his lips. For this very reason he is ill-adapted to the great mass movements of classic campaigns. He is impeded by correct formations and bewildered by the mechanics of complex manœuvres. It is a torture to him to be obliged to fight in strict adherence to the rhythm of bugles; and, while he will readily enough obey orders in the execution of broad strategic plans, going along uncomplainingly under the most trying conditions, yet, when the enemy charges him at the point of the sword, he wants to fight in his own way. And he does fight then, without any hard feelings, noisily, blusteringly, rejoicing in the rain of bullets and the play of swords, taking foolhardy risks and holding his courage cheap. All the while, however, he has his eyes fixed on his commanding officers, and his very life appears to hang on the energy which they exhibit. Let them waver ever so little, and all his daring is gone; he is instantly downcast and falls prey to a discouragement which he is powerless to overcome.

On the present occasion everything pointed to a victory for the expeditionaries. With such a commander as theirs, defeat was out of the question. And so it was with a firm stride that they made their way to the front, impatient to come to grips with this stubborn enemy. What they would do to these backwoodsmen was something scandalous; they would give them a dressing-down. They were already picturing their anticipated exploits; the stories they would have to tell would scare the wits out of the timid ones back home, who believed all you told them; what tragi-comic scenes there would be—up there in that monstrous weed patch, when they charged it with their rifles. They went on making bizarre plans, premature ones, and they all began with the same naïve preliminary, 'When I go back. . . .'

At times one of them would come out with some extravagant idea, only to be greeted with a ripple of suppressed laughter as the babble of voices stopped for a moment.

What was more, the glow of this resplendent morning cheered them. Above them was the beautiful blue-arching sky of the backlands with its rainbow tints, shading gently, imperceptibly, from the deep blue of the zenith to the dazzling purple in the east. Besides, had not the enemy left the road clear for them up to now, failing to take advantage of the most favourable stretches to attack them? There was but one thing that worried them: what if they should find this nest of rebels empty when they arrived? This likely disappointment proved an alarming thought: the entire campaign transformed into a long forced march; and then, their inglorious return, without having fired a single cartridge.

It was in this admirable frame of mind that they reached 'Pitombas'. The small, deep, winding stream which is found at this point now flows alongside the highway and now crosses it, finally leaving the road before reaching the farm to which it gives its name, making a long, bowed curve, almost a semi-circle, with the highway as the chord.

It was along this stretch of road that the troops came; and, as they reached the middle of it, there were half a dozen shots. It was the enemy at last. It was some scout who had been accompanying the expedition, or who, lying in wait for it there, had taken advantage of the favourable conformation of the terrain for a sudden attack from the side and then had safely fled, protected by the banks of the stream. His aim had been a sure one, and one of the subalterns of the rifle company, Lieutenant Poly, fell mortally wounded, and six or seven soldiers besides. The cannons of the Salamão Division were quickly loaded, and machine-gun bullets tore into the weedy undergrowth, the shrubbery bending as it does when swept by harsh winds. Before the echoes had died down, there came the sound of rhythmic rifle fire and, detaching itself from the column where it had formed part of the other rifles, the right wing of the Seventh now charged in the direction of the enemy, plunging into the weeds at top speed, slashing them down with their bayonets. It was a swift and glorious sally, but the enemy fled the encounter. Minutes passed, and the detachment returned to the line amid general acclamations, while the bugles gave the traditional signal of victory by playing the 'trinities', their notes ringing out loud and vibrant. The commander-in-chief, in an impulsive manifestation of sincere joy, embraced the fortunate officer who had given this repulse to the enemy; he looked upon the engagement as an auspicious beginning. It was almost too bad, all this fine equipment, all these men, all this impressive setting for a campaign that was to be ended with the firing of half a dozen shots.

The weapons of the jagunços were ridiculous. As spoils, the soldiers came upon a 'woodpecker' rifle under the riverbank; it was light in weight, with a very slender barrel. The rifle was loaded, and, taking it in his hand as he sat on his horse, Colonel Cesar discharged it in the air. As a weapon, it was insignificant, good for killing a bird.

'These people are unarmed,' he observed tranquilly.

3*

The march was then resumed at a more rapid pace, the surgeons and the wounded being left behind in 'Pitombas', under the protection of the police contingent and the rest of the cavalry. The majority of the men were already disappearing in the distance, at a double-quick step. The spell of the enemy was broken. The riflemen in the vanguard and those who guarded the flanks were now beating the brush alongside the road and plunging deep into the caatingas in search of any spies that might be lurking there, bent on routing them from their likely hiding-places or overtaking the fugitives who were making for Canudos.

This engagement was like an electric shock. The troops as they continued their rapid advance were animated by the irrepressible lust of battle; they were in that highly dangerous state of mental intoxication in which the soldier feels doubly strong, through the certainty of his own strength and the knowledge that he will be permitted an absolute licence in the indulgence of his most brutal instincts.

In a pursuing army there exists the same impulsive automatism as in one that flees. Panic and a foolish bravery, extreme terror and an extreme audacity, are in either case intermingled. There is the same dazed bewilderment as the men stumble forward headlong in the face of the most formidable obstacles, the same nervous tremor running through the ranks, the same painful anxiety which stimulates and hallucinates with equally forceful effect the individual who is fleeing death and the one who is out to kill. The explanation lies in the fact that an army is, first of all, a multitude, a 'mass of heterogeneous elements in which one has but to strike a spark of passion, and there is a sudden metamorphosis, a kind of spontaneous generation, by virtue of which thousands of different individuals become a single animal, a nameless monster of the wilds, going forward to a given objective with an irresistible finality'. Only the moral strength of a commander can prevent this deplorable transformation, by clearly and firmly imposing a directive which will bring order out of chaos. The great strategists have instinctively realized that the first victory to be won in war lies in overcoming this violent emotional contagion, this undependable state of feeling on the part of the troops, which with equal intensity will impel a man to face the gravest of perils or to take refuge in flight. A plan of war as drawn up with a compass on a map calls for passionless souls—killing machines—steadily functioning within lines that are pre-established.

Moreira Cesar's soldiers, however, were far from having attained this sinister ideal; and their commander, in place of repressing the nervous excitement in the ranks, made it all the worse by the example of neurasthenia which he himself set. An opportunity had occurred, meanwhile, for bringing the situation back to normal. They had reached 'Angico', the point which had been determined upon as their last halt. Here, their schedule called for a night's rest, and on the morning of the following day, they were to strike camp and, after a two hours' march, fall upon Canudos. The impulsive inclinations of the troops, however, were still further increased by those of their commander, and they were obsessed with one desire: to come to grips with the enemy. The halt at 'Angico', accordingly, lasted but a quarter of an hour, barely time enough to summon the staff officers for a consultation, which was held upon a small hill affording a view of the panting troops drawn up round about. Forgetful of the maxim that nothing can be accomplished with tired soldiers, the leader of the expedition then proposed that they go on and attack at once.

'My comrades! As you can see, I am a sick man. I have not eaten for days. But we are very near to Canudos now—let us go on and take it!'

This suggestion was adopted.

'We will have breakfast in Canudos!' he shouted and was met with a true soldierly ovation.

The march continued. It was eleven o'clock in the morning. The company of marksmen up ahead was scattering out through the thickets, from which now and then a distant shot could be heard, as the enemy fled with the one purpose, seemingly, of luring the troops on to the settlement, where, weakened and exhausted by their six hours' march, they would have to fight under unfavourable conditions—such was the sum of their clever strategy.

It was a mad impulse, depriving the men of their rest like this on the eve of battle; and, as a consequence, so long as it did not slow down the advance of the infantry, they had to be permitted to discard their knapsacks, canteens, ration kits, and all the equipment they carried, with the exception of their weapons and cartridges, to be picked up by the cavalry in the rear. This fact speaks for itself.

Advancing hastily in this manner, they reached the small plain on top of the Umburanas Hills. Canudos must be very close, within range of their artillery. The troops came to a halt.

The guide, Jesuino, upon being consulted, pointed out the direction in which the settlement lay; he was quite sure of it. Moreira Cesar thereupon called the Pradel Division into battle and, setting the aim at one and four-fifths miles, ordered two rounds fired in the direction indicated.

'There go a couple of visiting cards for the Counsellor,' he said, half-jestingly, with that superior sense of humour which a strong man possesses. The phrase ran down the ranks and was greeted with acclamations. A feverish attack was at once launched. The sun was beating straight down upon them as the battalions, overcoming the last difficulties of the terrain, went into action beneath a heavy, stifling cloud of dust. They now suddenly had a view of Canudos. They were on top of Mount Favella.

Here at last was that enormous weed patch which previous expeditions had not succeeded in reaching. It came into view all at once, lying there in a broadened depression of the rolling plain. At first glimpse, before his eye had become accustomed to this pile of huts and labyrinth of narrow alleys, some of which came out on the wide square where the churches stood, the observer had the precise impression of having unexpectedly stumbled upon a large city. Forming a huge, deepened moat to the left, at the foot of the highest hills, the Vasa-Barris half-circled the village and then took a sharp turn directly to the east, as the first waters of the flood season rolled slowly along. The compact cluster of huts about the square gradually spread out, sprawling over the hills to the east and north, with the last of the outlying houses taking on the appearance of scattered sentry boxes; and, meanwhile, there was not a single white wall or rubble-strewn roof to break the monotony of this monstrous collection of five thousand shacks dropped down in a furrow of the earth. The two churches stood out sharply. The new one, on the observer's left, was still unfinished, and its main walls, high and thick, could be seen covered with scaffoldings, with wooden joists, beams, and planks, while from this maze there emerged the rigid outlines of the cranes with their swaying pulleys. This structure towered above the others in the village and overlooked the broad expanse of plains; it was large, rectangular, solidly built, its walls consisting of great stone blocks laid one upon another with perfect skill, which gave it the exact appearance of a formidable bastion. More humble in aspect, built like the common run of back-country chapels, the old church stood facing it. Still farther to the right, roughly circular in shape, dotted with little rudely fashioned crosses, but without a single flower bed, a single bloom, a single shrub, was the cemetery of levelled graves. And there on the top of the mountain were the troops.

The vanguard of the Seventh was the first detachment to arrive, along with the artillery; they were engaged in repulsing a violent attack on the right while the rest of the infantry climbed the last slopes. They paid little attention to the settlement itself, meanwhile. The cannon were aligned in battle formation, as the first platoons came up, their ranks in confusion, the men panting; and a cannonading then began, with all the guns firing at once, without co-ordination. There was no missing a mark as big as this one. The effects of the initial rounds were visible at various points: huts were shattered, ripped apart and buried in débris by cannon balls exploding in their midst; the splintered roofs of clay and wood were sent hurtling through the air; the adobe walls were pulverized; the first fires were started.

The bombarded village was now enveloped in a dense cloud of dust and smoke which hid it completely from view. The rest of the troops could not be seen. The solemn thunder of the artillery rent the air, awakening a far, deep resonance throughout the breadth of the desert lands, as the deafening echoes came back from the mountainsides.

But, as the minutes passed, there were to be heard, sounding clear above the roar of the cannons, the sudden silvery notes of a bell. It was the bell of the old church down below, summoning the faithful to battle.

The battle had not yet started. Apart from a light flank attack made by a few guerrillas upon the artillery, the sertanejos so far had put up no resistance. The troops spread out over the sloping summit without their manœuvres being disturbed by a single shot; and when the shooting did begin, it was a sustained but aimless running fire. Eight hundred rifles blazing, eight hundred rifles aimed in a rasant line down the drop of the hill.

As the smoke cleared away now and again, the settlement could be glimpsed. It was a beehive in commotion: innumerable groups here and there, weaving in and out of the square, scattering down the paths along the riverbank, making for the church, dashing down the alleyways with weapons in their hands, climbing up onto the roofs.

A few, at the far end of the village, appeared to be in flight; they could be seen wandering along the edge of the caatingas and disappearing behind the hills. Others displayed an incredible nonchalance by crossing the square at a leisurely pace, oblivious to the tumult and the stubborn spatter of bullets from the mountain.

One whole company of the Seventh at this moment trained its fire for several minutes upon a jagunço who was coming along the

Uauá Road, but the sertanejo did not so much as quicken his step; indeed, he even came to a dead stop at times. His impassive face could be seen in the distance as he raised his head to gaze at the troops for a few seconds and then went tranquilly on his way. This was an irritating challenge. In surprise, the soldiers nervously concentrated their fire upon this exceptional being, who had now become the bull's-eye for an army. At one moment he seated himself beside the road and appeared to be striking a light for his pipe. The soldiers laughed. Then he got to his feet and, still at the same leisurely pace, was gradually lost from sight among the outlying houses.

From the village not a shot was fired. The commotion in the square had died down. The last of the stragglers were now coming in, among them a number of women with children in their arms or dragging them by the hand, as they went on in the direction of the arbour, seeking the barrier afforded by the big walls of the new church.

The bell had finally stopped ringing. The troops now began the descent along the gentler slopes, hundreds of bayonets gleaming in the sun. As he surveyed them, the commander-in-chief of the expedition remarked to the commanding officer of one of the companies in his own regiment, beside whom he happened to be standing: 'We're going to take the town without firing another shot—at the point of the bayonet!'

It was one o'clock in the afternoon. When the descent had been made, a part of the infantry took up its position in the vale. The artillery was in the centre, upon the last spur of the hills, in an advanced position directly above the river, facing the new church on a level with its cornices.

The battle began heroically, with all the troops moving into action at once and with all the bugles blowing. The church bell was once more ringing, and an intense rifle fire had broken out from the walls and roofs of the dwellings nearest to the river, while the blunderbusses of the guerrillas massed within the new church produced the effect of a single explosion. With the advantage of a favourable terrain, the Seventh Battalion marched forward on the double-quick, amid a hail of lead and pebbles, down to the river; and it was not long before, having climbed the opposite bank, the first of the soldiers were to be seen at the entrance to the square; they were in small groups, without anything whatsoever to suggest battle formation. Some of them fell at the river crossing, or tumbled into the stream to be swept away by the current, which was streaked

with blood; but the majority continued to advance under heavy
fire from the front and sides. A pitched battle was now raging
around the column which was advancing in so rash a manner; and
from then on, there was not the simplest military movement or
joint manœuvre such as might have revealed the presence of a
commander.

The battle was now breaking up into smaller skirmishes which
were at once futile and dangerous, with much fine bravery inglori-
ously thrown away. This was inevitable. Canudos, less than a
couple of yards from the square, became a hopeless maze of alleys,
winding and crossing in all directions. With its mud-built huts, the
town may have given the impression of fragility, but this was an
illusion; it was in reality more formidable than a polygonal citadel
or one protected by strong armoured walls. Lying wide open to
attackers, who might destroy it with their rifle butts, who might
with a blow knock down the clay walls and roofs or send them
flying in all directions, it yet possessed the lack of consistency and the
treacherous flexibility of a huge net. It was easy to attack it, overcome it, conquer it, knock it down, send it hurtling—the difficult
thing was to leave it. A complement to the dangerous tactics of the
sertanejo, it was formidable for the very reason that it offered no
resistance. There was not so much as a hard-surface tile to break the
percussion of the grenades, which fell without exploding, piercing
dozens of roofs at once. There was nothing to cause the smallest
band of attackers to waver, from whatever side they might come,
once they had crossed the river. Canudos invited attacks; it exerted
an irresistible attraction for the enemy who would bombard it;
but when the invaders, drunken with a feeling of victory, began
separating and scattering out down the winding lanes, it then had a
means of defence that was at once amazing and tremendously
effective.

In the sombre story of cities taken by storm, this humble village
must stand out as an extraordinary and a tragic instance. Intact, it
was very weak indeed; reduced to a rubbish heap, it was redoubtable. Yielding in order to conquer, it suddenly appeared before the
victor's astonished gaze as an inexpugnable pile of ruins. For while
an army with its iron grip might shake it, crush it, rend it asunder,
leaving it a shapeless mass of mud walls and wooden stakes, that
same army would of a sudden find itself with its hands tied, trapped
between the tottering partitions of timber and liana stalks, like a
clumsy puma powerfully but vainly struggling to free itself from
meshes of a well-made snare. The jagunços were experienced

hunters, and this it was, perhaps, which led them to create this 'weed-trap citadel'.

Colonel Moreira Cesar's troops were now engaged in springing that trap upon themselves.

At first, after they had crossed the river in spite of a few losses, the attack appeared easy enough. One detachment, led by valorous sub-alterns, boldly assaulted the new church, but without any compen-sating effect, and with the further loss of two officers and several men. Others, making a detour about this nucleus of resistance, fell upon the outlying houses along the river. They took them and set fire to them, as the inhabitants fled for shelter elsewhere. The latter were pursued as they fled by the soldiers; and it was in the course of this tumultuous pursuit that the one very grave peril of this mon-strous undertaking became apparent: the platoons began to break up. The men now dashed down the narrow lanes, two abreast, in great confusion. There were hundreds of corners to be turned, one after another, from house to house, and the soldiers rounded them in disorderly fashion, some of them without making use of their weapons, while others fired at random, straight ahead. In this manner the entire outfit gradually became split up into small wandering detachments, and these in their turn broke up into bewildered groups with numbers diminishing all the while as the forces became more and more scattered, until finally they were reduced to isolated combatants here and there.

From a distance the spectacle was a weird one, with whole battalions being suddenly swallowed up among the huts, as in some dark cave, while over the clay roofs there hovered a dense cloud of smoke from the first of the conflagrations. All in all, the attack was anything but military in character. It was no longer a battle but a series of skirmishes at the corners of the lanes and in the doorways of the houses.

Here, however, the attack was a fierce one, for there were no obstacles in the way. A blow from a rifle butt would effect an entrance through doors or walls, shattering them to bits and opening a free passage from any side. Many of the houses were empty. In others, the intruders would unexpectedly find a musket barrel against their chests, or else they would drop, riddled with bullets fired at close range from chinks in the wall. Their nearest comrades would then run to their assistance, and there would be a brutal hand-to-hand struggle, until the soldiers who outnumbered the inmates had forced their way through the narrow doorway of the hut. On the inside, crouching in a dark corner, a lone remaining inmate would fire his last shot at them and flee. Or it might be that he would stand his ground and stubbornly defend his humble dwelling, fighting terribly—and alone—to avenge himself on the victorious ruffians, boldly having recourse to any weapons at hand, repelling them with knife and bullet, slashing at them with scythe or cattle prong, hurling the wretched household furniture at their heads, or, weak and gasping for breath, rushing upon them in an effort to strangle the first on whom he could lay his brawny arms. The womenfolk, meanwhile, would burst into sobs and cower in the corner, until at last the bold warrior lay on the ground, pierced with a bayonet, clubbed by gunstocks, trampled under the soldiers' boot heels. Scenes such as these were many.

Almost always, after capturing a house, the famished soldier was unable to resist the longing he felt to have breakfast—at last—in Canudos. Suspended from the ceiling were the food containers, and these he would search. In them he would find sun-dried meats, clay cups filled with passoca (the sertanejo's wartime flour), and bags brimming with the savoury fruit of the urucuri. In a corner would be pouches with the moisture standing on them, swollen with water crystalline and fresh. The temptation was too much for him. Rashly, he would fall to for a minute's repast, topping it off with a large drink of water. Sometimes, however, he had a dessert of a cruel and bitter sort—a volley of lead.

The jagunços, coming in at the door, would fall upon him, and the struggle would be repeated with the roles reversed this time, until the imprudent warrior lay on the ground, slashed with a knife, clubbed, trampled by the sertanejo's coarse sandals.

Many became hopelessly lost in the alleyways. Hot on the heels of the fleeing woodsman, they would find themselves suddenly, as they rounded a corner, surrounded by a band of enemies. In their astonishment, they barely had time to take a bad aim and fire, then turn and run, dashing into the houses where, frequently, others lay in wait, ready to leap upon them; or else, they would attack and disperse the enemy group—whereupon the same scenes would be repeated all over again. And all the time they were buoyed by the illusion of a victory attained with dizzying ease. Was it not evident enough from all this disorder, all this fear and hubbub, all this terror on the part of the wretched, ugly little town? Why, the inhabitants were as frightened as the animals in a stable when the fierce and famished jaguars attack.

What was more, there were no insuperable obstacles in the invaders' way. The bold heroes who put in an appearance now and then, by way of defending their homes, had womenfolk to think about, driven out by fire, sword, and bullet, fleeing in all directions as they shrieked and prayed, or that armed legion of crutches— trembling old men and women, the lame and the halt of every description, the sick, the weak, and the maimed.

The upshot of it all was that in the fury of the chase many lost their way in that labyrinth of lanes and, in attempting to rejoin their companions, wandered farther astray than ever, as they madly dashed around a thousand little corners, only to become completely lost in the end in this enormous and convulsive-appearing settlement.

Stationed in front of his headquarters on the right bank of the river, the commander-in-chief of the expedition was observing the attack, without quite being able to come to a decision regarding it. All he could make out was his men disappearing from sight among the thousand and one holes and hiding-places of Canudos, followed by a great uproar in which curses and shrill cries mingled with the sound of rifle fire. All that he could see was small groups, detachments of soldiers without any formation and small bands of jagunços suddenly coming into view now and then in the open space of the square, only to disappear once more amid the smoke, in a confused hand-to-hand struggle.

That was all, but it was enough to alarm him; the situation was now a disquieting one. There was nothing to indicate that the sertanejos were giving up the struggle. The sharpshooters at the new church were standing their ground, and were able with practical impunity to fire in all directions; for the artillery had finally ceased, from fear of striking some of the soldiers with a stray ball. And now, above all the din of battle, the bell of the old church was steadily ringing out once more. Only about half the village was involved in the fray; the other half, on the right, where the Geremoabo Highway came in, was unaffected by it. Less compactly built, it was at the same time less open to assault. Spread out over a large elevated plain, it could be defended on a line of fire level with the enemy, obliging the latter to the dangerous expedient of trying to take it by storm. Consequently, after the other part of the village had been stormed and taken, it still remained intact, and this, perhaps, meant that an even greater amount of effort must be expended here.

The truth is, while there were not the winding lanes to contend with, as down below, these scattered houses nonetheless, by the nature of their distribution which was vaguely reminiscent of a chessboard, afforded an extraordinarily good opportunity for cross-fire, so that a single marksman might command all four points of the compass without leaving his own small square. When one took this portion of the town into consideration, the full gravity of the situation became apparent. Even assuming that they had met with success in the centre of the village, the victorious but exhausted troops would have to engage in a futile attack on that slope, which was separated from the square by a deep gully. Colonel Moreira Cesar's eye took this in at a glance. Accordingly, when the rearguard consisting of the police detachment and the squadron of cavalry came up, he ordered the police to proceed to the extreme right and attack this unscathed portion of the settlement as a complement to the action which was taking place on the left. The cavalry, meanwhile, was to attack in the centre, in the vicinity of the churches.

A cavalry charge in Canudos! This, surely, was an eccentric procedure. The cavalry is the classic arm of the service for use on open plains; its strength lies in the shock of a charge, when the mounted force comes in suddenly after a spirited attack by the infantry. Here, however, its movements were restricted by the walls of the huts and it had to charge, one man at a time, down those narrow corridors.

The cavalry—their winded mounts swaying on their unsteady legs—set off at a half-gallop down to the river's edge, where bullets were spattering in the water. That was as far as they could go, for their frightened steeds baulked there. By digging in their spurs and lashing the animals with the flat of their swords, the cavalrymen barely succeeded in making it to the middle of the stream, where, rearing and bounding, taking the bit in their teeth and sprawling their riders from the saddle, the horses made a wild rush for the bank from which they had started. The police for their part, after crossing the river in a downstream direction, in water up to their knees, came to a halt when they beheld the deep and slippery bed of the gully which at this point runs from north to south, separating from the rest of the town the 'suburb' which they were supposed to attack. The complementary movement was thus frustrated at the very start; and it was then that the commander-in-chief of the expedition left the place where he had been stationed.

'I am going to put a little mettle into those fellows,' he said.

He started off but was no more than half-way there when, letting go the reins, he lurched forward over the saddlebow. A bullet had struck him in the abdomen. His staff now gathered about him.

'It is nothing,' he said, 'a slight wound,' endeavouring to allay the fears of his devoted comrades. He was, as a matter of fact, mortally wounded.

In the meantime the police in their attack had adopted the tactics of their comrades in the other part of the town by knocking down houses and setting fire to them. Disorder prevailed everywhere, without the slightest sign of any military manœuvres, which indeed were inconceivable under the circumstances. This was not an assault; it was merely a rash battering of a monstrous barricade, which became all the more formidable every moment as it tumbled in ruins and went up in smoke, for the reason that beneath the litter in the streets, the fallen roofs and the smoking timbers, the lurking sertanejos were all the better able to slip away in safety, or else found hiding-places there that were more secure.

And then there came a major misfortune, an inevitable one, as night suddenly swooped down on the mêlée of combatants, exhausted from five hours of fighting.

Already, however, before night came, the troops had begun falling back. On the left bank of the river scattered groups, the first of the fleeing detachments, could now be seen running about in confusion, and they were soon joined by others; breaking ranks entirely, dashing out from the corners of the churches and from behind the huts along the riverbank, officers and men together, filthy-looking, singed, their uniforms ripped to pieces, took to their heels in whatever direction seemed most favourable, depending upon the rifle fire of the enemy, a crazed, shouting, terror-stricken, staggering, fleeing mob.

Beginning on the left wing, this impulse spread to the far right. Compelled to retreat to its original positions, the entire battle line, raked by enemy fire, fell back in a writhing mass to the river's edge down below. Without anyone to give the word of command, it was every man for himself. As they came to the river, a few small groups would split off, still, to set fire to the nearest houses or to engage in brief skirmishes, while the others, wounded or with no weapons left, were only interested in crossing the stream. It was a veritable rout.

And then, of a sudden, having fallen back to their last positions, under the hypnotic spell of panic and amid an indescribable tumult, the men, deserting their platoons, leaped headlong into the level-flowing current of the river! Struggling with one another, trampling the wounded, brutally beating off the maimed and exhausted, pushing them under and stifling them, the first of the fugitives made their way to the right bank and started to scramble up it. Getting such a hold as they could on the scant grass, propping themselves on their weapons, grasping the legs of their fortunate comrades ahead of them who were already clambering over the top, they became once more on the other side of the river a clamouring, fleeing mass. All that could be seen was a swarm of human bodies up and down the river, accompanied by loud, discordant cries. It was as if, as the result of some downpour, the Vasa-Barris had suddenly risen and leaped from its bed, bubbling, foaming, raging.

At this moment the bell ringer in the tower of the old church broke in upon the confusion. Night was falling, and in the half-light of dying day there came the melodious notes of the *Ave Maria*.

Baring their heads, tossing their leather hats or bright blue caps to the ground, the jagunços let fly one parting shot, as they murmured their accustomed prayers.

Having crossed the river, the soldiers gathered about the artillery. They were now a panic-stricken mob, without any resemblance whatever to a military force; they were an army in an advanced state of decomposition, all that was left being a number of terrified and useless individuals whose one thought now was to avoid the enemy with whom they had previously been so anxious to come to grips. The hill where they were at present was much too close to that enemy, who might, possibly, attack them there under cover of darkness, and it was accordingly necessary to abandon it. Still without any kind of order, dragging the cannons after them, they accordingly made their way to Mount Mario, four hundred yards farther on. There they improvised an incorrect square formation, with their broken ranks, their officers, the ambulances with the wounded, and the artillery and supply trains. In the centre of their 'camp' were the ruins of the 'Old Ranch House', and here their commander-in-chief lay dying. All that was left of the expedition now was this hodge-podge of men, animals, uniforms, and rifles, dumped in a fold of the mountains.

Night had come, one of those intensely bright nights which are common in the backlands, when every star—fixed, not twinkling—seems to radiate heat, as the cloudless horizons light up from moment to moment with the reflected lightning gleams of distant tempests.

The settlement was invisible now; or, rather, all that was visible was a few smouldering fires where the wood beneath the mud walls and roofs was still being consumed, or the pale glow of a lantern shimmering in the darkness here and there and moving slowly about, as if the bearer were engaged in a mournful search of some sort. These lights showed that the enemy was keeping watch, but the firing had ceased and there was not a sound to be heard. The

brilliant starlight made it barely possible to discern the faint outlines
of the church buildings, standing out from the rest; but the compact
mass of huts, the hills round about, the distant mountains—all were
lost in the night.

The disorder of the camp afforded a contrast to the peaceful surroundings. Huddled in between their comrades more than a
hundred maimed and wounded men, tortured with pain and thirst,
writhed in agony or crept about on their hands and knees, in grave
peril of being trampled by the frightened, neighing horses of the
supply train. It was out of the question to undertake to treat them
here in the darkness, where the careless lighting of a match would
have been an incredibly foolhardy act.

What was lacking, above all, was a commander possessed of the
requisite firmness. The burdens laid upon him were too heavy for
Colonel Tamarindo, who inwardly cursed the turn of fate which
had forced him into this catastrophic position.

'The time has come to die; every man for himself. . . .' That was
his only order of the day. Seated on a drum case, sucking on a pipe
in proud but stoic discouragement, he gave a similar reply or muttered a few monosyllables to all who sought his counsel; he had
entirely abdicated his function of bringing order out of this dis-
heartened mob by performing the miracle of dividing them into
fresh combat units.

The majority, however, took a dispassionate view of the matter.
They were under no illusions. They had but to picture to themselves the troops as they had arrived a few hours before, enthusiastic
and confident of victory, and contrast that picture with the one
before them; when they did this, it was clear to them that there was
but one solution possible—a retreat.

But this very night the backlands conflict had begun to take on
that mysterious aspect which it was to preserve until the end. The
majority of the soldiers were mestizos, of the same racial stock as the
backwoodsmen; and in their discouragement over the inexplicable
defeat which they had suffered and the loss of their commander who
had been reputed to be invincible, they readily fell victim to the
power of suggestion and, seeing in it all an element of the marvellous and the supernatural, were filled with an unreasoning terror
—a terror that was further increased by the extravagant stories that
were going around.

The burly and brutal jagunço was now transformed into an
intangible hobgoblin. Most of the combatants, even those who had
been wounded in the recent engagement, had not so much as laid

eyes on a single one of the enemy. And to all of them, even the most incredulous, there did begin to appear to be something abnormal about these ghostlike, all but invisible fighters with whom they had struggled so impotently, having had no more than a glimpse of a few of them here and there, dodging boldly in and out among the ruins and dashing unscathed through what was left of the blazing huts. Many of the soldiers were from the North, and they, upon hearing Antonio Conselheiro's name, were inclined to associate him with the heroes of childhood tales. The extravagant legend which had grown up about him, his miracles, his unrivalled exploits as a sorcerer, now appeared to them to have been overwhelmingly verified by this tremendous catastrophe.

Along towards midnight their apprehensions were greatly increased, when the drowsing sentinels who had been posted to guard the laxly organized camp suddenly awoke in terror, uttering cries of alarm. The silence of the night was broken by a strange sound coming up the mountainside. It was not, however, the dull tramp of an attacking party. It was something worse than that. The enemy down below, in that invisible town—was praying. This extraordinary occurrence, at this time of night—mournful litanies, with feminine in place of masculine voices predominating, welling up from the ruins of a battlefield—all this was formidable indeed. The effect was heightened by contrast. As the astounded soldiers whispered in fear, those sorrowful-sounding tag ends of 'Kyrie's' seemed worse to them than forthright threats would have been. In this eloquent manner they were being told that there was no contending with an enemy who was thus transfigured by religious faith.

Retreat was now more of a necessity than ever; and at dawn the next day a disturbing piece of news rendered it most urgent. Colonel Moreira Cesar had died.

The retreat was in reality a flight. Advancing over the summit, in the direction of Mount Favella, and then descending the steep slopes on the other side by the road which runs there, the expeditionaries spread out over the hills in a long and scattering line, without any semblance of military formation. In thus turning their back on the enemy down below, who, though alert, was not troubling them as yet, they appeared to be trusting solely to the swiftness of their movements to get them out of their plight. There was no defensive-offensive alignment by successive stages such as is the characteristic procedure in military crises of this sort. All that they did was to rush down the roads at top speed, with no thought of order or direction. They were not falling back; they were taking to their heels. One division alone, with two Krupp guns, under the command of a valorous subaltern, and strengthened by an infantry detachment, stood its ground for some time on Mount Mario by way of holding off the inevitable pursuit.

When it did finally get under way, this self-sacrificing detachment was fiercely assaulted. The enemy now had the impetus that comes from taking the offensive and was further aware of the dread he inspired in the fleeing troops. To the accompaniment of loud and enthusiastic *vivas* he attacked violently from all sides, in a circling movement. Down below, the bell was ringing wildly, and there was a burst of rifle fire from the new church, as the entire population of Canudos thronged into the square or dashed over the hilltops to view the scene, conferring upon the tragic episode an irritatingly mocking note, as thousands of throats gave vent to a prolonged, shrill, deadly intentioned whistling.

Once again, the fearful drama of backlands warfare was ending in lugubrious hoots and hisses.

The ranks were now completely broken. Eight hundred men were engaged in flight, throwing their rifles away, dropping the litters on which the wounded were writhing, abandoning their equipment, undoing their belts that they might be able to run the faster—running, running, in any direction, without weapons, in small groups and wandering bands, running down the road and along the intersecting paths, making for the depths of the caatingas, terrified, out of their senses, leaderless.

Among the burdens deposited along the side of the road when the panic broke out was—mournful detail!—the body of the commander. There was no effort to protect his remains, not the slightest effort to repel the enemy whom they had not glimpsed, but who made his presence known by noisy shouts of defiance and by scattering shots at irregular intervals, like those of a hunter in the brush. At the first sound of those shots, the battalions melted away.

Having concluded their search of the roads and trails, and having gathered up and brought in all the weapons and munitions of war that they found, the jagunços then collected all the corpses that were lying here and there, decapitated them, and burned the bodies; after which they lined the heads up along both sides of the highway, at regular intervals, with the faces turned towards the road. Above these, from the tallest shrubbery, they suspended the remains of the uniforms and equipment, the trousers and multicoloured dolmans, the saddles, belts, red-striped kepis, the capes, blankets, canteens, and knapsacks.

The barren, withered caatinga now blossomed forth with an extravagant-coloured flora: the bright red of officers' stripes, the pale blue of dolmans, set off by the brilliant gleam of shoulder straps and swaying stirrups.

There is one painful detail which must be added to complete this cruel picture: at one side of the road, impaled on a dried angico bough, loomed the body of Colonel Tamarindo.

It was a horrifying sight. Like a terribly macabre manikin, the drooping corpse, arms and legs swaying in the wind as it hung from the flexible bending branch, in these desert regions took on the appearance of some demoniac vision. It remained there for a long time.

And when, three months later, a fresh expeditionary force set out for Canudos, this was the scene that greeted their eyes: rows of skulls bleaching along the roadside, with the shreds of one-time uniforms stuck up on the tree branches round about, while over at one side—mute protagonist of a formidable drama—was the dangling spectre of the old colonel.

WITH THE DEFEAT *of the Cesar expedition, the Brazilian government prepared a large and well-equipped force with which to conclude the affair at Canudos. This time, using a careful plan of attack and dynamite, they levelled every one of the five thousand dwellings. But the jagunços never surrendered. Antonio Conselheiro died, but the fight went on until the last man was killed.*

As an observer writing of the strange war, Cunha very carefully went over the scenes and the actions. Then he returned to his home and wrote his book. The Brazilian military officials were shocked and furious at the detailed criticism. Cunha was a well-trained military man and knew what he was talking about. Then the rumour started that he was writing another book. This was more than the army officials could afford. Cunha was assassinated before his next book was completed.

CAUCASIAN FERMENT

BY H. C. ARMSTRONG

FOR OVER TWO THOUSAND YEARS *the Caucasus have lain like an abatis on the crossroads of empire. Alexander got tangled there, so did Pompey and Genghis Khan. During these years the mountain tribes and the kingdom of Georgia met their invaders and hurled them back. However, at the beginning of the nineteenth century the Russians invaded the Caucasus determined to stay, and for almost fifty years they found themselves embroiled in a bloody guerrilla war. General after general gave up in despair and returned to the court of the Tsar to spread the legend of Shamyl.*

This colourful Moslem was the military and spiritual leader of his people in their unsuccessful war for independence, and he became an ally of England and France in the Crimean War. When that war ended, Russia turned with renewed fury and strength towards the Caucasus. Gradually they subdued the guerrillas, and in 1859 they captured Shamyl, but out of deep personal respect, they paroled him. He died a decade later on a pilgrimage to Mecca.

The defeat and capture of Shamyl gave the Russians an uneasy fifty years of peace. With their own long tradition of freedom, the Christian Georgians intrigued, armed, and fought sporadically. But they never had a great leader, a man who could see guerrilla warfare as more than the outlaw band pricking at the Russians. If a single figure stands out during these years, it is Leo Kerreselidze.

Kerreselidze, a manor-born Georgian, devoted his life to freeing his country. At twenty, with a price on his head, he ran an illegal boatload of arms from Holland through the Black Sea. After years as a terrorist, he fled to the hills, leaving behind his Russian mistress, Tatiana, wife of the chief of the Russian secret police.

Kerreselidze told H. C. Armstrong the following story of the rescue of a friend that took place while he was a guerrilla chief in the mountains.

O NE evening a villager—Leo had been resting two days, in the valley, and was in his tent—came in haste to say that the Russians had taken Levan Jakeli. How it happened no one knew, but he himself, he explained, and several others had seen a squadron of Cossacks come into Dousheti from the east, and with them they brought Jakeli tied across a horse. He was wounded, for when they untied him in front of the cavalry barracks, he had been unable to walk and had fallen down. A sergeant had kicked him to make him get up, but eventually a couple of Cossacks had carried him in. Next morning they had taken him out along the road towards Tiflis, though no one knew what had happened after that. They had also brought three dead men in a cart, but they had left the bodies in Dousheti. He had himself, he said, seen all this. He had, in fact, waited outside the cavalry barracks, watching all night, but got no chance to speak to Jakeli, and as soon as the Cossacks had gone off down the Tiflis road he had come as fast as possible to report.

Leo calculated quickly. He cross-examined the villager.

How did he know Levan Jakeli?

He had seen him often the previous year in his village, the man replied, and besides, everyone in the countryside knew Levan Jakeli.

Why had he not come at once, the minute he saw the Cossacks? he asked.

He had thought it better to bring the whole story. He was not of Dousheti, and had only gone into the town to sell some eggs and chickens, so he knew very few people there, and could find no one to help him, so he had waited by the barracks to see what would happen. The Cossacks had left just after the sun rose, and he had come as soon as they were gone. He had done his best.

Leo realized that the story was true. A week ago he had sent Levan with three men to the other side of Dousheti to get news of the leaders round Zakatali. The Cossacks must have ambushed them. Three dead, and Levan in the hands of the Russians! They would certainly hang Levan. For more than a year he had been outlawed with a big price on his head, and only the previous month he had raided the court-house at Koutais, where they had been trying some of his men, killed two judges, the gendarme and all the police on duty and got the men away.

Somehow, if any power on earth could do it, he would save Levan from the Russians.

It would be impossible to intercept the Cossacks. They would be almost in Tiflis by now. If the villager had only come last night he could have done something—but useless to think of that. Tatiana must help. He would go at once to Tiflis and get the news.

Travelling fast and without resting on the way, he reached Tiflis before dawn, and himself found the priest. The girl came the same morning to the chalet. She had heard that they had caught Jakeli: he was wounded but would recover: the best doctor had been sent to attend him, as the Russian authorities had decided to stage a big trial and make an example of him, and they wanted him fit to plead before they began. Nothing would be done for some days.

She herself would not be able to see Leo for a week, as her mother-in-law with two daughters was staying in the flat. She could not leave them again without rousing suspicion, and she must go back almost at once. It would be best if he returned to the mountains and kept ready. It was too dangerous for him to remain in Tiflis. She would send him any news, and she would be sure to get it in plenty of time.

For several days Leo waited. As time went by he grew restless and impatient. Each day he expected a message. Levan was in the hands of the Russians and he was doing nothing. He sent a man to Tiflis who brought back word that the whole city knew that Jakeli was in the prison, and was talking of it. Every café was agog with the news. It had been published in the newspapers, 'Capture of Well-known Rebel': the Viceroy had issued a proclamation offering a free pardon to those who submitted within a week, but excepting certain rebels by name, and this list was headed by Leo Keresselidze of Akressi. But of Jakeli himself, how or where he was, and what was to happen to him, there was no news. No one had been able to get near him.

At last Leo could stand it no longer. He must at least do something. He certainly could not sit here up in the mountains idle and without a word—Tatiana must have failed—while they might be torturing or hanging Levan. If nothing came during the next day he would go again to Tiflis.

He lay down in his tent, but he only turned and tossed from side to side. There was no sleep for him. His men were ready to do anything he ordered, raid into Tiflis itself if he thought it best, but they did not understand his inaction. Levan's brother had been to him that evening begging him to save Levan. The lad had become hysterical and cried, and said that they were leaving Levan in the lurch: that, though it was untrue, had hurt Leo, but what could he do? He thought of a dozen schemes but all were useless, when suddenly he heard the sheep dogs baying on the edge of the forest.

Someone had arrived. And as he went out to see who it was, a man came running to him.

'The Russian woman has come,' he said, and Leo realized that all the camp knew. He had not realized before how they watched everything he did. 'We are holding her and the priest. What are the orders?'

Leo stifled the exclamation that came to his lips, and without a word made along the valley past the lake to where the path went down through the rocks and the forest to Gori.

The moon was at its full, so that in the black shadow under the edge of the forest he could see a group, and above it, silhouetted against a patch of light beyond, a figure on a horse.

The men made way for him—and one silenced a dog with a curse —as he hurried past them without giving them greeting, and came to the girl.

'You?' he said, and put up his hands to her, and she, leaving the reins loose on her horse's neck, leaned down close over him.

She had round her shoulders a cloak that covered her to the knees, and over her head a *bashliq*, a peaked cap like a monk's cowl—such as the Lazz fishermen wear on the Turkish coast when the weather is bad—which hid her face. A strand of her hair swept across his cheek as she bent lower.

'Yes!' she replied. 'I came because I could not find a messenger I could trust, and I had not time to look for one. I had news that was urgent. I promised you I would send you word. It has been difficult, but I have kept my word and not failed you.'

'Are you all right? It's a very rough road here. Had I known I would have come for you. You must be worn out. Weren't you afraid to come alone?'

'I was afraid—but I made Theodorus come with me. Poor Theodorus. He's over there, still shivering with fright,' and Leo saw that a little to one side, on a mule, sat the gaunt Greek priest. 'Theodorus was afraid of everything. He didn't want to leave Tiflis, but I made him. He was sure we should be caught by Cossacks or killed by brigands. He was terrified when a jackal cried, and when a bat began hunting close to his beard he was sure it was a vampire going for his throat—but his fear killed mine, and'—she laughed gently— 'and—I was coming to you.

'When we reached Gori they held us up, but after a while sent us on with men to here—and I am come,' and she sighed softly with a little gasp in her throat. 'But listen! On the third day from to-day, that is on Wednesday, they will take Levan Jakeli by train from

Tiflis to Koutais. The train will leave from the big platform at ten o'clock in the morning, and on it will be an officer and twenty men as guards. Levan will be paraded through the streets of Koutais. The streets will be lined with soldiers with orders to shoot if anyone resists. He will be tried and condemned to death there, and hung in the square of the town as a warning. You have not much time. . . .'

'You must rest,' he interrupted, and led her horse by the bridle across to the camp.

Behind them came the Priest. He had picked up his black gown, which bellied out round him over the saddle, and his long legs, in white bloomer trousers that reached to his ankles and there should have been tied with tapes but had come undone, and slopped over his feet with the tapes dragging on the ground, dangled down the sides of the mule. He was not used to riding, and the mule had bucked and bumped him so that every bone in his body was an ache and his hide was so full of sores and rubbings that he groaned at every step. And if the mule went steady, one of the Georgians, with a grin at his comrades, would prod it in the stern so that it capered again, when the priest would let out a yell, and call on God and the Holy Saints for help, and curse all women, especially those who forced quiet, peaceful men to go riding about in the mountains in the dark; and all the Georgians would chuckle and crow at his discomfort, and slap their thighs with delight, and again prod the mule until it capered once more.

At his tent Leo lifted her out of the saddle. She was limp with weariness and clung to him. For a minute he held her close, realizing all her body, and kissing her gently he laid her down on the rugs that made his bed, drew a skin over her and going out called his men and held a consultation.

He had his plans made quickly. He would attack the train where the line ran into a narrow gorge after a tunnel, about half-way between Tiflis and Koutais, and he sent out messengers to collect up all the help they could, and scouts to watch the railway.

He went back to the tent, and drawing the flap, looked in. She was lying as he had laid her down, but the *bashliq* off beside her and one hand under a cheek. She was sleeping as peacefully as a child, her lips parted and her breasts rising and falling with her even breathing.

He let the flap fall and walked up the valley. The great moon was sailing high over Kazbek, so that the glacier below the peak gleamed white. The stream on its way down to the placid lake, to be absorbed and to lose its voice in the still water, came racing past him, swirling and laughing between its rocks. The forest was still: only now and then it stirred under the fingers of a light breeze. An owl called. Overhead he could hear the shrill crackle of bats, and once, far away, the baying of a wolf-pack hunting.

Because of the woman asleep down there, all these had taken on new forms for him. They had become personal. The moon was looking down, wide-eyed, at him. The stream laughed and shared his thoughts. The forest was singing with his delight. His eyes and ears were open, seeing and hearing what had been hidden from them before.

By the tent he stopped. He was held back by a sudden shyness. He knew her with all the intimacies of a lover, but he did not know her at all.

He stepped in quietly and leaned down over her, and she stirred and drew him down beside her.

During the next two days a few men straggled in, until there were fifty in all. They had been difficult to find, for most of them were in hiding and their villages picketed with Cossacks. With these, late in the afternoon of the second day, Leo set out, taking the road towards Gori, and Tatiana went with them.

Leo had begged her not to go back to Tiflis, but to stay with him. He would, for her, give up this life. They could go away to Europe, anywhere she wished, as long as she would go with him.

But she refused. All his arguments she met with a quiet, persistent refusal which he could not beat down. She loved him, she said. She would do all she could for him, but she would return to her own people. That he should mate with a Russian was as impossible as that a wolf should mate with an eagle. If she took him from Georgia, he would hate her. This was a little madness which would pass. He was young and he would forget very soon. She would not change and she would treasure each hour she spent with him as a great memory.

When he seized her and held her to him, and swore passionately that nothing would change him, that he would not let her go, that he could not live without her, she stroked his hair with steady hands and drew his face down and kissed his eyes with lips cool and without passion, and loosened his hands with soft fingers that were stronger than all his great strength, putting a barrier between them through which he could not break.

She must go, and that night, she repeated. She had told the manservant that she would stay with friends for a few nights only. Her husband was away in Moscow, but might be back at any time, and if he came back while she was away he might suspect her—and then she could be of no more help. 'That would be silly, wouldn't it?' she said with a gay little laugh.

With them also went the priest. And he, poor man, so far from being relieved by the rest, was as stiff and sore as if he had been flogged with a knout, and sat on his mule all hunched up, his tall hat like a drunken chimney-pot over his nose, a bundle of misery. He shifted his position continuously, now sitting astride, now side-saddle, tucking his robe under him as a cushion now under one ham and now under the other, trying to find some part of him that did not ache. And all the while the Georgians made a butt of him and laughed at his discomfort. A man who could not ride a horse was for them a freak and no man.

Where the forest ended and the path ran down through the vol-canic rocks straight to Gori, they parted, abruptly, with a close pressure of hands, neither looking back. She went with the priest and three men who were to take her into Gori, and then to follow her across the plain in the dark and see her safe into Tiflis. While Leo with the rest made westwards through the foot-hills, keeping parallel with the railway line until they came near the gorge they had selected, and from where they would attack the train.

Leo rode in silence. Tatiana was gone, the night had swallowed her up, and he was oppressed with loneliness. He would turn there and then, go after her, and force her to come back, but he knew it was useless. He might be her lover, but she would not stay with him. The mating of the wolf and the eagle! Russian and Georgian! He could not even see her safe to Tiflis. He must get on and save Levan from the Russians.

As they came near the gorge his thoughts came back to what was ahead. In the early hours of the morning he reached the rendezvous which he had arranged with his scouts. The moon with a slice cut away was half down the sky. It had been wide-eyed and full that night she came to the valley: long ago! it was only two days, not sixty hours. He put such thoughts away from him with an effort. He had man's work to do.

His scouts reported that the railway ran up a slight gradient into the tunnel, where the train would slow down, and then out of the tunnel into the gorge. The hills above the tunnel, and the sides of the gorge, were covered with thick forest, which came almost down to the line. There was a picket at one end of the tunnel and a sentry at the other, who was visited and changed every two hours. There appeared to be no travelling patrol along the railway, and no communication by telephone or signalling between the picket and any other picket or military post. They had searched and watched carefully, they said, and got the password for the sentry.

There was a camp of woodcutters high up. He could, if he looked over there, see in the distance the glow of their fires. They were Georgians and all loyal. Some of them had joined up with rifles, and the rest would help in any way wanted.

Leo made his plans. The first thing was to settle with the picket and the sentry on the tunnel. Leaving the horses with two men, he sent four men to deal with the sentry, and himself took ten men for the picket.

They crept silently through the forest above the tunnel until they were close to the picket. The moon was gone behind the hill-top and left only a faint glimmer, but they could see the Russians sprawled out asleep, their blankets over their heads, for the night air was cold. One, on guard, sat with his rifle across his knees, humming a song to himself and swaying his body backwards and forwards. A mountain stream near by leapt over a waterfall and, crashing into a pool below, covered all sounds.

With their daggers and bare hands they rushed the picket. It was all over in a few minutes and hardly a sound—the man singing sobbed suddenly as a dagger went through his throat: another gurgled as he was throttled inside his blanket: the thud of a blow and a groan: silence except for men breathing hard after great effort. The sentry was finished in the same way, before he could fire or give the alarm. One man dressed in his clothes and took up his post as sentry. Others dressed as the picket and the picket commander.

Sending for the woodcutters, Leo made them prepare two trunks of trees in such a position that they could be pushed across the line at a moment's notice. Then placing his men on both sides of the gorge, with two in each direction to signal anything fresh, he sat down to wait.

The hours before the dawn moved on leaden feet, and the men round him nodded sleepily while he sat tense and unrelaxed, waiting. Far overhead, between the sides of the gorge, the light began to show, and from the earth came up a shaft of cold air that made him shiver suddenly and then was gone.

Word came up that the train to Tiflis was in sight. As it passed, the Georgian who was posing as the Russian sentry saluted, and the picket commander looked down from above, one hand hiding his face, and made a signal to the driver that all was well.

Two hours more, and then a third and fourth. No morning

4

patrol came inspecting. Leo had arranged to deal with that; but the Russians were very easygoing and did not bother to inspect the line every morning.

The sun was up now, lighting all the peaks and climbing down the opposite side of the gorge. The man above the tunnel was signalling —a train was in sight, the train from Tiflis. It was a mile away. It was coming up the gradient. It was just entering the tunnel. He heard the engine whistle a warning. At a word from him the wood-cutters heaved over the trunks, which rolled with a roar of loose stones onto the line, breaking a rail and blocking the permanent way.

The train was in the tunnel. The Georgians were ready. They crept to the edge of the gorge, hiding behind trees and rocks, lying close and unseen, silent, eyes intent and unblinking like those of snakes. The engine was coming out of the tunnel, snorting at the gradient; the carriages, the whole train was out. The engine driver had seen the trunks on the line, was sounding his whistle and forcing on his brakes in a great cloud of steam. The train had stopped with its buffers touching the trunks.

With a shout Leo fired, killing the engine driver and his mate, and the Georgians let fly a volley into the carriages. From the train the Russians, led by an officer, leaped out, and, running for cover to the steep lips of the gorge, began to fire back. The gorge, the whole valley, the mountains, echoed and re-echoed with the rifle shots. The Russian officer was down, and his men were running for the cover of the tunnel. They had no prisoner with them: Levan must be in the train.

With a dozen men Leo ran, regardless of bullets, down to the train. The passengers were cowering under the seats. In the first carriage after the engine was Levan Jakeli, handcuffed and chained to a soldier on each side of him. These made no resistance. They were not only chained to Levan, but were themselves chained to the carriage seat.

Leo tore at the chains. His men would have hacked off the hands of the soldiers at the wrists to free Levan had not one found the key of the padlocks on the body of the officer.

In a few minutes they had lifted Levan out and carried him gently to the horses.

He lay where they put him down, weak, pale and unable to stand, talking in a whisper. His wound had healed: he had been shot through one side and had two ribs smashed, but they had joined up all right. But he had been flogged and tortured just before starting, in the prison at Tiflis, to make him talk. A big gash across his scalp and down his cheekbone to the chin, where an officer had hit him with a knuckleduster, was new and had a crust of freshly dried blood over it.

Leo turned back. He had been about to call off the men. Now he would kill every Russian: not one should escape.

Those who were left of the train escort were in a culvert. A bomb drove them out, and as they ran across the open for the mouth of the tunnel he shot them down one by one, in cold, silent fury.

WITH THE FREEING *of his friend and companion, Kerreselidze brought increased reprisals on the Georgians, and he knew that the movement for a time was dead. He fled to Switzerland, where he studied law. But the thought of a free Georgia plagued him, and in 1914 he returned to take up arms with the Turks against Russia.*

After Russia's withdrawal from World War I, Kerreselidze aided in the setting up of a free Georgia, and for a time he served successfully as a general against the White Russians Denikin and Wrangel. But he could not hold off the Red Army when it turned to the Caucasus, and he fled into exile for the last time to Switzerland.

WITH SMUTS ON COMMANDO

BY DENEYS REITZ

To the Boer-Dutch in 1899, commando meant a small military unit of the type they used that October to invade British territory in South Africa. The war started by the commando invasion had a long and tortuous background. The shy, slim State Attorney of the Boer Republic described the Boer position in a peevish pamphlet called A Century of Wrong. He pointed out such injustices as the abortive Jameson Raid on the Transvaal Republics approved by Cecil Rhodes, and he made it clear that the large numbers of English miners swarming into his country were unwelcome. There were, of course, other incidents which he neglected to mention. After writing his pamphlet, the State Attorney turned back to his legal work and left the fighting to his countrymen. But in a short time the formal Boer forces were smashed and the Boer capital occupied. The attorney contacted General Louis Botha and offered his services. Botha, desperate to keep the war going, turned over to veteran guerrilla chief de la Rey the young volunteer—Jan Christian Smuts.

Lord Kitchener pressed his drive into Boer country to stop Botha's guerrilla operations, and Botha acted quickly. In July, 1901, he gave Smuts four hundred men and ordered him to cross into British Cape Colony and force Kitchener to withdraw to protect his own areas.

Smuts, eluding the British on his way south, was joined by small groups of Boer guerrillas. In one of these was eighteen-year-old Deneys Reitz, son of the Boer President. Young Reitz was already a veteran by this time, and he tells the story of the journey into Cape Colony and what was done there.

THE place of our meeting with General Smuts and his commando was in sight of the little village of Sastron, about fifteen miles from the Orange River, and his intention was to march nearer that day, and cross during the night. By noon a start was made, and towards five in the evening we could see a dark line in front of us marking the gorge, at the bottom of which runs the river between high mountain walls.

Unfortunately this was not all that we saw. Our side of the canyon was held for miles in each direction by a cordon of British troops, stationed there to bar our way. Whenever a footpath led down the cliffs, there stood a tented camp, and the intervening ground was patrolled by strong bodies of mounted men who clearly knew of our coming.

On seeing this, General Smuts led us back into a range of hills, where we waited until next day, while men were sent in search of some neighbouring outpost to act as guides.

At dusk a young officer named Louis Wessels arrived with fifty men, a hard-bitten crew, with whom he had been operating for over a year.

He reported enemy columns closing in on us from the rear, and said that unless we were able to effect a crossing that night, we should be trapped. He said, moreover, that the river was everywhere difficult, owing to the depth of the gorge and the perpendicular cliffs, but he had brought with him a veteran of the Basuto wars who knew of a path which might be practicable.

General Smuts decided to start at once, and in the falling dark our force rode out, accompanied by Wessels and his men, who agreed to enter the Colony with us. We travelled on, hour after hour in the dark, over rough ground, and then, towards three in the morning, we caught a glint of white far below, where the Orange River boiled and eddied in its narrow channel. It was yet night when we commenced the final descent, but after toiling down the precipitous path to which our guide had brought us, and along which assuredly no other mounted troops had ever passed, we reached the edge of the water. In single file we began to cross the river, a strong and turbulent mountain torrent, not broad, but so swift that our horses could scarcely maintain their footing, and as dawn lit the cliffs above, the hindmost man was through, and I stood in the Cape Colony at last.

After a short halt we took a path that led to the top of the cliffs opposite, by a deep cleft, up which we tugged our leg-weary animals, until, far above, we emerged on a wide grass-covered tableland, pleasantly dotted with native villages and herds of cattle at pasture.

We were now actually on British territory, but the country here lies in an angle between the Free State, Basutoland, and Cape boundaries, and the region seemed exclusively occupied by Basutos, for there were no European habitations in sight.

As soon as we gained the top, we scattered into small parties, riding from one native village to another, in quest of tobacco and fodder for our horses. While we were thus ranging, a body of mounted Basutos, about three hundred strong, came moving swiftly towards us. Some were armed with rifles, others carried battle-axes, assegais, and knobkerries, which they brandished in the air as they approached. We did not know what to make of this, but we thought that they could not be contemplating an unprovoked attack on a white force equal to their own. General Smuts, therefore, contented himself with sending word for the various foraging parties to close in, and the commando continued on its way without paying much attention to the horsemen, who at a shouted word from their leader came to a halt on a knoll close by, where they sat their horses in silence, watching the Boers pass.

At this stage, my uncle and I, with five others whose names I did not know, lagged behind to feed our horses from the grain baskets to be found in every native village, and as we were not frightened by the Basuto parade, which we put down to curiosity, we allowed the commando to get a considerable way ahead of us. At length, seeing that we were being left too far behind, we mounted and followed our men, the last of whom were just vanishing over the edge of the tableland by a road leading to the plain below.

By the time we could look down, the bulk of the commando was already at the bottom. They were riding along a road flanked on the left by a ledge of overhanging natural rock, part of the footwall of the tableland which they had just quitted, and on the right by a Mission Church and a long rubble fence, separating the road from fields and gardens. A force moving down this enclosed alleyway could be easily ambushed, and we were alarmed to see that the Basutos had left their horses above, and were scrambling down the final shelf of rock overhanging the road, crawling forward to the edge, to look straight down on our men riding unconsciously below. We expected to see them open fire on the crowded ranks at any moment. Indecision, however, came over the natives; they began nudging one another as if each wanted someone else to start shooting, and by the time that they had made up their minds the opportunity was gone, for the commando was already debouching from the confined space of the road into the open plain. My fellow stragglers and I were worse off, for although the Basutos had hesitated to attack the larger force, their intentions were clearly hostile, and we wondered how they would deal with our little band left isolated in the rear.

After hurried consultation we decided to follow on, and attempt to catch up with the commando, so we began to descend the slope. We reached the bottom unmolested, but as we passed the church beside the road we caught sight of many dark faces pressed against the windowpanes, and white eyeballs peering at us from within.

Then came a deafening crash, as a volley was fired at us point-blank from the building, sending showers of splintered glass about our heads. Fortunately the native is a notoriously bad marksman, for he generally closes his eyes when he pulls the trigger, so not one of us was hit, although the range was under ten yards. When the Basutos lying on the rocky shelf overhanging the road heard the volley, they took courage and also opened fire. The five men with us did the only reasonable thing under the circumstances. They dug their spurs in and rode off as fast as they could, but my uncle with his usual impetuosity loosed his pack animal, swung his horse in behind a massive boulder that had calved from the ledge above, and jumped to the ground. I had to follow suit, relinquishing my own led-horse, and riding in behind the rock, a huge cube that leaned against the parent crag in such a manner as to give us cover against the Basutos overhead as well as from those firing through the shattered windows of the church across the way. We opened fire in turn at the church, but we saw at once that our position was untenable. Immediately above, the natives were excitedly shouting as they fired at our retreating companions, and at such of the rearmost commando men as were still within range.

Already we could hear the voices of several of them craning over to get at us from above. With some of the enemy standing on the roof, as it were, and others shooting from the church not fifteen yards off, we realized that to remain here could have only one ending, and we prepared to mount once more, although our chances of escape seemed desperate.

Looking down the road, we could now see only two of our men, riding for their lives across the fields, for they had succeeded in leaping the dividing wall. The other three men were nowhere to be seen, but two dead horses lay on the road, and a third was galloping riderless in the distance. This looked bad, but no other course was open to us, so we leaped into the saddle and rode out from the sanctuary of the fallen rock. The moment we did so, the natives in the church saw us, and redoubled their fire, while those on the bank above raised bloodcurdling yells and also fired.

As we sped past, more natives rose from behind the fence lining the road. Fortunately these last were armed only with assegais and knobkerries, which came whirring about our ears. In this pandemonium we took every moment to be our last, but we ran the gauntlet safely for perhaps sixty yards, when the road fell suddenly into a deep spruit which neither of us had noticed in our excitement. It meant salvation, although at first it looked as if it only meant more danger, for, riding down, we saw some fifteen or twenty natives squatted in a circle, intent upon something that lay on the ground between them. Before they could do more than spring to their feet and strike blindly at us, we were through. Instead of riding up the opposite bank of the spruit, where we should come under fire again, we galloped along the bed under cover of the high banks, until we were able to emerge out of range.

Of the five men who had been with us, the two whom we had seen making across country got clean away, but the other three were either killed on the road, and then dragged into the spruit, or else they were destroyed on reaching there, for we learned long after that their bodies were found on the causeway, dreadfully mutilated by the natives for medicine, in accordance with their barbarous custom. I have little doubt that when my uncle and I rode down among them, they were busy at their grisly task of dissection, which we ourselves so narrowly missed.

We were out of danger now, but the prospect was not reassuring. True, we had got off without a scratch, but our pack animals were gone with most of our gear, and looking over our saddle horses, we were dismayed to find that they were both badly wounded. My brown mare had been hit by a jagged missile that had smashed her lower jaw, and my uncle's horse had a bullet through the crupper and another through the hind leg. I put my poor animal out of her misery at once, but my uncle thought that his might recover (which it did). I shouldered my saddle, and, leading the injured horse, we advanced on foot, dolefully speculating upon our future, for we had only a wounded horse and a handful of cartridges between us in this inhospitable country.

Far away we could see the commando posted on a ridge, to cover the retreat of those who were still in danger, for some of the men had been within range when the firing started on us at the church, and there were several wounded making their way across the plain.

When at last we reached the commando and had time to look around, my uncle and I had a pleasant surprise, for there stood our two led-horses safe and sound, with our blankets and cooking tins intact. They must have fled straight on when we loosed them on the road, and they had overtaken the commando while we were fighting below the shelf. Now they were contentedly ranged in line with the rest of the horses behind the hill, as if nothing out of the common had happened, so at any rate we still had a riding horse apiece.

While we were halted here, we saw that another party of ten or twelve men was in difficulties. They, too, had got separated from

our main body, while foraging on the tableland earlier in the morning, but no one had missed them until now when we heard the
sound of distant firing and saw them riding into view two miles
away, hotly pursued by numbers of mounted Basutos. They were
in grave danger, for between them and ourselves ran a deep ravine,
towards which they were being shepherded, and as the ravine
seemed impassable, it looked for a time as if we should have to
stand by helpless and see them killed. In order to do what we could,
the whole commando mounted and rode to the edge of the chasm,
and here, fortunately, we found a piece of high ground from which
we overlooked the scene on the other side, and were able to drop our
bullets among the advancing natives with such good effect that they
reined in. This gave the cornered men time to search the cliff for a
way down, which they succeeded in finding under cover of our
fire, and ultimately they rejoined us without casualties.

This final episode reduced my ammunition to four rounds, and
indeed many of the rest were no better off, for the long chase to
which they had been subjected during their dash through the Free
State had depleted their bandoliers to such an extent that the question was becoming a very serious one for a column such as ours,
starting to invade hostile territory.

After this we halted for an hour to give the wounded men a rest,
and to enable those whose horses had been killed to get remounted.
There were seven men hit, and, as we had no lint, bandages, or
medical supplies, there was little that we could do for them.

After a while the injured men were placed in their saddles, and we
trekked away, with several bands of natives hovering in our rear, as
if they contemplated a further attack, but in the end they retired.
After a wearisome ride we got beyond the area of the Native Reserve,
and towards afternoon we came across the first European farmhouse, where we left our wounded to be fetched in by the British.

We rested our exhausted animals till dusk, and then, saying good-
bye to the wounded men in the house, we rode on for five or six
miles before camping.

For months past we had experienced an unbroken spell of fine
weather, bitterly cold at night but cloudless sunshine by day. Now,
however, there was a change, and it came on to rain heavily, so that
we spent the long hours of darkness dismally lying in mud and
water. This weather, coming on top of the crowded events of the
last twenty-four hours, gave us our first taste of what was awaiting
us in the Cape Colony, and thus early we began to appreciate the
fact that our road was likely to be a thorny one.

4*

Next morning the sky cleared somewhat, although a penetrating drizzle continued for most of the day, through which we rode shivering, our thin clothing being but little protection. My own wardrobe was typical; a ragged coat and worn trousers full of holes, with no shirt or underwear of any kind. On my naked feet were dilapidated rawhide sandals, patched and repatched during eight months of wear, and I had only one frayed blanket to sleep under at night. Few of the men were better off, and we looked with apprehension on the change of weather, for it meant that the rainy season was upon us, with its attendant hardships, the full extent of which we were yet to learn.

Our course during this day took us through more settled parts, and for the first time we looked at farms and homesteads untouched by the hand of war. There were men peacefully working in the fields, and women and children standing unafraid before their doors as we passed, a very different picture from that to which we were accustomed in the devastated republics.

The people were almost exclusively of Dutch origin, so they gave us unselfish hospitality. In the matter of clothing they were hardly able to assist us, on account of the military embargo which prevented them from buying more than certain quantities, but gifts of coffee, sugar, salt and tobacco were ungrudgingly made, and the first slice of bread and butter and the first sip of coffee I had tasted for a year almost made the long journey worth while.

In spite of the bad weather, our first day among a friendly population was a pleasant experience, which put the men in good spirits, and I dare say we posed a little before the womenfolk, laughing and whistling as we rode along.

Our course, later in the afternoon, took us up a mountain pass, and when we reached the top towards evening, we could see in the distance the comfortable hamlet of Lady Grey nestling to the left, while in a glen below was the old familiar sight of a British column, crawling down the valley. This gave us no anxiety, for, being without wheeled transport of any kind, we turned across the heath and easily left the soldiers far behind.

That night it rained again, and a cold wind drove against us from the south. Our commando presented a strange appearance as we wound along; we had no raincoats, so we used our blankets as cloaks against the downpour, and the long line of draped horsemen looked like a tribe of Red Indians on the warpath.

Long after dark we came to a halt, spending a wretched wet night, and at dawn, cold and miserable, we trekked over bleak country, the biting wind in our faces, until at four in the afternoon we came to rest near a place ominously called Moordenaar's Poort (The Murderer's Way). The rain now ceased, and, a passing herdboy having told us that English troops were camped a few miles off, General Smuts decided to go and see them for himself. He took with him two young Freestaters who had joined him on the way down, and another man named Neethling from Pretoria, an old friend of mine. With these he left, saying that he would be back by dark. At sunset he had not returned, and for hours we anxiously waited for him until, shortly before midnight, he walked in among us on foot and alone. He had been ambushed by a British patrol, who had killed all three of his escort and all the horses, he alone escaping down a nullah. Had he been killed I believe that our expedition into the Cape would have come to a speedy end, for there was no one else who could have kept us together. The commando was divided into two portions commanded by Jacobus van Deventer (later Sir Jacobus van Deventer in World War I) and Ben Bouwer, respectively, both good fighting men but neither of them possessing the personality or the influence over men that General Smuts had, to save us from going to pieces during the difficult period upon which we were now entering.

We spent the night where we lay, and there was more trouble before daylight, for a porcupine came grunting through our lines, with the result that the horses stampeded in a body. They thundered off in the dark, crashing through fences and undergrowth in blind terror, and at sunrise there was not an animal to be seen.

With an English force in the vicinity this was a serious predicament, for they would make short work of us if we were dismounted, so all hands turned out to hunt for the horses. Luckily a few of the men had hobbled their mounts, which prevented them from going as far as the rest, and as these were run to earth in a hollow not far away, they were used to track the others, and after three or four uneasy hours, expecting to see the English appear at any moment, we brought back all the missing horses safe and sound.

We now travelled on for the next three days across windy barrens, heading south-west. The weather grew more and more tempestuous as we went, and we suffered severely from the cold, and from the intermittent rains that accompanied us. Both horses and men began to show signs of distress. The animals looked thin and gaunt, and the men sat on their saddles pinched, shivering, and despondent, for South Africans are peculiarly susceptible to the depressing effects of bad weather. They can stand cold and other hardships as well as anyone, but continued lack of sunshine soon makes them miserable, and for the time being we were a dispirited band, wishing we had never come.

By day we were wet and cold, and the nights were evil dreams. Dry fuel was almost unprocurable, and after a weary day we had to spend the hours of darkness cowering together to snatch a little sleep on some muddy mountainside, or in an equally sodden valley.

Soon we were losing horses freely, and not a trek was made without some wretched animals being left behind with tuckered flanks and drooping heads, waiting for the end.

We had three days of this, but our troubles were only beginning.

Towards sunset one evening we came in sight of the village of Jamestown, and saw a strong English column to our right, so General Smuts moved us on. It grew pitch-dark, and a driving rain smote straight in our faces. The night was so black that it was impossible to see even the man immediately before one, and the cold so bitter that we became stiff and numbed, and it was only with difficulty that we could drag our horses along, for we were ordered to go on foot to husband their strength.

When I was crossing a spruit, my sandals stuck in the heavy pot clay and came to pieces when I tried to withdraw them, and it was only by cutting corners from my blanket and wrapping one about each foot that I was able to go on at all. Our guide, a young man from a local farm, had lost his bearings, so we had to grope our way through icy rain for five hours, until we could continue no longer, and stood huddled together ankle-deep in mud and water, praying for sunrise.

When it grew light, over thirty horses lay dead from exposure, besides others abandoned overnight, and our spirits, low before, were at zero now.

The rain continued pitilessly until midday, when the sky cleared and the blessed sun shone upon us once more. We moved forward, and not far away saw a large farmhouse and outbuildings containing plenty of fuel. Soon we were warming our numbed bodies, and cooking our first hot meal for days.

The housewife at the farm gave me a pair of old-fashioned elastic-sided boots, and I unearthed an empty grain bag in which I cut a hole for my head, and one at each corner for my arms, thus providing myself with a serviceable greatcoat. My appearance caused much laughter, but I noticed that during the next few days, whenever we passed a barn, grain bags were in great demand, and soon many of the men were wearing them.

As the people here told us that there was an English force in the neighbourhood, we moved on later in the afternoon, first saying good-bye to Louis Wessels, the young Free State officer and his men, who turned back from here, as they had only come thus far to see our force well launched into the Colony. I believe that they reached their own country again in safety.

We continued for an hour, and then halted in a valley. Whilst we were idly resting in the grass two field guns banged at us from a hill, and shells came tearing overhead. More followed and, taken by surprise, we leaped into the saddle and made for the cover of a line of hills to the rear. The artillery was poor, and neither man nor horse was hit. Once in safety, we put our animals out of harm's way, and climbed up to see what the English meant to do. We could now see a column of horse coming down towards us, around a spur that had previously hidden them from view.

There were about six hundred of them, and they had with them two fifteen-pounder Armstrong guns, and several pom-poms which unlimbered and opened fire, while their horsemen cautiously approached us. After a time they quickened pace as though to attack, but, coming under our fire, they took cover behind some farmhouses and kraals. In spite of the shelling, and a lively exchange of rifle-fire, there were apparently no casualties on either side, and the affair terminated after dark. I did not fire a shot on account of the state of my cartridge belts, and the others fired no more than was necessary to stave off the enemy, because, as I said before, the ammunition question was an exceedingly serious one.

When the light went out, we withdrew to a farm close by, hoping for a real rest this time as we had not enjoyed a full night's sleep since we crossed the Orange River, more than a week before.

We did not get that night's rest, for at three o'clock next morning we were ordered up in the dark, and started in a cold drizzle of rain on a record march. Our men were weakened by long privations, our ammunition had dwindled to vanishing-point, and our horses were in the last stages of exhaustion, yet during the next six days, beset on all sides, we marched and fought, and in the end successfully got through.

When the sun rose and the rain ceased, we found ourselves crossing a high shoulder of land with a wide expanse of mountains to the south of us, and there, in every valley and on every road, stood the white tents of English camps, to bar our progress.

General Smuts surveyed the blocking forces for a while, and then led us due east across the front of the enemy posts. Our road took us through rough country, and he ordered every man to go on foot to spare the horses. The English made no attempt to come after us, their orders apparently being to hold the roads and exits, so we trekked all day, seeking to turn their extreme right flank. Throughout the expedition into the Cape we had no difficulty in getting local sympathizers to act as guides, and on this occasion a young farm hand volunteered to lead us. He picked his way so unerringly that towards nightfall we had not only succeeded in finding the end of the British line, but had even got round behind them, and could see the town of Dordrecht in the distance. We must have covered nearly thirty miles since getting out that morning, but as we were not yet out of danger of being headed back, we continued after dark, and, hungry and weary but in good cheer, we trudged all through the night, with only an occasional halt, mostly along steep mountain paths, wet and slippery from the rains. When daybreak came our young guide had done his work with such skill that we were well beyond the cordon, and there now lay before us the long mountain chain of the Stormbergen, stretching east to west as far as the eye could see. He told us that we could cross almost anywhere, so he was allowed to return home, and we made for a large farm lying at the foot of the range, where we turned our horses into the fields, and set about preparing a meal, once again hoping to spend the rest of the forenoon in sleep, for we had been on the move for twenty-four hours. But we had scarcely slaughtered a few sheep and broken our fast, when the well-known cry of 'Opsaal! Opsaal!' sent us scurrying to fetch our unfortunate animals, for coming down the slopes was a long column of English horse making our way. Nearby ran a pass up the mountain, and as it seemed clear of troops, we made for it, and in an hour stood on the top of the Stormbergen, with the enemy force slewed round and following us. The summit was a grassy tableland about three miles wide, sloping gently to where the southern face of the mountain fell abruptly down to the plains below.

There was no sign of troops up here, but as those in the rear were coming after us, General Smuts disposed his men to hold them back while we of the 'Rijk Section' were ordered to ride forward to the far edge of the plateau, to see whether the way in that direction was clear. We set out in couples, making for different points from which to look down on the Karroo. My companion was Henry Rittenberg, and when we reached the rim of the plateau we saw the narrow ribbon of a railway track winding across the plain at our feet, with train after train steaming up to a village station and disgorging numbers of soldiers.

The British, having failed to stop us at their first barrier, were now hurrying troops round by rail to establish a second, and already several mounted columns had detrained, and were beginning to climb up the mountain. One body was so far advanced that their scouts were appearing on the tableland itself, so Rittenberg and I rode nearer to examine their strength. We had not gone half a mile when some two dozen troopers rode at us from behind a roll in the ground, firing from the saddle as they came. We whipped round and galloped away, but had not the balance of the 'Rijk Section' come to our aid we should have been shot or captured, for there was no cover in which to make a stand, and our horses were in no fit state to compete with the well-fed English chargers.

We now returned to General Smuts, to report what we had seen, and he looked grave enough, for, with the original column of that morning closing in behind and all those fresh troops coming up in front, we were almost invested.

A strong north wind, which had sprung up earlier in the day, had steadily increased to a violent gale, and most of the men were crouching with their backs to the storm to escape the flying grit that stung like buckshot.

General Smuts, with Commandants van Deventer and Bouwer, was, however, on the lookout, standing well forward near the head of the pass up which the commando had come. While we were explaining the situation, about three hundred soldiers appeared on foot, having left their horses below. They did not seem to be expecting us here, for, when our men sprang up at a shout from van Deventer, they turned and ran back.

They were out of sight almost at once, and when we reached the edge we saw them scrambling down, but the wind in our faces made accurate shooting impossible, and I do not think any were hit. The soldiers only fired a few shots in reply, and a young man standing near me, named de la Rey, a nephew of General de la Rey, threw up his arms and dropped dead with a bullet through his brain. We left him where he fell, for we had no spade or other implement, nor had we time to bury him, for looking back we could now see more and more English horsemen emerging on the tableland, until we were practically encircled, although they were not yet strong enough to prevent us from moving freely inside the wide ring that they had formed about us.

Nevertheless we could not break out, for soon there were machine-guns at every point of vantage, so commanding the terrain that a burst-through during daylight would have cost us more men than we could afford, and our only course was to try to stave off the pressure until after dark. To that end, with the gale roaring about our ears, General Smuts led us hither and thither all the afternoon, now pushing back one portion of the enemy line, and then another, avoiding the machine-gun fire by using dead ground, and generally preventing them from hustling us too closely. With our tired horses and men the strain was great. Ammunition was at such a low ebb that some had not a round left, and when, towards evening, many more troops had come up our case seemed hopeless.

We and our horses had marched for forty hours on end, and we were all but finished for lack of sleep and rest, while the noose around us had slowly tightened, until by dusk we were at bay around a small farmhouse and kraal, lying somewhat in a hollow, where for the moment we had comparative shelter, but where our speedy capture seemed certain.

When the English troops saw us preparing to make a stand they stayed their advance, in the belief, no doubt, that having cornered us, they could afford to wait for our surrender in the morning.

General Smuts stood before the homestead in whispered consultation with his two lieutenants, while the rest of us leaned on our rifles, too weary to care very much what happened. Then out of the house came a hunchbacked cripple, who said that he would lead us through the English troops to the edge of the tableland, by a way which was unlikely to be watched, for it ran through boggy soil. His offer was eagerly accepted and orders were given to mount at once. Six or seven men had been wounded during the day, two of them so badly that they had to be left behind, but the others chose to accompany us, and in a few minutes we were silently filing off into the darkness, the cripple crouching insecurely on a horse at our head. He took us along a squelching path, that twisted for a mile or two so close to the investing troops that we could hear voices and the champing of bits, but at the end of an anxious hour he had brought us undiscovered to the escarpment. From here the mountainside fell sharply away into black depths below, how steeply we could not tell, but our guide warned us that it was very steep indeed. Dropping from his horse, he plodded off into the night on his crutches, carrying with him our heartfelt thanks, for he had risked his life and goods on our behalf.

We now began to descend what was probably the nearest approach to the vertical attempted by any mounted force during the war. I doubt whether we could have accomplished it by day, but horses are more tractable and surer-footed in the dark, so we pulled them over the edge and went slithering down. At times whole batches of men and horses came glissading past, knocking against all in their course, but luckily the surface was free of rock, and covered with a thick matting of grass which served to break the impact, and after a terrible scramble we got down without serious damage. For the time being we had shaken free of the enemy once more. Our most insistent need now was sleep, but this was still denied us. Somewhere on the plain before us ran the railway line on which we had looked down that morning, and many miles beyond that lay still another track, both of which had to be crossed before sunrise, if we did not wish to have the troop trains hurrying up more men. So General Smuts implacably ordered us on, and, leading our horses, we tramped obediently but wearily forward, little dreaming that another twenty hours of unbroken marching lay before us, and several days of even greater trials to come.

It was about ten o'clock by now, and the storm that had been raging throughout the day was subsiding, though the aftermath still blew cold; a blessing perhaps, for it served to keep us awake, and it made us step out to keep warm. After an hour we reached the first railway, a branch line from the Indwe Coal Mines. As we approached we saw the lights of a train, but General Smuts would not allow us to pile boulders on the metals nor to fire as the engine thundered by, for fear of killing civilians, so we stood aside, catching a glimpse of officers and others seated in the dining car, smoking and taking wine, all unaware of the men looking at them from the darkness. General French, the English cavalry leader, told us long after that he was on board that train with his staff, hurrying round by rail to control operations on the *berg* where he imagined us still to be, so unknowingly we missed a great opportunity.

After crossing the rails, we went on mile after mile, dazed for want of rest. Whenever there was delay at a fence or a ditch, whole rows of men would fall asleep on their hands and knees before their horses like Mohammedans at prayer, and it was necessary to go round shaking them to their feet to prevent them being left behind. Save for occasional halts we continued thus all night, for it was imperative to cross the remaining railway. As we had no guide we travelled by the stars, and the sun was rising before we struck it at a small siding about five miles east of Sterkstroom village, where, from the activity at the station, it was obvious that our escape from the mountain was known. Several trains were unloading troops, and there was no time to be lost. So mounting, we galloped as fast as we could across the rails for fear an armoured train might cut us off.

Commandant van Deventer and a few of us remained behind to search the railway buildings for anything that might come in useful, and while we were busy at this a long goods train came clanking up, and we brought it to a standstill by switching the points. It was an empty coal train in charge of a driver, stoker, and brakesman, whose faces were a picture when they saw what we were doing. As the train consisted of nothing but incombustible steel trucks, we let them proceed, after extracting a mailbag from the guard's van. The letters were all private ones, seemingly written under censorship, for not one of them made any reference to the war, but the newspapers were less reticent, and in one of them was unflattering mention of ourselves, for it said that General Smuts had invaded the Cape Colony 'with the riff-raff of the Boer Armies', which caused much merriment when later on I was able to read it to the men.

There was another surprising feature in the mailbag in the shape of a Proclamation by Lord Kitchener, wherein every burgher under arms after September 15 was sentenced to perpetual banishment from South Africa. This was news to us, and seeing that it was the 13th of that month by now, we were left with a bare two days in which to comply. This announcement was received with equal derision, when made known to the commando, and from what I have heard since, it had equally little effect up north in the Republics, where the 'paper bomb', as it was called, got treated with the scorn it deserved.

After speeding the goods train on its way, we overtook the commando at the Klaas Smits River, where we halted for about an hour, to give our poor horses a chance to pluck a few mouthfuls of grass, and to prepare a hasty meal for ourselves. Longer than that we were not given, for a column of troops with guns came up, and kept us on the move all day, slowly retiring from hill to hill, half dead with fatigue, but keeping them at arm's length until sunset, when they turned back and left us free to camp at last at a large farm, where we lay like dead men until morning after sixty hours of continuous marching.

This full night's rest was a great relief, but the strain was by no means over, and the worst was yet to come.

Towards nine o'clock next day, an English column appeared from the direction of Sterkstroom, so we saddled up and rode away, skirting the base of some hills running south. The column contented itself with following us slowly, apparently having been sent to keep us under observation, and they dogged our steps until sunset, when it came on to rain and we saw them go into camp.

We halted in a patch of thorn trees and, as it poured heavily till dawn, we had another of those wet and miserable nights which had been so frequent since our entry into the Colony.

Daylight saw the troops once more coming after us, and, owing to the shortage of ammunition and the condition of our horses, we had no option but to give way. The going was heavy, and at times the swollen spruits and dongas held us up, but we were in no great danger of being overhauled, for the column had wagons and guns, which impeded them so much that we had miles to spare.

In the afternoon the English camped again, and we halted for the rest of the day at a small farmhouse standing out on the plain. The rain had ceased since morning, but it was cold and threatening; black clouds hung low in the sky, and there was every promise of more dirty weather to come.

We could see smoke curling from the English camp four miles behind, where whole streets of comfortable tents had sprung up, at which we gazed wistfully, for there were warmth and rest, whilst we stood shivering in the biting wind, wondering how it was all to end. The English numbered about a thousand, and it was useless to attempt an attack in our present condition, for we were wet, cold, and in low spirits, and our ammunition was almost finished. So, when darkness fell, General Smuts gave orders for us to saddle up, intending to make for a larger farm where there was said to be ample shelter.

As we started, hard rain came down once more, and the darkness was so intense that we could not see a yard ahead. We had not gone three hundred paces before we heard horsemen splashing through the mud in front, and ran into the tail of an English patrol or column, we could not tell which, evidently making for the same farm. Neither side was prepared to risk a fight in the rain and dark. The troopers galloped away, and we sheered off, too, but with this difference, that they were able to continue on to the shelter of the farm, whilst we were adrift on the open veld.

The night that followed was the most terrible of all. Our guide lost his way; we went floundering ankle-deep in mud and water, our poor weakened horses stumbling and slipping at every turn; the rain beat down on us, and the cold was awful. Towards midnight it began to sleet. The grain bag which I wore froze solid on my body, like a coat of mail, and I believe that if we had not kept moving every one of us would have died. We had known two years of war, but we came nearer to despair that night than I care to remember. Hour after hour we groped our way, with men groaning who had never before uttered a word of complaint, as the cold searched their ill-protected bodies. We lost fourteen men that night, and I do not know whether they survived, but we never again had word of them.

We also lost a large number of horses, and I remember stumbling at intervals over their carcasses. We went on till daybreak, dragging ourselves along, and then, providentially, came on a deserted homestead and staggered into shelter, standing huddled together in rooms, stables, and barns until dawn, still shivering, but gradually recovering from the dreadful ordeal. When it grew light, some fifty or sixty horses lay dead outside. My little roan mare was still alive, but both my uncle's horses died here, and he, with thirty or forty more, was now a foot soldier. (As practically every man had crossed the Orange River with two horses, the number of dismounted men did not necessarily correspond to the number of horses that were lost.)

This night's 'Big Rain', as we named it, left such a mark on all of us that later we used to call ourselves 'The Big Rain Men' (*Die Groot Reent Kerels*) to distinguish us from those who had not experienced it, and for my part I passed through no greater test during the war.

The day was cold and wild, but the rain stopped. We broke up the floors and windows, tables and chairs, and everything else that would burn, and made great fires to dry our clothes and blankets, and to warm our chilled limbs. Towards noon, General Smuts ordered us on to another large farm, eight or nine miles away, which had, a native told him, plenty of fodder for the horses.

No attempt was made to send back for the missing men, because we were too exhausted, and they had to be abandoned. We plodded over the waterlogged country, a quarter of our number on foot, and the rest soon likely to be, for there was not a fit horse in the commando.

We found this farm also deserted, but there was protection for all, and a good store of oat sheaves, as well as sheep for slaughter, so that, although the rain came down again, we spent a comfortable night.

Although we had managed to avoid the different cordons thrown in our way and had eluded the columns sent in pursuit, we were not yet out of danger, for local natives now told us that southward every road, valley, and outlet was blocked by English troops. This meant that they were once more trying to head us back out of the Cape; but, with so many enemies in our rear, our only alternative was to go forward. Next morning, we set out on what was to be an eventful day (September 17, 1901).

Our road ran south down a long valley. The sky was clear, and the sun warm and bright for the first time for weeks, so that the men were cheerful again, although there was little other cause for optimism.

As a fighting force we were on our last legs. In front walked those who still had horses, dragging scarecrows behind them; then came a trail of footmen in twos and threes, their saddles slung across their shoulders, and in the rear rode the wounded in charge of their friends.

However, the sun was shining after the wet and cold and we went hopefully along. After a few miles General Smuts ordered the 'Rijk Section' to scout ahead of the commando, so those of us who still had horses mounted and rode forward as fast as our weakened animals could carry us. When we got to where the valley widened into more open country, a Dutch farmer rushed from a cottage beside the road and, in a voice hoarse with excitement, told us that English cavalry were waiting for us lower down. He said that they had mountain and machine-guns, and he estimated their strength at two hundred men, with over three hundred horses and mules, all of which proved substantially correct.

Edgar Duncker was sent back to report, and before long he returned with General Smuts, accompanied by Commandant van Deventer and a dozen men. General Smuts immediately decided to attack, and I heard him say that if we did not get those horses and a supply of ammunition we were done for. He ordered van Deventer forward with the men who were with him and the 'Rijk Section', to locate the British force, while he himself waited here to bring up the rest of the commando. We set off at once, and in a few minutes reached the banks of a small river which we crossed. As we were going through the fringe of thorn trees on the other side, we rode straight into fifteen or twenty troopers cantering towards us. Most of our men were still among the trees, but four or five of us were in advance, and when we leaped to the ground the soldiers were not more than ten yards away. Opening fire, we brought down several, and the rest turned and galloped back along the road. I fired my last two cartridges here, and my first thought was to run to a dead soldier and seize his rifle and bandolier, abandoning my own rusty weapon, then I rushed for my mare and joined in the chase.

The troop horses were in much better condition than ours, but the soldiers were delayed by a gate, so we got close again, dropping two or three more from the saddle.

At the gate van Deventer himself and half a dozen men turned aside to a kopje for observation, but the rest of us, about twelve in number, followed the retiring patrol to a ridge farther down the road.

They got there several lengths ahead of us and, abandoning their horses, took to the rocks. It was too late for us to retire back across the open plain behind, so we galloped on.

Before we reached their outcrop the soldiers opened fire almost point-blank, and worse still, a mountain gun unexpectedly fired on us from a point to our left, not thirty yards off, and a machine-gun rattled into action close by. So near was the mountain gun that smoke from the discharge billowed over us although the shells went wide. It was astonishing that any of us escaped, but, owing no doubt to our sudden appearance behind the flying patrol, the firing was wild, and only three men and some horses went down before we reached the rocks in which the soldiers were. Here we, in turn, loosed our horses and ran up, to find ourselves within a few feet of our original quarry and a number of others, who had been posted here before.

Now that we could look over to the far side, we were surprised to see a large English camp less than a stone's throw away, buzzing like a disturbed ant heap. Officers were shouting orders, and men tumbling out of their tents, some running towards us, others going to the right and left to take their stations.

This placed us in a remarkably tight corner, as we were so far ahead of our main body that they could not help us, for the English, having recovered from their first surprise, were sweeping the plain with gun and rifle fire. The result was that our little party was stranded on the very edge of an armed encampment, and practically mixed with the English soldiers. Fortunately General Smuts had hurried the commando on, and in a few minutes they opened fire from a hill in the rear, thus preventing us from being overwhelmed, for our opponents were forced to take cover and could not surround us. Those before us were in rough alignment along the bank of the ledge, so we were able to form a similar front, with a space of two or three yards separating us, while along the perimeter of the camp lay the rest of the troops in a half-moon. A young Transvaler named Muller and I lay at the end where the rocks ran dead, and from here we could see the mountain gun close by, busy shelling our commando. The gunners could not fire on us as they would have to hit their own men, and in any case they did not seem to realize that we were so near, for they were unconcernedly loading and firing at our men on the hill six hundred yards back. Standing behind the gun was a tall man handing shells to the three at the breech. I fired at him, and he spun round and sank in a sitting position against the wheel, where I found him dead when the fight was over. The

other three ran for the camp at their backs. I fired at one, and he
pitched forward dead, while Muller brought down a third, but the
last man got away among the tents. Having disposed of the gun-
crew in a matter of seconds we turned to the other work in hand.
The place we were fighting in was an outcrop of loose rocks,
jutting up like a reef, nowhere much higher than a man, although
the rear slope fell somewhat more steeply into the English camp.
In this narrow space, where we were facing each other almost at
handshake, a grim duel began. As the soldiers raised their heads to
fire we brought them down, for they were no match for us in short-
range work of this kind, and we killed twelve or thirteen and
wounded several more, at a distance of a few yards. We did not
suffer a single casualty, except for the three men hit as we rode in.
Of these, one was Edgar Duncker with a bullet through his foot,
and another a Jew named Cohen, with a smashed ankle. These two
had been able to crawl forward to the firing line and were taking
part in the attack, but the third man, Raubenheimer (a brother of
Vera, Countess of Cathcart), lay out in the open with his thigh
broken, and his dead horse pinning him down.

Before he could reach his men, I hit a sergeant who came running
up from the camp, a big heavily built man. He doubled up like a
knife, and rolled about, shot in the stomach; then he died.

Nicolas Swart by my side shot two other soldiers in quick succession, as they tried to join those in the rocks. There was a young
lieutenant a few feet from me. I found out afterwards that his name
was Sheridan, and they said he was a cousin of Winston Churchill.
Twice he rose to fire at me and missed; at his second attempt I
grazed his temple, and he dropped out of sight, but only dazed, for
in a moment he was up again, swaying unsteadily on his feet, with
his face streaming with blood, but still trying to level his rifle at me.
While I was hesitating what to do, Jack Borrius shot him through
the brain. Another soldier fired several hasty rounds at me, and I
put a bullet into his heel, which was protruding from behind the
rock near which he was lying. The sudden shock made him leap up,
and again Jack Borrius, who was wonderfully quick, shot him dead
as he rose.

In this manner the fight went on, until a mile beyond the camp we
saw a small force of English troops approaching from the south.
There were not many of them, but for all we knew they were the
advance-guard of a relief force and, should sufficient reinforcements
arrive to drive off our commando, those of us here in the rocks
would be marooned, so we decided to clear the rocks by charging.

After a whispered consultation from man to man, Jack Borrius gave the signal, and, rising together, we leaped in among the surviving soldiers. There were only ten or fifteen left, and so far as I can remember not a shot was fired on either side. Our sudden onslaught took them unprepared, and they surrendered at once. Without troubling about our prisoners we ran down shouting and cheering into the camp, before the rest of the defenders knew what had happened. When they saw us among the tents in their rear, something like a stampede set in. Soldiers went running in all directions, some making away into the thorn trees, others coming towards us and throwing down their arms. One man rushed to the horselines, and mounting barebacked, flourished a revolver and tried to ride off. I shouted to him to halt, but as he gave no heed I shot him dead. When the commando saw us enter the camp, they came galloping across, and the fight was over.

I took part in a final episode, for William Conradi and I, walking through a patch of trees to disarm some soldiers, came on a stone cattle kraal, in which a dozen men were holding out. When we looked into the kraal, they were leaning on their rifles on the far wall and firing at some of our commando men moving in the distance. We called out 'Hands up! Hands up!' but they turned instead and blazed a volley into our faces. Only our eyes were showing or we should both have been shot. Conradi killed one man and wounded another with a single bullet, and I wounded one, but even now they did not surrender, for, rushing across the kraal, they ranged themselves against the near wall, which alone separated us, and one of them thrust his rifle so near my face that his shot scorched my cheek and neck with cordite, fragments of which had to be picked out for days afterwards, with the point of a knife. When I seized the muzzle he gave an oath and jerked it back so forcibly that the sharp foresight gashed the ball of my thumb and the palm of my hand, and I had to let go.

The situation was fast becoming dangerous, when, to our relief, we heard the sound of voices through the trees, and a number of our men came running up to see what the firing was about. The soldiers now threw their rifles over the wall, but even this was not the end, for, as I hastened round to the entrance of the kraal to receive the prisoners, I collided with a soldier who came crouching along to get us in the flank. He did not know that the fight was over, and if I had not rammed him when I did, in another moment he would have been round the corner, shooting us down while we were engaged with the men inside. He said I was a 'surprise packet', offered me a cigarette, and came with me to join his captured companions in the kraal with his hand amicably on my shoulder. The whole incident had not lasted five minutes, but it had been sharp enough, and Conradi and I reckoned ourselves well out of it as we hastened back to the camp to take part in the looting. The commando was up and there was a great ransacking of tents and wagons. The small relieving force that had given us cause for alarm turned out to be only a patrol, and it had the doubtful satisfaction of watching us from afar as we turned the camp inside out.

When we had done we were like giants refreshed. We had ridden into action that morning at our last gasp, and we emerged refitted from head to heel. We all had fresh horses, fresh rifles, clothing, saddlery, boots and more ammunition than we could carry away, as well as supplies for every man.

Moreover, we had renewed confidence in our leader and in ourselves, a factor of considerable importance to a body of men in a hostile country.

In the fight we lost only one man, who was killed when we rushed the camp, and six wounded, whereas the enemy had thirty killed, many wounded, and many taken prisoners.

I did not count the number of soldiers opposed to us, but there must have been about two hundred. They belonged to the 17th Lancers, one of the crack regiments of the British Army. Among their wounded was their Commander, Captain Sandeman, and Lord Vivian, whom I found among the rocks where we first rushed them. He it was who told me the fate of the three men killed and mutilated by the Basutos, the day that we crossed the Orange River. He pointed out his little bivouac tent, and said that it would be worth my while to have a look at it. I was not slow to take the hint, with the result that having started that morning with a grain bag for my chief garment, a foundered horse, an old rifle, and two cartridges, I now appeared in a handsome cavalry tunic, riding breeches, etc., with a sporting Lee-Metford, full bandoliers and a superb mount, a little grey Arab, which his coloured groom said had been the property of Lieutenant Sheridan. I also selected a strong riding-mule in preference to another horse, for my experience during the past fortnight had taught me that a good mule for long marches and a light pony for use in action were the ideal combination. After I had completed my equipment, commissariat, and ammunition supply, I walked around the camp.

We considered that the taking of it was chiefly the handiwork of our original storming party, for while we could not have done it without the protection and covering fire of the commando, yet by riding in on the heels of the English troopers and taking post on the very edge of the camp, we had served as the spearhead that made success possible. I also saw the dead gunners and other men whom I had shot, and I looked on them with mixed feelings, for although I have never hated the English, a fight is a fight, and though I was sorry for the men, I was proud of my share in the day's work.

Lastly, I went to see what had become of my roan mare. She was still patiently standing where I had left her at the ledge. On each side of her lay a dead horse, but she had escaped unharmed. The gallant little beast was, however, so exhausted that when I tried to lead her away she could scarcely put one foot before the other, so I unsaddled her, throwing the saddle aside, for it was old and worn with much use since I had taken it from General Clements's camp ten months before. Removing the bridle and halter, I turned her loose in the hope that some neighbouring farmer would look after her, for she too had shown the mettle of her Free State pasture, and the marvellous endurance of the South African horse.

General Smuts now ordered us to set the tents and wagons on fire, and to destroy the mountain and machine-guns, as well as such surplus ammunition and other supplies as could not be removed. Then, leaving the prisoners, mule drivers, and native servants to shift for themselves, we rode off in triumph.

IN THE MONTHS *that followed the raid, Kitchener ordered all Boer guerrillas shot when captured. It was a long time afterwards that Reitz learned that wearing the enemy uniform had changed the guerrilla's status and lost him any rights as a prisoner.*

With the war's end, Reitz went into exile. Smuts made his peace with the English, and when he heard that his young friend was working as a mule driver in Madagascar, he sent for him. Reitz was ill, and while nursing him back to health, Smuts convinced him of the possibility of working with England. Together they fought General Lettow-Vorbeck in East Africa during World War I, and Reitz went on to become a colonel on the Western Front.

In the years after the First World War, Smuts became prime minister of the Union of South Africa, and Reitz became deputy prime minister. World War II found Field-Marshal Smuts directing operations against the Axis in Ethiopia, and Reitz a High Commissioner in London.

Reitz died in 1944, and Smuts, after his appointment as Chancellor of Cambridge University, died in 1950.

LAWRENCE AND THE ARABS

BY T. E. LAWRENCE

LEGENDS HAVE GATHERED *about the slight trim figure of Lawrence of Arabia. Some men label him a genius while others point out his idiosyncrasies and label him lucky. Those who admire him point out his archæological accomplishments, his excellent translation of the* Odyssey, *his acceptance in an alien world, his ability to tie the loose elements of the nomadic Arabs into an effective fighting force, to give guerrilla warfare new dimensions, and finally to write the great classic of that warfare—* The Seven Pillars of Wisdom.

Those who belittle him point out that he had every advantage a guerrilla chief could want—a mobile and friendly population with which to work, men who had nothing to lose by fighting and little to fear from reprisals, all the space in the world in which to fight and hide, a unifying force in the spirit of rising Arab nationalism, and in the Turks a decadent and unimaginative enemy.

There is truth in both assertions, for Lawrence was a complex person who lived in a strange world partly of his own making, who saw the advantages that lay in the situation, and with imagination and courage, capitalized on them.

There is an elusive, an almost mercurial quality about Lawrence's personality. Perhaps the answer to this enigma lies in the chameleon element which made him an Arab among Arabs, an 'other rank' in the peace-time Air Force, and a power among such powerful persons as Emir Feisal and General Allenby. He was able to give life as much as it demanded of him, and after that one greatest demand during World War I, he withdrew from life.

In the following selections he tells the effects of this greatest effort upon himself, reports in detail on three of his operations, and, finally, ingeniously analyses the strategy of guerrilla warfare. The first and last selections are from The Seven Pillars of Wisdom. *The others are from his original reports in the* Arab Bulletin, *written during his operations.*

SOME of the evil of my tale may have been inherent in our circumstances. For years we lived anyhow with one another in the naked desert, under the indifferent heaven. By day the hot sun fermented us; and we were dizzied by the beating wind. At night we were stained by dew, and shamed into pettiness by the innumerable silences of stars. We were a self-centred army without parade or gesture, devoted to freedom, the second of man's creeds, a purpose so ravenous that it devoured all our strength, a hope so transcendent that our earlier ambitions faded in its glare.

As time went by our need to fight for the ideal increased to an unquestioning possession, riding with spur and rein over our doubts. Willy-nilly it became a faith. We had sold ourselves into its slavery, manacled ourselves together in its chain gang, bowed ourselves to serve its holiness with all our good and ill content. The mentality of ordinary human slaves is terrible—they have lost the world—and we had surrendered, not body alone, but soul to the overmastering greed of victory. By our own act we were drained of morality, of volition, of responsibility, like dead leaves in the wind.

The everlasting battle stripped from us care of our own lives or of others'. We had ropes about our necks, and on our heads prices which showed that the enemy intended hideous tortures for us if we were caught. Each day some of us passed; and the living knew themselves just sentient puppets on God's stage: indeed, our taskmaster was merciless, merciless, so long as our bruised feet could stagger forward on the road. The weak envied those tired enough to die; for success looked so remote, and failure a near and certain, if sharp, release from toil. We lived always in the stretch or sag of nerves, either on the crest or in the trough of waves of feeling. This impotency was bitter to us, and made us live only for the seen horizon, reckless what spite we inflicted or endured, since physical sensation showed itself meanly transient. Gusts of cruelty, perversions, lusts ran lightly over the surface without troubling us; for the moral laws which had seemed to hedge about these silly accidents must be yet fainter words. We had learned that there were pangs too sharp, griefs too deep, ecstasies too high for our finite selves to register. When emotion reached this pitch the mind choked; and memory went white till the circumstances were humdrum once more.

Such exaltation of thought, while it let adrift the spirit, and gave it licence in strange airs, lost it the old patient rule over the body. The body was too coarse to feel the utmost of our sorrows and of our joys. Therefore, we abandoned it as rubbish: we left it below us to march forward, a breathing simulacrum, on its own unaided level, subject to influences from which in normal times our instincts would have shrunk. The men were young and sturdy; and hot flesh and blood unconsciously claimed a right in them and tormented their bellies with strange longings. Our privations and dangers fanned this virile heat, in a climate as racking as can be conceived. We had no shut places to be alone in, no thick clothes to hide our nature. Man in all things lived candidly with man.

The Arab was by nature continent; and the use of universal marriage had nearly abolished irregular courses in his tribes. The public women of the rare settlements we encountered in our months of wandering would have been nothing to our numbers, even had their raddled meat been palatable to a man of healthy parts. In horror of such sordid commerce our youths began indifferently to slake one another's few needs in their own clean bodies—a cold convenience that, by comparison, seemed sexless and even pure. Later, some began to justify this sterile process, and swore that friends quivering together in the yielding sand with intimate hot limbs in supreme embrace, found there hidden in the darkness a sensual coefficient of the mental passion which was welding our souls and spirits in one flaming effort. Several, thirsting to punish appetites they could not wholly prevent, took a savage pride in degrading the body, and offered themselves fiercely in any habit which promised physical pain or filth.

I was sent to these Arabs as a stranger, unable to think their thoughts or subscribe their beliefs, but charged by duty to lead them forward and to develop to the highest any movement of theirs profitable to England in her war. If I could not assume their character, I could at least conceal my own, and pass among them without evident friction, neither a discord nor a critic but an unnoticed influence. Since I was their fellow, I will not be their apologist or advocate. Today in my old garments, I could play the bystander, obedient to the sensibilities of our theatre, but it is more honest to record that these ideas and actions then passed naturally. What now looks wanton or sadic seemed in the field inevitable, or just unimportant routine.

Blood was always on our hands: we were licensed to it. Wounding and killing seemed ephemeral pains, so very brief and sore was life with us. With the sorrow of living so great, the sorrow of punishment had to be pitiless. We lived for the day and died for it. When there was reason and desire to punish we wrote our lesson with gun or whip immediately in the sullen flesh of the sufferer, and the case was beyond appeal. The desert did not afford the refined slow penalties of courts and gaols.

Of course our rewards and pleasures were as suddenly sweeping as our troubles; but, to me in particular, they bulked less large. Bedouin ways were hard even for those brought up to them, and for strangers terrible: a death in life. When the march or labour ended I had no energy to record sensation, nor while it lasted any leisure to see the spiritual loveliness which sometimes came upon us by the way. In my notes, the cruel rather than the beautiful found place. We no doubt enjoyed more the rare moments of peace and forget-fulness; but I remember more the agony, the terrors, and the mis-takes. Our life is not summed up in what I have written (there are things not to be repeated in cold blood for very shame); but what I have written was in and of our life. Pray God that men reading the story will not, for love of the glamour of strangeness, go out to prostitute themselves and their talents in serving another race.

A man who gives himself to be a possession of aliens leads a Yahoo life, having bartered his soul to a brute-master. He is not of them. He may stand against them, persuade himself of a mission, batter and twist them into something which they, of their own accord, would not have been. Then he is exploiting his old environment to press them out of theirs. Or, after my model, he may imitate them so well that they spuriously imitate him back again. Then he is giving away his own environment: pretending to theirs; and pre-tences are hollow, worthless things. In neither case does he do a thing of himself, nor a thing so clean as to be his own (without thought of conversion), letting them take what action or reaction they please from the silent example.

In my case, the effort for these years to live in the dress of Arabs, and to imitate their mental foundation, quitted me of my English self, and let me look at the West and its conventions with new eyes: they destroyed it all for me. At the same time I could not sincerely take on the Arab skin: it was an affectation only. Easily was a man made an infidel, but hardly might he be converted to another faith. I had dropped one form and not taken on the other, and was become like Mohammed's coffin in our legend, with a resultant feeling of intense loneliness in life, and a contempt, not for other men, but for all they do. Such detachment came at times to a man exhausted by prolonged physical effort and isolation. His body plodded on mechanically, while his reasonable mind left him, and from without looked down critically on him, wondering what that futile lumber did and why. Sometimes these selves would converse in the void; and then madness was very near, as I believe it would be near the man who could see things through the veils at once of two customs, two educations, two environments.

I left Akaba on September 7, with the two British gun instructors, and two sheikhs of the Ageilat Beni Atiyah, from Mudowarrah. My hope was to raise three hundred men in Gueira and take Mudowarrah station.

We rode gently to Gueira, where were a large camp, little water, and great tribal heartburnings. The three sub-tribes I was relying on were not yet paid, and Audah abu Tayi was making trouble by his greediness and his attempt to assume authority over all the Huweitat. It was impossible to get either men or camels, so I moved to Rum, five hours S.S.E. of Gueira. There are good springs, difficult of access, at Rum, some pasturage, and the most beautiful sandstone cliff scenery.

At Rum the Dhumaniyah came in on September 12, mutinous. The situation became unpleasant, so I rode to Akaba, saw Feisal, and returned on the 13th with the promise of twenty baggage camels, and Sherif Abdullah ibn Hamza el-Feir, who tried to smooth over the local friction.

On September 15 the camels arrived, and on the 16th we started for Mudowarrah with a force of one hundred and sixteen Bedouins, made up of Toweiha, Zuweida, Darausha, Dhumaniyah, Togatga and Zelebani Huweitat, and Ageilat Beni Atiyah. Sheikh Zaal was the only capable leader, and Audah's pretensions had made the other sub-tribes determined not to accept his authority. This threw upon me a great deal of detailed work, for which I had no qualifications, and throughout the expedition I had more preoccupation with questions of supply and transport, tribal pay disputes, division of spoil, feuds, march order, and the like, than with the explosive work which should more properly have been mine. The Sherif with me, Nasir el-Harith, went blind the first day out and was useless.

We reached Mudowarrah well on September 17, in the afternoon, after thirteen hours' march and went down at dusk to the station about three miles further east. We got within three hundred yards of it, but could find no position for a Stokes gun. The station is large and the garrison seemed to be between two hundred and three hundred men, and I was doubtful whether it would be wise to take it on with the rather mixed force I had; so in the end I went back to the well and on the 18th moved southward into sandy country. It is hoped to make Mudowarrah the object of further operations.

In the afternoon of September 18, I had an electric mine, in about five hours' work, over a culvert at kilo. 587, on the outside of a curve towards some low hills, three hundred yards away, where Stokes and Lewis guns could be placed to rake the lengths of either north- or south-bound trains. The position was too high for the best machine-gun work, but the presence of a British machine-gunner made safety play advisable.

We slept near the mine, but were seen by a Turkish watching post near kilo. 590 in the afternoon, and at 9 a.m. on the 19th about forty men were sent from Haret Ammar to attack us from the south, where the hills were broken and difficult to keep clear. We detached thirty men to check them, and waited till noon, when a force of about one hundred men moved out from Mudowarrah and came slowly down the line, to outflank us on the north. At 8 p.m. a train of two engines and ten boxwagons came up slowly from the south, shooting hard at us from loopholes and positions on the carriage roofs. As it passed I exploded the mine under the second engine, hoping the first would then go through the culvert: the Lewis guns cleared the roof meanwhile. The mine derailed the front engine, smashing its cab and tender, destroyed the second engine altogether, and blew in the culvert. The first wagon upended into the hole and the succeeding ones were shaken up. The shock affected the Turks, and the Arabs promptly charged up to within twenty yards, and fired at the wagons, which were not armoured. The Turks got out on the far side, and took refuge in the hollow of the bank (about eleven feet high) and fired between the wheels at us. Two Stokes bombs at once fell among them there, and turned them out towards some rough country two hundred yards N.E. of the line. On their way there the Lewis gun killed all but about twenty of them, and the survivors threw away their rifles and fled towards Mudowarrah. The action took ten minutes.

The Arabs now plundered the train, while I fired a box of gun-cotton on the front engine and damaged it more extensively. I fear, however, that it is still capable of repair. The conditions were not helpful to good work, for there were many prisoners and women hanging on to me, I had to keep the peace among the plunderers, and the Turks from the south opened fire on us at long range just as the train surrendered, our covering force on that side having come in to share the booty. The baggage in the train was very large and the Arabs went mad over it. In any case a Bedouin force no longer exists when plunder has been obtained, since each man only cares to get off home with it. I was therefore left with the two British N.C.O.'s and Zaal and Howeimil of the Arabs, to ensure the safety of the guns and machine-guns. It was impossible to complete the destruction of the first engine or burn the trucks. We destroyed twenty rounds of Stokes shells and some S.A.A. whose detonation kept back the Turks for a time. The north and south Turkish forces were both coming up fast, and our road back was commanded by hills which they were already occupying. I abandoned my own baggage and got away the men and guns to a safe position in the rear. Zaal was there able to collect thirteen men, and at 3 p.m. we counter-attacked the hills and regained our camping ground. We then managed to clear off most of the kit, though some of it, in the most exposed positions, had to be left. Sergeant Yells came up with a Lewis, and we retired ridge by ridge from 4.30 p.m. with no losses except four camels.

The Turkish killed amounted to about seventy men, with about thirty wounded (of whom many died later). We took ninety prisoners, of whom five were Egyptian soldiers captured by the Turks near Hadiyah, ten were women, and nine were Medina men, deported by the Turks. An Austrian Second-Lieutenant, who (with about thirteen Sergeant Instructors) was on the train, was killed: only sixty-eight of the prisoners were brought into Akaba.

From 5 p.m. we rode hard northward, and on to Mudowarrah well, at 8 p.m. We watered that night, without interruption from the Turks, which was good fortune, for the station is only three miles away and the Arab camels were so loaded with booty as to be useless for a fight. We left the same evening, and got to Rum on the night of September 20.

The promptness of the Turkish attack, the smallness of my force, and the amount of spoil made our retreat inevitable. I had hoped to hold up the line for a considerable time, and still hope that, with proper arrangements, it may be possible. The country about Mudowarrah (whose station well is, I feel sure, the key of the Maan-Tebruk railway) is so bare of grazing, that the maintenance of a large blockading force is not feasible; but the water difficulties for the Turks make a heavy attack by them, if Mudowarrah is once lost, improbable.

The Arab casualties were one killed and four wounded.

The mine was a sandbag of fifty pounds of blasting gelatine kneaded into one lump. It was set between the ends of two steel sleepers, in contact with each and with the base of the rail. Four inches of sand and ballast was laid over it. The spot chosen was over the south haunch of a three-metre arched culvert, and the contact wires were buried down the embankment, across a hollow, and up a low rocky ridge beyond. A naval waterproof detonator was used, as army detonators were not available. The burying of the contact wire took nearly four hours, since stiff single wires were supplied. A very light twin cable would be more use. It proved extremely difficult (on the score of weight) to carry off the wires after use.

The length of cable available was two hundred yards, but for reasons of observation I had to stand at one hundred yards only. The shock of the explosion was very severe, and parts of cylinders, wheels, pistons and boiler plating fell all over the place to a radius of three hundred yards from the locomotive. The whole side of the engine was blown off and half the culvert brought down. People in the trucks complained of shock. Had I fired the mine under the front engine I think both would have been wrecked. One was a Hejaz locomotive and one a D.H.P. (Damascus–Aleppo Railway).

I left Akaba on September 27, to test an automatic mine on the Hejaz railway. In view of the possibility of wider operations in October, I took with me Lieutenant Pisani, of the French section at Akaba, and three educated Syrians, in order to train them in anti-railway tactics.

We marched to Rum on September 29, where we stopped three days. Lieutenant Pisani had fever, and I spent the time in showing him and the others the preliminary work of mining and arranging with Sherif Hashim, a Shenabra, who is O.C., Rum, details of the Bedouin force required. Feisal's orders to him were to go where, when, and as I wanted. In an endeavour to get over the difficulties caused by Audah Abu Tayi's pretensions, I appointed Sheikh Salem Alayan to be O.C. Bedouins, and asked for only Dumaniyah and Darausha tribesmen, about forty in all. This number would have been enough to deal with a wrecked train, and easy to handle in the Fasoa district (for which I was bound), where the wells are small. However, the enormous haul of booty in the train blown up early in September near Mudowarrah had completely turned the heads of the Huweitat, and hundreds clamoured and insisted on taking part in my new expedition. We had a great deal of difficulty, and in the end I accepted nearly one hundred Darausha, and fifty Dumaniyah, including every sheikh in the two sub-tribes. All others were refused.

A feature of the Huweitat is that every fourth or fifth man is a sheikh. In consequence the head sheikh has no authority whatever, and as in the previous raid, I had to be O.C. of the whole expedition.

This is not a job which should be undertaken by foreigners, since we have not so intimate a knowledge of Arab families, as to be able to divide common plunder equitably. On this occasion, however, the Bedouins behaved exceedingly well, and everything was done exactly as I wished; but during the six days' trip I had to adjudicate in twelve cases of assault with weapons, four camel thefts, one marriage settlement, fourteen feuds, two evil eyes, and a bewitchment. These affairs take up all one's spare time.

We marched up Wadi Hafri to its head near Batra, where we watered with some difficulty owing to scarcity of supply, and the numerous Arab families at the well. The area between Batra and the railway is full of Arab tents. From Batra we marched on October 3 to near kilo. 475, where I meant to mine; but we found Turkish guard posts (of fifteen to twenty-five men) too close to the suitable spots. At nightfall, therefore, we went away to the south, till midnight, when we found a good place, and buried an automatic mine at kilo. 500.4. The nearest Turkish post was 2,500 m. away on the south. On the north there was no post for nearly 4,000 yards. The mine-laying took the five of us two hours, and then we retired 1,500 yards from the line and camped. On the 4th no train passed. On the 5th a water train came down from Maan at 10 a.m., and went over the mine without firing it. I waited till mid-day and then, in two hours, laid an electric mine over the automatic. The Turks patrolled the line twice daily, but one may usually reckon on their all sleeping at noon. We then disposed the Arabs to attack the train when it should come, and waited till the morning of October 6 for one to arrive.

The line here crosses a valley on a bank twenty feet high, and five hundred yards long. The bank is pierced by three small bridges, at intervals of about two hundred yards. We laid our mines over the southernmost of these, took the cables along the track to the midmost (the firing position), and put two Lewis guns in the northernmost, from which point they were in a position to rake the embankment. From this northern bridge ran up westward a two-foot-deep torrent bed, spotted with broom bushes. In these the men and guns hid till wanted.

On the 6th a train (twelve wagons) came down from Maan at 8 a.m. It arrived only 200 yards in advance of the Turkish patrol (of nine men), but this gave us time to get into position. From the open bed of the valley in front of the line, where I was sitting to give the signal for firing, it was curious to see the train running along the top of the bank with the machine-gunners and exploders dancing war dances beneath the bridges. The Arabs behind me were beautifully hidden, and kept perfectly still.

The explosion shattered the fire-box of the locomotive, burst many of the tubes, threw the l.c. cylinder into the air, cleaned out the cab, warped the frame, bent the two near driving wheels and broke their axles. I consider it past repair. Its tender, and the front wagon were also destroyed, with one arch of the bridge. The couplings broke, and the last four wagons drifted backwards down-hill out of fire. I was too late to stop them with a stone. A Kaim-makam, General Staff, appeared at one window, and fired at us with a Mauser pistol, but a Bedouin blazed into him at twenty yards, and he fell back out of sight and I hope damaged. (We have heard since he got back safe to Maan: he was one, Nazmi Bey.) The eight remaining wagons were captured in six minutes. They contained about seventy tons of foodstuffs, 'urgently required at Medain Salih for Ibn Rashid', according to waybills captured with the lot. We carried off about a third of this, and destroyed another third or more. The Turkish killed amount to about fifteen. Some civilians were released, and four officers taken prisoner.

The plundering occupied all the energies of our Bedouins, and Turkish counter-attacks came up unopposed from N. and S. I rolled up the electric cables first of all, and as they are very heavy and I was single-handed, it took nearly three-quarters of an hour to do this. Then two chiefs of the Darausha came to look for me. I went up to the top of the bank, hoping to fire the train, but found about forty Turks coming up fast and only four hundred yards off. As the nearest Bedouins were one thousand yards away and they were all on foot, driving their laden camels at top speed westward, I felt that it would be foolish to delay longer alone on the spot, and so rode off with two Arabs who had come back for me. We all reached Rum safely on the 7th, and Akaba on the 8th, where I found telegrams asking me to go to Suez and on to G.H.Q., E.E.F.

The raid was intended as an experiment only, and was most successful. The automatic mine failed, but I proved able to keep one hundred and fifty Bedouins in a camp one thousand five hundred yards from the line for three days without giving the Turks warning of our presence, in spite of the regular patrols passing up and down the line. This means that the rank and file of the Arabs, as well as the sheikhs, did as I ordered. The complete destruction of a cap-tured train, and annihilation of relief parties, will be easy, as soon as I have the Indian M.G. section to support me in the actual action. The Lewis gunners on this occasion were two of my Arab servants, trained by me in one day at Rum. They killed twelve of the enemy's casualties, but of course went off to get booty immediately afterwards.

I left Akaba on October 24, with Captain G. Lloyd, Lieutenant Wood, R.E., and the Indian Machine Gun Company. The Indians took two Vickers, and I took two Lewis guns with me.

We marched to Rum (October 25) and thence across El-Gaa and up W. Hafir to near Batra. We crossed the railway just south of Bir el-Shedia and reached el-Jefer on October 28. Captain Lloyd returned to Akaba from there. Sherif Ali ibn Husein overtook us, and the party marched to Bair, picked up Sheikh Mifleh el-Zebn and fifteen Sukhur and reached Amri on November 2. On November 5 we camped at Kseir el-Hallabat, and on the 7th failed to rush the bridge at Tell el-Shehab, and returned to Kseir. Thence the Indian M.G. Company with Lieutenant Wood, returned to Azrak. I went with sixty Arabs to Minefir, blew up a train at kilo. 172 on November 11 and reached Azrak on the 12th.

My intention had been to reach Jisr el-Hemmi on November 3, but this proved impossible, since rain had made the Jaulaan plain too slippery for our camels, and the Turks had put hundreds of woodcutters in the Irbid hills. This closed both the north and south roads, and left Tell el-Shehab (Bridge 14) the only approachable bridge in the Yarmuk valley. My first plan was to rush it by camel marches of fifty miles a day. This idea also failed, since by their best efforts the Indian Machine Gun Company were only able to do thirty to thirty-five miles a day, and even this pace cut up their camels very quickly, owing to their inexperience. They all did their best, and gave me no trouble at all, but were simply unable to march fast.

I decided, therefore, to raise an Arab force, and descend on the bridge in strength. The Abu Tayi refused to come, only fifteen Sukhur would take it on, and I had to rely mainly on thirty Serahin recruits at Azrak. They were untried men and proved little use at the pinch. For the last stage to the bridge, as hard riding was involved, I picked out six of the Indians, with their officer, and we got actually to the bridge at midnight on November 7. It is a position of some strength, but could, I think, be rushed by twenty decent men. The Indians with me were too few to attempt it, and the Serahin, as soon as the Turks opened fire, dumped their dynamite into the valley and bolted. In the circumstances I called everyone off as quickly as possible and went back to Kseir el-Hallabat. The Indians with us were very tired with the ride, which was a fairly fast one, of ninety miles in twenty-two hours. The Bedu and the Sherif wanted to do something more before returning to Azrak, and had the Indians been fitter, we could have put in a useful raid; but they were tired and had only half a day's ration left, since all extra stuff has been placed at Azrak.

The situation was explained to the Sherif, who said it would be enough to mine a train, without making a machine-gun attack upon it. The Bedu agreed, and we went off together. The party was composed of Sherif Ali with ten servants, myself with one, twenty Sukhur and thirty Serahin. None of us had any food at all. We went to Minifir, to kilo. 172, where I mined the line in June last. As the Bedu had lost my dynamite at the bridge I was only able to put thirty pounds into the mine, which I laid on the crown of a four metre culvert (about eighteen feet high) and took the wires as far up the hillside toward cover as they would reach. Owing to the shortage of cable this was only sixty yards, and we had to leave the ends buried, for fear of patrols. A train came down before dawn on the 10th, too fast for me to get to the exploder from my watching place. In the morning of the 10th a train of refugees came up at four miles an hour from the south. The exploder failed to work, and the whole train crawled past me as I lay on the flat next to the wires. For some reason no one shot at me, and after it had passed I took the exploder away and overhauled it, while a Turkish patrol came up and searched the ground very carefully. That night we slept on the head of the wires, and no train appeared, till 10 a.m. on November 11. Then a troop train of twelve coaches and two locomotives came down from the north at twenty miles an hour. I touched off under the engine and the explosion was tremendous. Something must have happened to the boiler for I was knocked backwards and boiler plates flew about in all directions. One fragment smashed the exploder, which I therefore left in place, with the wires. The first engine fell into the valley on the east side of the line; the second upended into the space where the culvert had been, and toppled over on to the tender of the first. The frame buckled, and I doubt whether it can be repaired. Its tender went down the embankment west, and the first two coaches telescoped into the culvert site. The next three or four were derailed. Meanwhile I made quite creditable time across the open, uphill towards the Arabs, who had a fair position, and were shooting fast over me into the coaches, which were crowded with soldiers. The Turkish losses were obviously quite heavy. Unfortunately many of the Serahin had no rifles, and could only throw unavailing stones. The Turks took cover behind the bank, and opened a fairly hot fire at us. They were about two hundred strong by now. Sherif Ali brought down a party of twenty-two to meet me, but lost seven killed and more wounded and had some narrow escapes himself before getting back.

The train may have contained someone of importance, for there were a flagged saloon car, an Imam, and a motor car in it. I suspect someone wanted to go via Amman to Jerusalem. We riddled the saloon. The Turks, seeing us so few, put in an attack later which cost them about twenty casualties, and then began to work up the slopes to right and left of us. So we went off, and reached Azrak next day.

About ten days I lay in that tent, suffering a bodily weakness which made my animal self crawl away and hide till the shame was passed. As usual in such circumstances my mind cleared, my senses became more acute, and I began at last to think consecutively of the Arab Revolt, as an accustomed duty to rest upon against the pain. It should have been thought out long before, but at my first landing in Hejaz there had been a crying need for action, and we had done what seemed to instinct best, not probing into the why, nor formulating what we really wanted at the end of all. Instinct thus abused without a basis of past knowledge and reflection had grown intuitive, feminine, and was now bleaching my confidence; so in this forced inaction I looked for the equation between my book-reading and my movements, and spent the intervals of uneasy sleeps and dreams in plucking at the tangle of our present.

Now, in the field everything had been concrete, particularly the tiresome problem of Medina; and to distract myself from that I began to recall suitable maxims on the conduct of modern, scientific war. But they would not fit, and it worried me. Hitherto, Medina had been an obsession for us all; but now that I was ill, its image was not clear, whether it was that we were near to it (one seldom liked the attainable), or whether it was that my eyes were misty with too constant staring at the butt. One afternoon I woke from a hot sleep, running with sweat and pricking with flies, and wondered what on earth was the good of Medina to us? Its harmfulness had been patent when we were at Yenbo and the Turks in it were going to Mecca: but we had changed all that by our march to Wejh. Today we were blockading the railway, and they only defending it. The garrison of Medina, reduced to an inoffensive size, were sitting in trenches destroying their own power of movement by eating the transport they could no longer feed. We had taken away their power to harm us, and yet wanted to take away their town. It was not a base for us like Wejh, nor a threat like Wadi Ais. What on earth did we want it for?

The camp was bestirring itself after the torpor of the midday hours; and noises from the world outside began to filter in to me past the yellow lining of the tent canvas, whose every hole and tear was stabbed through by a long dagger of sunlight. I heard the stamping and snorting of the horses plagued with flies where they stood in the shadow of the trees, the complaint of camels, the ringing of coffee mortars, distant shots. To their burden I began to drum out the aim in war. The books gave it pat—the destruction of the armed forces of the enemy by the one process—battle. Victory could be purchased only by blood. This was a hard saying for us. As the Arabs had no organized forces, a Turkish Foch would have no aim? The Arabs would not endure casualties. How would our Clausewitz buy his victory? Von der Goltz had seemed to go deeper, saying it was necessary not to annihilate the enemy, but to break his courage. Only we showed no prospect of ever breaking anybody's courage.

However, Goltz was a humbug, and these wise men must be talking metaphors; for we were indubitably winning our war; and as I pondered slowly, it dawned on me that we had won the Hejaz War. Out of every thousand square miles of Hejaz nine hundred and ninety-nine were now free. Did my provoked jape at Vickery, that rebellion was more like peace than like war, hold as much truth as haste? Perhaps in war the absolute did rule, but for peace a majority was good enough. If we held the rest, the Turks were welcome to the tiny fraction on which they stood, till peace or Doomsday showed them the futility of clinging to our windowpane.

I brushed off the same flies once more from my face patiently, content to know that the Hejaz War was won and finished with: won from the day we took Wejh, if we had had wit to see it. Then I broke the thread of my argument again to listen. The distant shots had grown and tied themselves into long, ragged volleys. They ceased. I strained my ears for the other sounds which I knew would follow. Sure enough across the silence came a rustle like the dragging of a skirt over the flints, around the thin walls of my tent. A pause, while the camel-riders drew up: and then the soggy tapping of canes on the thick of the beasts' necks to make them kneel.

They knelt without noise: and I timed it in my memory: first the hesitation, as the camels, looking down, felt the soil with one foot for a soft place; then the muffled thud and the sudden loosening of breath as they dropped on their forelegs, since this party had come far and were tired; then the shuffle as the hind legs were folded in, and the rocking as they tossed from side to side thrusting outward with their knees to bury them in the cooler subsoil below the burning flints, while the riders, with a quick soft patter of bare feet, like birds over the ground, were led off tacitly either to the coffee hearth or to Abdulla's tent, according to their business. The camels would rest there, uneasily switching their tails across the shingle till their masters were free and looked to their stabling.

I had made a comfortable beginning of doctrine, but was left still to find an alternative end and means of war.

I wondered why Feisal wanted to fight the Turks, and why the Arabs helped him, and saw that their aim was geographical, to extrude the Turk from all Arabic-speaking lands in Asia. Their peace ideal of liberty could exercise itself only so. In pursuit of the ideal conditions we might kill Turks, because we disliked them very much; but the killing was a pure luxury. If they would go quietly the war would end. If not, we would urge them, or try to drive them out. In the last resort, we should be compelled to the desperate course of blood and the maxims of 'murder war', but as cheaply as could be for ourselves, since the Arabs fought for freedom, and that was a pleasure to be tasted only by a man alive. Posterity was a chilly thing to work for, no matter how much a man happened to love his own, or other people's already-produced children.

At this point a slave slapped my tent door, and asked if the Emir might call. So I struggled into more clothes, and crawled over to his great tent to sound the depth of motive in him. It was a comfortable place, luxuriously shaded and carpeted deep in strident rugs, the aniline-dyed spoils of Hussein Maberig's house in Rabegh. Abdulla passed most of his day in it, laughing with his friends, and playing games with Mohammed Hassan, the court jester. I set the ball of conversation rolling between him and Shakir and the chance sheikhs, among whom was the fire-hearted Ferhan el Aida, the son of Doughty's Motlog; and I was rewarded, for Abdulla's words were definite. He contrasted his hearers' present independence with their past servitude to Turkey, and roundly said that talk of Turkish heresy, or the immoral doctrine of *Yeni-Turan*, or the illegitimate Caliphate was beside the point. It was Arab country, and the Turks were in it: that was the one issue. My argument preened itself.

The next day a great complication of boils developed out, to conceal my lessened fever, and to chain me down yet longer in impotence upon my face in this stinking tent. When it grew too hot

5*

for dreamless dozing, I picked up my tangle again, and went on ravelling it out, considering now the whole house of war in its structural aspect, which was strategy, in its arrangements, which were tactics, and in the sentiment of its inhabitants, which was psychology; for my personal duty was command, and the commander, like the master architect, was responsible for all.

Here was a pompous, professorial beginning. My wits, hostile to the abstract, took refuge in Arabia again. Translated into Arabic, the algebraic factor would first take practical account of the area we wished to deliver, and I began idly to calculate how many square miles: sixty: eighty: one hundred: perhaps one hundred and forty thousand square miles. And how would the Turks defend all that? No doubt by a trench line across the bottom, if we came like an army with banners; but suppose we were (as we might be) an influence, an idea, a thing intangible, invulnerable, without front or back, drifting about like a gas? Armies were like plants, immobile, firm-rooted, nourished through long stems to the head. We might be a vapour, blowing where we listed. Our kingdoms lay in each man's mind; and as we wanted nothing material to live on, so we might offer nothing material to the killing. It seemed a regular soldier might be helpless without a target, owning only what he sat on, and subjugating only what, by order, he could poke his rifle at.

Then I figured out how many men they would need to sit on all this ground, to save it from our attack-in-depth, sedition putting up her head in every unoccupied one of those hundred thousand square miles. I knew the Turkish Army exactly, and even allowing for their recent extension of faculty by aeroplanes and guns and armoured trains (which made the earth a smaller battlefield) still it seemed they would have need of a fortified post every four square miles, and a post could not be less than twenty men. If so, they would need six hundred thousand men to meet the ill-wills of all the Arab peoples, combined with the active hostility of a few zealots.

How many zealots could we have? At present we had nearly fifty thousand: sufficient for the day. It seemed the assets in this element of war were ours. If we realized our raw materials and were apt with them, then climate, railway, desert, and technical weapons could also be attached to our interests. The Turks were stupid; the Germans behind them dogmatical. They would believe that rebellion was absolute like war, and deal with it on the analogy of war. Analogy in human things was fudge, anyhow; and war upon rebellion was messy and slow, like eating soup with a knife.

This was enough of the concrete; so I sheered off ἐπιστήμη, the mathematical element, and plunged into the nature of the biological factor in command. Its crisis seemed to be the breaking point, life and death, or less finally, wear and tear. The war philosophers had properly made an art of it, and had elevated one item, 'effusion of blood', to the height of an essential, which became humanity in battle, an act touching every side of our corporal being, and very warm. A line of variability, Man, persisted like leaven through its estimates, making them irregular. The components were sensitive and illogical, and generals guarded themselves by the device of a reserve, the significant medium of their art. Goltz had said that if you knew the enemy's strength, and he was fully deployed, then you could dispense with a reserve: but this was never. The possibility of accident, of some flaw in materials was always in the general's mind, and the reserve unconsciously held to meet it.

The 'felt' element in troops, not expressible in figures, had to be guessed at by the equivalent of Plato's δόξα, and the greatest commander of men was he whose intuitions most nearly happened. Nine-tenths of tactics were certain enough to be teachable in schools; but the irrational tenth was like the kingfisher flashing across the pool, and in it lay the test of generals. It could be ensued only by instinct (sharpened by thought practising the stroke) until at the crisis it came naturally, a reflex. There had been men whose δόξα so nearly approached perfection that by its road they reached the certainty of ἐπιστήμη. The Greeks might have called such genius for command νόησις had they bothered to rationalize revolt.

My mind see-sawed back to apply this to ourselves, and at once knew that it was not bounded by mankind, that it applied also to materials. In Turkey things were scarce and precious, men less esteemed than equipment. Our cue was to destroy, not the Turk's army, but his minerals. The death of a Turkish bridge or rail, machine or gun or charge of high explosive, was more profitable to us than the death of a Turk. In the Arab Army at the moment we were chary both of materials and of men. Governments saw men only in mass; but our men, being irregulars, were not formations, but individuals. And individual death, like a pebble dropped in water, might make but a brief hole; yet rings of sorrow widened out therefrom. We could not afford casualties.

Materials were easier to replace. It was our obvious policy to be superior in some one tangible branch; guncotton or machine-guns or whatever could be made decisive. Orthodoxy had laid down the maxim, applied to men, of being superior at the critical point and moment of attack. We might be superior in equipment in one dominant moment or respect; and for both things and men we might give the doctrine a twisted negative side, for cheapness' sake, and be weaker than the enemy everywhere except in that one point or matter. The decision of what was critical would always be ours. Most wars were wars of contact, both forces striving into touch to avoid tactical surprise. Ours should be a war of detachment. We were to contain the enemy by the silent threat of a vast unknown desert, not disclosing ourselves till we attacked. The attack might be nominal, directed not against him, but against his stuff; so it would not seek either his strength or his weakness, but his most accessible material. In railway-cutting it would be usually an empty stretch of rail; and the more empty, the greater the tactical success. We might turn our average into a rule (not a law, since war was antinomian) and develop a habit of never engaging the enemy. This would chime with the numerical plea for never affording a target. Many Turks on our front had no chance all the war to fire on us, and we were never on the defensive except by accident and in error.

The corollary of such a rule was perfect 'intelligence', so that we could plan in certainty. The chief agent must be the general's head; and his understanding must be faultless, leaving no room for chance. Morale, if built on knowledge, was broken by ignorance. When we knew all about the enemy we should be comfortable. We must take more pains in the service of news than any regular staff.

I was getting through my subject. The algebraical factor had been translated into terms of Arabia, and fitted like a glove. It promised victory. The biological factor had dictated to us a development of the tactical line most in accord with the genius of our tribesmen. There remained the psychological element to build up into an apt shape. I went to Xenophon and stole, to name it, his word *diathetics*, which had been the art of Cyrus before he struck.

Of this our 'propaganda' was the stained and ignoble offspring. It was the pathic, almost the ethical, in war. Some of it concerned the crowd, an adjustment of its spirit to the point where it became useful to exploit in action, and the pre-direction of this changing spirit to a certain end. Some of it concerned the individual, and then it became a rare art of human kindness, transcending, by purposed emotion, the gradual logical sequence of the mind. It was more subtle than tactics, and better worth doing, because it dealt with uncontrollables, with subjects incapable of direct command. It considered the capacity for mood of our men, their complexities and mutability, and the cultivation of whatever in them promised to profit our intention. We had to arrange their minds in order of battle just as carefully and as formally as other officers would arrange their bodies. And not only our own men's minds, though naturally they came first. We must also arrange the minds of the enemy, so far as we could reach them; then those other minds of the nation supporting us behind the firing line, since more than half the battle passed there in the back; then the minds of the enemy nation waiting the verdict; and of the neutrals looking on; circle beyond circle.

There were many humiliating material limits, but no moral impossibilities; so that the scope of our diathetical activities was unbounded. On it we should mainly depend for the means of victory on the Arab front: and the novelty of it was our advantage. The printing press, and each newly-discovered method of communication favoured the intellectual above the physical, civilization paying the mind always from the body's funds. We kindergarten soldiers were beginning our art of war in the atmosphere of the twentieth century, receiving our weapons without prejudice. To the regular officer, with the tradition of forty generations of service behind him, the antique arms were the most honoured. As we had seldom to concern ourselves with what our men did, but always with what they thought, the diathetic for us would be more than half the command. In Europe it was set a little aside, and entrusted to men outside the General Staff. In Asia the regular elements were so weak that irregulars could not let the metaphysical weapon rust unused.

Battles in Arabia were a mistake, since we profited in them only by the ammunition the enemy fired off. Napoleon had said it was rare to find generals willing to fight battles; but the curse of this war was that so few would do anything else. Saxe had told us that irrational battles were the refuges of fools: rather they seemed to me impositions on the side which believed itself weaker, hazards made unavoidable either by lack of land room or by the need to defend a material property dearer than the lives of soldiers. We had nothing material to lose, so our best line was to defend nothing and to shoot nothing. Our cards were speed and time, not hitting power. The invention of bully beef had profited us more than the invention of gunpowder, but gave us strategical rather than tactical strength, since in Arabia range was more than force, space greater than the power of armies.

I had now been eight days lying in this remote tent, keeping my ideas general, till my brain, sick of unsupported thinking, had to be dragged to its work by an effort of will, and went off into a doze whenever that effort was relaxed. The fever passed: my dysentery ceased; and with restored strength the present again became actual to me. Facts concrete and pertinent thrust themselves into my reveries; and my inconstant wit bore aside towards all these roads of escape. So I hurried into line my shadowy principles, to have them once precise before my power to evoke them faded.

It seemed to me proven that our rebellion had an unassailable base, guarded not only from attack, but from the fear of attack. It had a sophisticated alien enemy, disposed as an army of occupation in an area greater than could be dominated effectively from fortified posts. It had a friendly population, of which some two in the hundred were active, and the rest quietly sympathetic to the point of not betraying the movements of the minority. The active rebels had the virtues of secrecy and self-control, and the qualities of speed, endurance and independence of arteries of supply. They had technical equipment enough to paralyse the enemy's communications. A province would be won when we had taught the civilians in it to die for our ideal of freedom. The presence of the enemy was secondary. Final victory seemed certain, if the war lasted long enough for us to work it out.

AFTER THE WAR, *Lawrence was a lost and lonely man. He went to the peace conferences as an authority on the Middle East and then disappeared from the public view. He tried to live for a time as an aircraftsman in the Royal Air Force under the name of Ross and even served briefly in India. He wrote the famous* The Seven Pillars of Wisdom *and the abbreviated version entitled* Revolt in the Desert, *and the recently published* The Mint. *He tried to return to classical learning and undertook a translation of Homer for Oxford University Press. But something was wrong. As he himself wrote, something had gone out of him. He legally changed his name to Shaw. It was rumoured that he planned to return to public life as an aide to Winston Churchill, but he never lived to do so. He was killed in May,* 1935, *while riding a speeding motor-cycle.*

TUNNEL WARFARE

BY HARRISON FORMAN

TWO THOUSAND *Chinese guerrillas came out of the west. At their head was flat-nosed, nervous General Nieh Yung-Chen. Nieh, sometime scholar in France and Moscow, came to Hopei in 1937 to establish a guerrilla army behind the Japanese invader. Nieh had taught tactics at Whampoa Military Academy before he deserted Chiang Kai-shek, and one of the things he knew was that 'it takes two to make a fight'. The Japanese were not going to fight him until he was ready. Then he would meet them on ground of his own choosing and on his own terms.*

During the next year he chose to meet the Japanese in two major clashes. The second time the enemy could count among its dead one lieutenant-general. When word of this reached the invaders' headquarters, fifty thousand crack troops were dispatched to eliminate Nieh and his growing forces. But the guerrilla leader did not choose to fight. Instead, he waited until their encirclement tightened. Then he slipped through their lines, leaving them nothing for their pains. In fury they decimated the countryside.

Then the Japanese began their 'silkworm tactics'. They established a large circle of blockhouses connected by barbed-wire fences and started nibbling inwards, systematically reducing Nieh's area of mobility. But this was a tedious process, unsuccessful by 1940, when the Japanese gave it up, and they brought in one hundred thousand troops to wipe out Nieh. His forces went underground—literally underground.

This story was told to Harrison Forman, during the war, by two guerrillas who were introduced to him by General Nieh.

'THEN began a new type of warfare—tunnel warfare.' And old Wang rolled up his sleeves, took a sip of hot tea, and motioned young Chao to silence. Wang was a specialist in subterranean warfare.

In the early days of the war the villagers dug cellars under their houses, in which to hide from the enemy. The Japs easily found these and rooted out the people, raping, torturing, murdering at will. The villagers then connected their cellars, until a whole village would become a veritable warren of tunnels. But when the Jap came again he would surround the village and make a careful search for every tunnel entrance, driving the people to the surface with fire, smoke, and water. Some of the villages then held council and decided to connect each village's tunnel system with that of the next. It was a staggering undertaking; but if it would save them from slaughter by the Japanese it would be well worthwhile.

So there exists in Central Hopei today an amazing system of tunnels linking hundreds of villages for miles and miles around, built on a scale that makes New York's subway system seem a child's toy railway by comparison. The tunnels are big enough to house the people together with their livestock and their possessions and are equipped with sufficient food and water for an extended siege.

When the Japs discovered that the tunnels ran in straight lines from one village to the next, they dug deep lateral trenches in the fields so as to cut through and expose these tunnels. Thus they were able to isolate one village from its neighbours.

At Peitan, about thirty miles south of Paoting on the Peiping-Hankow Railway, the Japanese decided to teach the tunnel fighters a lesson they would remember. Sectioning off a half-mile of tunnel, they pumped gas into both ends, asphyxiating eight hundred villagers. Undaunted, the Central Hopei villagers devised new tunnel designs. Tunnels were built zig-zag, and up and down; they connected, through emergency entrances, with wholly independent subsidiary tunnel systems at different levels going off in all directions. All the entrances were furnished with simple anti-gas devices, and provision was made to wall up and section off any portion of a tunnel system entered or exposed by the enemy.

Now, when the Japs were able to force their way into the opening shafts they ran into innumerable traps. Crawling single file through a narrow tunnel opening, a Jap might well set off a hidden mine, or be trapdoored into a spiked pit, or have his head lopped off by a village husky wielding a big sword. Sometimes a whole party would be lured into a chamber and a partition would be dropped behind them, trapping them. Then strings would be pulled and mines would go off or a grenade would be tossed into the confined space.

'Look here,' I interrupted. 'Perhaps I'd better not write about these things. The Japs might get hold of this information, and it might not be so good for your friends in Chin-Cha-Chi.'

Old Wang snorted. 'Pu yao *chin*—it doesn't matter. It wouldn't do them any good anyway. Besides, we have actually scores of different types of tunnel systems, and hundreds of different kinds of booby traps. So, go ahead and write about anything we tell you.'

He paused for a moment while I slipped a fresh sheet of paper into my typewriter. I asked him if he'd ever seen a typewriter before. He shook his head. 'I'm only a country bumpkin. I know nothing of such modern marvels.' As an afterthought he added, 'Though I do know something about fighting Japs.'

He wasn't boasting. He just didn't think too much of that accomplishment. Anyone with ordinary brains could fight the Jap—this was what he was trying to say.

The tunnels were a challenge to the Japs, and they tried in countless ways to force an entrance into the tunnels, or to drive the villagers to the surface. Captive villagers would be sent down at the point of a bayonet to detonate hidden mines. But watchers below learned to provide for this with safety gadgets on the mines, to be released by remote control when the Japs followed the captives. If puppets were forced down behind captives they, too, were spared on condition of surrendering their rifles. The defenders had an understanding about this: in the less developed tunnel openings the watchers at the bottom could tell friend from foe by the footwear of the one coming down—a bare or a rope-sandalled foot meant a captive villager or a puppet, while a leather shoe could denote only a Jap.

Since every bit of food, every bit of fuel, everything of possible value was taken underground, the Japanese found little comfort in burning the houses. Moreover, they dared not remain long away from their strong points, since at any moment there might be a sudden concentration of Paluchun regulars, or the ubiquitous guerrillas might appear. (Thousands of Paluchun in the populous areas of Central Hopei live in the tunnels by day, and come out to attack the nearby Jap strong points by night.)

The Japs tried tying a canister of gas to a pig's tail, then pouring paraffin on its back; they would then set this afire, sending the screaming pig down a tunnel ramp. But the villagers merely built water traps across the tunnel floor, drowning the pig and neutralizing the gas. Of course, every such counter-measure was devised only after the Japs tried some new and devilish trick which often took its toll of lives before a counter-measure was found.

Once the Japs tried a Hollywood stunt to lay siege to the tunnels in one district. They brought with them a gramophone with a loud-speaker operated by a suicide squad playing sound-effects records of trucks passing to and fro, to suggest to the villagers underground that their village was still under occupation with considerable military traffic overhead. After a few days the villagers noted a queerness in the sound of moving vehicles without the attendant vibrations which should have been felt in the tunnels. Surfacing, the villagers discovered the trick, captured the Japs, and now use the gramophone for village entertainments.

'Suppose I tell you,' suggested Wang, 'of the battle at Tachuti village. It was typical of scores of such battles the villagers have been fighting in the never-ending People's War.'

'By all means, yes,' I said eagerly.

Old Wang lit a cigarette, took another sip of his scalding tea, and began.

'The villagers in Kaoyang hsien, about thirty miles from the Hopei provincial capital of Paoting, had become especially defiant of the Japanese after they had perfected their tunnel and other defences. The Japs, deciding to put an end to this, sent a strong punitive expedition under the command of a brigade commander, Shangban. [Old Wang didn't know his Japanese name; Shangban, he explained, was the Chinese pronunciation of the two Chinese characters the Japanese commander used to write his name.]

'Shangban first established his headquarters in the occupied city of Kaoyang, the county seat. Then, one day, with a force of three hundred men, he started for the village of Tachuti, about six miles from Kaoyang. The villagers prepared for the attack by mobilizing their militia force—about four hundred strong—while the rest of the village's four hundred families were turned over to the tunnel command.

'The militia commander then inspected the village defences. There were two wooden cannons trained on each of the four entrances to the low mud wall surrounding the village. All roads and trails leading in were mined. The streets were mined and booby traps set. When he was satisfied that all was in readiness, the militia commander took up his post on the roof of the highest building to direct the battle. He used a gong for giving commands. One beat on the gong meant "emergency at the north gate"; two for the south; three for the east; and four for the west. He gave orders that the cannons were not to fire until the Japs were within at least fifty yards.

'Shangban approached the village warily, suspicious of the silence. He deployed his men to surround the village and then, after some hesitation, he gave the order to charge all gates simultaneously. The militia commander beat his gong. Mines detonated—cannons went off—grenades showered. It was one big explosion! When the smoke cleared, Shangban had retreated in dismay, leaving behind dozens of corpses.'

Old Wang lit another cigarette. 'We thought at first we'd finished off Shangban himself, but we were disappointed to find it was one of his officers we'd killed.'

' "We", did you say? Were you in that battle?' I asked.

'Oh, I guess I forgot to mention that, didn't I?' He smiled, embarrassedly—he hadn't thought it important. 'Yes, I just happened to be there—I was the political director for that district, you see.'

Shangban, angered and afraid, gathered the remnants of his repulsed force and sent out a rush call for reinforcements. He was determined to annihilate this village and so wipe out his disgrace. When the reinforcements came, bringing artillery with them, he circled the village looking for a likely place to set up his guns. The village cemetery on a little height safely outside the north gate appeared to be the best spot.

'But we had mined that cemetery for just such an eventuality,' Wang chuckled. 'Shangban was furious when he saw anti-Japanese slogans on the fence posts, and he ordered them torn down immediately. When a guard stepped forward, the first fence post he touched blew up in his hands, killing him and two others. But Shangban must have borne a charmed life—he was only knocked down.'

If Shangban had been angry before, by now he was enraged. He set up his cannon and ordered a barrage of tear and gas shells to be laid on the village.

'But we had had some experience with this gas before, and we'd found that garlic and cold water considerably lessened its effect on us. However, when the gas got to be too much for a militiaman, we sent him down into the tunnels and a tunnel guard came up to take his place.'

In the meantime, news of the battle had been signalled to all the surrounding villages. Wuniu, two miles away, sent its militiamen up through the tunnels; the militiamen from Shaowan and Nanchi also came. And when a strong unit of full-time guerrillas appeared suddenly to attack Shangban in his rear, the Japs took to their heels. 'We captured more than a hundred rifles from this battle,' old Wang said with satisfaction. 'But the steel helmets we gathered from the field afterward were not distributed for use as cooking kettles, as in the old days—we turned them over to the guerrillas for use in their "sparrow warfare".'

After the battle the villagers held a meeting. It was decided that the Japs would be sure to return, if only to recover their dead, whose souls would not rest easily if the bodies were not properly buried or cremated. So the corpses were loaded into carts and sent to a point about a mile from Kaoyang, where they were piled neatly by the side of the road. A flag fluttering from the top of the pile was inscribed: 'Don't come back if you want to live. We've been polite this time and sent your dead back to you. Next time we'll feed them to the dogs.' Then, to soften the effect of this, another flag beside it read: 'You soldiers are also farmers and workers back home. Why do you fight us? We wish you no harm. We want only to live in peace, with you and all the world.'

Shangban marched his men out of Kaoyang and silently collected his dead. Soon afterward he was transferred from that district, and Tachuti was never attacked again.

For several minutes Chao Fang had been trying to interrupt—ever since Wang's mention of 'sparrow warfare'. Now, as Wang paused for another sip of tea, Chao Fang began eagerly to tell me about his friend Wang Ming, whose father had been killed in the Peitan tunnel gas attack. The surviving relatives of the Peitan victims had formed the 'White Suit Corps' (white being used for mourning), a special group of guerrillas sworn to vengeance on the Japs, and Wang Ming was a member of the corps. One day he discovered the identity of one of the traitors who had betrayed the secret of the Peitan tunnel system to the Japanese. The traitor lived in a walled compound close to a Japanese strong point. Undaunted, Wang Ming sneaked into the traitor's house one night and took him prisoner at the point of a pistol. The traitor was brought before the Hsein government for trial, condemned, and shot. Unfortunately, shortly after this, Wang Ming was apprehended by the Japs; knowing that he was in for a bad time, he slipped his bonds, by a desperate effort, jumped his jailor, and grabbed the guard's rifle and bayoneted him. The dawn was just breaking and he was discovered as he fled to a rooftop near by. Surrounded, he fought bravely until noon, killing many of the Japs and puppets below, before using his last bullet to commit suicide.

The 'White Suit Corps' continued to harass the enemy like a swarm of angry hornets. A type of warfare they initiated became very popular. This was 'sparrow warfare'. Like sparrows they were everywhere, picking off a Jap here and a puppet there. A straggler behind a column of Japs on the march would be quietly dispatched by a knife in the hand of an innocent-looking *laopaishing* walking down the road. A handful of shots fired from ambush would kill two and wound three, the ambushers then scattering so as to afford no target for revenge.

A refinement of sparrow warfare is segmented-worm warfare. An ambush is laid, and when the Japs recover from the first shock they start chasing the ambushers down the road. Unobserved, the ambushers drop a few men in each village they pass through. Soon the pursuing Japs discover that they are chasing the wind, though the people in each village have convincingly told them, 'They've just passed through, heading *that* way.' More than that, on their return they may well be ambushed again by the collected segments; and so the game keeps up until the Japs get wise and stop taking the bait.

Often the partisans disguise themselves as Japs or puppets, and boldly march down the highway. Sometimes a group of a dozen or more will do this, primarily to observe and deceive the Japs in their blockhouses. At times as many as a hundred or more may form such a disguised company, eighty in puppet uniforms, twenty in Jap—the usual proportion. They march for miles, picking up all Japs and puppets they meet on the road. The frightened puppets usually make no trouble. The Japs are quickly disarmed, stripped, gagged, and dressed in *laopaishing* dress, as if they were prisoners. Meanwhile, other partisans line the highway in hiding prepared to support this column should it suddenly meet a strong enemy force. The purpose of this trick is to intercept messengers bearing documents, to seize important puppets travelling from place to place, to capture goods in transit, and to collect weapons, ammunition, and medicines —all at a minimum cost. Such disguised partisans have secret signs which they give to identify themselves so that they may not be attacked by their own people—a rifle periodically raised three times into the air, for example.

'I was with one such company,' Chao said, 'when we met a string of carts coming down the road. We stopped them. They proved to be a puppet magistrate travelling with a lot of valuable cargo and protected by an escort of thirty Japs and puppets. Seeing our Jap flag, the magistrate got down from his cart and began to kow-tow. He was going to Pochun, he said, on official business. We said we'd like to inspect his goods. At this, the escort got suspicious. A fight developed, but the escort soon fled down the road. Before reinforcements could come up we had looted the cargo and dispersed.'

A simple, old-as-the-hills ruse that worked well for quite a while was this one. A party of disguised partisans would appear before a Jap strong point, escorting bound captives, allegedly Paluchun men. The unsuspecting Japs would let them in, and immediately be wiped out and the blockhouse destroyed. There was a time when the Japs often took this particular leaf from the villager's book, disguising themselves as Eighth Routers in order to ferret out Paluchun sympathizers in the villages. It never worked, however, for the villagers spotted them quickly, and hugely enjoyed themselves hurling abuse or throwing stones at the 'unwelcome Paluchun'.

When the Japs discovered that village fighters rarely attacked the puppets, saving their mines and precious bullets for the *Jih Pen kwei tze*—the Japanese devils—they tried exchanging uniforms with the puppets. But as these 'puppets' marched through a village the people would ask them if they wanted a drink of water—and of course the 'puppets' would be immediately identified as Japs, whether they replied or not. In addition, the real puppets—being dressed in the dangerous Japanese uniform—had to declare their own nationality.

'If the column was off at a distance, how were you able to spot the fact that the uniforms had been exchanged?'

'Easily—the Jap can never disguise his waddling, bowlegged gait.'

To deceive the everwatchful villagers as to their numbers, Chao said, the Japs frequently sent trucks to run the gauntlet of road mines with blockhouse 'reinforcements'. A passing truck would seem to be loaded with men, though there might only be half a dozen living figures in it—the rest would be rubber dummies. When the truck reached the blockhouse the balloon soldiers were secretly deflated and the empty truck was sent back through the villages, having dropped its 'reinforcements'. The villagers, Chao told me, were highly amused by this childish trick, and frequently some sharpshooter contemptuously wasted a precious bullet on the dummy soldiers.

The Japs also used wooden cannon. These were dummies, however. Covered with tarpaulins they were hauled around to delude the Paluchun's intelligence service into overestimating the Japanese armament. These dummy cannon would often be dragged into battle and set up beside real guns. Boxes and crates, filled with pebbles and stones and prominently marked AMMUNITION were often ostentatiously moved from place to place.

Psychological or nerve warfare, both Wang and Chao said, was being waged on a grand scale by the North China villagers, and was proving tremendously successful. One of the quite unfailing devices was to spread false rumours of Paluchun movements—rumours reinforced by the imparting of 'confidential information' to known spies. For example, a Japanese agent would be told that secret orders had been received to prepare stores of food in order to provision the (mythical) Paluchun concentrations; and sometimes the villagers would support the fiction with elaborate pretences. Then the Japanese local officers would put in urgent requests for reinforcements, thus confusing their superiors into diverting troops from one point to another. When the Jap reinforcements arrived, they would rush about here and there in search of the Paluchun, with the villagers soberly leading them on: 'They've just left here.' 'They've gone this way.' 'They've gone that way.' A power like Japan which employs traitors and puppets is particularly vulnerable to this form of warmaking.

Meanwhile, to keep up the fictitious threat, the villagers would blow bugles, don clothes that from a distance looked like Paluchun uniforms, and march up and down with their shotguns and blunderbusses on their shoulders—convincing the worried Japs, watching them through their binoculars, that the Paluchun were gathering in force.

At night, particularly, the war of nerves was waged with notable success, with literally thousands of Japanese strong points and blockhouses being besieged by the villagers. There might be perhaps no more than a handful of them attacking out there in the dark—but the Japs could not be sure of this, and so preferred to remain inside their fortified shelters. Sometimes the attackers would set off strings of firecrackers, accompanied by a few rifle shots to convince the Japs they were being subjected to real fire. Often the Japs would answer with a furious fusillade, firing blindly into the night. When their firing died down, a few more of the real shots would touch off a repetition of the display. Or a few dogs might be tossed into the moat surrounding the blockhouse. Their floundering about, their efforts to scale the slippery walls, would suggest an attacking party storming the blockhouse, and the worried Japs would open fire. With the dawn, the nerve-strained Japs might discover the tricks and so would come to ignore them in time—whereupon the guerrilla commandos would steal up and really attack the place and inflict losses before melting away.

Often the people would co-operate actively with the Paluchun regulars in attacking larger strong points. One place, which had been besieged for twenty-eight days, was finally taken after the villagers, who had first carefully mined all the highway approaches to prevent the arrival of reinforcements, collected dogs for miles about, slaughtered them, and laid their carcasses all around the fortress. In the blistering summer sun the carcasses quickly decayed, enveloping the strong point with such an overpowering stench that the Japs were eventually forced to abandon their fortress and fight their way through the encirclement, suffering heavy casualties.

'And now how would you like to hear something about our naval warfare?' Old Wang looked perfectly serious.

'You mean *water* warfare?'

'Yes—war on the water.'

'Fine. Let's have it!'

'Well, it was this way. . . .'

In September, 1943, the Japanese army headquarters in Peiping issued an order forbidding the villagers in the Peiyangtien Lake area—about fifty miles south of Peiping—to shoot any more of the wild ducks which yearly flock there in great numbers. When the villagers refused to heed the order, the Japanese sent a fleet of specially constructed motor-boats and steam launches to police the shallow marsh-like lake.

For their duck-hunting the villagers had developed 'big shoulder-fire guns'—ten-foot tubular weapons operated like a bazooka and firing a scattering charge of about a pound of scrap metal. These were now pressed into military service. Hidden in the lake shore's tall reeds, the villagers would pot away at the passing motor-boats. After some thirty of these had been sunk or badly damaged, the Japs became annoyed. In the middle of the lake they built a huge fortified raft—a veritable battleship—bristling with machine-guns and deck cannon. Watchers in crow's nests atop the tall masts scanned the shores with powerful binoculars. When the slightest movement was detected in the reeds, machine-guns and cannon opened fire; or, if the range was too great, then one of a fleet of armoured launches standing by was immediately dispatched to investigate.

With the Japs' adoption of these tactics, the bazooka-sniping lakemen came out only at night. The battleship's searchlights then tried in vain to find them in the reeds, while charges of old nails, of scrap from broken kettles, pots, and pans, from rusted tools, ploughshares and such, continued to sweep the battleship's deck or rattle fiercely against its sides. When the crops in the fields adjacent were harvested, thousands of villagers gathered one night and quietly opened the dykes, allowing the lake water to spill into the fields. With the dawn the Japanese observed with horror that the water level had dropped alarmingly. Hurriedly they stripped the battleship of guns and equipment and escaped by launch through the lake's outlet toward Tientsin lest they be left high and dry. Before they left they set fire to the battleship, the spectacle being viewed by thousands of gleeful villagers. They lined the shores shouting, dancing, and clapping their hands like pleased children. When the dykes were repaired, the lake filled up, the ducks returned, and the villagers were once again free to use their home-made bazookas for duck hunting.

WITH THE CHINESE *divided by the war between Mao Tse-tung and Chiang Kai-shek, the Japanese envisioned an easy victory. But the two Chinese leaders turned from each other to face the invasion. Chiang met it directly on the battlefield and his strength diminished, while Mao, fighting a guerrilla war, grew steadily stronger. By the war's end their positions were reversed, and Mao, taking the offensive, conquered the Chinese mainland.*

All through the first decade of their conflict, Chiang, refusing to dignify Mao by acknowledging him as a rebel or guerrilla, labelled his opponent a 'bandit' and the war a 'bandit action'. Mao, victorious, labels Chiang's operations 'bandit actions'.

COMMANDOS AT VAAGSO

BY JOHN DURNFORD-SLATER

THE AMPHIBIOUS GUERRILLA *has a long tradition in Europe and particularly in England. Perhaps Lieutenant-Colonel Dudley Clarke recalled the Vikings, Drake in the West Indies, Howard at Cadiz, and all the other raiders from the sea that dark night of June 4, 1940, when Dunkirk fell. In any case, as he looked towards the unfriendly coast across the Channel, he thought of something in particular, and as he later wrote, 'before I went to bed I tried to marshal my ideas into the outline of a plan jotted down in note form on a single sheet of . . . writing paper'.*

By the twelfth of the month, Clarke's ideas had taken form and the amphibious guerrillas were organized under the name Commando, after the mounted Boer raiders in the South African war. On the night of the twenty-third of June, after rounding up the necessary equipment—there were only forty tommy-guns in all of England at this time—the first raid was made on the French coast. Dudley Clarke, along as an observer, was the first Commando wounded in action, and the returning raiders, dishevelled and grimy, were mistaken for deserters and arrested. From this dubious beginning the Commandos grew into one of the great raiding forces of World War II. In conjunction with the Royal Navy and the Royal Marines, the Commandos developed the invasion techniques which were to be copied around the world.

The Commandos themselves raided the Channel ports and North Sea areas, landed in the North African invasion, fought as shock troops in Sicily and Italy, and helped the Yugoslav partisans on the Island of Vis. They participated in the invasion of Europe, pushed on to the Elbe, and were finally shifted to the Far East to fight the Japanese.

Brigadier John Durnford-Slater tells the story of his raid on Vaagso, one of a series designed to prevent the Germans from making use of the small Norwegian ports and coastal industries.

WE sailed from Scapa Flow on Christmas Eve. The first leg of our journey, to the Shetlands, was a rough one. Our cross-Channel steamers were not designed for the battering given by these northern seas. Parts of our ship which should have remained solid came loose. The walls of my cabin, for instance, began to slide and make strange metallic noises. To prevent sickness, I took Joe Brunton's remedy of beer, cheese, and pickled onions. It worked fine for me, but, although I passed it on to my brother officers, they seemed to find the cure more distasteful than the illness itself. I don't think any of us will remember this as our most cheerful Christmas. Yet discipline was in no way relaxed.

Every soldier was turned out on deck while we inspected the mess decks. The ship rolled to sixty degrees. We could hear our men singing the Vera Lynn favourite, *Yours*. I had to admire their guts. These men were on their way to do battle; many were seasick; yet they sang.

When we arrived at Sollum Voe, in the Shetlands, an inspection revealed that everything forward in the ship was flooded to a depth of fourteen feet. Guard rails on the forecastle were smashed. The forward gun support was stove in and stores were flooded. The forward decks leaked and water was up to the doorsills of the sergeants' mess and elsewhere. At four in the afternoon of Christmas Day the Hunt-class destroyer *Chiddingford* came alongside and helped pump 145 tons of water out of *Prince Charles*. We were seaworthy again.

As many other ships had sustained damage it was decided to wait a whole day in the Shetlands to complete the necessary repairs and to give everybody a night's sleep. The soldiers had had their Christmas dinner and were all fully recovered. All our officers were in great spirits. I had a drink with Algy Forrester and said to him:

'These Germans at Vaagso won't be so happy to-morrow night.'

Algy said, very quietly, 'I personally intend to see that there won't be any to be happy.'

As night fell, on Boxing Day, the ships sailed again for Vaagso, Admiral Tovey covering our approach with the major units of the Atlantic Fleet, including his flagship, *King George V*. The submarine *Tuna* had preceded us and was lying off the entrance to Vaagsfjord to act as a navigational beacon on our way in. H.M.S. *Kenya* led our particular convoy, flying the flag of Admiral Burrough. She was followed by the destroyer H.M.S. *Chiddingford*; then came the *Charles* and *Leopold* carrying the troops with the destroyers *Onslow*, *Offa* and *Oribi* following close behind.

We were called at 4 a.m. I had often read in descriptions of naval battles that the sailors wore clean underclothes so as to minimize the risk of infection from wounds, so I put on a clean vest and pair of pants and told all the others to do the same. I took great trouble to check up on every item of my equipment. On this operation I carried a Colt .45 pistol with three spare magazines. All these magazines were discharged by the end of the day but I never again went into action carrying a pistol only, as these weapons do not give confidence when opposed to a man with a rifle. We had a good breakfast at 5 a.m. and carried with us a small compact haversack ration. In my case, and in nearly all other cases, this ration was untouched when we returned to the ship at 3 p.m. The excitement was too great to allow time off for eating.

Off Vaagsfjord at 7 a.m. we picked up the *Tuna* as planned. The surge of excitement which was running through our ship had erased all thought of seasickness. We entered the fjord, a spectacular passage between great, snow-covered hills. We were to land at first light, ten minutes to nine. The *Prince Charles* and *Prince Leopold* pulled into a small bay. The troops filed into the landing craft and these were lowered to the cold waters of the fjord. Then *Kenya*, two hundred yards behind us, opened the bombardment of Maaloy Island where the Germans manned a coast defence battery. We started the run-in in our landing craft.

About a hundred yards from our landing place, I fired ten red Very light signals. This told the ships to stop firing and the aircraft to come in with their smoke bombs. As I leaped from the leading landing craft three Hampden bombers passed over me at zero feet with a roar. As they did so they loosed their bombs, which seemed to flash and then mushroom like miniature atom explosions. Some of the phosphorus came back in a great flaming sheet. Next thing I knew both my sleeves were on fire. Fortunately I wore leather gloves and beat the flames out before they could eat through my four layers of clothing to the skin. The beaching had been made, dry, against snow-covered rocks which rose thirty or forty feet in an almost sheer wall. For the moment, we were unopposed and hidden from the enemy by smoke.

Unfortunately, however, one of the Hampdens was hit by anti-aircraft fire as she came in. Out of control, she dropped a bomb on an incoming landing craft. Bursting, the phosphorus inflicted terrible burns among the men. The craft, too, burst into flames. Grenades, explosives, and small arms ammunition were detonated in a mad mixture of battle noises. We pushed the emptied craft out to sea where it could do us no harm, and Sam Corry, our big, efficiently calm Irish doctor, taking charge of the casualties, sent them back to the *Prince Charles*. The rest of us turned to the battle.

Vaagso is built on one narrow street, three-quarters of a mile long, which runs parallel to, and about fifty yards from, the fjord. Behind the street, which was lined with unpainted wooden buildings, nearly sheer rocks rose to several hundred feet. I heard Johnny Giles yell, 'Come on', and saw him disappear with his No. 3 Troop into the smoke.

That was the last I saw of Johnny. Fifteen minutes later he was dead, killed in an assault on the back of a house. He and his men had shot three Germans who had been firing on them from the house, then rushed it. They went through the rooms and as Johnny entered the last room a fourth German jumped in front of him and shot him.

At about the time Johnny met his death I went into a large oil factory near our landing beach. I was looking for Johann Gotteberg, who had been named to us as the chairman of the local quislings and was the owner of this factory. Meanwhile Bill Bradley prepared the factory for demolition. I saw a middle-aged man who seemed to be attending the machinery with extraordinary concentration, considering the circumstances.

'Who is that man?' I asked my Norwegian guide, a native of Vaagso.

'That is Gotteberg, the owner.'

I had him arrested. A few minutes later he had a first-class view of his factory being blown up.

Algy Forrester went off like a rocket with his No. 4 Troop down the street of the town, leaving a trail of dead Germans behind him. The troop had just lost Arthur Komrower, who had suffered severe leg and back injuries when he was pinned between a landing craft and a rock. The third officer of 4 Troop was Bill Lloyd, who, with Algy, had developed the technique of landing on rough and rocky shores. Bill hardly got going before he was shot, clean through the neck. That was the end of him for this operation.

Algy waded in, shouting and cheering his men, throwing grenades into each house as they came to it and firing from the hip with his tommy-gun. He looked wild and dangerous. I shouldn't have liked to have been a German in his path. He had absolutely no fear. He led an assault against the German headquarters, in the Ulvasund Hotel, and was about to toss a grenade in when one of the enemy, firing through the front door, shot him. As he fell he landed on his own grenade, which exploded a second later. This rough landing at Vaagso was the first time we had put into operational practice the system he and Bill Lloyd had developed. For Algy it was also the last.

Other casualties in Algy's troop were heavy. Captain Martin Linge, my Norwegian friend, had also been attached to No. 4. When the attack was briefly held up after Algy's death, he kept things moving, but only for a few minutes. He was killed in exactly the same way as Forrester, shot as he tried to force open a door. I had spoken to Martin just as he left the beach.

'This is good, Colonel,' he had said, laughing. 'We'll have a party at the Mayfair to celebrate when we get back.'

He was a very gallant and fearless ally and would have made an ideal Commando soldier.

The Germans had a tank in a garage near the Ulvesund Hotel, about 150 yards up the street, a fact of which we were aware through our intelligence. The tank was an old one, but if it were brought out on to the street it could wreak havoc among us with its gun. After Martin Linge's death, Sergeant Cork and Johnnie Dowling of 1 Troop managed to reach the tank, still in the garage, and blow it up. Unfortunately Cork used too heavy a charge and didn't get away quickly enough. He was caught in the explosion and died of wounds. Johnnie was untouched. Corporal 'Knocker' White was left in command of Forrester's troop. He performed the job so gallantly that he was to earn a Distinguished Conduct Medal for it.

From our out-of-doors, snow-covered headquarters near the landing place, I could see everything that took place on Maaloy. Nos. 5 and 6 Troops, only fifty yards from the beach when the naval barrage lifted, were up the slopes of the island like a flash. I saw them advancing through the smoke in perfect extended order. Jack Churchill, who had played them in with his bagpipes, was leading them with considerable dash. On landing, Peter Young saw a German running back to man his gun position. 'I was able to shoot him,' Peter told me later. Ten minutes after this, Young reached the company office on Maaloy. One of the German company clerks made the literally fatal mistake of trying to wrest Peter's rifle from him. Small pockets of resistance were quickly cleaned up and many prisoners were taken, including two Norwegian women of easy virtue who had been consoling the German soldiers.

The fighting in the town was still hot and heavy, however, and I had Charlie Head, my Signals Officer for this raid, send a message to the headquarters ship asking for the floating reserve, and another to Jack Churchill on Maaloy asking if he, too, could help. Jack promptly sent 6 Troop under Peter Young; and Charles Haydon ordered the floating reserve to the far end of Vaagso. We were now attacking on two fronts.

Back in the main street, where our attack had been stalled, Peter Young with 6 Troop got things moving again. I left the Adjutant to control our headquarters and joined him. It was very noisy: there were the different sounds from the various calibres of small arms; artillery exchanges between *Kenya* and a coast defence battery somewhere down the fjord; anti-aircraft fire from the ships against the attacking Messerschmitts; the demolitions; and the crackling roar of flames. I heard one signaller complaining how difficult it was to receive messages.

'This is bloody awful! A man can hardly hear himself think!'

Our opposition was much stiffer than I had expected. It was not until later that I learned that about fifty men from an exceptionally good German unit were spending Christmas leave at Vaagso.

As I tried to catch up with Peter Young I saw him and George Herbert throwing grenades through windows and doors. They appeared to be enjoying themselves. I finally joined them in a timber yard which had only one entrance off the main street. Part of our plan had been to dump many sacks of grenades near the landing place. Our Administrative Officer had organized a gang of loyal Norwegian civilians who followed close behind the leading troops, carrying these sacks, and offering the troops replenishments of grenades as often as they were needed.

Suddenly, in a strange interval when artillery and demolitions seemed to pause for their second wind, there was an eerie, unexpected stillness. Half of No. 6 Troop were clustered in the timber yard. A single rifle shot rang out and a man fell dead beside me. I thought the shot had come from a house, about twenty yards away, on the other side of the small yard. We all started firing furiously at the windows of the house. I emptied my revolver, feeling strangely helpless, for there was only one exit to the yard and unless we did something quickly it seemed certain the sniper would pick us all off, one by one. Another shot came from the house and another man fell dead. I think this was the first time in warfare that I truly felt fear. I didn't like it.

We crouched behind a pile of timber. The sniper fired whenever one of us moved. Soon he picked off a third of our number. He was shooting right down at us from a first floor window.

There was a shed just behind our cover and George Herbert disappeared into it. 'Captain Young,' he called, 'I've found a tin of petrol!'

'Put some in a bucket, Sergeant,' Peter called back. 'When you've done that we'll all stand up and give you covering fire while you toss it into the house.'

Herbert obeyed, and the others followed the petrol up by lobbing grenades through the windows. There was a great burst of flame. Very soon the wooden house was burned to the ground, a funeral pyre for the sniper. I wasn't sorry to leave that timber yard.

It was just about then that Lieutenant Denis O'Flaherty was wounded. He had been leading assault after assault on enemy-held houses and was leading an attack on the steamship wharf when a sniper, concealed in a warehouse, hit him in the eye. The bullet came out through his throat. O'Flaherty, a brave soldier, had been wounded twice before. This most serious wound was to cost him eight major operations and two years in hospital. He lost his eye but never his spirit. Later, still fighting for Britain, he was decorated by the Americans for gallantry in Korea.

After the affair of the timber yard, when the attack got moving down the main street again, a door on the fjord side of the street suddenly opened and a German lobbed out a grenade. It rolled between my feet and stopped. I was standing on a corner and instinctively took a tremendous dive for shelter round the edge of the building. I landed on my face, just in time to hear the grenade go off. I escaped with a couple of small bits of the grenade in my palm, but my orderly was badly wounded.

About thirty seconds later, the same door opened and the German who had tossed the grenade came out with his hands up and expressing his earnest desire to surrender. I was prepared to accept this, but one of my men thought otherwise. He advanced on the German: 'Nein! Nein!' the German yelled, a small man, yellow and scared.

Our man was so angry that he shot the German dead, through the stomach. This, of course, is one of the tricky problems in warfare. Can a man throw a death-dealing grenade one second and surrender the next? I hardly think he can expect much mercy.

Then I saw Bob Clement organizing an attack on another building farther down the street. With Lance-Sergeant Culling, he led the way. As they approached the front door, a German threw a percussion grenade at Culling's face, killing him instantly. Clement kept a brisk fire going into the building and called for Sergeant Ramsey and the mortar detachment, posting men all around to prevent any German from escaping. Ramsey got a direct hit on the roof with his third round and then pumped several dozen mortar bombs through the hole. The place was soon blazing. On my way back, when the flames had died down, I counted twelve German corpses inside.

This incident was to end the most severe phase of the fighting. We were now well on top, and I felt sure we would achieve every objective of the raid. I remember marvelling at the courage of the newsreel and press photographers, who never roamed far from the leading soldiers. Harry Regnold, the army movie cameraman, Jack Ramsden of Movietone News, and E. G. Mallandine, an army stills photographer (now with *Illustrated* magazine) were continually in the forefront of the battle.

All this time there had been a good deal of air activity. The R.A.F. fighter cover consisted of Blenheims, which, although no match for the Messerschmitts, nevertheless put up a gallant performance. It was a heartrending sight to see two or three of the Blenheims shot down by the Messerschmitts, which were able to out-manœuvre their slower and heavier opponents. However, they were successful in their main objective of keeping the enemy bombers away from the ships.

When we got to the end of the street, I looked at my watch. It was 1.45 p.m. I was astonished to realize that I had been away from my headquarters for two hours. It was nearly time to make our withdrawal. I called a troop commanders' meeting to issue final orders.

'We'll not be going any further,' I said. 'We'll withdraw a troop at a time. No. 2 troop with Clement will go first; then No. 6 with Young; and No. 1 with Bradley will cover, coming last.'

On the way back down the main street, I found many houses were now burning fiercely. Pieces of burning wood fell on the road. I was wryly amused to notice that many of my men, who had been entirely without fear in battle, were now scared to death by the flames. I took the lead.

'Come on with me! You won't get hurt!'

And I ran quickly through the avenue of fire. When we were nearly back to headquarters I saw a handsome young German lying in the gutter, seriously wounded in the chest and obviously near death. He smiled at me. When he beckoned, I walked over and spoke to him. He could speak no English, but indicated that he wished to shake hands. We did. I think what he meant, and I agreed, was that it had been a good, clean battle.

While the street fighting had been going on, the destroyers *Oribi* and *Onslow* had not been idle. They had set about destroying enemy

6

shipping in the anchorage. The original intention was to bring the larger ships back to England; but the Germans were too quick at scuttling to make this possible. Nevertheless, it was some satisfaction to see ship after ship settling to the bottom. *Onslow* and *Oribi* often had to administer the *coup de grâce*. Boarding parties, moving quickly, were able to recover valuable documents. Ten ships, totalling eighteen thousand tons, were sent to the bottom.

During the fighting Charlie was flashing messages from our beach headquarters through to Brigadier Haydon. When Charlie was not up to the latest fighting progress he did the best he could to reassure the Brigadier. 'Everything going well', 'progress satisfactory', were the phrases he used again and again when, for all he knew, we might all have been massacred.

'I couldn't see any point in interrupting you at your work,' he said to me later.

At the peak period of the battle Charlie was passing signals at the rate of forty an hour.

Snipers made the evacuation of the wounded a considerable problem, but Sam Corry and his medical orderlies did a wonderful job. Sam was a man with a great fighting heart. He could not resist the temptation to take part in the battle. I saw him several times, first attending to his wounded, then seizing their rifles to get a few shots at the enemy. Handcarts were used as far as possible to transport the wounded to Sam Corry's regimental aid post, just off the beach. From this point they had to be carried on stretchers down the almost sheer rocks leading to the boats.

We carried out demolitions so effectively that we used most of the stores we brought ashore for this purpose, 300 pounds of plastic explosive, 1,100 pounds of guncotton, 150 pounds of ammonal explosive, 150 incendiary bombs, 60 guncotton primers, and 1,400 feet of fuse. Before any German-occupied building was blown up, a member of our intelligence section searched through it for documents. This precaution paid off beautifully when we found the master code for the whole of the German navy. For many weeks to come, as a result of this priceless discovery, the Admiralty in London was able freely to decipher all German naval signal messages. This, of course, helped us greatly in the conduct of the war at sea.

The withdrawal and re-embarkation was now going smoothly and silently. Charlie Head and I were the last two on the beach, and I could see that he wanted to be the last man off.

'Go on, get in!' I said, in a tone which indicated that this was an order, not a request.

He grinned and obeyed, thus giving me, beyond dispute, the honour of being first in, last out, on this operation which was to be described in *The Times* a day or two later as 'the perfect raid'.

The two Norwegian tarts found on Maaloy were taken with other prisoners on board the *Prince Charles*. Laughing as if it were a great joke, I think they hoped to carry on their business without interruption, despite the changed fortunes of war. They were put in the doctor's cabin; he was so busy attending the wounded that there was no chance of his needing it. They were quick to replace their battle-stained clothes by helping themselves to two pairs of the doctor's best pyjamas, and wore them with necklines which plunged far below the demands of decency. I am glad to say their sentries ignored them.

Despite all the events of the day, the news had not reached every German-held port, and as we pulled out a large German merchant ship was coming in. The *Prince Charles* joined in the bombardment, but I fear her fire was inaccurate. The ship was soon sunk by H.M.S. *Kenya*.

I went up to the bridge and saw her Captain, and he said that I had a very warlike appearance as blood from my hand had spread to a good many portions of my clothing, my tunic had a large burn in it, my pistol was still in my hand, and three grenades were lying on top of the Mae West inside the tunic. The Mae West, blown up hard, makes a very convenient lodging place for things of this kind.

We pulled out to sea at a good speed and the resourceful Charlie Head soon conjured up a bottle of whisky. The day was not quite done. Before leaving Scapa Flow we had all been taught a few phrases of Norwegian and Charlie had added one of his own. Just before going to bed I took a walk round the boat deck and saw a lovely Norwegian girl who had embarked with us to go back to England. We got talking, and I could not resist the temptation to try out Charlie's phrase, '*Yi ilsaka di*', which means 'I love you'. To my surprise she understood despite my curious accent, and replied in English, 'Me too.' However, this promising episode soon came to an end as some sentry or other interfering person arrived on the scene.

No. 3 COMMANDO *had to fill about eighty vacancies after Vaagso. It was about this time that the Prime Minister, Mr. Churchill, decided the Commandos were 'to be in the hunter class'. From this point on they wore green berets. Some units even wore them into battle where the heavier steel helmets would hamper their activities.*

THEY SOUGHT OUT ROMMEL

BY HILARY ST. GEORGE SAUNDERS

GOOD MILITARY *men have always known the advantages of striking at the leadership of the enemy. In the field, lieutenants and captains have long been a primary target, and the few instances when senior officers have been killed or captured have lent themselves well to propaganda. If the death took place in the middle of a battle, it was expected that the leaderless troops would become disorganized and demoralized. However, in modern times, formal armies are hydra-headed, and disorganization is unlikely. Because of this, assassination seems unjustified unless there is propaganda value in the fact that such action is possible.*

The actual kidnapping of rear-echelon leadership is almost commonplace. In recent wars, Mosby kidnapped Union generals, Mao Tse-tung captured Chiang Kai-Shek, W. Stanley Moss kidnapped the German commander of Crete, and Fitzroy Maclean brought in General Zahidi of Iran. Despite the willingness to resort to such action, military assassinations have been rare. One of the deterring factors is probably fear of retaliation. This may also explain why there have been so few wartime attempts on the lives of national leaders.

However, in World War II the British Commandos made a carefully planned and clearly cold-blooded attempt to dispose of their most able opponent—Field-Marshal Rommel.

In the strange war that see-sawed across the top of Africa and was fought in wide-open space that permitted tactics almost more naval than ground, Rommel proved himself a genius and became a symbol of German invincibility. The decision was therefore made to capture or destroy him. Hilary St. George Saunders, the official historian of the Commandos, wrote this account of that attempt.

EARLY in October, 1941, six officers and fifty-three other ranks of the Scottish Commando, with Keyes, now a lieutenant-colonel, at their head, were placed under the operational command of the 8th Army. It was decided that they should make a bold attempt to strike at the brain of the enemy by landing far behind the lines and attacking Rommel's headquarters.

On the evening of the 10th of November they set sail from Alexandria in two submarines, the *Torbay* and the *Talisman*, and moved westwards in fair weather. During the voyage the men of the Commando were in high spirits, 'all ranks were greatly interested,' runs a report, 'in what was to us a novel method of approaching our objective, and the soldiers were high in their praise of the way in which we were fed and accommodated.' Laycock commanded them and Geoffrey Keyes, at his own request, was in charge of the detachment detailed for the most hazardous part of the raid, the attack on Rommel's headquarters. How hazardous this was had been made very clear by Laycock during the preliminary stages of planning. 'I gave it as my considered opinion,' he said, 'that the chances of being evacuated after the operation were very slender, and that the attack on General Rommel's house in particular appeared to be desperate in the extreme. This attack, even if initially successful, meant almost certain death for those who took part in it. I made these comments in the presence of Colonel Keyes, who begged me not to repeat them lest the operation be cancelled.'

The Commando soldiers carried in H.M. Submarine *Torbay* landed first. The submarine had reached the chosen spot, a desolate stretch of coast, on time, and a moment later the flashing of an electric torch from the shore enabled the landing to begin. The torch was in the hands of Captain J. E. Haselden, an Intelligence officer of great coolness and daring, who, disguised as an Arab, had been dropped by the Desert Reconnaissance Group to await the advent of the Commandos. It was only with great difficulty that they reached shore. A considerable swell was running, and to launch small rubber boats, each holding two persons, from the rolling deck of the *Torbay* was no easy task. 'An extra large wave,' records Captain Campbell, Keyes' second-in-command, 'washed four of our boats into the sea with several men. We were delayed a long time by this accident.' Eventually Keyes got on shore with Sergeant Terry, his gallant and pertinacious partner. They were followed by Campbell and some of the other men, but two had to be left behind, one of them injured. The small party made for a roofless stone ruin where Haselden had lit a fire.

In the meanwhile Laycock with his detachment was seeking to land from H.M. Submarine *Talisman*. The weather was growing steadily worse, heavy seas capsized most of the boats, but Laycock and seven other ranks reached the shore. Morning found the small party bivouacking in a wadi chosen from the map as a good place in which to lie up during the following day, for it was naturally not possible to move during the hours of daylight. The sun shone; the men's clothes dried, and an ambulance aircraft painted with red crosses flew overhead but its crew failed to observe them. Only half the force detailed had got ashore and a new plan had therefore to be made by Keyes and Laycock. It was finally decided to divide the depleted force into two, Keyes to lead the first detachment and attack Rommel's house, and Lieutenant Roy Cook with six men to lead the second, to cut the telephone and telegraph wires at the crossroads south of Cyrene. Laycock himself was to remain behind in the wadi, with a sergeant and two men, to form a beachhead and keep guard over a dump of rations and ammunition. They would also be at hand to receive the remainder of the detachment should the *Talisman* be able to land them on the following night.

During the day the weather turned rainy, which added to the general discomfort. At 2000 hours, Keyes set out. 'On that night,' says Captain Campbell, who in captivity wrote a full account of the raid, 'we marched inland over extremely difficult country, mostly rock-strewn sheep tracks. Our guide left us at about midnight, fearing to go any further in our company.' Keyes then took the lead, and with the aid of a compass and an indifferent Italian map, established them just before dawn on the top of a small hill where all except the sentries disposed themselves for sleep in the scrub. They awoke 'in drizzling rain to the sound of excited shouting'. Arabs 'brandishing short Italian rifles appeared', and Keyes was presently in close converse with their leader, 'a very villainous-looking Arab with a red headcloth wound round his head at a raffish angle, through the medium of Corporal Drori, a Palestinian, one of the party, who spoke perfect Arabic'. So winning was Keyes' personality that the 'seedy brigand' chief promised to provide food and, when night fell, to act as a guide to a cave which was a few hours' march away from the objective. He was as good as his word, and at midday brought cooked kid's meat and soup. This, the first hot meal they had had for thirty-six hours, did much to revive their spirits, dampened, like their bodies, by the frequent rain which continued to fall. They were also able to obtain cigarettes bought with Italian money provided by Keyes.

As soon as it grew dark they set off again with the 'brigand', who took them to the cave in about two and a half hours. It proved to be 'fairly roomy, quite dry and, apart from an appalling smell of goat, an ideal place to spend the rest of the night and the next day'. They had, however, to move before dawn, for the Arab warned them that goatherds would probably drive their flocks into the cave since the weather was bad. Their next hiding place was a small wood 'where a lot of wild cyclamen was growing'. Here Keyes, Cook and Sergeant Terry breakfasted off 'arbutus berries that look and taste like strawberries and are called by the Senussi "the Fruit of God".' They then made a reconnaissance and returned in a thunderstorm, which induced Keyes to take the risk of returning to the cave so that his men might 'keep as dry as possible during the trying hours before the final march and attack'. He had been able to catch a glimpse of the escarpments near which lay Rommel's headquarters. His next move was to despatch an Arab boy, who had been with the guide, to spy out the land 'in and near Sidi Raafa, which the Italians called Beda Littoria. This proved a brilliant move . . . for when the boy returned . . . Geoffrey was able to draw an excellent sketch map of the house and its surroundings.' But while the boy was away, thunderstorms succeeded each other, 'and the country we had to march over turned to mud before our eyes . . . spirits were sinking, at least I know mine were, at the prospect of a long, cold, wet, muddy march before we even arrived at the starting point of a hazardous operation.' Keyes, however, encouraged them by pointing out that in such foul weather their approach would be unheard and that therefore they would meet with less opposition since everyone who could would be under cover.

The attack had been planned for midnight 17th-18th of November, 1941, so as to coincide with the opening of General Auchinleck's offensive against Rommel. Six hours before, the Commando soldiers 'fell in with almost parade-ground precision' for the final stage of the operation. They moved off, leaving behind them one man who had run a nail from the sole of his boot into his foot, to guard the spare rations. 'It was pouring with rain, and we were most of the way walking ankle-deep in mud. It was not long before we were wet to the skin.' So bad were the conditions that they were soon compelled to move in single file 'to avoid knocking one another over as we slipped and staggered through the mud' and the streaming darkness. About 2230 hours they reached the bottom of the escarpment, rested a short while and then began to climb its two hundred and fifty feet of muddy turf and rock. Half-way up, their passage roused a watchdog and a stream of light issued from the door of a hut '. . . a hundred yards on our flank. As we crouched motionless, hardly breathing, we heard a man shouting at the dog. Finally the door closed.'

At the top of the escarpment they found a muddy track which the guides had told them would lead them straight to the back of Rommel's headquarters. Here Cook departed with his detachment to find a pylon from which the telephone wires ran, and which he was to blow up. This task he successfully accomplished, but was captured on his way back to join Laycock, and spent the rest of the war a prisoner in Italy.

The remaining men, about thirty, then moved off, Keyes with Sergeant Terry about fifty yards ahead, followed by Captain Campbell and the rest. After covering a quarter of a mile, the guides refused to go further and they were left behind, Keyes 'impressing upon them that they must wait for our return and they would then be rewarded for their services'. So the raiders pushed on, 'weapons at the ready to deal with any interference'. About 2330 hours they reached some outbuildings within a hundred yards of the house thought to be the headquarters. A dog began to bark furiously, and an Italian in uniform, accompanied by an Arab, came out of a hut. He immediately saw Campbell and his men, but Campbell addressed him 'as imperiously as I could' in German, telling him that the party were German troops on patrol. The Palestinian interpreter repeated these remarks in Italian, and the Italian turned away just as Keyes and Sergeant Terry, who had made a final reconnaissance, came back. The moment had now come.

The men formed up for the assault moving to the places assigned to them in the plan drawn up by Keyes. Then Keyes, with Campbell and Sergeant Terry, pushed through a hedge into the garden of the house and went round the corner 'on to a gravel sweep before a flight of steps at the top of which were glass-topped doors'. Tommy-gun in hand, Keyes ran up the steps and Campbell pushed open the door. 'Just inside we were confronted by a German, an officer, I think, in steel helmet and overcoat.'

'Geoffrey at once closed with him, covering him with his tommy-gun. The man seized the muzzle of Geoffrey's gun and tried to wrest it from him. Before I or Terry could get round behind him he retreated, still holding on to Geoffrey, to a position with his back to the wall and his either side protected by the first and second pair of doors at the entrance. Geoffrey could not draw a knife and neither I nor Terry could get round Geoffrey as the doors were in the way, so I shot the man with my .38 revolver which I knew would make less noise than Geoffrey's tommy-gun. Geoffrey then gave the order to use tommy-guns and grenades, since we had to presume that my revolver shot had been heard. We found ourselves, when we had time to look round, in a large hall with a stone floor and stone stairway leading to the upper stories, and with a number of doors opening out of the hall. The hall was very dimly lit. We heard a man in heavy boots clattering down the stairs, though we could not see him or he us as he was hidden by a right-angle turn in the stairway. As he came to the turn and his feet came in sight, Sergeant Terry fired a burst with his tommy-gun. The man turned and fled away upstairs.

'Meanwhile Geoffrey had opened one door and we looked in and saw it (the room) was empty. Geoffrey pointed to a light shining from the crack under the next door and then flung it open. It opened towards him and inside were about ten Germans in steel helmets, some sitting and some standing. Geoffrey fired two or three rounds with his Colt .45 automatic, and I said: "Wait, I'll throw a grenade in." He slammed the door shut and held it while I got a pin out of a grenade. I said "Right", and Geoffrey opened the door and I threw in the grenade which I saw roll to the middle of the room. Before Geoffrey (who said "Well done" as he saw the grenade go in) could shut the door, the Germans fired. A bullet struck Geoffrey just over his heart and he fell unconscious at the feet of myself and Terry. I shut the door and immediately afterwards the grenade burst with a shattering explosion. This was followed by complete silence and we could see that the light in the room had gone out. I decided Geoffrey had to be moved in case there was further fighting in the building, so between us Sergeant Terry and I carried him outside and laid him on the grass verge by the side of the steps leading up to the front door. He must have died as we were carrying him outside, for when I felt his heart it had ceased to beat.'

Campbell returned to the hall of the building, and then went round to its back, but while he was approaching it one of the Commando soldiers posted at the back entrance mistook him for a German and shot him through the leg, (it was amputated later, when Captain Campbell was a prisoner), thus making it impossible for him to return to the beach. The men offered to carry Campbell back across the twenty-five miles, but he refused. They left him lying there, withdrawing under the command of Sergeant Terry. Campbell was presently found and taken by the Germans to hospital. Geoffrey Keyes they also took away and buried with military honours in the cemetery close by, the chaplain of the garrison church at Potsdam performing the ceremony. He was posthumously awarded the Victoria Cross.

General Rommel was not at the house attacked, and it is now known that he had never used it. Our Intelligence was faulty. The

6*

house was the headquarters of the German and Italian supply services. Nor, as was thought at the time, was Rommel in Rome attending a birthday celebration; he was close to the front line, then about to be attacked by General Auchinleck.

The raiders, with Sergeant Terry in charge, made their way, not without difficulty, back to Laycock who was awaiting them in the wadi; and then, still hoping, though in vain, that Cook and his men would arrive, sat down to await the return of the *Torbay*. She arrived off the coast after dark on the 20th and flashed a message in Morse, which Laycock was able to read, saying that the sea was too rough and that she would return on the following night. She then moved off after successfully floating ashore a rubber dinghy containing food and water. This was thankfully received. The party prepared to spend the remainder of the night and the next day ashore, and to pray for better weather.

At first light a defensive position was formed, the main detachment remaining near the caves while two small detachments protected the eastern and western flanks of the position. The morning wore on; all was quiet; the wind and sea were abating; the hopes of the party were rising. But at noon shots were heard. They came from the westernmost sentry groups, who were in action against some Italian native levies, known to be in the neighbourhood. Colonel Laycock was not unduly worried. He felt confident that he and his men would be able to keep off the Arabs until darkness and then retire to the beach. Two small parties were sent out to outflank the enemy, but did not succeed in doing so, for by now German troops had appeared, while beyond them was a considerable party of Italians. These remained on the skyline about a mile to the north, and took no part in the fighting.

One of the small parties presently came back, having been able to advance only a quarter of a mile before coming into action. After their tommy-gun jammed, the officer with them, Lieutenant Pryor, continued to advance alone until wounded. With great difficulty he crawled back to the main position.

The Germans were by now maintaining a sustained fire, and about two o'clock in the afternoon it became evident that it would be impossible to hold the beach against such superior forces. When the enemy were no more than two hundred yards from the caves, Laycock ordered the detachment to split up into small parties, dash across the open and seek the cover of the hills inland. There they could either try to get in touch with H.M.S. *Talisman*, which they knew would be lying off an alternative beach that night, or they could hide in the wadis which abounded, and await our forces. Lieutenant Pryor, who was grievously wounded, was left behind with a medical orderly and ordered to surrender. He eventually did so and was taken off to captivity on the back of a mule watched 'by a lovely great red-backed shrike sitting on a juniper bush'.

After the party had scattered, Laycock found himself with Sergeant Terry. They crossed half a mile of open country, being continually sniped, but neither of them was hit. Once in the shelter of the Jebel, which offered the excellent cover of thick scrub, they set out together to join the 8th Army. After the first few days they made friends with various members of the local Senussi tribes, who helped them and hid them each night in the wadis which the enemy were known to have searched during the day. 'Neither of us,' records Laycock, 'could speak Arabic, and our conversation was mostly carried on by means of broken Italian and by making signs to each other. For instance, a Senussi holding up his five fingers pointing at us and then drawing his forefinger across his throat, meant that five of our original raiding party had been murdered by the Arabs and handed over to the Germans. Our greatest problem,' he continues, 'was the lack of food, and though never desperate we were forced to subsist for periods, which never exceeded two and a half consecutive days, on berries only, and we became appreciably weak from want of nourishment. At other times we fed well on goat and Arab bread, but developed a marked craving for sugar. Water never presented a serious proposition as it rained practically continuously.'

One evening they were making a thin stew out of some goat and bones—mostly bones—which they had flavoured with wild garlic picked by Laycock. As they were about to eat it a friendly Arab arrived, gave one loud sniff, and overturned the pot. He subsequently explained to the enraged and hungry pair that the garlic would have destroyed their sight. They ate all that goat, returning to dig up the lungs and entrails which they had buried.

Eventually the colonel and the sergeant joined the British forces at Cyrene, forty-one days after they had originally set out. 'On joining them we fell upon the marmalade offered to us and polished off a pot each.' They were the only members of the party to reach Cyrene.

IT WAS REPORTED *later that the Germans had quickly found their way to the rendezvous from a carefully marked map dropped by one of the raiders.*

Colonel Laycock, who eventually rose to major-general and chief of Combined Operations, reported in at Cairo on Christmas Day, only to be rushed back to England where he was given command of the Special Service Brigade.

ÉQUIPES BOULAYA

BY GEORGE MILLAR

IN THE MONTHS *following Marshal Pétain's surrender, France was quiet for a time. Its soldiers and civilians were stunned and bewildered. It was hard for a Frenchman to believe that Paris was German. Then slowly out of the confusion came anger and revulsion as Frenchmen reacted to the occupation and the humiliation of defeat. And out of the anger came the Maquisards—the French irregulars. They took the name Maquis from the Corsican smugglers who 'live in the bush'. They banded together with two objectives 'Armed assistance to an Allied landing in France' and 'co-operation with the political action groups of the Resistance in over-throwing the Vichy regime and setting up a liberation government'.*

The recruitment notices circulated in the cities and the farm com-munities were dramatic in their simplicity.

NOTICE

Men needed in the Maquis to fight. They will live badly and dangerously. Food will be scarce. They will be completely separated from their families until the end of the war. Violations of this rule of isolation will be punished. No pay will be guaranteed. Efforts will be made to help their families, but no promises can be made. All correspondence is forbidden.

And Frenchmen answered the call to take arms in a secret army. Royalists, Communists, Democrats, Catholics, Protestants, and Jews all remembered they were Frenchmen and together they fought the Germans. Liaison was set up with the French in exile, with the British and the Americans. Supplies were dropped in along with demolition experts, radio operators, and Allied-trained guerrillas.

Captain Millar, an escaped prisoner-of-war, was one of these, and under the field-name of 'Émile', was dropped near Dijon just before D Day. There he was introduced to Boulaya, otherwise Joseph Barthelet, a swash-buckling captain of the Resistance, and with him made his way eastwards to Vieilley in the valley of the Ognon. There was organized one of the most successful, and most human, of the Maquis groups, a group which became known as the 'Équipes Boulaya'.

WHEN we reached the Maquis I asked to be shown the dump of parachuted material which I knew existed near by. Georges led us up a path so nearly perpendicular that I had great difficulty, and Boulaya even greater, in getting up at all. I made up my mind there and then that I must have nails put in the soles of the square-toed shoes London had given me. I remembered as I struggled up the path that when I got my clothes in London the French-English captain had tried to insist on my taking one pair of heavy boots. I had refused because I hate wearing heavy boots, even for hard walking in rough country. I wondered if the captain had not been right. Certainly the Maquisards were surprised at my light shoes, and my feet would often have been drier in boots.

At the top of the small hill he had climbed Georges dived into seemingly impenetrable brush, and he soon disclosed the arms and explosives depot, a part of the material from one small parachutage. The material was in a bad state. It had been exposed to the weather for some months, stored merely in sacks shoved under a ledge of rock and covered over with moss. Bit by bit, crouched double to avoid the branches, with muscles already creaking from my climb and now cramped maddeningly, I pulled out the material. Rage consumed me as I handled rusted grenades and explosives soggy with moisture. Everything was in such a wet condition that in England it would have been unconditionally scrapped.

I was careful to conceal the main seething of my anger, but my questions and exclamations grew colder and more bitter. Georges' face grew long, and Boulaya injected the strained talk less frequently with his maddeningly optimistic remarks.

'There is not enough explosive to do much work,' I said at last. 'And from the look of it, I doubt if it will work. We shall have to take the lot down to the Maquis and dry it. Then I shall test it. It's quite hopeless to store this material out in the woods without protection. Why was it not stored in the container cells? They were designed for that purpose.'

Georges was unable to keep quiet any longer.

'That is all that remains of that parachutage,' he said coldly. 'Except for the Sten guns and pistols, all of which were given out, it was split into three parts. The other two parts were stored as you advocate in the woods on the other side of the côte in the container cells. And this part is the only part that remains. The Boche captured the other two dumps. All this was carted in rucksacks over the hill, a distance of sixteen kilometres through the snow by myself and Barbier of Thise. Weinmann helped us to begin with, but he was ill and he had to stop after one trip because he was spitting blood. If you think it was easy. . . .'

I interrupted him:

'It looks as though you might as well have spared yourself the trouble. Or taken a little more trouble and endeavoured to make this dump waterproof. Now if we can get all this down into the sun we shall see whether some of it will still work.'

They agreed with frigid politeness.

While the atmosphere was strained I decided to strain it further.

'In the British Army,' I began maddeningly. 'In the British Army we have a rule for any formation, no matter how small, that goes out by itself. Say it is a section. The section arrives to take up a position. The first thing to be done is to post sentries. What is the next?'

'Next they make some tea perhaps,' suggested the intelligent Boulaya.

'No. They dig two holes. One is for rubbish and the other is a latrine.'

'Exactly,' said Boulaya. 'We have the same procedure in the Army. But of course it is impossible in the Maquis to have quite the same standards.' He had understood. We left it at that.

Down in the Maquis they organized carrying-parties with three men, the whole strength apart from Philippe, who was 'attempting', they said, to cook the meal. Buhl had departed to see his wife, but another man had returned, Maurice. When the material had all been spread out in the sun to dry, a sorry sight, we ate squatting on our hunkers like savages beside the beds of pine branches. The food was revolting, for Philippe was no cook and all the cooking utensils and the French Army dixies from which we ate were greasy and horrible. There were two fried eggs for each of us, followed by segments of tough rabbit burned nearly black.

It was getting hot and airless in the woods and we were thirsty after the work. We drank water from the old water-bottles, water with a queer dead taste. After the meal, while I worked with the explosives we had spread out to dry, I began to instruct the four young Frenchmen in the use of these strange things.

And suddenly, from their eager questions and their enthusiastic attention, I picked a flicker of hope. All through the long afternoon I talked to them in my halting technical French. Talked to them until I was hoarse, asked them questions to see that they understood, made each of them handle the explosives, and finally listened to their talk, struggling with their strange language spiced with the *argot* of the Maquis.

Who were these four young men? They were four youths of the working classes. Their faces and hands and habits were rough, none rougher. When they talked a girl was called a *gonzesse*, a hand-grenade was an 'orange' or a 'lemon', a Sten gun might be a *petrolette* or a *clarinette*, and the big Colt automatic was a *chassepot*. They were dressed in a mixture of clothes with khaki from the French and German armies, the predominant motif. All four wore khaki trousers of cheap stiff German cloth, trousers stolen from the Wehrmacht. Their boots were in a terrible state, although Georges had recently had them patched in the village. Toes and heels showed through holes in the leather. They had no socks.

They were dirty, all four. They sprawled over the ground, and when they came close to me I smelled their bodies. Especially that of the Pointu, who wore no shirt.

The Pointu was thus called because he was a tall, lanky youth, of the type that has outgrown his strength. He was an unnaturally serious twenty-year-old. His weapons were well-cared-for, and I noticed that he was careful, though clumsy in his work.

Philippe was still younger. He was a handsome boy, his blond good looks were just beginning to coarsen with his environment. He had a strangely deep and resonant voice for his age.

The Frisé (I suppose in our Army he would have been called 'Curly') had been a sailor in 1940. He was an old twenty-two-year-old, tough and cheeky but intelligent. I saw that he was the only one who had closely studied the instruction booklets which were parachuted in every container. The Frisé really knew something. Boulaya and Georges, who had also read the pamphlets, still knew nothing. The Frisé learned easily. And his personal weapons, a Sten and a Colt, were in perfect condition. He was a strange-looking young man. Powerfully built but with short legs and a huge head that looked even bigger because of the enormous thickness of dust-coloured curls surmounting his high forehead. He spoke some English too, and maddened me frequently by flinging mispronounced English words into our conversation.

While the Frisé, in his odd tough way, gave me a perfectly correct first impression of brilliance, it was Maurice who interested me most of the four. He was older than the others, in the middle or late twenties, and he had a family in Besançon, a wife who was enceinte. He had been a house-painter, and a Communist. But he never spoke about these things. He had been in the Army, a noncommissioned officer in the *Corps Francs*, the volunteers who did patrols against the German lines and outposts in the opening 'dead' period of the war. He often spoke about his life in the Army. He was single-minded and solid. He had already paid the price of his front teeth in the battle. The stumps of them and some ragged, strangely white edges showed when he smiled, which was frequently. The Germans had broken his front teeth with hammers to teach him a lesson when they had caught him trying to sabotage in Besançon station. Maurice was a wide man. He was not short, but the great width of his shoulders made him look almost squat, and his face was round and wide, so that when I remember him it is as though I remember him in one of those convex mirrors that broaden every object they reflect.

Those were the four young men who formed that day the Maquis of Vieilley. Georges was not really a part of the Maquis. He made its existence possible by holding the goodwill of the village and by getting food and supplies for the Maquis. But he was no more a part of it than I, a foreigner, was part of it. Georges was a poacher, a man who walked alone.

Something about them inspired me. They were ordinary young men. They were the youth of France. And they were good material because they were excited and eager and fresh.

That was it. They were fresh. The whole situation suddenly turned round like a revolving stage in my mind, a stage that showed one instant a gloomy set, dark and hopeless, and the next instant a fine light set with a wide road leading into the distance. I saw that Boulaya had done me a favour in bringing me here to work with him. Here was the best way to begin his celebrated 'Équipes Boulaya', to begin them with only ourselves and the four youths who lay around me in the pine-trees.

Everything fell into the picture. Perhaps in the gloom of the previous night's sleep my mind had already been working things out.

We would build Vieilley into the centre of our area. Then we would strive to dominate, first by sabotage, later by force of arms, the two valleys, the big valley of the Doubs running north-east from Besançon to Belfort and the valley of the Ognon, which runs approximately parallel to the other. The two valleys were the key to the town of Besançon. We would make Besançon our objective. Boulaya would march through it at the head of his men—perhaps.

The first thing was to get the confidence of the Maquis. We must sleep there that night, Boulaya and I. And we would do a sabotage

attack with them the following day. If the attack succeeded my
new plan was on.

I questioned and requestioned the Frisé about the big station and
railway depot at Besançon. He had worked there as a *garde voies*
for the Germans before he had run away to the Maquis. He was
able to draw me plans of the depot.

The others began to pay thrilled attention to my questions.
Excitement grew under the pine-trees.

After talking over with the Frisé all possible targets in the depot,
I decided that the best would be two big turn-tables (called by the
French *plaques-tournantes*) used to empty the locomotives from the
round-houses.

I chose the turn-tables for several reasons. Both the Frisé and
Maurice knew that part of the depot well and thought that the job
could be done. The Frisé had a friend who owned a small café
just across the wall from the turn-tables, and whose son was a
cheminot employed in the depot. The son would be able to give
them last-minute information on the positions of the German
guards. And the turn-tables were an important target. If they were
put out of action up to seventy big locomotives vital to the Germans
would be imprisoned in the round-houses.

So that evening I sent the Frisé away to study the situation. He
left in a rush and flurry on a brand-new woman's bicycle that he
had 'found' in Besançon. To go to the city he altered his toilet only
by perching an extremely dirty beret on top of his curls. Maurice
was to join him in the morning to make the final reconnaissance,
then they were to return in the afternoon to report to me. They
swore that they would be able to examine the turn-tables from close
to. I wanted an actual description and drawings and the diameter in
centimetres of each of the big central pivots. A turn-table works on
balance. There is a central pivot underneath and there are two outside wheels, one at each end of the platform. When the locomotive
is driven on to the turn-table it balances on the pivot and the two
wheels do not touch the steel runway beneath them. One charge on
the pivot therefore can knock out the whole turn-table, and repairs
are extremely long and difficult.

I wondered if the Frisé and Maurice would come back and say
that the job was impossible. It was not unlikely that this would
happen. But I had a feeling that they were determined young men.

At two o'clock the following afternoon they returned. Maurice
was a shade nervous about things. But the Frisé swept all objections
aside. There were fifty-six big locomotives in the round-houses and

more expected in the evening. What if there were German guards in the round-houses? They never stirred outside, did they? He had not seen them come out once the night before. And there were only three, or five at the most, if the other two from lower down came up that way to chat to their friends. As for the *gardes voies*, they would not dare to interfere. And they would take the Pointu with a *clarinette* to guard the gate into the lane, and Philippe with another to stand well down the lane and give warning if a patrol came. He described the vital pivots in some detail. I had the impression that he was lying when he stated categorically that he had seen them from close to (why, he had 'even touched the thrice-defiled things'). But he gave me a careful description of them with dimensions which I have now forgotten. The Frisé was irresistible.

By this time I had checked over and tested most of the material rescued from their dump, and I was staggered and proud to find that all of it worked, a mute tribute to the British armament industry, which I had hated so much in peace-time. I reckoned that this would give us in all about fifty 'standard' 1½ lbs charges—enough to hit the railways a good thump while I was trying to get some more explosives.

Squatting in the middle of the pines, with the excited Frisé breathing anxiously down my neck, I made up the two big charges. I made them as neatly as we had been obliged to make them in the training schools, each charge a long and perfect cube of explosive, with two nice white primers nestling inside and a two-foot tail of detonating cord coming out of its end. Now there was a small problem. In England we always wrapped our charges in waterproof material and fixed this up solidly with rubber solution and adhesive tape. Here, in the field, there was hardly any adhesive tape and there was no material and no solution. So I cut up an old French Army linen flea-bag, had the Pointu dye it with ink, and sewed the charges into two solid little bags.

They dressed themselves up for the long walk over the hill, over past the Vauban fortress of 'La Dame Blanche' at the top, and then down through the other side of the forest of Chailluz until they struck the suburbs of Besançon. They would reach Besançon before curfew and would carry their weapons and charges through the back streets in two haversacks. By curfew-time they would be hidden with the Frisé's friend, the café owner. From the upper windows of the café they could watch movements in the depot. They were to attack at 2 a.m. Pointu and Philippe gave their Stens a last rub and polish, broke them down into three pieces, and packed them with their magazines, one in each haversack. The Frisé and Maurice carefully adjusted their massive charges in the haversacks on top of the Stens. They ate a light meal of bread and cheese, standing up, looking at each other and at us excitedly.

Boulaya and I walked with them as far as the fields.

'Remember now,' I said. 'Place the charges properly inside the steel lattice-work and against the pivot proper. Wedge the charge against the surface of the pivot, then light your fuse, and don't pull on the fuse as you light it. The moment it is lit move away individually for the gate. Don't run away. Walk. Once at the gate, run down the lane. And take cover when you see the flash of the explosion in the sky, those charges are big, there will be much metal flying.'

'Yes, Émile. Thank you, Émile. Au revoir.'

I watched the four of them cross the field, striking up diagonally towards the forest that came pouring down the side of the ridge towards us. Boulaya put his hand on my arm.

'Well, Émile,' he said. 'To-night a start is being made.'

He was dreaming again that Besançon would one day be free. The four Maquisards had disappeared from view. The evenings were still chilly, and dew was beginning to fall. I closed the fastener on the front of my leather jacket. Boulaya had the great hooded blue cape that he had worn as an officer in Morocco. He used this to cover him when he lay down on the pine branches beside me. I was in my sleeping-bag. We used the 'bed' of Maurice and Philippe since it looked like rain and their bed appeared to have the most scientific 'roof' over it.

Before going to sleep I set the alarm clock in my head. For twelve-thirty. I set it, just in case it worked unsatisfactorily, or in case the Frisé and Maurice got impatient and decided to do the job before two o'clock.

I awoke at midnight. Boulaya still slept, but uncomfortably. A light drizzle was falling. Not enough to penetrate our roof of pine branches, but the kind of drizzle that is normally prelude to something worse.

At twelve-thirty to the second I heard the first thump. It was like someone beating a giant metal tray in the distance, and it was followed immediately by its own echo. I timed it on the luminous face of the watch London had given me. Thirty seconds passed. One minute; the second one should go now. Ninety seconds. Two minutes. Something had gone wrong. I tore myself from the sleeping-bag, and sat up naked in the cold. But I still gazed despair-ingly at the dial of my watch. Two and a half minutes. I strained to hear small arms fire, although I knew that the depot was much too distant for that to be possible. I pictured the four youths there, surrounded perhaps. Perhaps even at that moment being clouted to the ground by brutal *Feldgendarmes*. Two minutes forty-five seconds. Even as I decided to wait till three minutes had elapsed I heard the second explosion. It was much louder than the first, but there was no echo. A wave of gratitude to the young Frenchmen swept over me, a warm feeling that possessed me and gave me peace and a longing for sleep. Should I waken Boulaya? No, I would keep this to myself. If I woke him he would want to talk, and he would certainly roll himself a cigarette and drown the smell of the pines.

Why had the second explosion been louder than the first? The charges were exactly similar. Possibly one or both had been badly placed. But I realized that, bad soldier as I am, I did not care so desperately whether or not the two turn-tables were destroyed, what mattered was that the Frenchmen had not failed. They had the courage to do big things.

They came in at six-thirty. In the rain. The hair hung damp on their foreheads. Their feet were blistered and their leg muscles were reacting in the almost drunken way you see when unfit men are exhausted. None of that worried me. But there were only three of them.

'Where is the Frisé?' I asked.

'Oh, we left him coming through the forest, in the woodcutter's hut beside the well. His feet and legs were so bad he couldn't keep going.'

'How many people are there in the hut?' Boulaya asked.

'Oh, not many. The father and mother and the son and his wife and three or four children.'

'Children! But the Frisé might shoot his mouth off.'

'He will, indubitably.'

'Name of God, why did you leave him there?'

'How were we to stop him?' Maurice asked. 'As for talking. I was greeted when I arrived at my home in Besançon yesterday morning by my wife, greatly excited. "Maurice, my cabbage," she cried. "It is too dangerous. I forbid it. Think of the unborn child." "Forbid what?" I asked. And she answered: "Don't go trying to deny it now, idiot. Why, all Besançon knows that you and Frisé are going to blow up the turn-tables to-night, and that you have an English officer with you who is planning your coups. Why, half the young men in Besançon were queueing up in the bistro by the depot last night to buy drinks for the Frisé."

'And it was quite true,' Maurice added, with a smile (for he did not appear to dislike the notoriety). 'Frisé has only the one vice. He is a gabber. No use trying to shut his mouth. As for women or drink, he is just not interested, but talk will be his downfall.'

'That must be changed But the turn-tables. Why did the second charge go so much later than the first?'

'Well,' said Maurice, a little timidly. 'We realize now that your plan was the best. I mean for me to go into one pit and the Frisé into the other and light the charges almost at the same time. But, as you may realize, it's one thing to agree before or after which plan is best, and it's another to do the actual job.

'Suddenly we decided two things. That it would be too long to wait until two o'clock, and that the Frisé and I would lay the charges together. Lighting the first and then going on and doing the second. So we did that. Another thing. Philippe wanted to actually come into the depot instead of waiting outside in the lane. So we let him. The poor kid was going to feel kind of out of things.

'It was no easy job wedging the charge in behind the steel lattice-work. Frisé held the charge while I lit the fuse. Then we went on to the next. Philippe stopped a little by the first turn-table to see that nobody interfered with it.'

'My God.'

'Yes, but there were quite a lot of workers about. Some Schloks too, but they paid no attention to us. They were playing cards in the hut. We had tied white handkerchiefs around our sleeves, so they would think we were *gardes voies*. Well, we could not run from the first turn-table to the second. There were too many people around. We walked across together and we had not got the second charge in place when the first one went off. Name of God, what a bang. There was metal clattering down for nearly five minutes, it seemed. We lay under the shelter of our turn-table, and when the metal stopped falling around us we placed the charge and I lit the fuse.

'Frisé now made his big mistake. That boy really is indiscreet. "Philippe," he shouted across the station. "Are you all right?" As though half the *cheminots* in the depot did not know young Philippe. Then he shouted to the station at large: "Keep in cover, there's worse coming." Just then the air-raid sirens went, for they thought the first explosion was a bomb. There was not a soul, not even a Schlok to be seen around. They had put out the lights. We beat it for the gate, picked up the Pointu, and threw ourselves down in the lane when the second explosion came.'

'It was louder than the first?'

'Yes, much louder.'

'Were the two charges placed the same?'

'Yes, exactly the same.'

'Do you think the attack succeeded?'

'Yes.'

On this we shook hands all round, and realized that there was nothing, absolutely nothing, to eat for breakfast. Boulaya, beside himself with joy that the first attack had succeeded, was sorely vexed that he could not feed his men.

'One of the great events of the war for Besançon,' he exclaimed. 'And the men who did it return to find that there is not a crust of bread, not even a drop of warm coffee for them.'

But the men who did it were going to their rude beds, too tired and too happy to talk much or to mind the rain. Before they slept Boulaya produced a small bottle of extra-strength Marc, made by his old father from the fine grapes of Salins. In this wonderful beverage we all toasted the successful beginning of Boulaya's campaign to liberate Besançon.

And later Georges arrived with eggs and bread and ground and roasted wheat for making 'coffee'. While the others ate *breakfast à l'Anglaise*, Boulaya and I discussed with Georges plans to put the Vieilley Maquis on a more permanent basis. The three Maquisards ate like wolves, especially the Pointu, who needed a lot of nourishment. Before they had finished the Frisé came hobbling in. He had news of the result of the attack.

There were sixty-three locomotives in the trap. One turn-table had been lifted right up in the air, its pivot was smashed to bits. The other, the second to be attacked, had suffered more damage to the structure as a whole, but it was judged that the pivot could be repaired. The German engineers thought they could have that one moving with hand-gear in a few days. The other would be immovable until a new pivot could be cast and transported, that would certainly take weeks, perhaps months.

All eyes were turned on me while the Frisé recited this.

'The charges were not big enough,' said the Frisé.

I turned this statement over in my mind. It was fairly clear to me that one charge, the first one, had been properly placed, and the other had been less carefully placed, because the pair were interrupted by the first explosion and the turmoil that it caused. But if I made public this opinion I would only arouse a storm of argument, and I would lose some of their faith and liking. Much better to turn the Frisé's accusation (for that was what it amounted to) to my own profit. Accordingly, I replied with every appearance of sincerity:

'I am very sorry indeed. I would like to congratulate you all and thank you all for a fine achievement and a brave deed.'

A stunned silence greeted this. They tried to work it out for themselves. Was the foreigner actually accepting the responsibility? They had been certain of a good argument.

'They seemed on the small side, those charges,' Pointu said, just to make sure.

'Yes, perhaps they did,' I answered at once. 'One is always liable to make a mistake. Explosives are queer things.'

'And pray do not let us quibble,' Boulaya said. 'For the coup of the *plaques-tournantes* will long be remembered. Émile and I must leave you now, but soon we will both return, and then deeds, military actions, will prove to the Boches that there is a serious menace for them hidden in the forest of Chailluz. We shall make the Maquis of Vieilley famous for all time.

'But not famous now, Frisé. I am appalled at your lack of discretion in Besançon. Do you realize that your loud mouth has endangered the whole Maquis and especially our friend Émile? You go around telling every low person of your acquaintance what you and your comrades have been ordered to do, and worse still, you declare that those orders were given by *an officer in the Intelligence Service*. Don't you understand that if the Boche has wind that there is a British officer in the forest he will encircle the forest, if it takes three thousand men to do it, and he will tear it apart, branch by branch, until he has got every one of us, Émile included.'

The Frisé was too tough a bird to be put out by words.

'Who says that I said anything in Besançon,' he said through the mixture of egg, bread, butter, and coffee that filled his mouth. He allowed his hard grey eyes to play around our circle.

Nobody said anything.

Maurice led the way. We were a party of five. As we walked towards the forest I looked at the men with me and ran over once more in my head the tasks they would have to perform.

I planned to approach the station by the small back roads, walking in three pairs fairly widely spaced and arriving near Control Post No. 3 just before the 11 p.m. curfew. There we would hide in a convenient private garden. At midnight we would move out together and do the job, entering by the gate which the Frisé and I had used to cross the *cœurs d'aiguilles* that morning. The men carrying the charges were myself and Maurice, who had six each, and the Frisé with four. When we got to the *cœurs* I would begin to work across from the Control Post side, while Maurice would first cross all the lines and then begin working back towards me. The Frisé, who knew the station best, was to go on up the line towards the station and place his four charges on the Belfort line points. The other three carried Stens with three magazines per gun. They were to dispose themselves with Buhl watching and if necessary interfering with the Control Post, the Pointu watching the *Bahnhof's* hut and guarding Maurice and me from surprise from the open end of the tracks, and Philippe was to go in with the Frisé and protect him, and at the same time our rear. I calculated that the whole attack should take not more than ten minutes, that would give us roughly twenty minutes to get clear of the station before the first charges blew. And it would take us about forty minutes to clear the suburbs and reach the edge of the friendly woods. We would have to withdraw by the approach route. I did not like the withdrawal, and I could see plenty of holes in the whole plan. I sincerely wished that it was all over, and I simply could not imagine what had bitten me, what had made me so determined to initiate the thing.

At ten o'clock we were at the rendezvous, but there was no sign of the Frisé. We climbed through the hedge, and sat under the exact pylon that had been fixed for the meeting. It was now dark, but not pitch-black. We waited for an hour and a half. Spirits which had been reasonably good up to ten o'clock, sank completely to the lowest possible limit. All of us now had bad headaches from handling the '808'. It is at such times that you see what men are made of, when you are cold and there is an uneasy feeling in your stomach, and all the worst part of the job to be done lies right ahead. Maurice, Philippe, and the Pointu were surly and annoyed, but they held staunch. Buhl, the self-styled leader, the oldest man of the four, was the one who turned sour.

'Well,' he said at eleven-thirty. 'All that long walk for nothing.'
'What do you mean, nothing?' I answered angrily.
'Obviously, we can't go on now.'
'And why not?'
'The Frisé isn't here.'
'Maurice and I can still lay our twelve charges.'
'Yes, but if the Frisé isn't here it means he's been picked up by the Boches on the road here. With all that stuff on him. They'll know he's only one of a gang. The whole town will be watched. Even if he doesn't shoot his mouth off.'

'The Frisé wouldn't talk,' said the Pointu. 'We're not all like you.' Ordinarily the Pointu was the Frisé's bitterest critic.

'There is nothing to suggest that the Frisé has been taken,' I said, although secretly I thought it might be so. 'He has slept in at the camp, or he has gone straight to the depot on his bicycle before the curfew. Well, there is nothing for it but to go on without him.'

'But it's long past the curfew time, and we've nearly seven kilometres to walk through the streets,' said Buhl.

'What about it. We must go as a patrol, that's all. Maurice and Philippe will go ahead as scouts. I will follow a hundred metres or slightly less behind them. You will follow on my heels, and Pointu behind you. No talking. The scouts will stop every few hundred metres to listen; we should hear the Boche easily. When the scouts stop we stop. If surprised by the Boche, fire and fall back. Let the scouts come back through us, and give them covering fire. Walk only on the edge of the road.'

We set off, gingerly at first, and then, as the scouts gathered confidence, at a rattling pace. Buhl behind me kept up a constant flow of whispered remarks. I pointedly paid no attention.

'Madness,' he said. 'One needs to be too well trousered for affairs like this. Why shouldn't we do sensible sabotage in the country? Let the Bisontins look after Besançon. It's not sensible, that is all I complain about. Throwing ourselves away like this. Listen to the noise we're making. Oh, God. A regiment of Dragoons would make less noise. . . .'

With his last remark I secretly agreed. I had already made up my mind on two things; that I would never again venture on a job with Monsieur Buhl, and that for future night operations I would insist on everybody wearing *espadrilles* or rubber-soled shoes. I had wanted to wear ordinary footwear to the place where the Frisé should have met us and then change into something more silent, but I had been over-ruled by the others who clung to their heavy boots. Never again.

After thirty minutes' swift progress we were in the town proper. And two policemen in dark uniforms, wheeling bicycles, came round a corner and face to face with Maurice and Philippe. It happened that we were close behind the scouts at that point. I heard young Philippe say something to the pair in his low, hoarse voice. At the same time he made a sweeping motion with the fierce muzzle of the Sten he carried in both hands, and the two *agents* dashed up an alleyway and out of sight. I heard Philippe laugh, and the scouts moved swiftly on, so I did not interfere with them.

Next, as we were gingerly coming down the last slippery hill between high walls before the station (I could already see the blue lights of Control Post No. 3) the beam of a headlight swung around the corner and a small motor-cycle came panting up the hill. An enormous man sat stiffly upright in the saddle. All of us flung ourselves face downwards in the gutter. The motor-cycle panted on, and stopped about two hundred yards up the hill. The rider appeared to adjust his coat, then he continued on his way. This reassured me. If the man had seen us he would not have dared to have stopped. On the other hand, he was almost certainly a German. No Frenchman would use a motor-cycle at that place and hour. For a second or two I actually thought of turning, I am ashamed to say. But I soon urged the men on, and we found ourselves by the spot where Frisé and I had first looked at the night's objective.

All the landmarks were clearly discernible as I pointed them out to the four men. But the station seemed a million times more busy and noisier than in the morning. This was largely due to one engine, which was shunting carriages and trucks about directly in front of us. There were three or four railwaymen engaged on the shunting work as well as the driver and fireman of the engine. We saw the door of the *Bahnhof's* hut opening and closing fairly continuously, and Buhl, who had his eyes riveted on the Control Post, reported that he had seen a man looking out from there over the great fan of the *cœurs d'aiguilles*.

I had no intention of keeping either myself or the men waiting too long here. It was bad for the nerves. My watch said twelve-thirty. When we had tied handkerchiefs around our arms in imitation of the brassards of the *gardes-voies* I said to Maurice:

'Right, Maurice. You see your *cœurs*?'

'I think I see where they are.'

'We'll go first. Go straight across the line and begin working opposite me. Don't forget to wedge your charges against the V-shaped casting, either inside the V or, if it's blocked with wood, on one of the wings. Let's go and get it over.'

We slouched into the lights, walked down the railway line, and with a brief glance around, I got to work. I felt for the first charge or two as though I were working on the stage of the Palladium. Then I got used to the lights, the noise and bustle. And I had all six charges down and wedged and initiated in less than three minutes. I stood up. Maurice was crouched over the points and working slowly towards me, his haversack holding the unused charges hanging in front of him. Philippe was far down the lines towards the station, leaning casually against a hut. Buhl, his Sten gun held along his leg so that it did not show, was facing the big Control Post, and the Pointu was lurking in the shadows by the *Bahnhof's* hut. But they were not isolated figures in an empty scene. The place was fairly busy. There were people moving about everywhere. Far from frightening me, the bustle of the place gave me confidence.

Maurice had finished. Good and conscientious workman, he was nervous about his work.

'Hope I've done the right ones,' he said. I gave the whistle that was the agreed signal for withdrawal. Pointu, being the nearest, was with me first. I told him to go and tell the *cheminots* working on the shunting to clear off, that the station would go up in the air in twenty minutes. The lanky youth did this with alacrity, showing his *petrolette* a little more obviously than was necessary as he did so.

As we made for the gate there came an announcement from the control-tower:

'All *cheminots* leave this area at once and return to the depot. This is urgent.' And then, very faintly, the metallic voice added: '*Vive La France.*' The men doing the shunting had chosen this method of spreading the Pointu's warning. Frisé met us at the gate.

'Where have you been?' I asked him, and followed the question with some vile French.

'I was at the rendezvous,' he lied. 'But this is not the moment for conversation. A Cossack patrol has just passed the railway bridge at the corner. When are we going to do the job?'

'The job is done, or at least our part of it. The charges will begin to go in fifteen minutes.'

'Name of God, and me with my detonators not even attached yet. I must be off.' He placed his bicycle against the wall, and went slowly through the gate fiddling about as he went with a tangle of charges and adhesive tape.

'Where are you going?'

'To place my charges, of course. Like to come along, Philippe, in case I need protection?'

'We'll wait at the rendezvous,' I told the Frisé. 'Philippe knows how to find it.' I knew it was useless trying to stop him, and two men would do better for the job than a greater number. So the four of us set off on the long way back through the town. We had done nearly a quarter of an hour's hard walking, and were not far from the Cossacks' barracks when the first charge went off. The whole town was in a hollow, so the noise sounded particularly impressive. There was a vivid flash too. From then on, at irregular intervals spaced over nearly forty minutes, the explosions came. As I counted thirteen, fourteen, fifteen, sixteen, I knew that the Frisé also had succeeded. And not one charge had failed.

The sound of machine-gun firing came from the Cossacks' place. We learned later that they thought it was an air-raid, and they were proving to their German masters that they were awake by firing a few bursts into the air. I was glad that they did fire, the noise sobered my men a little. They were inclined to get too jubilant, and too noisy despite my injunctions before we had started that the with-drawal was the most dangerous part of the whole operation, and must be performed in silence. The good suburbanites of Besançon were crowding to their garden gates to stare down-hill into the dark bowl, watching for the flashes. Most of them thought it was Allied bombers. This annoyed the young men with me. So much so that passing one house the Pointu waved his Sten at the inhabitants and shouted:

'Enough of this goggling. Get inside. And don't say that you saw us.'

The people stared at him with amusement. A little fat man and his wife and four children.

'Would you gentlemen not care for a glass of indifferent wine?' asked the little man. And his button-eyed stare said: 'So it was you who did it, eh?' Stupid Pointu. When I thought of the boastful Frisé following behind without my controlling presence I went hot and cold.

He and Philippe did not keep us long at the rendezvous. We divided a small ginger-bread cake that Buhl carried into six pieces and ate it, drinking water from a water-bottle. First I asked the Frisé where he had been.

'I was here at the right time,' he said.

'You were either at Vieilley, asleep at that time, or you were with your friends in the café in Besançon. You risked the success of the whole expedition and the lives of your comrades. Why can you not work for the others as well as for yourself?'

'Émile, I am sorry. I was so ill to-night. I had a dreadful head-ache. I will never do it again.' He was nearly in tears. But he did not say where he had been. And he suddenly burst out in a suffocat-ing snarl. 'And don't let any one say that I did not do my part.'

'There was no need to shout your name around the station,' said Philippe. It appeared that no sooner had the Frisé placed his charges than he shouted into the station itself (from where he stood he could just see its dark mouth):

'Stay in your holes, *couillons*. There are sixteen mines in position, and the first man to interfere with them gets filled with lead. I, the Frisé, guarantee it.'

'Another thing, Philippe,' I said, when I had stifled my laughter at the Frisé's stupidity. 'What did you say to the two policemen we met on the way in?'

'I told them that they had seen nothing, and that they were lucky that we had not the time to take their *velos* and their uniforms too.'

'But the *agents* are friendly to us. You must try to be more polite.'

'Polite to the *flics*!'

'Politeness would be going enormously too far,' said the Frisé.

From the look-out I could only see the farthest roofs of Vieilley, the nearer roofs ran too close into the swelling hill-side. If the '8.10' had wakened me the peasants would be already on their way out to the fields, and the fires would not yet be lit in the village. The peasants were an hour behind the clock. They refused to accept the advanced 'German time'.

What a splendid view it was. Over the shining and rich landscape I was able to see traces of our handiwork. That black stain just north of Vieilley, for example, was where we had crashed the two trains into each other. An almost bloodless little victory. They were empty trains that we set roaring at each other, face to face on the single line. One of them was a train with a cargo of rather sticky boiled sweets in cheap paper wrappings. The two trains met head on, with a noise that could be heard in the valley for many miles. For an instant the two big locomotives seemed to pause, buffers locked. Then they reared like two caterpillars meeting face to face, and both trains rolled clear of the line (unfortunately from the sabotage point of view).

When the villagers in the valley heard of the sweets spilling out of the railway wagons between the stations of Merey-Vieilley and Moncey, they sent scouts out to the spot. And following the scouts came long strings of lean children. Children who had scarcely tasted sweets in their lifetimes of war. Many of them had come, unthinking, with nothing to carry sweets away but their two hands. Others had receptacles like buckets, or even dolls' prams.

When we successfully attacked a train or a station we expected always to see one or two car-loads of Gestapo on the spot anything from half an hour to three hours after the train left the rails or the charges went. But this time, by a happy chance, the Germans were slow in getting to the trains. And early the following morning from my look-out high up on the hill I saw more strings of children winding their way by the paths from the villages to the railway. They came from Buthiers and Cromary, on the far side of the Ognon. From Devecey, Bonnay, Merey, Palise, Venise, and Moncey; from Chaudefontaine, Rigney, and La Barre, the children came to gather like ants around the fantastic train that lay still smoking in the Vieilley wheat-fields. And when the Germans came to the wreckage they found no sweets.

'And there is no tobacco,' said Frisé. 'What about letting me and Philippe go and stick up the *bureau de tabac* at La Bretenière. I heard they were expecting some supplies there.'

'By all means, go and *buy* some,' Boulaya said. 'No nonsense now. You must not even carry weapons.'

'Count on us,' said Frisé, and the couple departed.

We were in the middle of a stilted lunch with three influential citizens from Besançon and not enough eating utensils to go round when Frisé and Philippe, highly elated, returned. They had just derailed three locomotives in Rigney station in front of the crowds waiting on the platform for the two o'clock *voyageur* to Besançon.

'Afraid we had not the time to stick up the *bureau de tabac*, in fact we never got that far,' said the Frisé, putting both feet right in it.

'Only his way of talking,' Boulaya explained to the three Bisontins. 'Frisé is one of our best and most conscientious soldiers.'

'Passing under the bridge by Rigney station we saw the three *locos* standing there hitched together and with steam up,' Frisé went on. 'I says to Philippe: "Did you forget to leave your revolver in the Maquis as Boulaya said?" "I did," he answers. "That's strange. So did I," I reply. So we got into the station and I got hold of a *cheminot* standing there, and make him show us how to fix the points and wedge them so that a train approaching at speed will derail itself. Then we walk back to the three engines outside the station. I jump into the cab of the first one and show them my persuader, Philippe gets into the rear one. "Get going backwards," we tell our respective drivers. When we had backed to about one kilometre from the station we all get out. I give them all a cigarette while the three firemen stoke the fires up good. The driver of the middle one is a bad lot. He refuses my cigarettes. "O.K.," I says to the drivers. "Hop in and give them full tubes." They do as they are bid, jumping out as the engines get going. Only I noticed that the second one had not opened her full throttle. I give him a wipe across the nose and we move back to the station for our bicycles. The crowd at the station is jubilant. Three *gonzesses* kiss Philippe. Only one has the temerity to kiss me, but she does it better than his three put together. The Gestapo passed us on their way out to see the wreckage. They were going so fast they paid no attention to us.'

Nono interrupted my thoughts.

'Your pistol's hanging out again,' he said.

This time I turned it around and pushed it right up into my pocket until the butt stuck. I could not draw it quickly now, but I was tired of being told that it showed. Nono began to sing again. A charming song, which went:

> '*Sur la route qui va, qui va, qui va,*
> *Et qui ne finit pas.* . . .'

'How old are you, Nono?' I asked when he had finished.

'I'll be twenty in one month.'

'You'll just fall in for your military service when the victory comes.'

'Yes. I look forward to that.'

'What are you going to be?'

'A lawyer, like my father.'

'I would give a lot to be twenty again.'

'Why do you say that? It doesn't feel so good to be twenty.'

'I know, but so much lies ahead.'

We had begun to mount a longish hill with a curve at the top, and a wood on the left of the road. The slope was just negotiable on a bicycle. My *Griffon* groaned as it took the strain.

'What age are you?' asked the curious Nono.

'Thirty-three.'

'God, so old. One would never think you were so old.'

'I have never done one thing long enough, or loved one woman long enough to grow very old,' I said.

'What did you do in peace-time? I suppose you were a soldier, an officer.'

'No. I was a newspaperman.'

'For a newspaper in the provinces?'

'No, in Fleet Street. That is in London.'

'Which paper, Émile?'

'The *Daily*. . . .'

The words died on my lips as though my larynx had sucked

them back to silence. There was a German soldier in the wood on
the left. He was only a yard inside the bushes. He did not seem to
be paying any attention to us. We cycled on for two or three yards,
breasting the slope, then both of us saw what lay ahead—several
German lorries pulled into the side of the road and Germans in
uniform examining the civilian who had been riding a bicycle about
three hundred yards ahead of us—and both of us said simultaneously:
    'We must turn back.'
    Nono had been riding on my right. Now we swung round as
quickly as we could on the roadway and he was on my left. As we
turned one of the Germans bellowed down the road, obviously to
men concealed behind us:
    'Terrorists. . . .'
    And before we had got any speed up on the down-hill the man
we had seen in the bushes had come out to the side of the road,
slightly in front of us. He was a short, square German soldier, and I
shall remember his face as long as I live. It was a strong, shiny,
very-much-washed-looking face. It was pink and white, and the
paint-work on his heavy helmet was deeply scored with criss-
crossing scratches. There was no fear on it. Only satisfaction. I
struggled to get my pistol out, but, thanks to Nono's admonish-
ments, it would not move from my pocket. There was only one
thing to do—ride for it. The German had already raised his rifle to
the aim position. I would pass him at two yards' range. I was
between him and Nono, and I assumed that I was as good as
dead.
    We were side by side picking up speed, when the bang came,
close to my right ear-drum. I could not believe that I was still
careering down the hill, swerving my bicycle from side to side.
They were firing at me from behind and from both flanks, especially
from the left flank, where they had men hidden in the grain. I
could see them like scarecrows in the grain. They had come up to
the kneeling position to fire at me.
    'Poor Nono,' I said as I flew down the hill. 'Poor Nono.' And
something told me that I was going to get away, because they had
killed Nono instead of me. I had to get off this road though. There
was an up-hill beginning where the down-hill ended. They had got
some kind of machine-gun going now. The steel was zipping off the
road metal. If I slowed on the up-hill they would certainly knock
me over easily.
    There was only one piece of available cover. The wood on my
right. There were Germans in that wood, but probably they were

                                                              7

all higher up. At the bottom of the hill, without slowing down my *Griffon*, I swung it to the right into the deep ditch. As the machine dropped I tried to shoot myself up, and my momentum carried me sailing head first through the thick scrub bordering the wood.

For a fraction of a second I lay there, winded, grateful for the cover from fire. The firing was still wildly going on, but now the steel was cutting through the upper branches above my head. I heard shouting too, and the sound of a car's starter, and heavy boots running on the road.

At no ordinary time would I have bothered to walk through such a wood, even hunting for *chantrelles*. Now there was nothing else for it. I hoped that I was in a tongue of the southern part of the forest of Chailluz. On my left was an open glade running up to a small farm. I dare not run up the glade because it was observed by the Germans, and if they were at all intelligent, they would send a party up it and completely cut me off. On my right I could hear Germans smashing through the small trees and bushes. My only hope seemed to be to break through and get to the top of the 'tongue' and into the forest before they cut me off.

Although I was pouring with sweat, I kept my leather jacket on, since it protected my body from scratches. My face, hands and bare toes and ankles were soon running with blood, for much of the dense undergrowth was bramble. In places I had to slash a way through with my sharp parachutist's knife. It was a race all right. I could hear the Germans each time I stopped, and they were edging ever closer to me. To make the going harder, the wood ran up a steep hill. I had never in my life felt a more numbing physical exhaustion. Every branch seemed scientifically designed to claw at my arms, legs, and head, or to drive little dagger-like shoots into my eyes.

Georges' teachings helped me, for I came to a tiny clearing where wild boar had rooted in the ground. I followed their tracks, and so came on a path. It was extremely narrow and low, as paths go, but it helped me considerably. Now I seemed to be gaining on the Germans on my right and I was nearly opposite the head of the glade on my left.

When I reached the edge of the forest proper, I paused for a moment. The Germans were struggling through a thicket perhaps fifty yards behind me. After a second's reflection I drew my Colt and sent two .45 shells thudding into this thicket. There was an instant answering salvo with a sub-machine-gun and rifles, but when I had fired I had dropped down a bank and now, fairly silently on my rubber-soled sandals, I was running through much opener woodland.

With all their other faults, the bushes and trees through which I had torn my way had been hanging with moisture. My corduroy trousers were soaked through, and so heavy that it was difficult to run. I stopped to roll them up over my knees. While I stopped, I heard another party of Germans arrive at the farm in what sounded like two trucks. My line of escape was to circle to the left and try to cross the Marchaux road lower down. I must therefore try to make a circle round this second party. The first party had not stopped long after my shots. They were already on the move again. But I was confident of outstripping them. I got out the excellent compass they had given me in London, and checked up on my direction. Until I found a path I knew I would have to go through the forest by map memory. Then I set off at a steady run. I am fond of running long distances, and I was then extremely fit. But my breath was coming in the deep gasps of an animal that is hunted. The battle through the wood had taken a lot of the energy out of me.

After half an hour I struck a path that I recognized from our withdrawal that morning. If I had not known it I should have hesitated to take it, thinking that paths were dangerous since one might find Germans on them. But I knew that the entry to this one was fairly well hidden in the woods, and it was just what I needed to take me round the large German party that was now cutting deep into the wood from the farm. I continued, running down the path for perhaps two miles. All sounds of pursuit had now died, and I was nervous, for an unheard enemy is sinister. I had a feeling that we had bumped into an ambush set by the advance-guard of a large body of German troops. If they were very eager to get me it was possible that they had set guards along the Marchaux road which I was now approaching.

At the edge of the clear space that bordered the road at the point I intended to cross, I pulled out the small flask they had given me at the airfield in England. After drinking nearly half of the 'calvados' it fortunately contained, I felt equal to the crossing and the climb which now confronted me. Using all available cover, I worked nearer and nearer to the road. There were three young children there, but I was not going to bother about them. I tried to clean the blood off my face with a handkerchief damped with spittle, took off my tell-tale leather jacket, rolling it into a shape that was easily carried. I changed the magazine in my big Colt and thrust it loosely into my trouser pocket. As I did so I remembered with a twinge that if I had been able to draw this weapon Nono would possibly still be with me.

I strolled across the road, as though I were a cultivator returning from his work. No Germans were in sight. But the road was busy with peasants. As I mounted the hill, for I was now on the western end of the plateau between Marchaux and Champoux, I heard the church bell of Marchaux begin slowly to toll. I was sure that it was tolling for Nono. And perhaps for me too. I cut straight up the hill. At the edge of the forest I stopped to look west. I was astounded at what I saw. Two large bodies of Germans were working their way up towards the edge of the forest. That could only mean one thing. They were going to search the forest, and on our side of the Marchaux road, the northern bit of the forest. There were not more than two hundred Germans in these parties, however. Unless they had other parties operating on the other side of the *côte* from Vieilley, Bonney, or Devecey, the search could not be serious for me, though it might menace the Maquis.

Pushing myself to my fastest pace, I climbed the long hill to the path that I knew so well running along the summit. There was no sign of Germans on the top, and I made good time back to the cabin, and, since there was nobody there, down to the Maquis.

Nono's funeral was the biggest ever seen in these parts. There were more than three thousand mourners and every village sent its contingent. There was a guard of honour of our Maquisards dressed in their khaki uniforms and carrying Sten guns. They guarded the tomb, which was covered with wreaths and the beloved German-banned tricolour. Pinned to a cushion paraded at the funeral was the *Croix de Guerre*, awarded posthumously to Nono. Standing over the grave in the sunshine Colonel Fournier of Venise, who had been a great man in the Daladier war government of 1939, made an impassioned eulogy of the dead boy beginning:

'*Soldat de France, mort pour la Patrie*. . . .'

Nono was a youngster who had a talent for leadership. Even after death this talent seemed to persist. His dead body was an inspiration to the valley.

When I listened to all this, and later when I visited his two parents, leaving guards outside the house to see that there were no Germans about, I felt angrily that, had I been sufficiently energetic to walk to Thise, Nono would have been something better than a little hero of the Resistance. He would have been alive.

I told his parents that he had been killed instantly there, beside me on the road. But a cultivator of Marchaux who was working in some pear-trees on the hill-side and claimed to have witnessed the whole thing, said that Nono was only wounded on the roadway. He dropped his rucksack and ran across the field to a little wood, and from there managed to make his way to the forest at the bottom of the *côte*. He was tying up his leg wound when the Germans caught up with him. He fired with his revolver. They filled him with lead and dragged him back by his heels to the road. When they saw the contents of his rucksack they kicked his dead body. Then they threw it into a truck and took it to Marchaux. They also took my bicycle, the *Griffon*.

One day after lunch Philippe asked if he might take some of the others out and do a job on the Vesoul railway. We had just heard a train pass below us in the valley, and this was such an unusual sound that it roused us to action. Boulaya refused permission, but I persuaded him to let Philippe take out the Pointu and two new lads, Communists whom Maurice and Philippe together had rescued from imprisonment in the German hospital in Besançon, where they had been convalescing from German-inflicted wounds. The four of them departed happily on foot, carrying an arsenal of miscellaneous weapons and the heavy tools we used for unscrewing the railway lines. They promised to work as far afield as Miserey. Things appeared to go badly. That afternoon we heard the sound of firing, and the story came back to us that while they were derailing a train near Miserey a German truck full of soldiers passed on the road and opened fire. The Maquisards replied and then withdrew.

One by one that evening the young men dribbled back into the camp, bringing with them all their weapons and the tools. The story of the Germans was true, but Philippe had turned their arrival to our profit, for while the little battle was going on he had walked into Miserey station, found another train there and obliged the railwaymen to start it at full speed. This, crashing into the derailed train in the cutting, broke up the battle and allowed the other three Maquisards to withdraw in good order. On the way home Philippe and the Pointu seized a third train near Devecey, made all the occupants descend, and hurled this train on to the wreckage near Miserey. This was a wonderful day's work. I cycled out to see it, and I knew that if the enemy still had a crane he would need it for this, and it would be a long job. The cutting was deep, and the wreckage was well wedged in.

But our Philippe was irresistible. Boulaya gave him a holiday in Besançon to celebrate this important victory. He spruced himself up and left on a new bicycle. (We had just taken eight new ones from the police in Besançon, and Boulaya and I each bought one on the black market, so we were now astoundingly well off for bicycles.) Bronzed and bleached by the sun now, Philippe looked more cherubic than ever.

Unable to avoid the scene of his crime, he cycled past the still smoking remains where the Gestapo were examining tracks and questioning civilians and railwaymen. He saw another locomotive in Miserey station. Unarmed as he was, he cursed and swore at the railwaymen until they sent their engine rushing down the track. It hit the wreckage while the Gestapo were still there, and jumping, said onlookers, thirty feet into the air it landed upside down on the other side of the heap of twisted metal. Its wheels continued to revolve for some time. Already crowds were gathering for this fantastic sight. Cycling excursions were setting out from all the villages. Many of them were to have their money's worth. Philippe, tranquilly continuing on his way to Besançon, found another train and again, with only his gruff and determined voice to help him, succeeded in getting it launched at full speed on the right rails. In front of a large audience this train added itself to the heap in the cutting.

Sightseers were still visiting the place six weeks later. And it was known locally as 'the mountain of Miserey'. This closed the Vesoul line until (and, alas, after) the Allied Armies arrived.

The battle was going our way. The fame of Boulaya was growing in the land. We were expanding cautiously, as surely as possible. But there were annoying, maddening difficulties of supply.

Food for the Maquis was normally obtainable because the country people were generous, and the F.F.I. now usually had adequate finances sent out from the French headquarters in England. But there were other things that the Maquis needed desperately. Things like boots, bicycles, tyres, petrol, blankets, socks, grease, biscuits and tinned food or chocolate for emergency rations. We could not get those things from England, and when the parachutages began every cubic centimetre of container space would be wanted for weapons. But the German garrisons in our part of France possessed those things. Boulaya and I had to see how thefts, large-scale thefts, from the Germans could be organized.

Our existing Maquis were unsuitable for such work. They were

serious, almost military units. If we allowed them to become
gangsters for one week they would never return to their regular
work. It looked as though we must have another organization of
gangsters, separate from our ordinary, our 'respectable' terrorists.

Our old friend the Frisé became the first of the gangsters. In
reality, the Frisé had to be banished because his indiscretions grew
so grotesque that his presence endangered the whole organization
centred on Vieilley. He was sent with a friend named Marcel,
another ex-sailor, to form a new Maquis near Franois, west of
Besançon.

Frisé departed with an air of 'you just wait and see', and within
a few days he had produced fireworks, killing some Gestapo men
and making their *traction avant* his own car. Wearing captured
German uniform, he and Marcel began to tour the area. At first
they only had one uniform. So Frisé wore the tunic and Marcel
wore the hat. We expected them to get caught almost immediately, but they were a wily pair, the Frisé knew every road and
track in the area, and many times they passed through impossible
situations by sheer dash.

At first the Frisé confined his sorties to sabotage expeditions on
the railways and telephones. But soon the necessities of his cars
(after the first week he was not content with one, but always had
two or three Citroëns in his woodland 'garage'), obliged him to
make almost constant expeditions in search of what were now
necessities to him, petrol, oil, and tyres. Despite this, we began to
find the Frisé useful because he was mobile, and he was afraid of
nothing.

When Rioz was burned, the Frisé played the lead in what, for
him, was not an extraordinary incident.

Hearing that two friends of his were among the men rounded
up by the Germans inside Rioz, the Frisé took off with Marcel and
two others in their fastest car. They were able to direct themselves
on Rioz by the smoke that was already floating in a horrid, oily
column above the village. There were groups of Cossacks guarding
the roads with their shaggy ponies and little anti-tank guns. When
they saw the Frisé's German uniform they jovially waved the car
past. So they drove into the centre of the village, and by luck they
found the house where their friends were. When they had released
the prisoners and tied up the guards, they naturally took all the
German arms that they could find. And the Frisé saw something
that made his mouth water. It was a 9-mm. Italian sub-machine-
gun, and it seemed to the Frisé to combine the beauties of the little

American Winchester, the Sten, and the Schmeisser. He took it and checked that the magazine was full. Then he saw something else that interested him.

Sixteen Germans were sitting in a café across the street having a glass of Marc (or schnapps, as they called it, the barbarians). With the Frisé the two coincidences were strongly linked. Finding a dream weapon and seeing the dream target. The others had gone back to the car, for they were anxious to leave Rioz. The Frisé wiped his sweaty hands on the seat of his pants, took the new gun in his hand, walked across the road and kicked open the door of the café.

The Germans sat at marble-topped tables around the room.

One good swinging burst, and I have the lot, thought Frisé. His prospective targets sat frozen momentarily in terror, gazing at the figure in the doorway with its fierce frizz of hair.

Frisé squeezed on the trigger. Nothing happened. He had forgotten before he crossed the road to see how this weapon worked. Now it was obviously on 'safe'. He searched desperately for the safety-catch with his spare fingers. He was still searching when he noticed that the Germans were getting busy. Four or five of them were drawing guns. He leaped backwards and sideways out of the doorway, a stream of bullets following him. Doubling round the corner he found the car, started up and all ready to go. The same Cossacks who had waved them in waved them out. Sixty yards beyond their post the Frisé told Marcel to stop.

'What is it now?' asked Marcel and the others.

But the Frisé was leaning half his body out of the window. One shot rang out from his new sub-machine-gun, a pause, then a short burst.

'Drive on,' he said. But Marcel did not need to be told because the Cossacks had flung themselves on the roadway and were busily answering the Frisé's fire.

'I just wanted to see that it worked,' the Frisé explained. 'You see, it's got two triggers. The front one fires single rounds, and the other bursts. That will take a little getting used to.'

Apparently it did. The following day when he was explaining the new weapon to me he accidentally put a short burst within two inches of my right big toe.

Yes, the Frisé was wonderful. But Paincheau was the real discovery. Paincheau was supreme. For the bulk needs of our headquarters or the Maquis we fell back on him.

The first thing I desired to end was the tobacco situation. And

Paincheau ended it for us. He sent some men and trucks to Besançon and, working with a gang he ran in the town, they went to the place where French tobacco for the use of the German military garrison was stored. Breaking into the warehouse, these men coolly loaded their trucks with hundreds of cases of cigarettes. Germans passing in the street never imagined that anything illegal was going on. One night's work in the grand manner had provided enough cigarettes for all our Maquis for months. Paincheau had killed the *bureau de tabac* menace.

Next we asked him for boots, and these he supplied in the same grand manner. The Frisé also captured a truck-load of boots. All the Maquisards, including the officers, now appeared in brand-new lemon or banana-coloured boots. This became such a menace to security that we had to issue an order that all boots were to be dirtied or stained dark before worn. It was said that when a customer entered a shoe-shop in Besançon to ask for a pair of boots, the salesman said:

'But why not join the "Équipes Boulaya", monsieur? There you get boots without disbursement and without coupons.'

The next thing was petrol. Paincheau already had fairly large stocks of this which he had requisitioned. But he decided that these must be increased. With his Besançon gang he devised the following plan. The main German petrol supply in Besançon was kept in tanks which were in a guarded building. One night Paincheau's men drew up in a large tanker truck beside one wall of the building which was not guarded. One of the men was a mason. Scientifically and silently he cut a hole in the brick wall. His comrades ran a pipe through the hole and into a tank in the interior. All night they pumped petrol out of the German store into their truck. As the first light of dawn came over the hills surrounding the city they stopped pumping and the mason rebuilt the wall. The tanker returned to Rougemont to empty its precious load. The following night the operation was repeated successfully. But now the level of the petrol in the tanks had sunk so drastically that the Germans discovered the loss. Since there were always guards on the door of the building, the Gestapo arrested all German soldiers who had been on this guard in the past seven days. Paincheau decided that we would get no more petrol. So that night four of his men volunteered to go back into the store building, to put two hundred pounds of sugar into the remaining stocks. They entered the building by the same route. The same mason closed the hole after them. The operation was an entire success.

7*

Once Boulaya was short of money. All our Maquisards were paid like soldiers regularly by the week on a fixed scale according to the number of their dependants. Their pay was small, but it was important that it should not be interrupted. Paincheau could get anything from a bottle of absinthe to a funeral cortège with a black-and-silver hearse, lilies, and black Belgian horses. He met us in a wood between Devecey and Bonnay and unstrapped from the back of his 'petrolette' an enormous sack.

'What have you there?' Boulaya asked.

'Eight million francs,' he replied calmly.

It was Gestapo money deposited in banks in Besançon. Paincheau explained that four men had succeeded in getting this money by several visits to banks with an accomplice, a woman who worked for the Gestapo. But the story was so complicated that I could not follow it. Perhaps it was because he spoke so softly. At any rate, the men who did the coup had only, we understood, kept two million of the German money for themselves, and the rest they presented to the Resistance. They were real patriots. Boulaya and I were greatly touched by the patriotism of the experts. We laughed a lot.

Jacques Paincheau was a magician. With his help we were able to organize the food situation. Where lesser beings thought in kilos, he thought in terms of truck-loads, barge-loads, warehouses. He could produce sugar, rice, gruyère, yes, even tyres for vehicles and chocolate by the ton. And all taken from the enemy. Although, like a skilful prestidigitator, he produced all those valuable things without apparent effort, his coups were all the result of faultless planning and execution. He worked everything out to the minutest detail, and he was prepared to lead his men into anything that he planned. He and I became close friends. We were not able to meet very frequently because we were both too busy. But each time that I met him I found that his mind was packed with ideas for work, and each time they were new ideas. Like the Frisé, Paincheau wasted no time on women, or playing around.

When Laval fled to Belfort with his retinue of Darnan's Militia and German S.S., Paincheau sent up three of his best men in a car to see if they could get near to Laval. One of the men, the leader, was the young brother of Gros-Claude, a powerful, squarely-built young man, and a crack shot.

I happened to be with Paincheau in his Rougemont headquarters when young Gros-Claude returned.

'Hullo, he has a new car, anyway,' said Paincheau.

It was a small but smart black car with whitened tyres. A car that reeked of Paris (or Vichy)—and women, and furs, and perfume.

'Guess who this automobile belongs to?' shouted Gros-Claude. 'To Darnan himself. And we took two people in it, a man and a woman.'

They had found at Belfort that Laval was too well guarded. They could not get near him. But they picked up the black car and its occupants, who appeared to be stragglers from the entourage. Gros-Claude wanted the car, so he pushed his pistol in at the window and told the man sitting at the wheel to get into the back beside the woman. The driver appeared greatly perturbed, but he obeyed this command without recourse either to the handsome sub-machine-gun that lay all ready with a round in the breech on the seat beside him, or to the American Colt, also loaded, that filled the well-polished leather holster nestling under his coat. The woman had a gun in her handbag. But only a tiny, mother-of-pearl affair. There was nothing unusual in that. She was beautiful too, said young Gros-Claude. He had left one of his companions in the other car with orders to follow the black machine. He now took his place behind the wheel of this new one, and drove out of Belfort. His companion on the front seat turned half round so that he could watch the man and woman they had taken, and he held a pistol just in case they were troublesome, but they chatted and smoked all the way and assured their captors that they were charmed to be charmed away from the Laval entourage. They had wanted for a long, long time to join the Resistance. The Maquis was the life. . . . They had met continuous German convoys on the journey back from Belfort. One German officer had tried to stop them, but they had run past. There were two bullet-holes in the back car. . . .

'Where are the prisoners?' interrupted Paincheau.

'Up in the wood.'

'And their papers?'

'Also up in the wood. We took them from them at Belfort. I hadn't time to look at them.'

'Come on. We may as well see who they are. The car is pleasant. Well done.'

The wood covered only an acre or two. It was isolated, and had to be approached by rough farm tracks. People were brought here for questioning. It would have been dangerous to take even innocent strangers to an ordinary Maquis. And here La Marche and other traitors had been killed.

Two fat wallets and a woman's handbag lay on a tree-stump.

As Paincheau looked at the first wallet, an expensive affair in real
leather and silver, his breath came in a sudden hiss. He whipped
round, looking at the two prisoners who sat smoking on a bank.
And he spat at them one word:

'*Miliciens!*'

He went through document by document, photograph by
photograph, the contents of the two wallets. They were the records
of vile lives centred on Vichy for two years. Both the man and the
woman had possessed two identities, it appeared. Both had passed
to the 'Hôtel du Parc' at Vichy for their 'special police duties'. In
both wallets were addresses of 'suspected criminals', and following
each address were short notes such as: 'Denounced as listening to
British radio. Believed to have fifty thousand francs secreted in the
house in British and Swiss money.' What a picture of crime and
bestiality the two wallets showed. The man's wallet contained
photographs of his companions in uniforms and in over-smart
civilian clothes, and snapshots of women, many of them wearing
few or no clothes and posing lasciviously for the photographer.
And the woman's wallet held, among the pictures of cafés and
bathing-parties and young men, a signed portrait of Darnan himself.

'Stand up,' said Paincheau. His face and the face of every man
in the circle was full of loathing as he looked at the traitors who had
lived in the rich and gruesome slime of the Militia.

How did they look, the traitors? The man was weak. You
could see that by his effeminate pointed face and the little mouth
that had a homosexual look to it (despite his wallet). He was a
tall, and at first sight a strapping man. But his neck was too long,
and his legs were knock-kneed. His hair was greased back and
shone like a solid surface. At the back of his head the long hair
swept back from his ears, met in a kind of interlocking parting.
He was dressed a little like Paincheau, except that he wore a pale
tie to accentuate his olive tan. A brown leather glove, the top
folded carefully down so that it did not touch his shirt-cuff, encased
one of his hands, the other played incessantly with the buttons on
the front of his coat. It was a coarse hand, like a peasant's with a
slab of dead, immobile flesh on the back of it, and many black hairs
growing out of the flesh and lying along it like healthy creepers.
His nails were carefully kept, and they shone. His eyes wandered
round and round the clearing and its occupants, except for Paincheau. He avoided looking at Paincheau. You felt that his face
would have been more comfortable with a little worldly smile
fixed on it below the thin line of moustache, but that he was forcing

a more serious expression because he did not want to annoy the men who stood around him. He answered Paincheau's questions in a voice that was rough, with a lot of slang and bad grammar. You knew what he was feeling there in the middle of the circle. He was feeling: 'So this is what it is like to die.' And then: 'It cannot be me. This only happens to other people.'

The woman was not so frightened. She thought too: 'This cannot happen to me.' But then she had more reason for believing such a thing, even though she admitted to all the facts that her wallet declaimed. Oh yes, she had been in the Militia. Yes, Darnan had given her the picture.

She hoped that her physical attractions would still pull her out. Gradually as they were questioned she increased the space that separated her from her companion, as though she was dissociating herself from him, disowning him. He was going to be killed. But not her.

Her eyes did not avoid Paincheau, they scarcely looked at anyone else. You could see her weighing up his clothes, his side-whiskers, his softly persistent, controlled voice. Again and again her eyes sought his. And he occasionally looked into her eyes, but his look said neither yes nor no. This was a woman of the type that the French would call a *poule*, but that the English would hesitate to call a tart. Tall and rather beautiful and voluptuous, she was quietly dressed with no jewellery except for two rings. Her dark hair looked soft and expensive. Her face was heavily made up with a very dark, purplish mouth. She was proud of her strong teeth, for she chose every opportunity to open her lips in a wide smile. Her nails were very long and pointed and of some clever colour between pink and red. They failed to elongate her hands. Ugly hands, the hands of a woman who might cook and make love well, but who would dislike doing the flowers.

Paincheau finished questioning the man first. When he had admitted to the story that the papers told, Paincheau left him coldly and began on the woman. The man had been uncomfortable under the questions of course, but now that Paincheau was finished with him, he seemed to find it unbearable there, doing nothing.

So he was given a spade and a pick and told to dig a grave. Paincheau did not ask the woman many questions. Soon the two were digging under the trees while the others watched. They might as well have dug one grave for the two of them. But without being told, they worked on two separate graves. They had been lovers in life too. At least the man had said so. The woman had said nothing

when this question was put to her. It was surprising the trouble they
took with their graves. Was it only that they wanted more minutes
of living? Or was it that they desired to lie well-covered under the
trees in their traitors' graves?

The man asked for permission to go into the trees and ease himself.
Paincheau nodded. Two men went with him. He was a long time
there. The woman worked alone in the clearing. Occasionally she
gave a dry sob as she laboured. The earth was hard packed, and
there were many slender tree roots below the surface. She was
making so little impression on the roots that Paincheau told a man
to help her. She threw out the loose earth while the man worked
with the pick, loosening the earth and wood for her. The smell of
her perfume hung vaguely in the clearing. Her handsome, Chinese-
looking shoes were shapeless now with the wet earth that clung to
them.

When the man came back from the edge of the clearing, he stood
for a little time looking down into the hole he had made for his
body. Then a long shudder caught him. As though he were touched
by an electric shock that began a shaking between his shoulder-
blades and stretched out in both directions up to the greased hair,
and down the legs in their wide trousers. When the shudder stopped
he ran for it.

He ran perhaps fifteen paces and then Jojo shot him with a
pattern burst of the Sten gun, five rounds thudding into the small
of the back. When he fell he skidded for a bit along the surface of
the ground. His body was limp and disjointed. He had an easy
death.

Paincheau did not like a mess. He made two men put the body
in the grave. The woman now climbed out of her grave. You got
the impression that she had been waiting for this. Indeed, she said:

'Now that he is—gone. Now I can say that I tried for a long time
to leave the Militia. I hated them all and their brutality. I always
tried to help any of you boys. I always wanted to be on your side.
Take me in the Maquis. Please take me in the Maquis, Monsieur
Jacques. I will cook or fight or spy or anything. Please, please,
Monsieur Jacques.' As she spoke she took little swinging steps
closer to Paincheau. Now she was kneeling hands locked together
and forming a rest for her upthrust chin.

'Think of the ways I could help you,' she said hoarsely. 'I could
lead you to Militians who are hidden away. I could show you where
to find money, cars, jewellery. I will do anything. I will tell you
what I could do. I could get Darnan for you. Give me the car and

send someone with me to Belfort. I will deliver Darnan to you. Please, Monsieur Paincheau.'

'Perhaps there is something in what she says,' one of the men said.

'Get up from your knees,' Paincheau told her. There was no expression on his face or in his voice.

She rose slowly from her knees and her outstretched hands caught on Paincheau's clothes and pulled herself up towards him. He put his hands behind him, the two arms rigidly stretched backwards so that he would not touch her. But perhaps she did not notice.

'Please, Monsieur Jacques. Please.' Her voice was softer, more caressing. Paincheau jerked his head at a man standing behind her, and bringing one of his hands round her body, made a slight sign. The man approached quietly, and raising his pistol while the woman still clutched at the motionless Paincheau, he blew away the back of her head.

Frisé came in on his *petrolette* as we were retiring to our barn to sleep. He had a German prisoner sitting on the carrier behind him, arms clasped around his waist. The prisoner had a livid bruise near the point of his jaw. Frisé explained that he had taken this man near Cirey. Held up at the point of the Frisé's pistol, the German surrendered. But ordered to get on the back of the small motor-cycle he quailed. He was frightened, with perfect reason, of two things: firstly, of sitting behind the Frisé, and, secondly, of being ambushed or even seen by other Germans. So the Frisé had hit him once on the jaw.

'Then what happened?'

'He fell down, and when he got up he agreed to sit behind me,' answered the Frisé.

'That is untrue,' interjected the German, who spoke reasonably fluent French. 'When you hit me you wept tears and you apologized. Then I saw that you were a decent fellow, so I agreed to sit behind you.'

'Liar,' shouted the Frisé. ' "Cuistot," give this pig of a Schlok something to eat.' Then he handed me a message he had collected from Gros-Claude, the elder, who was leading a band that attacked the Belfort road. They had killed seventy-five Germans that morning. Gros-Claude was improving.

It was a good parachutage. There were a lot of rifles and Brens, which were what we needed for ambushes and sniping. At the end of the afternoon the whole dump was closed down and everything incriminating disposed of. The last convoy waited to go off. It was our own truck which was to run a selection of arms for one hundred men down to the country near Bouclans. There one of Boulaya's Besançon companies that had been waiting so long had finally taken to the Maquis, and they were without arms. The Pointu, the sergeant of Colonial Infantry, and little Démaï were in the back of the truck, sitting on top of the deadly cargo. Pointu had three phosphorus grenades rolling inside a captured German helmet handy to his right hand. A supply of these grenades had arrived in this parachutage and they were invaluable for this type of work, particularly if you were pursued.

Paul, the American radio operator, for example, had been chased a week or two previously in his car by a car-load of Gestapo men. Paul knocked out the back window with his pistol-butt, threw one phosphorous grenade out backwards, and the enemy, car, Gestapo and all, disintegrated in a cloud of white smoke with a stabbing flame. Paul was now a veteran gunman. He had established his headquarters in the cellars of the old château at Ronchaux, and he had killed two other Gestapo men with my small .38 Colt.

The Frisé was most keen to use the phosphorus grenade. He was really a child. When there was some new weapon he simply burst with curiosity until he had tried it out on the enemy. He was going to act as advance-guard for the truck—or the 'arms convoy', as they called it—by riding ahead alone on his little *petrolette*. In that way if there was any trouble the Frisé would buy it alone. He liked working like that. Before he left I searched the insecure carrying-bags of his machine. As I had suspected, they contained two ordinary hand-grenades and four phosphorous grenades. I took them out while he eyed me sadly.

'Fool,' I said. 'You want to burn yourself. Why do you take such stupid risks?' He laughed at that, for he was always quite pleased when you got angry with him. Then he rode away. I watched them skylined for a minute on the road to Venise. The Frisé jerking along on his little motor-cycle and the truck following five hundred yards behind. And my heart filled with joy and pride that these men undertook gladly such dangerous missions.

Back in the Maquis there was terrible news. Maurice and Philippe had been taken by the Germans. An ambush had been set for them inside Besançon. The enemy had caught them with explosives and weapons in their possession. The car they had taken to Besançon on the night of the parachutage still stood outside Maurice's house. Nobody dared to touch it in case there was another German ambush there. I would never see them again. They were two of the best men.

The Maquisards were preparing for the night in the church when I arrived with Georges. They were going to bed early because they had done clearing patrols in the forest starting at dawn. Over in one corner a man lay his head swathed in bandages.

'Who's that?' I asked.

'The Frisé.'

'How did it happen, Frisé, my friend?' I asked, sitting on the floor beside his bed. 'Was it at the bridge?'

'Bridge nothing,' he replied gruffly. 'I am in this trouble because of you and your damned phosphorus grenades, Émile. Now the least you can do is to get me out of it.'

'Yes, of course. What happened?'

'I was riding my *petrolette* through Venise. There must have been a phosphorus grenade lying in the roadway. Before I knew where I was I found myself enveloped in white vapour. I went to the fountain to wash it off. An agonizing pain began. There is only a little on my face, but it hurts.'

'Who had left a phosphorus grenade lying in the middle of the roadway at Venise?'

' Well,' he admitted. 'I had three or four in the bag behind on my carrier. Maybe one of them fell out. The road is hellish bumpy in Venise.'

The retreating German Army came pouring into the valley, until in many places saturation point was reached, and there was no small space that did not hold a German. In places the valley smelled of death, and the woods were stained with a stain that would not wash out in years of wind and wetness, the stain of human rot and blood and pus.

There were two American armies pushing at the Germans, sweeping them clear of France, the 7th sweeping from the south, beginning from the shores of the Mediterranean, and the 3rd sweeping down from the north-west.

Vieilley village formed a boulder against the grey tide that, obeying the eastwards surge towards the Fatherland, pushed up the Ognon valley. The main German traffic flooded the big roads that ran by Vesoul and Belfort. It was a backwash that flowed up our valley. Sometimes it flowed as far as Bonnay.

But the villagers of Vieilley, helped by our Maquis, went out in the night and felled the big trees across the roads. When all the men and boys were needed for the work or for fighting the young girls kept watch for the German convoys.

Normally when the convoys approached the blocks of felled trees they turned tail. If they tried to pass the rather pathetic barriers they were fired on by Gustave and Gustave's nephew and the thin boy with the squint, and all the others who were lucky enough to have weapons. Sometimes the villagers would be helped by the Pointu or the fierce Frisé with a band of Maquisards. They would lie in the ditches and blast the enemy with Mills grenades or burn him with phosphorus.

So, by a miracle, Vieilley kept itself entirely clean of the German waves. Not one house was burned, not one girl was outraged. And since Vieilley formed a brave little buttress to the tide the other villages that I knew immediately behind it, going as far as Rigney, were also saved. They helped to save themselves too.

MAQUIS NOTEBOOK

BY JOSEPH KESSEL

THE LEADERSHIP *of the Maquis was usually home-grown. From every social stratum men of courage came to the top. Generals de Gaulle, de Benouville, and others came from the army. Georges Bidault, a civilian, rose from obscure professor to Maquis leader and eventually became Premier of France.*

Many of these Frenchmen were withdrawn to England and specially trained in covert operations and then dropped back into their home country to organize the underground. Joseph Kessel's Notebook of Philippe Gerbier is the journal of one of these leaders. Kessel worked in the French underground for three years. He wrote this notebook during the war. For security reasons he had to change the names of people and places, but nothing can hide the integrity, ingenuity, and courage of those who worked with him.

BACK from England yesterday. At the moment of plunging from the plane into the black night I remembered J. He had made a bad landing and broken both his legs. He nevertheless buried his parachute and dragged himself five or six kilometres to the nearest farm, where he was taken in. In my own case a rather acute stricture about the heart when the pilot signalled to me. Afraid for no reason. Not a bit of wind. Landed in a ploughed field. Buried the parachute. Knowing the region, had no difficulty finding the small local railway station.

Got off the train at the small town of C. I didn't want to rejoin our headquarters of the southern zone directly. The last telegrams sent to London were disturbing. Went to an architect friend of ours who treated me like a ghost. 'You come from England, you come from England,' he kept saying. He had recognized my voice over the radio. I didn't realize that it was so unmistakable. There I committed a rather stupid and serious blunder. Indiscretions are due not so much to malevolence, the temptation to talk or even stupidity as to admiration. Most of our people are carried away by their enthusiasm. They like to magnify, to create a halo around our com-

197

rades, especially the leaders. It keeps them going, rouses them and gives colour to their monotonous little everyday work. 'You know, X has done a magnificent thing,' says one who is in the know to another. And the latter feels a need to share his enthusiasm with a third. And so on until the story reaches the ears of an informer. There is nothing so dangerous as this generosity of feeling.

So, because I've been to London I am in danger of becoming the object of a cult.

A country priest has come to say mass at the château. He spends his days and nights going from farm to farm. 'You,' he says to a peasant, 'you have room to hide three men who refuse to go to Germany.' 'You,' he says to another, 'you must feed two more,' and so on. He knows exactly what each one can do. He has a lot of influence and people obey him. He has been reported to the Germans and warned by the French authorities. 'I have no time to lose,' he says. 'Before I go to prison I should like to place three hundred.' It's become a kind of sport. A race against time.

A good day:
1. A radio transmitter is operating at the home of the farmer's wife who gave us shelter before our departure in the submarine.
2. Felix has left the clinic with his ankle quite cured and a flourishing beard. He reports that he is in touch with Lemasque.
3. Mathilde has arrived.

She escaped with sixty suspects from the Palais de Justice in Paris, where they had been taken for questioning. She doesn't know how it was arranged, nor by whom. Inside accomplices, most probably. At a given word they had only to follow the corridors as far as the door leading to the Place Dauphine, open it and walk out.

Mathilde remained in hiding in Paris for three days. She resisted the violent temptation to see her children. She maintains that she never has done and never will do anything so hard. She showed me a photograph which she managed to hide through every search. Six children, from the oldest, a girl of seventeen, to the baby whom Mathilde wheeled around for so long, lying on piles of forbidden newspapers. 'I'm sure my big Thérèse will take good care of the little ones,' Mathilde said. 'I won't be able to look after them till the war is over.' She took back the picture and hid it again. The way she did this gave me the feeling that it would be a long time before she looked at it again. She has asked for work right away, lots of work, dangerous work. I said I would think it over. I know she can do a lot and do it well. I must find the best possible use for her. Meanwhile she is staying at the château.

Long talks with Mathilde. I knew from the chief that she was a remarkable woman, but even so she astonishes me. She was born to organize, to command, and at the same time to serve. She sees things in straight, simple terms. Her will, her sense of method, her patience and her hatred of the German are all equally strong. Now that all her family ties have been cut by the enemy she has become a formidable instrument against him.

In prison Mathilde learned a lot about disguises, the ways of escape, the technique of assassination. I am taking her on as my second in command. She is going to tour the whole Southern Zone to make contact with the sector leaders. She will rejoin me in a large town. The liaisons here are much too slow.

News of Felix from Jean-François.
Felix was arrested in the street by two men who spoke perfect French, but were agents of the Gestapo. He was questioned without being too badly beaten. As he would not admit his identity, three of the Gestapo took him to his house in the middle of the night. His wife and his little boy, terrified as they were and knowing nothing of Felix's underground activities, made no bones about recognizing him. The German policeman beat him in front of his wife and child till he fainted. Then they began a search, smashing everything in the room. Felix came around again, but this time he didn't move. He had the presence of mind to lie still and recuperate, as Jean-François put it, and suddenly he dashed to the window, broke through the shutters and jumped into the street. His room was on the second floor. He sprained an ankle, but ran all the same. A patrol of French cyclist police was passing. Felix told the sergeant what had happened. They took him to one of our people. The next day he was in one of our clinics, the next in another, the next in still another. It was only there that the Gestapo lost trace of him. Felix has his foot in a light plaster and will soon be out. He has asked me for a new assignment. He won't be able to see his wife and child again till the war is over. He thinks his wife is very angry.

Was it accident, luck, premonition or instinct? I left the château a week ago. Two days after my departure the Baron de V. was arrested at the same time as our sector leader. Both have already been shot.

A resistance group removed many of the sewer gratings in Marseille one nightfall. The Germans and their friends being the only ones having the right to go out after the curfew, there was no one to regret among those who suffered broken bones at the bottom of the sewers.

At all the big railway stations, the Gestapo and the French police who are at their orders post men gifted with an exceptional visual memory, who have carefully studied the photographs of the patriots they are looking for. They are 'physiognomists' like the employees we used to see in the doorway of the gambling rooms in big casinos, whose job was to remember the faces of all the players.

Mathilde has come back from her tour. She has given me a complete report on our sector. She saw everyone. She spent every night in trains. It's less tiring, she claims, than looking after a large family when you are poor. To tell the truth she no longer looks like a housewife. I think her new way of life and a kind of cold, desperate fury have transformed her expression and her way of moving. But she has been working at it as well. She told me that she changed her personality several times in the course of the trip. Sometimes she would powder her hair and wear an austere black dress, at other times she would use a lot of make-up and dress conspicuously. 'I change fairly easily from the old lady bountiful to the old tart,' she says in her matter-of-fact way.

One of the most important things she did was to establish relations with the local chiefs of the other groups to avoid overlapping and interference in operations. It sometimes happens that two or three different organizations are simultaneously working for the same objective: sabotage, train-wrecking, a raid or an execution. If there is no contact the number of men involved in an assignment is uselessly multiplied, and so are the risks. And that makes one or two squads that might be used elsewhere. It is important, moreover, to avoid the risk of a minor operation bringing the police down on a district where a more extensive operation is in preparation. On the other hand the exchange of plans increases the chances of leakage and indiscretion.

This is the eternal problem of underground life. It is impossible to make recruits, to act, without taking people into one's confidence, and yet to take people into one's confidence is dangerous. The only remedy is to partition everything to limit the damage. The Communists are the great masters of partitioning, as in everything connected with the underground life. Mathilde has come back full of admiration for the strength, the discipline and the method which she found among them. But short of working underground a quarter of a century there is no way of catching up with them. They are professionals, we are still paying our apprentice fees.

Mathilde has found an attic in the house of a little dressmaker. She said she was a nurse. To-morrow she will have her papers. She is going to direct one of our fighting units.

The chief is in Paris.

I relayed to him verbally, via Jean-François, the contents of a large stack of mail. Jean-François is back. The chief agrees that Felix, Lemasque, and Jean-François take charge of the Maquis on the spot. He approves of my having entrusted Mathilde with her present post.

On his way to Paris Jean-François was carrying a valise full of tracts. He had also put a ham in the valise. He feels sorry for his brother. As a matter of fact, the chief is dying of hunger. . . . In the street Jean-François was suddenly grabbed by a *garde mobile* and had to open his valise. The guardsman examined the contents thoroughly. His face wore a hard look. Jean-François was preparing to drop it and run. But the guard merely said to him, 'You oughtn't to mix up the black market with the business of fighting the Boches. It's not right.' When Jean-François told his brother the story, the chief was deeply moved by it. Much more than by the adventures in which so many of our people lose their lives.

The Gestapo has enormous sums at its disposal for its informers. We know a small town of ten thousand population where the Gestapo budget is a million francs a month. With that it has been able to buy four well-placed informers. It would be easy to liquidate them, but I think it's better to keep them for the final settlement. Traitors whose faces are known are less dangerous.

The Bison is still unbeatable. Mathilde asked him for four German uniforms. The Bison got them. That means for certain the death of four German soldiers. We will never know how the Bison did it. He has the discretion of a Foreign Legionary.

Mathilde amazes him and inspires his respect. He says of her, 'She's somebody.'

Have moved again. Have taken an apartment under a fifth alias. My papers: A Colonial officer on leave. Inoculations against malaria. Mathilde, as a nurse, comes to give me the injections.

Mathilde's first operation.
One of our most successful group leaders had recently been moved from the prison where he was held to a hospital. Yesterday evening an ambulance with four German soldiers and a nurse drew up before the hospital. The nurse showed an order from the Gestapo to hand our group leader over to her. Neither Mathilde nor her men had to use their weapons.

Felix, Lemasque, and Jean-François are working all-out to organize a few mountain shelters where men who have refused to be deported are in hiding.
Visited Lemasque's sector.
I am not given to emotion, but I don't think I shall ever forget what I saw. Hundreds and hundreds of young people returning to a state of savagery. They can't wash. They can't shave. Their long hair hangs over cheeks burned by sun and rain. They sleep in holes, in caves, in the mud. Food is a terrible daily problem. The peasants do what they can, but it can't go on indefinitely. Their clothes fall off in tatters, their shoes go to pieces on the rocks. I saw boys shod with sections of old tyre or even strips of bark tied to their feet with string. I saw others who had on nothing but an old potato sack split in two and tied round their waist like a loin-cloth. It is becoming impossible to tell where these boys come from. Are they peasants, workers, clerks, students? They all wear the same hunger, the same wretchedness, the same hardness and the same anger on their faces. Those whom I visited were well disciplined under Lemasque and the helpers he had chosen. We get as much food and money as we can. But there are thousands of fugitives in the various 'Maquis'. No secret organization can take care even of their most elementary needs. Must they then die of hunger or take to looting or give themselves up? And winter has not yet come. Woe to those who put such a choice before our young men.

Lemasque has made amazing strides. The duties he had assumed when I was in London, his present job have taught him decision and authority. He controls his nerves. His enthusiasm is held in leash but shines through like a muffled fire. He exerts an unmistakable, powerful ascendancy over the instinctive kind of people he commands.

Felix has sent me a liaison agent with a whole list of things needed in his Maquis. At the bottom of the list the following note:

'Vichy has sent a company of *gardes mobiles* into this region to hunt us out. I have made contact with the captain. We have talked things over and we understand each other. He said to me, "Don't be afraid. I was an officer of the Republican Guard. I took my oath to defend the Republic. To-day the Republic is in the Maquis. I shall defend it." '

Mathilde has made a discovery which definitely confirms certain information about which we were not quite sure.

The dressmaker where Mathilde has taken an attic has a son of about twelve. Like all town children in our time he has a grey complexion, flabby muscles and a famished look in his eyes. He is very gentle and has great delicacy of feeling. Mathilde is very fond of him. This little boy works as a page at the Hotel T. The job is a good one, not so much for the wage that he gets as for the scraps from the restaurant that he is sometimes given. Mathilde was invited to share some of these feasts. She says nothing was more pathetic than to see the little boy pretending that he wasn't hungry so as to give as much as possible to his mother, and the mother enacting the same comedy when neither could take their eyes off the food.

Well, lately the little boy had been sleeping terribly. He would moan, weep, scream and choke in his sleep. The shivering fits that came over him were almost convulsive. He seemed delirious and he would call out, 'Don't hurt her. . . . Don't kill her. . . . Stop, *please* stop crying like that.'

The frantic mother consulted Mathilde, whom she still takes for a nurse. Mathilde spent part of the night listening to the boy's nightmares. Then she woke him up gently. She asked him questions. A woman who has had as many children as she has and who has loved them as much knows how to talk to youngsters. The dressmaker's son told her everything. About a week ago he was put at the disposal of the guests who occupy the fourth floor of the hotel where he works. He has to stand by on the landing and answer the bell. The whole floor, he says, is occupied by gentlemen and ladies who speak French well but are all Germans. They receive a lot of people. There are men or women who always come between two German

soldiers. And these French people always have an unnatural look
in their eyes, as if they were afraid and didn't want to show it.
And they are always taken to the same room, No. 87. Almost
always cries and peculiar noises and moans can be heard in this room.
The noises stop and then go on again and again. 'Till it makes you
sick, I swear to you, Madame,' said the child to Mathilde. 'The
voices of the women they are hurting are worse than anything.
And if you could see the state they're in when they bring them back.
Often they are taken into another room, and then brought back.
It begins all over again. I didn't want to talk to anybody about it
because I'm afraid to think about it.'

That is how we located the torture chamber for this town.

The following day Mathilde asked me what advice I would have
given the dressmaker about her son.

'Why, to take him away from the hotel right away,' I said.

'Well, I persuaded her to let him stay on,' said Mathilde. 'It is so
valuable to have a spy in such a place. Especially an innocent
one.'

Mathilde's lips contracted and she gave me a sad, questioning
look. I was forced to tell her she was right.

The captain of the *gardes mobiles* has kept his promise to Felix.
He had not found a single deserter from deportation in the Maquis.
He does, to be sure, execute a daily round of the woods and the
valleys, but he makes a point of sending out a motor-cycle scout
ahead of time who creates an infernal racket. This gives everyone
warning. But the captain has just advised Felix that two officers of
the S.S. have arrived to superintend and direct the manhunt.

A brothel owner said to one of his friends who operates a bar,

'My house has been requisitioned by the Boches. It has never been
worked so hard. But I don't want this money. It burns my fingers.
I should like to use it against the Boches.'

The bar-keeper communicated this wish to the Bison, who in
turn confided it to Mathilde. She saw the brothel owner.

'How will I know it is really being used against the Boches?' he
asked her. 'We will put out an agreed phrase over the London
radio,' Mathilde answered. We sent the phrase on. It was repeated
by the B.B.C. We have received five hundred thousand francs.
What is more, the brothel owner has put a wonderful estate at our
disposal. An old general who has helped us a lot through his con-

nexions in the Army and who is being hunted by the police has already taken refuge there.

An adventure of Felix's.

The captain of the *gardes mobiles* gave warning that the two S.S. officers were beginning to suspect the trick he was playing and that he would not be able to resist their pressure much longer. Felix set himself to studying the movements and habits of the two Germans. The company of the *gardes mobiles* is billeted in a fair-sized village. The two Germans have rented a chalet on the mountain slope. Getting up very early they always go and have breakfast in a little inn located between their chalet and the village. The path that leads to the inn has high embankments on both sides and at one point makes a sharp bend. It was a perfect spot for an ambush.

Felix has a tommy-gun in his armoury. He could finish the Germans off alone. But in the village there are two stout fellows who tell all and sundry that they are ready to do anything against the Germans. One is the postman, the other the harness-maker. Felix decides that this is his chance to try them out. If they are just café-braggarts it is better to know where you stand. If they are really able to act, they must be brought in. Felix suggests the job to the postman and the harness-maker. They accept.

At dawn the three men are at the bend in the path. Felix has his tommy-gun, the postman and the harness-maker their revolvers. The sun is coming up. The Germans approach. They are talking in their own language and laughing very loud. They have no anxiety. They are the masters in a conquered country. Felix appears and points his tommy-gun on them. The two officers look for a second at the short bearded man with his round red face. They put up their arms.

'They understood right away,' Felix told me; 'their faces didn't even move.' Felix had only to press the trigger to finish them. But he wanted the postman and the harness-maker to prove themselves and pass their apprenticeship. He ordered each of them to kill a man. They came up and fired several shots, closing their eyes a little, it appears. The Germans fell without losing their composure, quite simply. Their grave was prepared in advance. Felix and his accomplices threw the bodies in and put the squares of turf back on top. Except for these three men no one will ever be able to find the corpses of the two S.S. officers.

'It was a clean job,' said Felix. 'But between you and me, it sort of upset me. Those bastards really had guts. And that look they gave when they realized what was up sort of hit me in the stomach. We hid our arms and those of the S.S. and went and had coffee in the bistro where the Boches were going. I wondered how the postman and the harness-maker would react because I myself, though I've seen some pretty bad things, still felt a little yellow about the gills. Well, by Jove, they swallowed the black juice perfectly calmly and before long they were both snoring on the bench. In the afternoon the postman started off with his letters and the other went back to selling his junk as if nothing had happened.'

Felix rubbed his bald spot and remarked, 'They've certainly changed the French.'

A long talk with Louis H., chief of a group with which we often co-operate. We first discussed a very specific matter. Louis H. has three men in a concentration camp whom he highly values. The Gestapo has demanded the surrender of these three men. They are going to be handed over to the Gestapo via train in four days. Louis H.'s organization has had terrible losses in the last month, and he no longer has enough men to try to free his comrades. He came to ask me if we could undertake the operation. I shall give the necessary orders.

Mathilde and the Bison have left to organize the escape of the three prisoners with which Louis H. entrusted us.

An adventure of Jean-François'.

The Maquis region where Jean-François is working is not very far from a good-sized town where he often goes for provisions, liaisons, false papers, etc. He has gone too often, I suppose, for he was arrested there by the French police as he got off the train.

From his brief experience in the reconnaissance corps Jean-François has kept a taste for hand-grenades, of which he had three in his suitcase. As his two captors and he were making their way with the crowd of passengers through the narrow station exit, Jean-François was able to open the lock of his suitcase and dump the contents on the ground. In picking them up again he managed to slip the grenades into his pockets. While he was being taken to the Commissariat he stooped down twice to tie his shoelaces. The grenades were left in the gutter.

The police then grew a little suspicious of his movements and handcuffed him.

'Take those off a moment so that he can sign his deposition,' said the *commissaire* when Jean-François was brought before him. Hardly were the handcuffs off when Jean-François' two arms shot out and struck the officers on each side. They managed to seize him as they fell, but he shook them off, pushed the *commissaire* away and ran for the door of the police station. A priest was just entering at this moment.

'Stop thief, stop thief!' yelled the two policemen who had started after Jean-François. The priest blocked the doorway.

'Gaullist! Gaullist! . . .' cried Jean-François.

The priest let him pass and immediately barred the way for the two officers. They rolled all together on the doorstep. While the officers were extricating themselves from the priest's cassock Jean-François turned down one street, then another and still another and was at last out of reach.

But for how long? They had his description. His jacket had been torn in the struggle. By going to the home of any of the people he knew he ran the danger of putting the police on the track of the whole local organization. He must leave town as quickly as possible. But the station was more closely watched than any other spot. Jean-François decided to leave on foot, but first he had to change his appearance. He went into a barber's shop that was empty and called for the owner, who came shuffling out of the back room in his slippers. He was unprepossessing, weasel-faced, with cautious little eyes hiding behind flabby eyelids. A real informer's head. But Jean-François had neither time nor choice. He explained that he wanted his moustache shaved off and his hair, which was naturally ash-blond, dyed black.

'A joke I'm going to play,' he explained. 'A bet I made with my girl-friend.'

The barber made no reply and silently went to work. From time to time Jean-François tried to catch the barber's eye in the mirror, but never managed to. For a whole hour they did not exchange a word.

'It's all up,' Jean-François was thinking.

'How's that?' the barber asked at last.

'Fine,' said Jean-François. He was in fact quite unrecognizable. His hard, dark face was even painful for him to contemplate. He gave the barber twenty francs.

'I'll bring you the change,' said the barber.

'Never mind,' said Jean-François.

'I'll bring you the change,' the barber repeated. He disappeared behind a dirty curtain. Jean-François was so certain that he was about to be denounced that he hesitated between two alternatives—whether simply to escape or to put this man out of the way before he fled. He had no time to decide. The barber came back almost at once with an old raincoat over his arm.

'Put this on quick,' he said in a low voice, still without looking at Jean-François. 'The coat is no beauty, but it's the only one I have. You'd soon be noticed in those town clothes.'

The three comrades with whose escape Louis H. has entrusted us took the train yesterday at seven-forty-five. They were in a third-class compartment with handcuffs and guarded by five gendarmes. Mathilde got on the train at the same time. She wore a black coat and a scarf of the same colour on her head. She found herself in the prisoners' coach. The train passed through several stations, then it sped on through a deserted countryside. At eleven-ten Mathilde pulled the emergency signal, then slipped into the compartment adjoining the one where the prisoners were, went to the window and unfastened her black scarf. A few moments later, as the train was coming to a stop, the Bison and two of our men emerged from behind the railway embankment and through the outside door entered the compartment where the gendarmes and Louis H.'s comrades were. Our men had sub-machine-guns. The gendarmes took off the prisoners' handcuffs and then we made them take off their own clothes, which they did not seem to mind too much. Louis H.'s comrades and our men took the gendarmes' uniforms and their carbines and jumped out on the line. The guard appeared on the scene at this moment.

'You can go on now,' the Bison cried to him. The train got into motion again. Mathilde did not even get out.

The place selected for the abduction is about twelve kilometres from a fairly large estate. This property belongs to the big wine-grower who offered me the tank. He had been hiding on the other side of the embankment with a cart and two horses. In the cart there were some big empty wine barrels. Louis H.'s men and ours hid in the bottom of the barrels. The wine-grower took them home to his still-room. The Bison and his two comrades left at nightfall. The escaped prisoners are going to stay hidden away at the wine-grower's for a week. And also put a little fat on.

In the course of a trip down their way I spent an evening with them. The three men have no flesh left on their bones. The discipline in their camp was much more severe than in the one where I knew Legrain. No parcels allowed, a lot of useless hard labour, a constant surveillance, sentries at night in every hut. High-tension current in the barbed wire. The prisoners were so hungry that they ate the grass which grew in the camp. The commander made his inspection every morning with a riding-crop. That set the tone for the guards.

'However, one day the brutalities suddenly ceased,' one of the escaped men told me, 'thanks to the intervention of the most ridiculous of our comrades. This country squire in normal times spent his life writing adventure stories which were published by the local papers. He carried on his resistance in the style of his novels. The miracle is that he has not been shot. We have never seen a man more impulsive, loose-tongued, fantastical. But one day he told the commander that he had a wireless transmission set hidden in the very camp, that he was in communication with London and that he would have the commander executed if a single prisoner was struck once more. The old brute was frightened.'

There was in the camp a section for Communists. They were, as always, treated in a particularly appalling way. Somehow a few of them managed to escape. Three days later they came back and gave themselves up again. They had escaped *without the party's authorization*. The party was sending them back to the camp.

The plans I had taken had to be handed over by me to a large business office in Paris on the Avenue de l'Opéra. Two days later, having travelled only by small local lines, I presented myself there. As I was about to ring the bell the door opened of its own accord. A hand fell softly on my wrist and drew me inside. I found myself facing German policemen. Since morning the office had become a trap.

'Who are you? What have you come here for?' I made up a reason which fits in with the normal operations of the business. 'Your papers?' I showed my latest ones which were fabricated subsequently to my being shadowed by the two old men. One of the policemen went to the telephone and spoke with the Gestapo headquarters. I understand German and I followed the conversation. At the other end of the wire they asked the policeman to read a list of names. I heard the one which I went under only ten days ago. The policeman came back to me, gave me back my papers, pushed me to the door. I tried to go down as slowly as I could. In the concierge's lodge I thought I saw a man in spectacles. I went out, started walking and stopped before a shop window. A few paces from me was a man with glasses. Then I went as far as to a bakery that I know which has a double exit. In this way I gained a few minutes. I saw a fire station where I found some well-disposed people. They hid me in a fire-wagon and took me in their car to a second-hand furniture dealer on the left bank, one of our best agents. I handed him my plans and the next day I left Paris pushing a hand-cart full of old chairs.

Took a studio for our contacts.

In this house I pass for a painter who likes to paint when he pleases or entertain his friends.

This morning I had a rendezvous at the studio with Jean-François, Lemasque and Felix. It was months since I had seen them, and we had a lot of things to decide for their Maquis. As I was coming up to the house the concierge was on the doorstep desultorily beating an old rug. Seeing me cross the street she suddenly began to beat it with a kind of frenzy. This concierge has never been one of us and knows nothing of my activities. All the same, I did not go in.

This woman has deliberately saved my life. An extremely simple chain of circumstances has led to a catastrophe.

On leaving his region Jean-François delegated his command to an ex-officer who has plenty of authority but too much optimism and no conspiratorial sense. It became necessary for him to send a message to Jean-François and he sent him a liaison agent. He chose a very young chap without any experience and, instead of sending him to a relay, he gave him the street address and the number of the studio. The lad, while waiting between trains, fell asleep. He was awakened by a comb-out. They found my address on him and he was not able to invent a plausible explanation. A trap was laid and Lemasque, Felix and Jean-François were caught. It was only after this that the concierge thought of using the rug as an alarm signal.

News of Jean-François.

The police officer questioned him in the studio, having before him all the reports found on Jean-François, Lemasque and Felix. Jean-François answered whatever came into his head. Suddenly he bit the commissaire in the hand so violently that he took a piece of his palm off. He seized the documents, knocked over the two inspectors one on top of the other and went down the stairs like a hurricane. He got the reports safely to me and has gone back to the Maquis with my instructions.

News of Felix.

On a scrap of onion-skin paper Felix had the address of an emergency apartment rented in the name of a young girl, where I would go from time to time in the guise of protector. This address Felix had written in a code of his own. When questioned, he managed to interpret the signs as a rendezvous taken on a certain day and a certain hour in a public square with an important leader of the resistance. He let this come out with the hesitations, the evasions and the reticences which were needed for him to be believed. In the same way he agreed to lead two policemen to this supposed rendezvous.

He arrived in the middle of the square, leading the policemen by a few steps. A tram was just then passing. Felix jumped in, slipped through and out the other side, where he disappeared in the crowd.

Then he wanted to let me know and went to the emergency address. But in the meantime the girl who had rented it had come to the studio, where the police had been able to make her talk. Felix was recaptured.

He is locked up like Lemasque in Vichy in the cellars of the Hotel Bellevue which has been requisitioned by the Gestapo.

I saw in the factory a young worker who spent eight months without cause in the German quarter of the prison of Fresnes. He has two ribs broken and he limps for life.

What is most unbearable according to him is the heavy smell of pus which has spurted out over the walls of the cells.

'The smell of our tortured comrades,' he says.

I think of Lemasque. I think of my old friend Felix.

News of Lemasque.

He was shut up in the same cellar as Felix, with handcuffs and irons on his feet. Felix was considered the more dangerous. He had aroused the savage fury of the Gestapo by outwitting them. They questioned him the very first day. He did not return from the questioning, but that night, by the light of the bulbs in the ceiling, Lemasque saw Felix's corpse being dragged through the corridor by a rope tied round the neck.

There were no longer eyes in his face, no lower jaw. Lemasque was able to recognize him chiefly by the top of his bald head. Felix la Tonsure. . . .

Lemasque was so afraid of undergoing the same tortures that suddenly he *knew* that he would escape.

He succeeded (he will never be able to say how) in undoing the padlock that fastened the irons to his ankles. With his hand-cuffed hands he loosened the insecurely anchored bars of the cellar vent and, feet first, he wriggled out. There he was in the streets of Vichy with his hands still shackled. The only person he knew in Vichy was a ministry clerk who lived in a commandeered hotel. Lemasque had been to see him just once to obtain false papers. In the streets overrun by patrols of *gardes mobiles* and the Gestapo on their beats Lemasque, with his handcuffs, started off to look for the hotel. He would have to find it before dawn or he was lost. Hours went by. Lemasque kept wandering round Vichy. At last he thought he had found the spot. He entered the sleeping hotel. One last effort, a desperate effort of memory to recall the floor and the exact position of the room. At last Lemasque thought he remembered it. He knocked at the door, which opened. It was in fact the comrade he had been looking for.

That evening a friendly workman came with a hacksaw and freed Lemasque from his handcuffs. I have had the story confirmed by the ministry clerk and by the worker. Otherwise I should always have wondered if Lemasque had not weakened and thought up this escape in the interest of the Gestapo.

The resistance movement commits sabotage, attacks and kills, abundantly, obstinately and spontaneously. All the organizations have their combat groups. The guerrillas form a veritable army. The mass of German corpses has become so dense that the enemy has had to give up the hostage system. They can no longer line up one hundred dead Frenchmen for one dead German, unless they are prepared to assassinate the whole of France. The enemy has thus recognized publicly, as it were, that the country was triumphing over terror.

But the Gestapo goes on with its terrible work. It aims to replace hostages by suspects.

Lemasque, after his escape, took only a week of rest and got back to work. He has just been arrested again. By luck he is still, for the moment, in the hands of the French police. Mathilde has promised me that she will get him out of prison. However, as Lemasque knew where I live, I am changing my domicile.

Mathilde, with her hair dyed henna, heavy make-up and a cushion under her dress, has passed herself off as Lemasque's pregnant mistress. She has been given permission to see him. Lemasque's escape promised to be rather easy, thanks to inside accomplices, provided a rather dubious character who is Lemasque's cellmate can be got rid of. To this end Mathilde had slipped a small phial into Lemasque's pocket. Lemasque refused to poison the man, who is in all likelihood a spy.

Mathilde has passed Lemasque some chloroform. He refused to use it because he is afraid of giving an excessive dose. Yet time is pressing. The Gestapo is going to demand that Lemasque be handed over. I think he still remembers Paul Dounat.

Lemasque has been transferred to another prison. There he found one of our comrades who is in very bad shape from the questioning he has undergone. Mathilde had organized a rescue by main force for the day when Lemasque was led for the last time from the prison to the examining magistrate. Everything was ready. Our men were about to open fire. But Lemasque who was holding his comrade's arm gave Mathilde a negative shake of the head and continued to hold up the other who was dragging himself along with difficulty. On leaving the Palace of Justice both were handed over to the Gestapo. I felt an impulse of anger against Lemasque.

Felix's wife begs to be allowed to work for us. She had been in complete ignorance of Felix's underground activity. She learned of his end through one of our emissaries who was to give her a sum by way of financial relief, but who had explicit instructions to divulge no detail regarding the organization, no relay, no point of reference. Felix's wife refused the money and began to weep softly. 'My poor man,' she kept repeating. 'If I had only known, if I had only known.' She could not forgive herself for having so often reproached Felix for his absences, his apparent indolence.

I have no idea how she managed to ferret out one of our people. Through a series of intermediaries her request finally reached Mathilde, who alone knows my refuge and who has transmitted it to me. Felix's wife will be a liaison agent. It is the most dangerous work, but the wives of executed comrades have always accomplished these missions better than anyone.

We are assuming the responsibility for Felix's consumptive little boy.

Lemasque was taken to room 87. He fainted after half an hour of questioning. He regained consciousness. He swallowed a cyanide pill.

The most recent invention of the Gestapo questioners: They apply a dentist's drill to the gum till the point attacks the jawbone.

I have sent Mathilde and Jean-François to inspect our transmitting stations—or rather, what is left of them—one by one.

We have had a string of bad luck.

At the beginning of the resistance movement we could send out our dots and dashes without too great risk. The Germans were not in sufficient force to give full attention to the secret broadcasts and had little equipment. But at that time we lacked transmitting sets, experienced operators, continuous liaisons with England. The work was done in a rather disorganized and primitive way. To-day we are infinitely better equipped and trained. Only, as in every war, the enemy was quick to join the parade. He has a first-class technical personnel and his detection cars, disguised either as delivery, mail or Red Cross trucks, patrol, cruise, swarm and spy all over the country.

I happened to observe one of these cars coming close to its objective. It was travelling very slowly, at the pace of a man's walk. Before each house it would stop for a second and start off again smoothly and noiselessly. One felt that within an inexorable mechanism was reducing yard by yard the radius of approach. One had the impression that a choking monster was feeling out the dwellings one after the other and passing its tentacles through the walls.

It does not take much more than half an hour for a car, after it has caught the first waves, to reach the spot where the station operates. And half an hour is very short for getting contact with London and to transmit the messages. Then begins a struggle. While the operator works at his post a comrade stands lookout at the window, another comrade keeps watch in the street. As soon as he catches sight of the beast that is on the scent and feeling its way he makes a signal previously agreed upon to the man at the window. He in turn warns the operator. It is a game of speed and of luck. In the last week it has gone against us.

Ajax was taken completely by surprise. His watchers were keeping their lookout on the front of the house. The Gestapo came up an alley in the rear. This time the detection was concealed in a fire-wagon and it was by using firemen's ladders that the German police got in through the window. Ajax avenged himself as he could. He asked his assistant, 'What's happened to that time bomb?' The Gestapo agents were good and scared. Ajax took advantage of this to destroy his transmission code.

Of Diamant's arrest we have no details. We only know that in the midst of a message to London he suddenly tapped out the words, 'Police . . . police . . . police. . . .' And the broadcast was cut off.

Achille was the one I liked best. Before the war he was a waiter in a popular restaurant where I sometimes went. A little man, rather old, dark and gentle. He had learned to operate a radio very well. He was very conscientious and skilful. He always managed to get his messages through. Even when the detection car was spotted he would continue tapping. He knew how to stop just in time. He had an inner sense of seconds. Perhaps because he had been a waiter in a café. He must have miscalculated once. He was shot the day after he was caught.

When a man of the resistance movement is caught on simple suspicion he nevertheless has a chance to survive. But if this man is a Jew he is sure to die the most horrible death. In spite of this there are many Jews in our organizations.

Mathilde has wound up her tour of inspection at Augustine's farm, from which I left, last year, for Gibraltar. The operator, who is very young, had committed a gross blunder. His fiancée was spending a few hours at the departmental seat. He took the train to see her. He did not return. He was surely picked up in a raid and because of his age sent to Germany.

At the farm Mathilde and Jean-François found messages to be transmitted that had been brought by liaison agents. There was a bundle of them and some were extremely urgent. They studied the transmitting code and Jean-François, who is a good operator, began to tap out the messages.

The station was set up in one of the commons from which a long ribbon of road could be seen. Mathilde and Augustine stood by the window. A truck appeared. It was not going fast. It stopped for a moment in front of a deserted sheep-pen. 'Keep right on,' Mathilde said to Jean-François, 'but we've got to watch out.' The truck started moving again, stopped in front of an empty barn. 'Keep right on,' said Mathilde. The truck slowly grew larger. Jean-François was tapping very fast. The truck was skirting the fields of the farm. 'Another second and I'll be through with a telegram,' said Jean-François. 'Go ahead,' said Mathilde. The truck was coming. 'Take the set and run for it into the woods,' said Mathilde. Jean-François hesitated, he didn't want to leave two women alone. The men of the Gestapo were getting out of the truck. 'It's an order,' said Mathilde. When the German police entered the farm they found two silent women, dressed in black, quietly knitting. After a routine search they made their excuses and left.

Augustine's daughter, who is seventeen, has joined us. She had been wanting to for a long time. She took advantage of Mathilde's visit and of her authority to force her mother's consent. Madeleine will be paired as a liaison agent with Felix's widow, who is doing very good work.

When we ask people who, without belonging to an organization, help us to conceal arms, to take in comrades, when we ask them what would give them pleasure, they often answer, 'Have the B.B.C. say something for us.' This seems to them a wonderful reward.

Madeleine and Felix's widow have been arrested. Denounced by a militiaman. Mathilde has decided he must die.

One of our information agents ran into a patrol of four German soldiers in an absolutely forbidden zone. He fired fast and well. He killed them all and then committed suicide. He could have escaped. The way was free. We found this out through two Germans who survived and who were handed over to us. But he was too much afraid of being caught, tortured and made to talk. He had intended the last bullet for himself a long time before. He obeyed a reflex.

Felix's widow and little Madeleine have been taken to room 87. They were undressed completely. A man and a woman of the Gestapo (a married couple, it is believed) questioned them while sticking red-hot pins in their stomachs and under their nails. Felix's widow and Madeleine likewise underwent the torture of the dentist's drill which is sunk into the jawbone. They did not reveal anything. Between each of the tortures they sang the *Marseillaise*. This scene, which seems to be taken directly out of an absurd melodrama in the worst possible taste, is put down in an official German report. Leroux has transmitted a copy to me. He has likewise informed me that the two women vowed they would not talk.

This story has made a dreadful impression on Mathilde. Her face literally turned black. She keeps repeating endlessly, 'If I don't get Madeleine out of this God will never forgive me.' The thought that she persuaded Augustine to let her daughter go into the resistance movement is eating Mathilde's heart out. She does not think about Felix's widow. It's the features of the girl that haunt her. She is the same age as Mathilde's eldest daughter, whose gentle, regular features I have seen in a photograph.

Mathilde has committed an act of madness. She tried to rescue Madeleine by main force right out in the open street as she was being taken from the prison to be led once more to room 87. Mathilde had with her the Bison, Jean-François and three men of the combat groups. They are all fanatically devoted to Mathilde. They came close to succeeding, but a charge of the S.S. broke their attack. They fell back. A chase through the streets. Our men took to the roofs. Gunplay from behind chimneys. Several Germans killed but they got two of ours. The Bison and another wounded were caught. Mathilde and Jean-François succeeded in escaping. Mathilde has only aggravated little Madeleine's situation, and for a mere liaison agent she has broken up a whole combat group. And we have lost the Bison.

To lead the Gestapo to the location of a transmitting station which has never existed, the Bison had himself driven at night along a route which we had reconnoitred in advance. A chain was stretched between two trees across the narrow road. The dimmed-out head-lights failed to show it up in time. The car ran full speed against the chain. Mathilde and Jean-François cleaned out the Germans with tommy-guns. The Bison has a broken arm, but he will recover.

I went to a meeting of the resistance leaders. Leroux accompanied me with a warrant. I was Leroux's prisoner. An ideal safe-conduct.

The meeting lasted a long time. When it was concluded the chief said to me:
'There are fourteen of us here. Each one has risked his life in coming. I am not sure the practical results will justify this risk. But it

makes no difference. Underground France has held a council of war in defiance of the terror. That was worth while.'

And he said further:

'We are only fourteen, but we are borne up by thousands and probably by millions of men. To protect us combat groups are watching all the approaches that lead to this retreat, and will die before they let anyone get to us. Yet no one here feels pride or even a sense of power. We know that our soldiers change their names a hundred times and that they have neither a shelter nor a face. They move in secrecy, wearing shapeless shoes, on roads without sunlight and without glory. We know that this army is hungry and pure, that it is an army of shadows—the miraculous army of love and misfortune. And I have become conscious here of the fact that we are only the shadows of those shadows and the reflection of that love and that misfortune. That, above all, was worth while.'

Back at Leroux's. I transmit the warning to newcomers who wish to enter the ranks of our organization that they must not count on more than three months of freedom, that is to say of life. This will certainly not keep them out, but it is more honest.

MATHILDE WAS CAPTURED *by the Germans. They found the picture of her daughter and offered Mathilde a choice. She could reveal what she knew about the Maquis or have her daughter sent to a German Army brothel. Suicide was no solution so long as her daughter was in the hands of the Gestapo. Mathilde stalled for time and requested an opportunity to re-establish her contacts with the underground. She was released. Her companions loved her and realized her problem. They solved it for her when they shot her down from a speeding car.*

MISSION FOR A DICTATOR

BY OTTO SKORZENY

WITH ROMMEL CAUGHT *in the great nutcracker of the American and British forces in Africa and the defeat before Stalingrad, the German Staff saw the need for an emergency or special force. They sought to create such a force within the rigid frame of the Prussian military tradition.*

Karl von Clausewitz, the Plato of Prussia, had written scantily of irregular warfare. As a staff officer with the Russians, he had watched Tchernitchev's Cossacks and Lutzow's Black Rifles harass and confuse Napoleon. General Ludendorff's extension of the irregular cavalry techniques resulted in the blitzkrieg strokes which brought the easy German victories in the first years of World War II.

With a single exception, this was as irregular a tactic as the German military tradition developed. That single exception was the brilliant military leadership displayed by Paul von Lettow-Vorbeck in East Africa during World War I. Lettow-Vorbeck, with an initial force of two hundred and fifty Europeans and several thousand natives, out-generalled a vastly larger and better equipped force under the one-time guerrilla Jan Christian Smuts.

It was during this war that the first air-drop to guerrillas was attempted. Germany sent supplies to Africa by Zeppelin. The large craft returned from a 4,500 mile non-stop flight after being informed that East Africa was in British hands.

But in April, 1943, the Nazi generals were not thinking in terms of native troops, for whom they had nothing but contempt. Instead they called in a young Nazi veteran, Otto Skorzeny, to form a unit along the lines of the British Commandos.

After studying the tactics of their British counterparts, some of these German commandos were rushed, without Skorzeny, to Iran to aid in tribal attacks against the British. The tribes were quickly smashed and the Germans captured.

Skorzeny's first mission with his men was the release of Hitler's ally, Benito Mussolini. Il Duce had been imprisoned somewhere in Italy by his compatriots. No one knew exactly where.

Hitler saw the rescue as a propaganda coup and Mussolini as a rallying

*force for the disintegrating Fascisti. Skorzeny tells the story of Il Duce's
rescue himself.*

M^Y small 'personal information bureau' offered me almost
certain proof that Mussolini was in a hotel at the foot of the
Gran Sasso peak, and, of course, carefully guarded. For several days
we tried without result to obtain accurate maps of the region. As
the hotel was only completed shortly before the beginning of the
war, it did not figure on any map. We unearthed only two tips:
the report of a German resident of Italy who had spent his winter
holidays there in 1938 and the prospectus of a travel agency which
vaunted the beauties of this winter sportsmen's paradise in the very
heart of the Abruzzis.

Since these sources were certainly much too scanty to allow for
the preparation of so important a raid, we were obliged to take
photographs from the air at the earliest possible moment. General
Student lent me a plane equipped with an automatic camera and, on
the morning of September 8, I left the airport of Pratica di Mare,
near Rome, accompanied by Radl and the Information Officer of
Divisional G.H.Q. According to our plans, this officer was to play
an important part in our projected operation.

Since at all costs we must conceal our intent from the Italians, we
agreed to cross the Abruzzi range at a height of about 1200 feet.
Even the pilot was not in the secret; he had been told we were to
take photos of some Adriatic ports.

When we were about twenty miles from Gran Sasso we decided
to take several trial shots with the huge camera embedded in the
belly of the plane. We soon discovered that the grooves for the
bands of the film had been obstructed by the frost. The camera was
therefore useless. Luckily we had brought along a portable camera;
we would have to use it as best we might. Already we had begun to
suffer from the cold for we wore only light African Expeditionary
Corps uniforms. As it was impossible to open the large glass cupola
aft during flight, we were forced to gut one of the segments of
security glass in order to give us free play for the camera. This
proved a scarcely comfortable expedient since the photographer had
to thrust his head, shoulders and arms out through this opening.

I ventured to do so first. I could never have believed that the air
was so cold, the wind so biting. I passed my chest through the
opening while Radl held my legs. A few moments later we were
flying over the Campo Imperatore, a wild and jagged plateau,

situated about 6,000 feet or more above sea level; from it, in one single mass, the steep walls of Gran Sasso rose to a height of 8,500 feet. Grey and brown rocks, immense bare cliffs, a few névés, and then we passed over our objective, the hotel, a massive building even when viewed from this height. I took the first photo, then, holding the fairly heavy camera in my left hand, I turned the crank which advances the roll of film. Only at this precise juncture did I realize that in these last few instants my hands had grown numb.

Square behind the hotel, I sighted a little meadow, vaguely triangular in shape. Immediately I said to myself that this was where we would land. I took a third shot, and, by giving a rather nervous kick, I made Radl understand that it was really time to pull me back into the plane.

I was still trying to establish with the maximum of certainty whether Mussolini really was at Gran Sasso. The first indications had been furnished (involuntarily, I may add) by two Italians; but I would have liked to obtain confirmation, preferably from a German. It would have been foolish to send an emissary boldly to the hotel which was linked to the outer world by only a funicular running up from the valley. I had already racked my brains to find some means of approach that might appear perfectly innocent. The eve of the Italian capitulation, I had at last managed to lay my hands on the man I needed.

At Rome I knew a German Army medical officer, a very ambitious fellow who had been long dreaming of a handsome decoration. Deciding to exploit his thirst for glory, on the evening of September 7 I explained to him how he could win the favour of his superiors.

Until now German soldiers stricken by malaria—and they were legion—had gone to convalesce in the Tyrol. I therefore proposed that the doctor go 'on his own initiative' to the mountain hotel atop Gran Sasso, which I pretended to know quite well, and that he ascertain whether this establishment, on a site at an altitude of about 2,100 feet, could be transformed into a convalescent home. I insisted he discuss the matter on the spot with the hotel director; I urged him to note the number of beds available, the sanitary equipment, and so forth. Also, I told him, he must enter into negotiations at once.

My suggestion did not fall on deaf ears. On the morning of September 8, my good medico set off bright and early by car. At this moment, I began to feel anxious. Would he be able to return and would I ever see him safe and sound again?

Next day, my 'spy in spite of himself' returned, much crestfallen at the idea that, because of the Italian capitulation, his fine project had gone to pot. In great detail, he related how he reached Aquila and entered the valley which gave access to the funicular station. But all his efforts to push on further proved fruitless. The road to the funicular was blocked by a barrier, which, moreover was guarded by several Carabinieri posts. After lengthy discussions with these, he had been allowed to telephone to the hotel. But it was no hotel director who replied; from the other end of the wire, an officer informed him that Campo Imperatore had been declared a military training reservation and that all other use of the plateau or its buildings was forbidden.

According to the doctor's observations, this must betoken some very important manœuvres for in the valley he espied a radio car and the funicular was plying a busy trade. In the last village the natives told him incredible tales to the following effect: the hotel had only just been requisitioned quite recently . . . the whole civilian personnel had been dismissed overnight . . . the buildings were being transformed into billets for two hundred soldiers . . . higher officers were reported to have been seen in the valley . . . certain people, people 'in the know', even supposed that Mussolini was interned up there in the mountain fastness. . . .

'But this last,' the doctor averred, 'constitutes an untrustworthy rumour.'

I took care not to disabuse him.

Next day, September 10, 1943, our troops continued to hold Rome and its suburbs solidly. I could at last carry out my project, or rather its final preparations. These consisted in drawing up a detailed plan.

Admitting the raid in itself was feasible, I first discussed the diverse possible techniques. One thing was certain, we had not a moment to lose. Each day, indeed each hour of delay, increased the danger of the Duce's being transferred to still another place of confinement. Then there was that other eventuality which we dreaded most: Suppose the prisoner were handed over to the Allies who had doubtless requested this. (Later we were to learn that General Eisenhower had incorporated this request in the armistice conditions.)

An operation by land seemed to us to be irremediably doomed to failure. An attack up the steep slopes leading to the plateau would entail enormous losses. Besides, the Carabinieri would be alerted early enough to find time either to hide the Duce or to bear him off elsewhere. To prevent them from escaping with their prisoner, we would have to surround the entire range with a cordon of troops, which would necessitate an entire division. In conclusion, then, a land attack must be considered as unfeasible.

Out trump ace should be total surprise, for, beyond all strategic considerations, we feared the Carabinieri might have received orders to kill their prisoner rather than let him escape. (This supposition, too, proved correct later; only our lightning action saved the Duce from being put to certain death.)

We saw only two means worth considering: a raid by paratroops or a landing of planes and gliders near the hotel. After weighing the pros and cons of both these solutions for a long time, we chose the second. To avoid too rapid a descent of parachutes in this rarefied altitude, we would have had to possess special parachutes, and we had none. Moreover, given the rough ground, I foresaw a much too scattered arrival of men; thus a swift action carried off by serried troops would be impossible.

Our only solution, therefore, lay in the landing of several gliders. But was there any ground, close to the hotel, that would permit such a landing?

When on the afternoon of September 8 I had wanted to have our aerial photographs developed, the great laboratory at Frasquati had already been razed by bombs. Still, one of my officers managed to have a few copies printed in an emergency laboratory. Unfortunately this laboratory could not furnish us with large-format stereoscope prints which would have supplied us with clear relief view of the terrain. I had to be content with ordinary photos 4 x 4 inches; yet on them I could distinguish quite clearly the triangular field which had attracted my attention when we flew over the hotel. This field, chosen as landing place, formed the basis of my plan.

We must also devise a means of covering our rear guard and of assuring our retreat after the accomplishment of the mission itself. In our project, these two aims were to be carried out by a battalion of parachutists who in the course of the night were to float down into the valley and, at Zero Hour, seize the funicular station.

Having set down the main lines of the operation, I called on General Student. I was aware that for the last three days he had scarcely found a chance to rest for three minutes—nor indeed had I —but it was imperative to come to an immediate decision. I exposed my plan to him and succeeded in winning his assent. Truth to tell, the general was none too enthusiastic, he did not fail to voice his apprehensions; but he understood that, unless we intended purely and simply to abandon our mission, we must try the last chance left to us. However, before giving his official sanction, he insisted on consulting his chief of staff and another staff officer.

These two aeronautical experts proceeded to oppose our project flatly. According to their views, a landing at such an altitude, and on a terrain which had not been put into good shape, was a feat which had never been performed, for the very good reason that it was 'technically impossible'. A landing such as my programme called for, they opined, would entail the loss of at least eighty per cent of the effectives transported. The rest of the troops would then be too few to stand a chance of accomplishing their mission.

Against these arguments, I pointed out that I was fully aware of what danger we ran, but that certain risks must be considered when a new technique was being tried out. I went on to say that I considered that a cautious bellylanding along the very gentle slope of the triangular meadow would reduce the speed of the gliders upon landing. I recognized this speed was rather considerable in such a rarefied atmosphere but I insisted my plan would avoid heavy losses. In conclusion, I declared myself prepared to follow these gentlemen's counsel if they had any better plan to suggest.

After long reflection, General Student finally fell in with my theory and immediately issued orders:

'Send to southern France immediately for the twelve transport gliders you need. J Day is to be September 12, Zero Hour 7000. In other words on September 12 at 7 a.m. sharp the gliders are to alight on the high plateau and at the same moment the battalion is to seize the funicular station in the valley. I shall personally brief the pilots and recommend the greatest caution in landing. I believe you are right, Captain Skorzeny; the raid must be carried out just as you suggest, and not otherwise.'

Having managed to get my way, I studied the last details of the operation with Radl. We must calculate distances very carefully, we must decide on what equipment the men were to take, and especially, we must indicate, on a huge chart, the specific point where each of the twelve machines was to land. A transport glider can carry nine men exclusive of its pilot; these men are called a group. We assigned a particular task to each group; for my part I was to travel in the third glider in order to take advantage of the cover furnished by the two preceding groups before I attacked the hotel.

Everything being settled, we still weighed our chances once again. We knew that they were pretty slim. First, no one could possibly guarantee that Mussolini was still in the hotel or that he would remain there until daybreak. Second, it was not at all certain that we could overcome the Italian detachment quickly enough to prevent the Duce's execution. Third, we must caution the officers who foretold the irremediable failure of our raid.

Whether their pessimism was exaggerated or not, we must foresee casualties upon landing. Nor was that all because, even without allowing for any casualties, there were only 108 men in all. Nor would each group be available at the same time. We would be tackling at least 250 Italians who knew the terrain perfectly and who were entrenched in the hotel as in a fortress. In so far as equipment was concerned, we were probably on an equal footing with the enemy. Doubtless our automatic rifles would give us a certain edge on the Italians. This might to some extent compensate for our numerical inferiority, provided that our initial losses were not too high.

One point still worried me. Was there no way, I wondered, whereby to increase the surprise element which was our trump card. We puzzled over the matter for more than an hour without hitting upon anything useful. Suddenly Radl had an idea of genius: we should take a higher Italian officer with us! His mere presence would probably serve to create certain confusion in the minds of the Carabinieri, a sort of hesitation which would prevent them from resisting immediately or from assassinating the Duce. This would help us to strike before they found time to collect themselves.

General Student immediately approved this bold proposal and we looked for the best means of carrying it into effect. The plan was for General Student to receive this officer on the eve of J-Day and persuade him—no one knew quite how—to participate in the operation.

A high official in our embassy, who was thoroughly at home in Roman military circles, suggested he knew a man who might possibly consent to help us. This officer was in the higher ranks; he had been a member of the General Staff of the Governor of Rome. In the course of the fighting for the possession of the city, he had displayed a rather neutral attitude. At my request, General Student invited him to call on the evening of September 11 at his Frasquati headquarters to discuss 'certain problems' with him.

We were now provided for in this respect. But a new subject for anxiety arose: news received of the transport gliders September 11 was anything but satisfactory. The increasingly intense activities of the Allied air forces had forced our squadron repeatedly to make long detours. Further, the execrable weather hampered their flight considerably. Up to the last moment we hoped that they would arrive promptly in spite of all this, but it was not to be.

We had therefore to alter all the phases of our operation. J Day was still scheduled for Sunday, September 12, for we could in no case allow ourselves to lose a whole day; but Zero Hour was postponed from 7 a.m. to 2 p.m.

At the hour agreed the Italian officer arrived with exemplary military promptness. But General Student had been unexpectedly delayed. We excused ourselves and begged the Italian to meet us on the morrow at eight at the Pratica di Mare airport.

Worst of all, this postponement of Zero Hour lessened our chances of success even more palpably. On the one hand, the violent ascendant currents to be expected during the warmest hours of the day would make our landings even more dangerous; on the other hand, the detachment charged with seizing the funicular station would have a more difficult task because forced to attack in broad daylight. So be it, we would try to succeed anyhow!

Early in the afternoon of September 11, I had gone to the olive grove of a convent near Frasquati where the unit I commanded had set up camp. I had already resolved to accept only volunteers for our raid but I wished very frankly to warn them that they would face great dangers. I had them fall in and made a short harangue:

'Your long inactivity is coming to an end,' I told them. 'Tomorrow we shall accomplish an operation of the highest importance, one with which I was entrusted by Adolf Hitler himself. We must all of us expect heavy losses; they are unfortunately inevitable. I shall direct our commando and I assure you I shall do all in my power; if you do the same, if we fight side by side with all our might, our mission will succeed. Let the volunteers step forward.'

To my great joy all, without exception, took one step forward. My officers had a great deal of trouble to persuade some of them to stay back because I could take along only eighteen men. On orders from General Student, the other ninety must come from the Second Company of the Battalion of Cadet Parachuters.

Next I called on the commanding officer of this battalion to discuss the different phases of the operation with him. Designated by General Student, this officer was to lead the detachment detailed to seize the valley station of the funicular. That evening, the battalion of Cadet Paratroopers set out for the valley. The die was now cast.

In the early hours of the night, a news broadcast by the Allied radio caused us another great fright. The announcer stated that the Duce had just arrived in North Africa aboard an Italian battleship which had escaped from the harbour of La Spezia. Having stomached my initial shock—were we to arrive late again this time?—I took a naval map and worked out a little mathematical sum.

Since I knew exactly when a portion of the Italian fleet had left La Spezia, it was patent that even the swiftest ship could not have reached the African coast at the hour when the news was broadcast.

Consequently this was simply a vulgar hoax meant to lead the German High Command into error. But ever since that day I have greeted information from Allied sources with a prudent reserve.

Next day, Sunday, September 12, 1943, we left for the airport at 5 a.m. There we were informed that our gliders would probably arrive at about ten o'clock. Taking advantage of this delay I checked up on the equipment of my men. Each had received a five days' issue of 'paratroopers' rations'. As I had also ordered several crates of fresh fruit, an almost gay animation soon reigned in the shadow of the huts. To be sure we could feel that tension which inevitably grips even the bravest of men before a leap into the unknown, but we contrived to dispel any apprehension or nervousness the moment it appeared.

Yet by half-past eight the Italian general had not shown up. I therefore sent Lieutenant Radl to Rome with orders to bring him to us as quickly as possible and at all costs.

'Manage as best you can,' I told Radl. 'Bring him back here alive, that is all that matters.'

Presently after all sorts of difficulties Radl succeeded in unearthing our man and piling him into his truck. As soon as they reached the airport General Student tackled the Italian. I was present at this interview. We informed our ally that the Führer asked him to help us to free the Duce with the minimum possible bloodshed. Visibly flattered to learn that Hitler himself was appealing for his co-operation, the Italian found it difficult to refuse. He promised to do his best and this, I reflected, was of incalculable advantage.

At last at about eleven o'clock the first gliders landed. The engines of the aeroplanes which were to tow us were quickly fuelled. Then each plane and the glider assigned to it took up their positions on the airstrip. We lined up successively in the order in which, our flight done, we expected to land.

Meanwhile General Student, summoning the glider pilots, reminded them that a vertical landing was strictly forbidden; they must land horizontally only. Next, on the blackboard, I plotted out the map of the terrain and charted the spots where each of the machines was to ground. Finally, with the Information Officer who had taken part in our reconnoitring flight, I checked up on essential details such as the timing of our voyage, the altitude we were to observe, the direction we were to follow, and the rest. Since, save for Radl and myself, he alone was familiar with the configuration of the lofty plateau as seen from the air, he was detailed to fly the first plane and thus to guide our squadron to its goal. Our estimates called for us to cover some odd hundred miles in exactly one hour. Accordingly we arranged to take off at exactly 1 p.m.

Suddenly at half-past twelve the sirens blared an air raid warning. Enemy bombers hove into sight and, almost at once, we could hear the first explosions on the outskirts of the airport. While we scattered for shelter, I thought bitterly that this spelled the end of the magnificent operation we had devised. What hellish bad luck it was to suffer such a mishap at the last moment! Fortunately a few moments before 1 p.m. the sirens wailed the 'All Clear'. I rushed to the main airstrip and discovered that, though the cement had been bombed here and there, our planes had escaped damage. We could therefore take off on schedule.

As for the Italian general, I took him with me in the third glider and placed him exactly between my legs astride the narrow beam we sat on, squeezed together like sardines. We had barely enough space to park our weapons. Already the Italian, who had climbed in with me somewhat reluctantly, was regretting the promise he had made us. 'Who cares? To hell with him!' I thought, for at that moment I had no time to lose.

My eyes glued to my wrist watch, I raised my arm. It was exactly 1 p.m. The motors tuned up; soon we were rolling along the strip, and, almost at once, I felt us taking off. Slowly we rose to describe vast curves as our caravan soared into formation, heading north-east. The weather seemed ideally to favour our enterprise; immense white banks of clouds floated across space at an altitude of over 5000 feet. No wind rose to break up these dense cloud banks. Thus we were reasonably sure of attaining our objective without being detected and of making a happy landing despite the difficulties of the terrain.

A stifling heat filled our transport glider. Crowded as we were, not to speak of our arms and equipment, we found it practically impossible to budge. The Italian general was turning white about the gills; a while later, his complexion was as grey-green as his uniform. I realized beyond a doubt that travel by aeroplane did not agree with him. At all events he did not enjoy it much.

The pilot kept doing his best to inform me of our position which I immediately checked on my map. We flew over Tivoli. From the cockpit we could see almost nothing of the country because the narrow side windows were covered with virtually opaque cellophane and the slits were too small to look through. This glider of ours was indeed a most rudimentary vehicle of transportation: a few steel tubes for a frame, a canvas envelope, and that was all.

We flew through a massive cloud bank and reached a height of 12,000 feet. When once again we moved into the sunlight, the pilot of the plane towing us informed me that planes numbers one and two had disappeared.

'Who takes on?' the pilot asked.

It was a distressing piece of news. What, I wondered, had happened to the two planes? At the time, incidentally, I was not aware that we also had only seven planes behind us, not nine. Later, we found out that, as our squadron took off, two gliders struck a crater made by enemy bombs, and collapsed.

'I'll take command until we reach our objective,' I told the pilot. Then, with a penknife, I cut right and left and between my legs to make slits which would permit me to distinguish at least the main features of the land over which we were flying. I decided that the primitive structure of these gliders possessed certain advantages. Thanks to a conspicuous landmark here and there—a bridge here, a crossroads there—I managed to get my bearings. And I breathed more freely because I was confident that this piece of ill luck would not foil our operation. Of course, on landing, I would not be covered by the troops in the missing gliders, but I thought nothing of it.

A few minutes before Zero Hour, I clearly descried the valley of Aquila below us. Looking down on to the road, I could see our trucks bearing the vanguard of our paratroopers swiftly up the mountain towards the terminal station of the funicular. Obviously they had cleared every obstacle and were in a position to launch an attack at exactly the moment desired. Here was a lucky omen! I felt certain that we too, for our part, would succeed.

Already, below us, loomed the Hotel del Gran Sasso, perched high aloft on its mountain fastness. I ordered my men to stand by and told the pilot to release our glider.

Suddenly a great silence fell upon us, broken only by the flutter of the wind about our wings. The pilot flew in a series of wide circles, seeking, quite as anxiously as I, where exactly we were to land on the gently sloping meadow. I felt we were in for it now because the 'gently sloping meadow' was, in point of fact, a steep, indeed precipitous abyss. Triangular in shape, it was much like the platform for a ski jump.

Already we were much closer to the plateau than we had been on our observation flight. Moreover our tailspin turns afforded us a particularly plastic view of the topography of the terrain. I understood at once that to land here as ordered was impossible; the pilot understood this too, and turned towards me, questioning. Gritting my teeth, I wrestled with a terrible problem. My conscience told me to obey the formal orders my commanding officer had given me. Yet should I do this? If so, the operation must come to naught and I would have to land horizontally in the depths of the valley, supposing this to be possible; if, on the other hand, I refused to abandon my project, I would have to land vertically at all risk and cost, thus flagrantly violating all the orders I had received. What was I to do? I made up my mind quickly.

'Vertical landing as near as possible to the hotel!' I ordered.

'Without turning a hair, the pilot reduced the circles, veered and sheered vertiginously, and finally, side-slipping over his left wing, went into a fantastic tailspin. For a moment, my throat contracted as I speculated whether the glider could possibly withstand the pressure of such speed. Then, immediately, I banished all such fears, assuring myself now was no time to entertain such considerations. The whirring of the wind increased and rose to a howl as we approached the ground. I saw Lieutenant Meier loose the parachute brake. There was a violent jolt, a sound of something cracking and shattering. Instinctively I closed my eyes. Then I felt that we had touched earth and, after a final spasm, the glider stood its ground, stock still.

Already the first of my men was emerging through the opening, the door of which had been swept off. Arms in hand, I followed. We were about twenty yards from the hotel. The numberless rocks surrounding us had played havoc with our glider but they had acted as a bolster and favoured our descent. We had not rolled more than about twenty-five yards after hitting the ground.

At the corner of the hotel building, close to a slight bank, stood the first gendarme. Obviously stupefied, he did not even stir; no doubt he was still wondering how we could possibly have fallen out of the very skies. I had not time to bother about our Italian passenger who was somewhat dazed and who sidled out of the glider. I dashed towards the hotel, and, as I did so, I remember congratulating myself for having expressly ordered my men not to fire until I myself fired. The surprise of the enemy was therefore complete.

I heard my men panting behind me, I knew they were following me, and I was proud I could rely on them.

We swept like a whirlwind past the still stultified sentry, shouting 'Mani in Alto, Hands up!' We then entered the hotel. Passing through an open door, we noticed a broadcasting unit and an Italian soldier sending out messages. Having kicked his chair from under his feet, I smashed his radio with the butt of my tommy-gun. Then, of a sudden, we noticed that none of the doors led into the hotel proper. We therefore turned back and found ourselves outdoors again. We skirted the building at a run, rounded a corner, and faced a terrace some twelve feet high. In a trice, one of my N.C.O.s gave me a hoist; the other troopers followed me.

I looked carefully at the façade of the hotel. On the first floor, gazing out of the window, stood a man with a characteristic, massive head. It was the Duce. Seeing him, I knew our operation was to be crowned with success.

I shouted to him to withdraw from the window and we made for the main entrance of the hotel. There we met Italian gendarmes who were seeking to make their way out of the building. Two machine-guns commanded the spot but we put them out of circulation. Using the butt of my tommy-gun I thrust my way through a compact mass of Italians while our men kept shouting: 'Mani in Alto!' So far, no shot had been fired.

I reached the lobby of the hotel, alone. For the moment, I had no notion of what was happening behind my back; I had no time to look. On the right was a stairway which I scaled three stairs at a time. Reaching the second floor, I followed a long corridor, flung open a door, and found it to be the right one!

The occupant of the room was Benito Mussolini, flanked by two Italian officers whom I lined up against the wall. Meanwhile my plucky friend, Lieutenant Schwerdt, joined me. Taking in the situation at a glance, he forced the two officers out of the room. They were too surprised to dream of offering the slightest resistance. Having rid me of them, Schwerdt closed the door noiselessly.

Thus the first chapter of our exploit had succeeded. For the moment at least the Duce was in our hands. Within three or at most four minutes from the time we had landed, we had found him. From outside, through the windowpane, I glimpsed the faces of two of my N.C.O.s. Unable to push into the hotel lobby, they had scrambled up the lightning rod to come to my rescue, if necessary. I stationed them in the corridor to cover us on that side.

Looking through the window, I watched Group 4 coming up at

the double. My orderly officer, Lieutenant Radl, headed them: Lieutenant Manzl was crawling up on his belly, behind his men, because the landing of his plane had broken one of his feet.

'Everything is right as rain!' I told them. 'Police the ground floor.'

Gliders 5, 6, and 7 landed. Paratroops poured out of them. They took up their positions more or less as we had planned. Next, suddenly, I saw Glider 8, caught in a gust; to my horror it took off from its plane while the plane was still circling, and plummeted like a stone to crash into bits on a heap of rubble.

A few lone shots crackled in the distance; doubtless the sparse Italian posts on the plateau were alerted. I ran into the corridor and shouted for the Italian officer in command of the hotel. The latter, a colonel, reported immediately. I explained to him that all resistance was futile, and I insisted on immediate surrender. The Italian colonel requested a moment's reflection; I granted him sixty seconds. Then Lieutenant Radl, who had managed to cross the hotel portal, joined me, but I sensed that the Italians were still holding the main entrance because I was receiving no further reinforcements.

The Italian colonel returned, bearing in both hands a magnum crystal goblet, filled with red wine. Bowing briefly:

'To the victor!' he said.

A sheet hung from the window served as the white flag of surrender. I shouted a few further orders to the men massed behind the hotel. Then, at long last, I had a chance to turn towards Mussolini. Sheltered behind the heavy frame of Lieutenant Schwerdt, the Duce stood in a corner. I introduced myself:

'Duce,' I said, 'the Führer has sent me to set you free.'

Mussolini, betraying all his emotion, embraced me.

'I knew my friend Adolf Hitler would not abandon me,' he replied.

AFTER A RISKY TAKE-OFF, *Skorzeny delivered Il Duce to Hitler. Less than two years later, executed by Italian partisans, Mussolini was hung from a meat-hook in Milan.*

Skorzeny's commandos went on to capture Admiral Horthy of Hungary and ensure that country's continued 'loyalty'. During the Battle of the Bulge they infiltrated Allied lines in United States uniforms, confusing and harassing the American forces.

In the closing days of the Third Reich, Major-General Gehlen tried to form a patriot underground army—the Werewolves. But most of the Germans refused to fight without uniforms. Spontaneous guerrilla warfare was alien to the Germans.

SECRET ARMY

BY T. BOR-KOMOROWSKI

THE POLES BOAST *that theirs was one country that developed no quislings in World War II. This is amazing when one remembers how the crushing defeat of Poland in 1939 left that country without an Army or hope. Yet no Pole deserted to the enemy. And the underground army grew. When the Battle of Warsaw began in 1944, there were over 380,000 members of the Polish 'Home' Army alone, and a second army was fighting in Italy and France with the British.*

In the year following Poland's defeat, small guerrilla forces became active, and by 1941 they were welded into an underground army under the direction of General Grot Rowecki. Diversion and sabotage were the main objectives of the Home Army. German supply lines and production were kept in a constant state of confusion.

Administrative sabotage reached new heights with the Home Army issuing orders in the name of the Nazi commanders until those commanders informed all concerned to hold all orders suspect. Soon all inconvenient orders were disregarded, making effective German administration and production impossible.

In July, 1943, the Germans captured and executed General Rowecki. General Komorowski, assuming the code name of Bor, became the commanding general. Liaison with England was stepped up and supply drops became more frequent, reaching a total by the war's end of 488 flights from England and Italy. General Bor developed a working liaison with Soviet guerrillas and at the same time increased the elimination of key Nazi figures. In the first six months of 1944 the Home Army sentenced and executed 796 prominent German agents in the streets in broad daylight. The most difficult of these was the execution of one of Himmler's most trusted generals. The story of the execution and its aftermath is told by General Bor-Komorowski. It is a strange tale of discipline and courage as well as a revelation of the problems faced by a commander who knows his every action will bring calculated reprisals to large numbers of his people.

IN autumn of 1943 Himmler assigned Major-General Kutschera of the S.S. and police to Warsaw. He was only thirty, but he had already made his mark by massacres of civilians in the other occupied countries of Europe. His relations with Himmler were of some intimacy, Himmler's sister being his mistress.

Kutschera's tasks had been clearly defined. As the Polish countermeasures had begun to yield results and the German officials were in many cases giving way to fear in their dealings with the Polish Underground, he was to destroy Polish resistance at all costs. In other words, he was to drown Warsaw in a sea of blood.

At first he succeeded. Public executions became a weekly occurrence. That was a return to the German methods of 1939, especially in our western provinces, then incorporated into the Reich. From time to time they had used this method, but Kutschera made public execution his daily weapon. In the course of one month in 1943 the death toll for Warsaw alone was: October 16, 20; 17, 20; 19, 20; 20, 20; 22, 10; 23, 20; 25, 20; 26, 30; 30, 10. In these two weeks 177 people were publicly shot in the streets of Warsaw, among them five women. In all German-occupied Poland approximately 15,000 people were executed during the winter of 1943–44. Public executions of this kind were also customary to Cracow, Lwow, Radom, Kielce, Przemysl, Rozwadow, Jaslo, and dozens of other towns. Apart from public executions, firing-squads were active inside the prisons and the number of people who were summarily executed in captivity was infinitely greater.

I fully realized that were we to break under this new pressure and Kutschera be convinced that his methods were effective, the more intensified and frequent would his method of terror become and the more numerous would be his victims.

His method was to round up chance pedestrians in the streets, seize several hundred of them and then have their names posted on the billboards and announced by loudspeakers. Single lists numbered as many as two hundred at a time. The announcement of names would be accompanied by the information that if the families of the arrested people would disclose the names and whereabouts of members of the Underground, their relations would be released. In this way, he hoped to break our solidarity by forcing denunciations. His attempts, however, were unsuccessful.

Public executions would take place the next day, in broad daylight, in the streets of the capital. The victims were brought from the Pawiak Prison with plaster of paris gags in their mouths to prevent them from shouting patriotic calls as they died.

Once Renia, my wife, with her baby in the pram, passed Senatorska Street, where an execution had just taken place. The corpses had already been carried away, but blood was splashed all over the pavement and bits of brain were sticking to the walls. People were kneeling all around, and in a few seconds the whole place was covered with red and white flowers and burning candles. Flowers were put in every bullet hole in the wall. Renia stopped to pray. German police appeared and she made off. When she looked back they were shooting and beating people up—all in vain, for after a moment the crowd was back again, and new flowers and new candles had appeared. Kutschera had 2,000 of these victims on his conscience, to say nothing of the secret executions which took place within the walls of the burned-out Ghetto.

I decided that, cost what it might, Kutschera must be killed. The tactics of using terror to combat German terror seemed to be the only right solution. It was clear that, in view of his exceptional position, both in the senior ranks of the Gestapo and in his relations with Himmler, at least two hundred Polish hostages would have to pay the price for his death. I calculated, however, that the removal of such a notorious criminal would convince his successor that nothing could save him from death if he followed the same tactics. In the long run, I argued, his death would save many human lives and go far to stop the intensified German terror, although the immediate price would be heavy. Before I made up my mind that Kutschera must die, a warning had been sent to him informing him that, if he did not cease these atrocities, he would be killed. A second warning was sent, far more categorical, adding that, though he had evaded death in Belgium and Czechoslovakia, he would not do so in Poland.

The date of Kutschera's death was entered on the list three months before it was to take place. It was the most difficult operation of its kind that the special Kedyw units had undertaken. Various items of information had to be gathered, despite the efforts made by the German authorities to conceal them. We had to know Kutschera's exact mode of life, his habits, his time-table for lunch each day, the route he followed to his office and back, and so on. It was not easy. He used a variety of cars. Sometimes his escort would be in civilian clothes, at others in military uniform, and occasionally in police uniform. He himself wore various uniforms, but never the insignia of his rank as major-general.

Three attempts were made: two of them failed. The third and successful attempt took place on February 1, 1944, in the very heart of Warsaw. It lasted barely three minutes.

The officer in charge of the attack, Lieutenant Bronislaw Pietraszkiewicz, was chosen from among our ablest diversion soldiers. He went by the name of 'Lot'. He had previously been a Scoutmaster and was just twenty. He could preserve complete calm and self-control in situations demanding determination and coolness of action. Among his more striking earlier feats was the execution of a leading Gestapo official in the presence of his wife, who was unexpectedly accompanying him and was wheeling her child in a perambulator. To throw a hand-grenade at that distance would have killed the woman and child also. This was not included in Lot's orders and it was our principle that all our executions were on a judicial basis. Lot had to make a lightning decision in that split second. He took the added risk, drew a tommy-gun from the violin case he was carrying and shot the German dead at a distance of one yard.

The plans for the final attempt on Kutschera were worked out in detail. The scene was set just in front of S.S. and German police headquarters and only a few steps from Szucha Street and Gestapo headquarters. As a result of three previous attacks on Germans at this point, all the entries to the streets had been blocked by barbed wire and were guarded by S.S. patrols and concrete pill boxes.

It was 9.55 a.m. when Kutschera's car appeared at the turning from a side street some distance away. As usual, his A.D.C. was at the wheel, and Kutschera was sitting next to him on the front seat. Behind them was a car with his escort of four Gestapo men.

An innocent-looking girl pulled her handkerchief out of her pocket. It was a signal to two of the attackers, standing on the other side of the street with tommy-guns under their coats. It was also a signal for a 'German military car', driven by Lot with 'Cichy' (Corporal Marian Zegier) as passenger. Lot drove up to Kutschera's car, swerved left and blocked the way. Kutschera's A.D.C. jammed on the brake and stopped his car just as a collision seemed inevitable. A bare two yards separated the radiators of the two cars. Lot threw a filipinka; the explosion was so close that the door and part of the chassis of his own car were crushed. It took him and Cichy a few seconds to struggle out. Meanwhile, 'Sokol' and 'Juno' let fly two long bursts from their tommy-guns and wiped out the escort of four Gestapo men. Lot and Cichy were now clear of their car and rushed towards the general, who was still dazed by the explosion of the filipinka. Lot seized him by the lapels and dragged him out. He then fired a burst from his tommy-gun into Kutschera's head. Cichy finished off the A.D.C. in exactly the same way. Germans rushed up from all sides, firing at the 'executioners'. Firing came also from the pill boxes at the street corners. Lying on the ground, the Polish escort swept the street with short bursts from their tommy-guns.

While this was going on, Lot was busily searching Kutschera's pockets for his identity papers. But when Kutschera was dragged from the car, he had dropped his wallet under the car. Lot knew he had to get the papers—those were his orders—and it was his adherence to duty which proved fatal, since clearly every second was priceless. He was hit by a well-aimed shot in the stomach. Cichy had also been wounded. But both continued to search for the papers and finally found them. Then the four of them got into their car.

Sokol now took the wheel and Lot hunched beside him. They shot off at top speed along a pre-arranged route. Lot continued to give orders until they got about half-way, but then his strength gave out and he collapsed into unconsciousness. As they sped on another bullet grazed the driver's head, but it was only a surface wound, and Sokol drove on. Their destination was the Hospital of the Transfiguration in Praga, across the river. It was one of the Red Cross headquarters of the Home Army. Many of the doctors belonged to our organization, and we used to send there any of our soldiers who were wounded in and around Warsaw. They had been warned that their help might be needed that day. Both the wounded men, Lot and Cichy, were taken straight to the operating table on arrival.

Once their two wounded comrades were safely in the hospital, Sokol and Juno decided to get back to the left bank of the river. If they had driven eastwards, out of the city, they might have got clear. Here again operations routine and the adherence to a precise plan proved fatal. They had reckoned that a car driving westwards would not be suspected but in this they were mistaken. As they were crossing the Kierbedz Bridge, all the German patrols were notified. When they got half-way across they heard the wailing siren of the German emergency police squad. Just ahead, they saw a line of men in green uniforms barring the end of the bridge. That way was closed. Sokol decided to get back to Praga. He tried to turn sharply, but they were going too fast and the car hit an iron girder with terrific force. German police motor-cyclists now appeared at both ends of the bridge.

In a flash, Sokol and Juno leaped from the car, climbed the iron balustrade and jumped into the river 100 feet below. German rifles and machine-guns sprayed them from the banks and the bridge. They disappeared, came to the surface and started swimming rapidly downstream. Bullets splashed all around them. Sokol was the first to be killed. Juno continued to struggle on. Silent crowds watched with bated breath from the banks. Then the sound of a motor-boat was heard; the Germans had taken up the pursuit by water. But the swimmer refused to give in. The police boat gained on him swiftly. Shots fired at close range could now be heard. Once more the body of the mortally wounded man appeared on the surface. Then it sank.

These events took place in the near vicinity of the Hospital of the Transfiguration. The arrest of the two wounded men might take place at any time. Their commander decided to act at once.

At 6 p.m. a police car drove up to the hospital. Sentries were stationed at every entrance and gate. The 'Gestapo' rushed into the ward where the two men were lying after their operations. Doctors and nurses looked on with horror and despair as the 'Germans' took them away. But their faces cleared when, twenty minutes later, another batch of Gestapo men turned up to collect the Polish 'bandits'. They made a thorough search of the whole hospital, but failed to find their prey. Lot and Cichy were soon in a safe place. The same evening I received a detailed report of the day's events—the sentence had been carried out. Along with the report, a photo of Kutschera in smiling mood was put on my desk.

All four men were awarded the Virtuti Militari Cross, Poland's highest decoration for bravery to her soldiers. All the crosses were awarded posthumously. Both Lot and Cichy's wounds proved fatal. Lot died the same day and Cichy the following morning.

THE CHIEF ACTORS *of the drama were all dead but the tragedy was not yet concluded. Two funerals took place. A requiem mass was held for Lot and Cichy in a tiny chapel at the cemetery. Lot's comrade in arms, 'Wanda', sang his favourite* Ave Maria. *An hour after the two young men were buried, another funeral was held in the same chapel. In the middle of the service the Gestapo rushed into the chapel and tore off the lid of the casket. Being an hour later than they knew, they saw only the wrinkled face of an old woman.*

DANIELE—ČETNIK

BY CHRISTIE LAWRENCE

WHEN THE CROSSROADS *changes hands for the fourth time, who recalls those who died taking it the first time? If they were regular soldiers, the records are cleared and the families are notified. But if they were guerrillas who drifted into the woods and a war, no one knows who they were, why they came, and where they died. Their companions remember them as Maria, or the-man-with-the-green-cap, or by a cover-name as common as Smith. The guerrilla may be a shy girl with tremendous courage or a blustering old man afraid to die who dies anyway, but so long as the guerrilla fights, anonymity, like darkness, is a form of protection. The guerrilla who lives is a hero, but the one who dies, dies unknown.*

Christie Lawrence was a young British officer who escaped from the Nazis after being captured on Crete. He jumped from a train in the Balkans and joined a guerrilla band in Yugoslavia in the early days of World War II when the British were supporting Draža Mihailović's Royalist Četniks. Lawrence tells this story of a small guerrilla action during those days when the Četniks and Communist partisans were trying to work together. But it is more than a story of political strife and guerrilla warfare. It is the story of a girl with a strange talent who drifted into Lawrence's band.

WE moved off immediately an hour before dawn, and chose an excellent spot for an ambush about five miles from the town. There were several houses near the road which had been burned out, and Stanimir explained that between the two attacks the Germans had broken out and, as a reprisal, had burned all the houses within a kilometre of the road on either side for several miles. They had taken the Četniks by surprise and met with no resistance.

We chose a place for our road-block where the road ran through a shallow, narrow valley, with wooded slopes on both sides. Two ruined but stoutly built houses thirty yards from the road served as a strong point, and we mounted in them two of the light machine-guns (L.M.G.s). The block itself took us the rest of the day to build, and we used material from the torn-up railway track not far away. We used both sleepers and rails, and finally I judged that even a light tank might have difficulty in negotiating it. We disposed the men on the edge of the woods on either side of the road, with orders not to fire until the signal was given.

Two days passed quietly, and we spent them improving our block and reconnoitring the railway track to make sure that it was impassable. Most of the bridges had been blown and broken down, and we judged that the Germans would only use it as a last resort. Finally we posted scouts a kilometre along the road, and taught them to signal with their rifles the arrival of a convoy and the number of lorries. We had no food, and kept ourselves by visiting by turns the neighbouring vineyards, which covered every southern-facing slope, and eating grapes. They satisfied both hunger and thirst, and were very energizing, but the quantity we needed was surprising. I suppose I ate fourteen or fifteen pounds a day, gnawing them from the bunches like sweet corn. The rest of the time we sat nursing our rifles and watching the dusty white road, brilliant in the sun. The hillsides were deserted except for an occasional peasant, still working in his vineyard.

About two hours after dawn on the third morning, the scouts signalled six lorries, which almost immediately came in sight. I felt a wave of excitement, put a round up the spout, and took a trial sight along the road.

'Steady,' whispered Stanimir. 'Remember you have only twenty rounds.'

'Fifty,' I murmured to myself.

The L.M.G.s wisely held their fire until the leading lorry sighted the block and began to slow up. Then both of those in the houses opened up, and the other two followed suit from the hillside. I saw the windscreen of the leading lorry splinter. The lorry skidded into the side of the road, cannoned off the bank, and overturned. German soldiers began to crawl out, and then we all opened fire. The firing of the guerrillas sounded far too ragged to me to be coming from a hundred rifles, until I remembered—but only after I had fired about ten rounds—that rapid fire in guerrilla warfare is taboo, and you must pick your target very carefully.

The last two lorries turned round immediately and made off in the direction from which they had come, but the other three drew up behind the first, and the Germans began to jump out and take cover in the ditches. But they were at a serious disadvantage, for they could take cover only from one direction at a time, and were being fired on from three. Nevertheless, they quickly had three L.M.G.s in action. Presently, one of our L.M.G.s from the strong point stopped firing, and, soon after it, the other, which left the little force there with only two or three rifles. As soon as they saw this, a small party of Germans, who had escaped unhurt from the leading lorry, began to crawl up the bank towards it. Radevič ordered all the men within earshot to concentrate their fire on them as they worked themselves through the undergrowth. By careful sniping we managed to keep their progress very slow, and presently the body of the German fire began to slacken too.

'We must bring this to an end,' said Stanimir. 'In ten minutes the tanks will be here, and I must have their arms.' At that moment Radevič took up a Very pistol, which I did not know he had, and shot a white light up into the air. Immediately from two sides, shouting wildly, the guerrillas leapt from their cover and, brandishing their rifles (few of them had bayonets), they ran madly at the Germans on the road. I was borne along on the tide, and found myself running as though I had a fixed bayonet. I should have been at a loss had we caught up with the enemy, but the Germans stood up with their hands in the air, and we never made close contact with them.

The guerrillas descended on them and, in less time than it takes to undress, had stripped the live ones, wounded and unwounded alike, of their boots, weapons, and most of their clothes. In the four lorries there had been about forty men, of whom only eighteen remained unwounded, while eleven were dead. Those who were taken prisoner looked more frightened than I had ever seen men look.

We also stripped the lorries of their contents, which were mostly ammunition. There were four L.M.G.s and two small mortars which had never got into action against us. Radevič quickly loaded the guerrillas with as much as each man could carry, and then, leaving Stanimir and me with a party of five to destroy the lorries, they all set off to a rendezvous in the hills.

There was no time to lose if we were all to be away before the counter-attack. Quickly we pierced the petrol tanks of three of the lorries, and set fire to them. All the ammunition which the guerrillas had been unable to carry away was placed in the fourth lorry, which, we found, had not been damaged in the fighting, apart from a smashed windscreen. Stanimir leapt into the driving seat, and I clambered up after him. The other five piled into the back. Then we set off up the road straight towards Kruševac. Two hundred yards along the road we turned off to the right and went bouncing over a rutted track towards the hills. After a quarter of an hour's hectic driving, Stanimir pulled up under some trees. We had climbed about five hundred feet, and were looking down almost directly on the spot where the ambush had taken place.

A Stuka was already circling over the burned-out lorries. After about half an hour we saw four of the six light tanks arrive. They looked a very old pattern—not front-line stuff, I thought. Stanimir looked anxiously at his watch.

'If the others do not arrive quickly,' he said, 'the Boches will find out where we have taken their missing lorry, and might follow with the tanks. I am afraid of the tracks in the dust.'

'What will become of the prisoners?' I asked.

'Radević will march them barefoot into the hills for a few miles,' he said, 'and then let them go. I would not be in their position. All the peasants around are armed. Not many of them will find their way back to Kruševac.'

After the tanks, another and much larger contingent of Germans arrived in lorries, and began picking up the dead and wounded under cover of the tanks' guns.

About an hour later twenty of Radević's men arrived to take away the rest of the arms. This included the L.M.G.s and mortars, several boxes of ammunition, and some tommy-guns.

'Those are not much good to us,' said Stanimir. 'They use far too much ammunition and have no range.'

One of the men had a message for Stanimir, who grinned and turned to me. 'Novaković is looking for you,' he said. 'He wants you to go straight back to headquarters with this man. You'd better go. There won't be any more excitement to-day. I shall burn this lorry and then rendezvous with the others.'

When I had filled my haversack with spare rounds, I went with the man who had brought the message, to find headquarters.

The General was furious. He made me an unnecessarily long speech, I thought, considering that I could not understand it, in which the words 'officer' and 'discipline' kept recurring. My impression was that he was more jealous than pleased over our little action.

While we had been engaged, news had arrived asking him to deal with one of Kosta Pechanac's *vojvode* called 'The Stork', who had raised a company at Aleksandrovac, a rich wine-producing village south of the Morava between Kruševac and Kraljevo. 'The Stork' was known to have offered the services of his men to the Germans, and constituted a menace to the flank of the attacking forces.

Novaković and Keserović decided to march on Aleksandrovac with about a hundred of their combined forces, leaving Zakić and Radević to deal with the increased danger from Kruševac. Always intent on seeing as much new country as I could, I decided to go with the General. Keserović took only forty men, and the remainder of the company of a hundred had been made up from the Partisans, among whom were two women.

For food we continued to eat grapes.

During the march to Aleksandrovac, which was executed very slowly, and took nearly three days, I took the opportunity of getting to know some of the Partisans. I found that their leaders were all peacetime Communists, who had led double lives for many years. They were fanatical and ruthless. This little force also contained a number of students, one of them only sixteen. Nevertheless, more than half were simple peasants, who had joined the Partisans more by luck than judgment, because they wanted to fight the Germans. These men were subjected to a continual and subtle propaganda from their leaders and the students, which they had scarcely the education to resist, so that they very quickly became imbued with Communistic ideas.

'The government in Belgrade under Nedić is bad enough,' said one of them to me, 'but the government under Simović in London is worse. Why did they not stop and fight? Why did the King run away? He is a young man and not married, he could have fought. But it is always the peasant who pays. We have to fight and die for him, so that he can come back and live on us.'

This sort of talk, which might have come from a street-corner orator, went on continually among the Partisans, and the peasants among them were very soon convinced.

I was very careful not to get involved in political arguments, but I found all the time among the Partisans a sense of distrust. They alone of the Serbs seemed to have an active dislike of my nationality.

'England betrayed us,' they said. 'Without Russia, England cannot win the war. We were fools to ally ourselves to you. We should only have been the allies of Russia, which is our mother-country.'

Only the women of the company never tried to argue. One was a pretty, dark-eyed, brown-haired girl, who looked very sad, and seldom spoke at all.

9

'She joined us in order to be with her brother,' said one of the students. 'The other day he was killed. We had to carry her away, or she would have stayed and given herself up. Before the war she was a schoolmistress in Kruševac. We call her Boginja because she is so good.'

The other girl was a fair and strongly built woman of about thirty, with deep-blue, almost violet eyes. The most surprising thing about her was that her hair always looked as though she had just washed and brushed it, the way it shone in the sun. Her hands were more often clean than those of anybody else. Her name was Daniele, and she told me that she was a Jewess. She carried a heavy German L.M.G.

The battle of Aleksandrovac was a farce. We broke down the bridges leading to the town, and cut all the telegraph wires. Then we surrounded it, taking up positions in the vineyards and across the only two roads. Aleksandrovac is a little town of about two thousand inhabitants. It has one long main street, metalled with cobbles. It is very prosperous, for the wine produced there is some of the best in Serbia.

'The Stork' had collected a little band of twenty-five men, who were armed on the same scale as most of the guerrillas. But he had applied to the Germans for clothing and permission to requisition food officially for them.

When Novaković sent a courier into the town, 'The Stork' immediately surrendered. In an interview with the guerrilla leaders he promised to behave himself, and we all descended into the town and were fêted by its inhabitants.

The townsfolk were extremely kind to me. They gave me good meals, and offered me a bed in one of the best houses. Jošić, who had been detailed to 'look after' me, was always at my side.

We strolled along the street until we came to a barber's shop. I was trying to explain to the barber that I wanted a haircut and a shave when a woman's voice said in English:

'Can I be of any help?'

It was Daniele. I asked her to explain to the barber what I wanted. Then, when I was wrapped in a towel, 'Can I sit and talk with you?' she asked. 'I speak English quite well.'

She told me that her parents, who were Slovenian Jews, were in England, where they lived in the Lake District. She herself had once been in London, where she had stayed for a week at the Mayfair Hotel.

Looking at her interestedly in the mirror, I noticed that her eyes were beautiful and sad.

'You must have been rich to stay at the Mayfair Hotel,' I said.

'My husband was.'

I wanted to ask what had become of him and only just remembered my manners in time to refrain. But she told me.

'He is Romanian,' she said, 'and when the Germans came to Belgrade, where we lived, he was afraid because I am a Jewess. So he left me and went back to Bucharest.'

After a pause, she added: 'This is a filthy life.'

'Then why are you here?'

'There is nothing else, and I am a very good machine-gunner.'

'Do you mean to say that you work that thing in battle?' I asked.

'Yes. They used to give me and Boginja the ammunition to carry. When her brother was killed we were left alone with the gun, so I had to work it. I found I could do it very well. It was the first time I had ever fired anything except a little rifle, for sport.'

I asked: 'Do they always make you carry it? Isn't it very heavy?'

'Very. But, if you work it out, it is obvious that we must all carry our own weapons.'

'But why did you ever start this life?'

'It is a very long story,' she replied. 'One day I will tell it to you.'

The barber finished my hair, and we left the shop together.

'Do not walk up the street with me,' she said; 'they discourage it.'

'That must make life rather lonely for you,' I said.

'It is. But no more so than for you,' she replied. 'All the people who know enough French to talk with you do not like you because you are English.'

'What is your name?' she asked.

'Christie Lawrence.'

'I shall call you Krsta, because that is Serbian. It means 'a cross'. Krsta Lorenčić.'

And she was gone.

During the few days we stayed in Aleksandrovac I saw a good deal of Daniele and heard her story. Her parents had been rich, and as a child and young woman she had travelled over most of Europe. For many years their home had been in Austria, but after the Nazi invasion her father had had to flee for his life. Daniele went to Belgrade, where she met the Romanian who afterwards became her husband, and with him she travelled widely in the Balkans. He fled immediately after the German invasion, and left her in Bel-

grade, with very little money and some of her jewels. She sold
some of these jewels and made her way to Kruševac, where she had
a friend, a Jew, who was a doctor. But the Germans came and
arrested him, though, for the moment, they left her alone, for they
did not know who she was. Then, partly from fear and partly from
hate, she had joined the Partisans.

In Aleksandrovac, Novaković reorganized his forces. He formed
a small headquarters, and the remainder he split into platoons of
fifteen to twenty men. Each platoon had one L.M.G. Because he
was short of officers he offered me the command of one of the
platoons. I accepted, but on condition that I should have at least
three men who could speak French to act as interpreters. He gave
me two, and Daniele was one of them. The other was a young
Partisan from Montenegro, called Sima. He had been the most
friendly of the students. Of the rest of my men, half came from
Keserović's company and the others were recruited locally. They
had all volunteered to serve with me, and there were sixteen altogether.

Besides the L.M.G. we had two German tommy-guns and five
revolvers. I swapped one of the tommy-guns with Popović for a
dozen bayonets, and fitted most of the riflemen up with them.

With the aid of Sima and Rade Ćiraković, a miner who had
worked in the English mine at Kosovska Mitrovitsa, I rigged up two
bayonet sacks, and spent several days in giving my platoon bayonet
drill. I then made everyone pool his ammunition and divided it out
equally all round. Every man had eighty rounds, and there were
nearly two hundred rounds for the L.M.G. Half of this I carried
myself and the other half I gave to Rade, whom I made Daniele's
No. 2. He agreed at once that he would carry the gun most of the
time, and Daniele carried his rifle, but it seemed to be the accepted
thing that Daniele should be the gunner.

'She is the best shot I have ever seen,' said Rade. 'At two hundred
metres she can put a burst through a saucepan lid!'

During the third week in October, we had orders to prepare to
move. We were to take part in the battle of Kraljevo, where
Novaković hoped to take over command from Major Djurić.
Almost daily, while we had been at Aleksandrovac, we had heard
the sound of firing from the direction of the main Kraljevo-
Kruševac road, and we heard that Radević was being hard pressed
in his task of keeping the two German forces apart. Small detachments had from time to time succeeded in breaking through from

Kruševac to Kraljevo. Our task, said Novaković, would probably be to strengthen the attacking forces on the eastern side of Kraljevo, where we should also have the role of holding up anyone whom Radević let through.

We marched almost immediately. Kraljevo was the biggest battle that had taken place up to that time. The reinforced German garrison now numbered nearly two thousand, with the addition of a few hundred of Kosta Pečanac's Četniks. Outside were more than three thousand guerrillas. Both sides had artillery, and the guerrillas, in the early stages of the battle, had captured a dump of Yugoslav Army 50-kilogramme aeroplane bombs, but without their detonators. The guerrillas had three tanks, for which they only had machine-gun ammunition. Of these they had already lost two in a bold and successful action.

One night the Germans had been mustering for an attack and the guerrillas had received word of their rendezvous. The commander of their three tanks had conceived the bold plan of entering the town under cover of dark and driving up to where the German infantry was collecting. As he had hoped, the Germans had thought that the tanks were their own, and let them approach to within fifty yards of their massed troops. At this point the three tanks, which were moving in line ahead, had wheeled and, as they drew abreast of the Germans, opened up with their machine-guns. The element of surprise had been complete, and the attack had been broken up. But two of the tanks had failed to get back through the German defence system. The remaining one had shot away all its ammunition.

When we arrived within striking distance of the town there had been two or three days of pause in activities. The Germans had been sending out their Serbian levies (Kosta's Četniks) on reconnaissance, and fighting was confined to skirmishing on the outskirts of the town. The guerrillas were, meanwhile, regrouping for another attack.

Tactically, the battle for Kraljevo, which was the decisive engagement in the whole guerrilla operation of the autumn of 1941, developed very loosely. There was no rigid direction from the commanding staff, chiefly because communications between the scattered units were bad. Moreover the position of the nominal military commander, Mihailović's Major Djurić, was not sufficiently secure, and a disagreement with one of his subordinates frequently meant the latter's withdrawal from the action for several days, until he could be conciliated. This attitude is catching, and I found myself several times refusing to follow a course of action demanded of me by my superiors when it seemed to me inevitable that I should lose too high a proportion of my men. After the initial assault on the town, which took place during the second week in October, and failed owing to lack of co-ordination, the attacking forces had split themselves into three main groups, each of which worked almost entirely independently. Their attention was continually being diverted from the main objective, because of attempts by the Germans to break through from Kruševac and Kragujevac and reinforce their garrison. In this they were several times successful.

In the later stages of the battle the guerrilla command grew steadily weaker, and there was no single co-ordinated attack, although the forces on the south and west of the town penetrated as far as the centre, and for two days held the railway station, effectively sabotaged a factory making rolling stock, and destroyed several locomotives.

Jakčić, from the moment I began to serve under his command, used my platoon continuously. We were first thrown into the push which took us as far as the railway station. Progress in this attack was unbearably slow. Time and again the guerrillas outmanoeuvred the defending forces, but their chief weakness was that they had not the final thrust which would have pushed their advantage home. They were generally as averse to hand-to-hand fighting as the Germans were. Jakčić was not slow to discover the value of my dozen bayonets. If I had consented to provide the final assaulting force as many times as he had wished, I should have lost all my men in the first three days. As it was, I had far heavier casualties than any of the other platoons. My casualties were always quickly replaced, but I would never take a man who had no bayonet.

I quickly taught my platoon how to advance under the cover of fire from Daniele's L.M.G., admirably served by Rade Čiraković. With the detachment of a chef carving a steak, and a delicacy of touch that she might have acquired from playing the piano, she would place controlled bursts which kept quiet the hottest of defensive fire. The Germans used to search for her with mortars, but Rade always seemed to know when to move.

Those were exhausting days and nights, with little sleep and nothing much to eat. For a whole week we lived on pumpkin—a tasteless and unsatisfying diet, and not nearly so good as grapes.

When we had taken the railway station, and my platoon had con-solidated their small part of the defence of it, I sent Sima back to Jakčić to ask to be relieved. Of my original sixteen, I had only twelve, and four of those were lightly wounded. Although the seven replacements were promising men, I did not feel justified in keeping them there any longer, especially as the Germans had started to shell us, and a counter-attack seemed imminent.

Our relief consisted of a newly recruited platoon of peasant Partisans, and I remember thinking that they would not stand for long after hard pressure. But I handed them over all the ammunition I had left—it was not much—and we set off for the rear. As we started it began to rain. And the reaction was killing. Rade, Sima, and I took turns in carrying the L.M.G., for poor Daniele was almost finished. I remember watching her face, on which there were new lines, as she limped with blistered feet beside us. No woman, I thought, should ever be allowed to take part in active Partisan life —their physical disabilities are too great.

We had orders to report to headquarters—twenty miles back, in the Goć mountains. We had been relieved just before dawn, and during the day were joined by several other platoons, led by one of Jakčić's political commissars. The political commissars were important men in the Partisan ranks at that time. They were all leading members of the original Communist Party, and usually they had authority over all but the highest military leaders.

Nightfall found us on the edge of the Goć woods, with a full five hours' march ahead of us. The political commissar ordered a halt and said we would rest there the night. It was still raining, and he sent out some of his men to collect brushwood for a fire.

I suggested that we should post sentries, but the commissar said it was unnecessary. Soon there was a cheerful blaze, and the men disposed themselves around it.

All day I had been troubled by a nail in one boot, and as soon as everyone was settled I made my way to the light of the fire, to see if I could make it comfortable. I had taken the boot off and was working at the nail with a bayonet, when suddenly there was a burst of tommy-gun fire from the edge of the clearing in which we had halted. A man in my platoon, sleeping beside me, was hit, and half-reared himself up. In an instant everyone was awake. I dropped the boot, snatched up my rifle and bayonet, and made off for the undergrowth at a crouching run. All around me dim figures were doing the same. Ten yards into the undergrowth I paused to listen. There was firing from at least four tommy-guns, fifty yards away on the other side of the fire. The clearing was full of dim figures, but I could not tell whether they were friends or enemies. Then I heard Sima softly calling my name:

'Krsta, Krsta.'

I answered him, and we joined forces. The firing very quickly stopped. It seemed as though nobody from our side answered.

'Where are Rade and Daniele?' I asked.

'I don't know,' said Sima.

'Who attacked us?'

'Probably Kosta's Četniks. The Germans never come out at night,' said Sima.

We waited a few minutes, and then I said I was going back for my boot. Crouching low, I was approaching the fire when somebody from the edge of the undergrowth threw a bomb at me. It landed in the fire, and blew burning sticks all over the place.

'I befoul thy mother, fool,' shouted Sima from the bushes. 'It's Krsta.'

I stood up and approached the fire. There were several bodies on the ground, and among them one of my platoon. The Partisans had left their rifles behind, and I came upon an ammunition-belt, complete with bayonet, which I recognized as belonging to one of my men. I picked it up, and then I searched for my boot.

Meanwhile the rest of the Partisans were sorting out their equipment. The various leaders called a roll, and we found that nearly half were missing.

'Are we all here?' I asked Sima.

'Two men missing, and Dragi Kostić has lost his rifle,' said Sima. Dragi was one of the new recruits.

My boot was nowhere to be found. Only after half an hour's search did Daniele find its remains. When the bomb had landed in the fire, it had blown a burning log on to it, and set fire to the upper. It was now quite unusable, and this was a hard blow, because boots were scarcer than ammunition.

We scraped a shallow trench with our bayonets, and buried the dead man from our platoon.

Partisan headquarters was on the site of a sawmill, which, during the war, had not been worked. It was very well organized, with a doctor, a limited supply of medical equipment, and a number of Kraljevo girls who had volunteered as nurses. Before the action, the Partisans had laid up a large store of food and, though it was seriously depleted, troops who were resting were always fed with two good meals a day. Every day two sheep were butchered and their meat was used in a stew.

I slept for nearly forty-eight hours, and then mustered the platoon.

The missing man had arrived, also without a rifle. I made a little speech, partly in Serbian, and partly through Sima, in which I emphasized the importance of taking care of one's arms in all circumstances. I then said that I would not keep in the platoon the man who had run away, but Dragi could have the chance of staying with us to carry ammunition. His rifle, which Rade had found, and his ammunition belt would be given to a new recruit. I promised that the first rifle captured in battle would go to him. He elected to stay.

A stream of clean, soft water ran through the camp. It had previously provided power for the mill. And there, in the evening, I found Daniele, washing her hair. I watched her until she had finished and was drying it in a towel. Then I approached.

'You have beautiful hair,' I said.

'Thank you,' she answered rather coolly, but her eyes smiled.

'You are not as tough and masculine as you pretend,' I teased her.

'A compliment is a compliment at any time,' she replied. A pause, then she said:

'I am tough enough outside, but inside, I am not. I feel I am no longer really me.'

'What do you mean?' I asked.

'You men! This is all right for you. You kill a few Germans, and you take a town, and what then? Do you think you can hold it? Do you think that the Germans will allow you to hold it? Sitting right across their lines of communication? And if it is not across their lines of communication, what good is it to you? You, an English officer, you have seen the German Army, and you ought to know how useless and cruel all this is. We cannot pit ourselves against them. They must beat us in the end.'

I was a little taken aback. 'Cruel?' I said. 'All our men are volunteers, and, as for the Germans, they are our enemies, and soldiers, and after all——'

'After all, after all,' she replied scornfully. 'It's all right for *us*, *we* don't pay for it. The Germans will never catch *us*. But do you know what will happen? Sooner or later this attack will break down, and then the Germans will come out, and they will take hostages from all the villages we have occupied, and will shoot them. They will burn down the villages, as they did in Poland, and put the children into concentration camps. Have you never thought of the women and children in Kraljevo? What is happening to them? When we blockade the town, no food can get in, and the German

9*

garrison takes what is there already. Do you know what it's like to see a little child go hungry, day after day? And when it's all over, what have we accomplished? A few hundred Germans dead, a mere drop in the millions of their army. I tell you we accomplish nothing, nothing.

'We don't even keep the spirit of resistance alive,' she continued. 'These Communists, what do *they* want? They want to attract recruits and be strong, so that when Yugoslavia is liberated, as she will be one day by the English or the Russians (but heaven knows when that will be), they will be able to seize power. They are only working with Draža Mihailović because he is too strong for them at the moment. And *he* is as bad. He wants a Serbian dictatorship over the rest of the country. He is not a Yugoslav, he's a Serb. Power, power, that's all any of them want.

'Have you seen these petty little local leaders,' she went on more calmly, 'how they squabble about a man and a gun? Novaković went away because he wanted to be a commander, and Djurić let him go because *he* wanted to be commander. And Jakčić prefers Djurić to Novaković because Novaković is the stronger man.

'Then *you* look out. You're a pawn, but you have fifteen men, and most of them good ones. They will fight for your support, and try to murder you if they don't get it.'

At that moment Sima came running up.

'The Germans have counter-attacked,' he said. 'They have re-taken the railway station and routed the main force. They are driving along the Ibar valley, half-way between Kraljevo and Ušće.'

Ušće was a little town on the Ibar, twenty miles south of Kraljevo. It was in Partisan hands.

'Jakčić says he's got something for you to do. He wants you at once,' added Sima.

On the way to headquarters I asked Sima if he knew what I was to do.

'Do you know anything about aeroplane bombs?' he asked. 'They want a bridge blown. Could you do it with aeroplane bombs? Their detonators are missing, remember.'

'Is there any other explosive?' I asked.

'I should think so,' said Sima. 'There used to be some T.N.T.'

'Any time-fuse?'

'There's plenty of that, because I've seen it.'

'Tell him, then, that I'll have a crack at it.'

Jakčić explained that it was a high, single-span girder railway bridge across the Ibar. It was about fifty yards long and nearly seventy feet high, and spanned a deep gorge.

'We can't hold them much longer. They have been strongly reinforced from Kragujevac and are using mortars and artillery,' he said. 'We have destroyed some of the other bridges, and that has held up their tanks, but you must get there before dawn to-morrow, which gives you nearly ten hours. The bridge is thirty kilometres from here. You can have as many bombs as you like. I have brought them up by ox-wagon.'

'How many horses can you let me have?' I asked.

'Two,' he replied.

'Right. I'll take four bombs, some hand-grenades, and I want some ammunition for my rifles.'

'You can have a hundred rounds,' said Jakčić.

'And the L.M.G.?'

'Two hundred in all.'

Rade had assembled the men when I returned. 'I want five rifle-men,' I said, 'and someone to carry the ammunition for the L.M.G. Also two men to look after the horses.'

Rade picked the eight best men. 'Are you coming?' I asked Daniele, 'or shall I take the gun?'

It was the only time I ever saw her angry.

We slung a bomb on either side of the two horses, and I packed four pounds of T.N.T. in my pack. Rade also had a dozen hand-grenades of assorted makes. We took bread in our hands, and, with a guide from headquarters, we set out, eating as we marched.

All night, through the dripping trees, we made good progress. As we emerged from the forest, the whole sky on our right hand was lit up.

'What did I tell you?' said Daniele quietly, by my side. 'They are burning already.'

The road was especially bad for the horses. The bombs weighed fifty kilograms each, which made a heavy load for the little mountain ponies. I was still missing one boot, and had my foot wrapped in bandages, which kept wearing out.

We reached the bridge at last, about an hour before dawn. Already firing had started up the valley to the north—and not nearly far enough away to be to my liking. I told the two extra men to off-load the bombs and take the horses back to headquarters. I took the detonators out of the hand-grenades, and showed Rade how to extract the fuse and fix them with the time-fuse which we had brought. He did two perfectly, but the third he bungled, and blew a piece off the top of his finger. Daniele bound it tightly with a handkerchief. I had in the meanwhile prepared six detonators, and I thought that eight would be enough. On to each of the bombs I strapped with string a pound of T.N.T. I tied also two hand-grenades, into which I had reinserted the fuses, to each pound of T.N.T. I allowed two minutes of fuse to make sure of our getaway. Then we placed the four bombs end-to-end across the single track.

By the time we were ready it was dawn. The battle had flared up and I judged that it could not be more than a mile or two, if that, to the north. I posted the five riflemen, and Daniele, with the gun covering the road and railway to the north, though I judged that the Germans would not use the railway at that spot, because of the frequent tunnels. Then I lit the fuses. I ran the hundred and fifty yards to where the rest of the men were, and waited breathlessly. The fuses seemed to take hours to burn. Then there was a single, shattering explosion and, with a rending of steel, the bridge collapsed into the river below. It was perfect.

I had stood up to admire my handiwork when suddenly, beside me, Daniele opened fire. With her usual efficiency, she had not taken her eyes off the road. Three German scout cars had come round the bend. But, no doubt rendered jumpy by the sound of the explosion, they stopped when Daniele fired on them.

My men had ten rounds each, and Daniele a hundred and fifty. The scout cars sprayed the hill with machine-gun fire. Daniele silenced the first. She must have put a burst straight through the loophole. The range was about a hundred and fifty yards. Then, one by one, the men stopped firing as they ran out of ammunition,

'Retreat,' I shouted at them, and they did so, keeping under cover of the rocks.

Daniele went on firing until the belt was empty.

'That's the end,' she said, and raised herself on her elbows.

'Keep down!' screamed Sima. But it was too late. With a little cry, Daniele collapsed over the gun.

Rade and I lifted her, and eased our way up the hillside, towards the crest where we should be out of sight. We had about a hundred yards to cover and, though it normally would have been easy because of the rocks, we went slowly, for we carried Daniele between us.

When we had passed completely out of the line of fire we put her down, and I opened her shirt. A bullet had entered just above the left breast, and passed out below the shoulder blade, leaving a jagged hole. She was bleeding profusely from the wound in her back. I took out my only clean shirt from my haversack, and we bound her up as best we could.

Then Sima cut a couple of ash saplings, and we made a stretcher with Rade's blanket.

But, long before we reached headquarters, she had died. We went on carrying her automatically, each taking turns to rest.

Jakčić was not at headquarters when we reached there. The political commissar had been left in charge. I told him that the bridge was blown.

'Good,' he said. 'Who is that?'

'Daniele, my machine-gunner,' I answered.

'Is she dead?'

'Yes.'

'Have you brought the gun?'

'No.'

'Why not? What is the use of a body? A machine-gun is worth five live men, and five hundred dead ones.'

There did not seem to be anything to say. The commissar and I were poles apart. As I turned away he remarked that, had it been anyone else, he would have had him shot, which was boastful nonsense, and he knew it.

Rade, Sima, and I were very tired. Since we had set out twenty-four hours earlier, we had not slept or eaten. We took a spade and our rifles, and carried Daniele deep into the woods. Under a very tall beech we dug a hole and buried her. Sima wrapped her head in a towel, because, he said, he could not bear to think of the dirt in her hair.

Then by common consent we set out, not for the headquarters, but away from it.

RATWEEK FOR TITO

BY FITZROY MACLEAN

WHEN BRITISH BRIGADIER FITZROY MACLEAN *jumped into Yugoslavia in 1943 with orders to contact Tito and establish liaison, there were several theories concerning the identity of Tito. One group claimed that Tito was a title held at different times by different men. Others believed that he did not exist at all. They claimed the name was formed from the initials of* Tajna Internacionalna Teroristicka Organizacija, *or Secret International Organization. The more romantic theorists said that Tito was not a man but a 'young woman of startling beauty and great force of character'.*

Maclean, however, found a man called Tito, or Josip Broz, holed up in a ruined castle. Tito, a Croat veteran of the First World War and twenty years of exile, prison, and Communist agitation, had taken over his country's Communist Party in 1937. He had reorganized it, given the orders 'you will do this; and you that'—in Serbo-Croat, 'ti, to; ti, to'. By the summer of 1941, he had the Party so well organized it was able to start fighting the Germans with any weapons at hand.

When Tito's Partisans entered the field, they were prepared to serve under the more official Četniks, *a guerrilla group formed by the Royalist Government's Minister of War, Colonel Draža Mihailović. However, despite meetings between the two leaders, no working agreement was ever reached, and the two groups began to fight each other as well as the Germans.*

As German reprisals became more vicious, the Četniks *withdrew from the field, remaining neutral or finding common ground with the invader. With typical Communist ruthlessness, Tito disregarded the reprisals and waged one of the most effective guerrilla campaigns in history. He eventually held nominal control over much of the country with the exception of the cities and towns, and he aided the Allies by forcing the Germans to draw more and more troops from other fronts into Yugoslavia.*

Finally established on the Island of Vis and receiving extensive Allied support, Tito was prepared to consider Operation 'Ratweek'. Brigadier Maclean tells the story of 'Ratweek'.

EVERYWHERE the news was the same: the German offensive was slackening and, gradually, the initiative was passing to the Partisans. And now, from various sources, more and more insistently, came a fresh rumour—a rumour that the Germans were thinking of withdrawing from the Balkans, of cutting their losses and falling back on a more easily tenable defence line in the north.

If the war in Europe was not to be unnecessarily prolonged, it was important that they should not be allowed to carry out this intention unhindered. Taking advantage of the presence of both General Wilson and Tito within easy reach, I accordingly proposed to both a plan designed to ensure that, in the event of a withdrawal, as few Germans as possible would get away safely.

The scheme was called Operation 'Ratweek'. My proposal was that, for the space of one week, timed to coincide as closely as possible with the estimated beginning of the German withdrawal, the Partisans on land, and the Allies on the sea and in the air, should make a series of carefully planned, carefully co-ordinated attacks on enemy lines of communication throughout Yugoslavia. This would throw the retiring forces into confusion and gravely hamper further withdrawal.

I first put this plan to Bill Elliot. He and the other airmen liked it. With the help of the Americans, they could, they said, find the necessary planes. The Navy, always glad of an excuse for some sea raiding, agreed too, and General Wilson, after an hour or two spent going over the plan on the large-scale maps, gave it his final blessing.

The next thing was to make sure that Tito would play. It would have been understandable, if, now that there was a chance of the Germans withdrawing of their own accord, the Yugoslavs, who had suffered so much under the German occupation, had refused to put any obstacles in their way. But it was clear to me at once that this was not a consideration that weighed with Tito. He was all for going on fighting the Germans to the very end. Having listened to what I had to say and to my assurances that the Allied naval and air forces were prepared to co-operate to the utmost, he undertook to instruct his own staff to start planning at once jointly with my officers and representatives of B.A.F. As soon as a detailed plan had been drawn up, he said, he would send instructions to his commanders in the field to take the necessary steps to put it into execution, in consultation with my officers on the spot, whose task it would be to co-ordinate the operations carried out by the Partisans with those of the Allied air forces.

The detailed planning was done for the most part at B.A.F. Head-quarters and my own Rear Headquarters at Bari, where Peter Moore, recently returned from Slovenia, and John Clarke, who had just come back from Montenegro, were now in charge. The whole of Yugoslavia was divided up into sectors; a Partisan commander and the British officer attached to him were made responsible for each, and targets allotted accordingly. Any target, such as a bridge, a viaduct or a railway junction, which was too strongly held by the enemy for the Partisans to be able to attack it with any hope of success, was made the responsibility of the R.A.F. or of the heavy bombers of the United States Army Air Force. Where additional quantities of high explosive or ammunition were needed, special drops were arranged. Plans were made, too, for tactical and strate-gical air support to be given at the appropriate moment to the Partisan forces engaged. Meanwhile our destroyers and M.T.B.s would scour the sea routes.

In drawing up these plans, we had recourse to all available sources of information concerning the enemy's order of battle and the dis-position of his troops, while at every stage we consulted by signal the British officers and the Partisan commanders on the spot. Thus, the whole of the German line of withdrawal would be covered and every possible target accounted for. In the light of what we guessed the enemy's plans to be the attack was fixed for the first week of September.

If the Germans withdrew, their main line of withdrawal north-ward was bound to be along the Vardar Valley and the Belgrade-Salonika railway. For us, this now became the most important target of all. If their communications could be cut here, their situa-tion would indeed be desperate.

My plan was to join John Henniker-Major in southern Serbia, where Koča Popović had his Headquarters. There I should be within easy reach of the Belgrade-Salonika railway and in a good central position from which I could cover wide areas of country. Tito sent a signal to Koča, informing him of my impending arrival and instructing him to make his plans for 'Ratweek' in consultation with me, co-ordinating his operations through me with those of the Allied air forces. He furthermore undertook to send with me, as his personal envoy, General Sreten Žujović, or Crni—the Black—as he was usually known.

Crni, whom I knew from Bosnian days, was one of the outstand-ing figures of the Partisan Movement. Indeed, at this time, he was in effect Tito's Deputy Commander-in-Chief. A Serb by race, he had made himself a name as a guerrilla leader in the original rising in Serbia in the summer of 1941. In addition to his military talents, which were considerable, he was also extremely shrewd politically and possessed remarkable breadth of outlook. He was, too, a first-class organizer, and a good man in a tight spot. Tito used him as a kind of reserve, sending him to take charge in any part of the country where things were going badly for the Partisans or where a military or political crisis had arisen. In appearance he was tall and cadaverous, with lank black hair and pale hollow cheeks, which after midday were covered with a blue-black stubble, for, like most Serbs, he had a strong growth of beard. A continual dry cough showed that on him, as on so many of the Partisans, the sufferings and privations of the war had left a lasting mark. The sadness of his expression was relieved by a pleasant smile and by the vivid intelli-gence of his eyes. Like Koča Popović he spoke almost perfect French, having lived for many years in France. An older man than most of the Partisan generals, he had fought in the French Foreign Legion in the first war. His wide interests and pleasant manners made him an interesting companion, and he was sufficiently sure of his position in the Communist hierarchy to be willing to discuss any topic, however controversial. I was glad he was coming with me. His presence showed, too, the importance which Tito attached to the forthcoming operations in Serbia.

General Žujović was disgraced in 1948 in somewhat obscure cir-cumstances. According to the Russians the reason for his disgrace was his loyalty to them.

The next thing was to get ourselves in. The enemy's general offensive, which in the rest of Yugoslavia had petered out by the end of June, had lasted in Serbia all through July, keeping the Partisans constantly on the move and making it hard for them to receive para-chute drops. In August, however, there came a lull in the fighting, and with it the opportunity I required. John Henniker-Major signalled that Koča Popović's Headquarters were for the time being established on the thickly wooded slopes of the Radan, overlooking the German garrison town of Leskovac on the Niš-Skoplje railway, and that the Partisans were also holding a flat piece of ground near the neighbouring village of Bojnik, where an aircraft could land. There was no time to be lost, for it was impossible to say when the Germans, now thoroughly alarmed at the increased scale of Partisan activities in Serbia, would resume their attacks. I sent a most imme-diate signal to Henniker-Major to say I was coming and warned

Sergeant Duncan and my own wireless operator, Sergeant Campbell, to stand by to accompany me. In a few hours all arrangements
had been made for us to go in on the first possible night.

Before leaving Vis, I climbed up to Tito's cave on Hum to discuss
with him the final plans for 'Ratweek' and to say good-bye. The
broad outline of the plan was now complete and it only remained
to arrange the details with the local commanders. Already additional supply drops were being made and air support laid on for the
forthcoming operations. I found Tito cheerful enough, though, like
me, tired of life on Vis and making plans to leave it. After we had
finished with our maps, food and drink were brought, a plateful of
fried eggs and a bottle of sweet Dalmatian wine, and we talked of
Serbia, which Tito had not visited since the heroic days of 1941.
Then he wished me good luck and good-bye. We parted with
jocular assurances that we would meet again in Belgrade.

At first sight, landing by plane had seemed an infinitely more
normal and agreeable method of entering a country than what Mr.
Churchill called 'jumping out of a parachute'. But, when we
reached our destination and, in the pitch blackness of a moonless,
overcast night, began to circle lower and lower through the clouds,
over hilly country, towards what might or might not be a suitable
landing strip for a Dakota, I found myself wondering whether a
parachute jump would not after all have been preferable. Then,
through the mist, the signal fires flared up on the ground below;
we circled once or twice more; the flaps went down, the revolutions
of the propellers became slower, and soon we were bumping and
jolting to a standstill over the uneven soil of Serbia.

A Partisan, leading some horses, emerged from the shadows. We
had kept our personal kit to a bare minimum and, once the wireless
set had been strapped to a pack pony, we were ready to start. Then
the Partisan officer who had come to meet us took the lead and we
galloped off. As we left the flat open ground of the landing strip
and, crossing a little bridge, entered a clump of trees, some shots
were fired from nearby and the bullets whistled past us in the darkness. It was too dark to see anything, but clearly there were people
in the immediate neighbourhood who were not on the same side as
we were.

The ride that followed was long and dreary, through thick bush
and scrub, mostly uphill, but with occasional abrupt descents, slithering and sliding down the sides of stony ravines. There was still no
moon and the horses were anything but sure-footed, needing con-

stant helping and coaxing over the rougher patches. Their German
Army saddles, too, were far too big for them and threatened cease-
lessly to slide under their bellies or even over their heads. It was
with frayed tempers that we eventually reached our destination in
the early hours of the morning.

After a good deal of rather irritable groping about in the dark, I
found John Henniker-Major asleep under the trees in a kind of wig-
wam made of part of a parachute stretched over some branches. In a
few minutes I had fixed up a similar shelter against the steady drizzle
that was now falling, and, spreading out my sleeping bag beneath it,
lay down for a few hours' sleep.

When I woke, the sun was shining through the trees and Campbell and Duncan were busy frying a tin of bacon we had brought
with us. It smelled delicious. We were on the edge of a little clearing in the wood. Somewhere nearby I could hear the sound of
running water. Behind us, a great forest of oaks and beeches
stretched up towards the summit of the Radan. Immediately in
front of us, sloping downhill, lay a brief expanse of green turf, like
an English lawn. Beyond, the woods began again, covering the
lower slopes and the foothills with a blanket of foliage. Then,
beyond that again, for mile upon mile, stretching away to the
hazy blue of the horizon, the rich rolling countryside of Serbia was
spread out before us in the sunshine, a patchwork of green orchards
and yellow maize fields with, dotted here and there, the white-
washed walls of a village and the onion spire of a church. There
could have been no greater contrast with the austere uplands of
Bosnia or the stony barrenness of Dalmatia than this peaceful,
smiling landscape.

Crawling out of my sleeping bag and pulling on my boots, I spent
the next few minutes rousing John Henniker-Major, always a heavy
sleeper. In the course of the night he had rolled out of his improvised tent and half-way down the hill. There his progress had
been checked by the stump of a tree, round which he was now
curled, snoring peacefully. This was to repeat itself night after night
during the weeks that followed. The distance which he covered in
the course of his slumbers varied according to the steepness of the
hill on which we happened to be camping, but he scarcely ever woke
on the same spot where he had gone to sleep. He had had a bad
time of late and I suppose that the effect on his nerves showed itself
in this way. Certainly there was no other indication that his composure was in any way ruffled.

After breakfasting lavishly off black bread, crisply fried bacon and some freshly brewed tea, we sat down on the grass in the sun, and John settled down to give me some account of his experiences and impressions since first being dropped into Serbia four months earlier.

Next I discussed with Koča Popović the detailed plans for 'Ratweek'.

He was living nearby, and after breakfast we strolled across to where he was encamped under the trees. On the way John pointed out to me a wooded hilltop, standing out from the rest a couple of miles away across the valley, which, he said, was held by White Russians who were fighting for the Germans. To the west and the east, respectively, the Germans were installed in the Ibar and the Morava Valleys. To the north the Bulgars held Niš, Prokuplje and the valley of the Toplica. To the south were the Albanians, and the local Albanian minority, the Arnauts.

I found Koča sitting with Crni under the trees, a brisk, businesslike figure in his neat grey uniform with his large black moustache. When he talked the words came rattling out like bullets from a machine-gun, and his deep-set brown eyes sparkled with energy and intelligence. Very able and, for all his talk of only wanting to retire to study philosophy, extremely ambitious, he was clearly delighted with his new command and with the prospect which it brought him of being first into Belgrade.

Almost every day I spent an hour or two with Koča.

By the last days of August our preparations for 'Ratweek' were complete, and we started to watch with redoubled keenness for any signs of an impending enemy withdrawal. But still there was no indication that the Germans had made up their minds to move, and we reflected a little sadly that it would, after all, have been too good to be true if we had really guessed the enemy's intentions to within a few days. At any rate it was something that, when they did start to go, they would find their road and railway communications well and truly wrecked.

As the appointed day approached, I decided to make my way down to join the Partisan force which was to attack the railway in the Leskovac area. Having taken leave of Koča Popović, who was also moving off to supervise operations elsewhere, John and I set out, accompanied by Sergeant Duncan and by Sergeant Campbell, with his wireless set on a pack pony. The sun was shining as we started downhill towards the valley. It was hot and we marched in our shirt sleeves. Soon we came out from under the trees to find the maize turning golden in the fields and the trees in the orchards weighed down with fruit. From the clover came the hum of bees and a lark was singing somewhere high above us. The track under our feet was white and dusty. The scene had all the serenity of a late summer's day at home.

Then, suddenly, from the other side of the valley, came the crack and roar of an explosion, and, looking to where the sound had come from, we saw, against the blue of the sky, a great cloud of white smoke billowing up from the hill where the White Russians had been encamped. Other detonations followed the first and, as the smoke cleared away, we could see that something was burning fiercely. If these were the results of a Partisan attack, it had clearly been a most successful one. We were only surprised to have heard nothing of the preparations for it.

After we had gone some way, we met a Partisan riding hard in the direction from which we had come. We asked him if he knew what was happening. He said that he had come from a nearby out-post and was on his way to report. The White Russians had blown up their ammunition dump and set fire to their huts and were now evacuating the position.

It was only gradually that the full significance of what we had seen dawned on us. At the places where we stopped to rest, scraps of information reached us, all pointing to one conclusion, and, later, when we set up our aerial and made contact with Bari and with other parts of Yugoslavia, we received still more definite informa-tion to the same effect. There could no longer be any doubt about it. The German withdrawal had begun. By a piece of immense good fortune our timing for 'Ratweek' had, it seemed, been perfect. The knowledge filled us with a sense of agreeable anticipation.

Our first day's march brought us to Bojnik, where I had been landed a week earlier, and the following evening we reached the village where the commander of the Twenty-fourth Partisan Division, the formation responsible for the attack on the railway in the Leskovac area, had set up his headquarters. The Partisan Divisional Staff and Johnny Tregida, my liaison officer with the Twenty-fourth Division, were living in a rambling white farm-house opposite the little Orthodox church.

The place was in an uproar. A batch of Bulgar prisoners had just been brought in and were being herded into the courtyard. Dour, swarthy, stocky little men, in dark-grey uniforms and German-type steel helmets, they sat or lay about on the ground glumly while the

Partisans sorted out the officers from the other ranks. The Bulgar rank and file, the divisional commander explained, could sometimes be prevailed upon to join the Partisans, but the officers were for the most part hardened 'Fascists'. Until recently few Bulgars had been taken prisoner; they had fought with a determination and a brutality equal to that of the Germans. Now they no longer showed quite the same reluctance to surrender. I recalled what the German colonel had told us about the Bulgars at Koča's Headquarters and, remembering that in World War I Bulgaria had been the first of Germany's allies to crack, wondered whether something of the kind might not be happening now.

We had our evening meal that night in the Partisan commander's mess, a merry gathering which included two Orthodox priests with long hair and beards who seemed to have attached themselves to the Division as chaplains. The life and soul of the party was Brko (or 'Whiskers'), the Chief of Staff, a cheerful character with sandy hair and a flowing moustache in the best Serbian style. With him we discussed our future movements. He would, he said, take us himself to the headquarters of the brigade who were carrying out the main attack on the line north of Leskovac. If we started next morning we should just arrive in time.

It was hot down in the plain, and, not relishing the idea of a night indoors in a crowded room, I unrolled my sleeping bag outside in the yard. But there I was little better off: people stumbled over me; mosquitoes attacked me; while the Bulgars, anxious no doubt as to their prospects of survival, kept up a constant monotonous mumbling.

After riding all the next afternoon through rolling, park-like country, we came to the tiny hamlet where the brigade commander had established himself in preparation for his attack on the line. From the rising ground on which it was situated, the town of Leskovac could be seen, spread out in the valley below, at a distance of not more than a mile or two from where we were. A mile away to the south, fighting was in progress for the possession of a ridge, overlooking our present position, which the Partisans had captured and which the enemy were now seeking to win back. The issue was still in doubt and, as we entered the village, the noise of machine-guns and mortars could be heard, first nearer and then further away. Spasmodically, the sounds of firing continued to reach us during the night.

Next day, the first day of 'Ratweek', dawned bright and fine. The battle of the night before was over. The enemy had withdrawn, leaving the Partisans in possession of the ridge, and everything was now quiet. The attack on the railway was scheduled for that night. The Partisans were to attack two points to the north and south of Leskovac, blowing up bridges and demolishing as much of the permanent way as possible. Leskovac itself, the seat of a strong German garrison, including, it was rumoured, a good deal of armour, was to be left to the Allied air forces. Apart from the actual damage which an air attack would do to transport and installations, it would, it was hoped, shake the morale of the mixed German and quisling garrison and help to soften them up in preparation for the Partisan operations against the railway that night.

As we sat at breakfast, Sergeant Campbell came running down from the hillside where he had set up his wireless, with a most immediate signal. It was from Bill Elliot. Air reconnaissance, he said, confirmed the presence of a strong concentration of armour and motor transport of all kinds in Leskovac, and it had accordingly been decided to turn the heavy bombers on to it. A force of fifty Fortresses would attack it at eleven-thirty.

We had not expected anything on this scale. It seemed rather like taking a sledge hammer to crack a walnut. Up to now the 'Heavies' had not been so easy to come by, being needed for the really big targets in Austria and northern Italy. But evidently 'Ratweek' was going to be done in style as far as the Allied air forces were concerned.

As the appointed hour approached, we gathered in a little group on the hillside and stood waiting. Seeing that we were watching for something to happen, some peasant women and an old man or two from the village came and joined us, looking out across the valley. A mile or two away we could see the white houses of Leskovac spread out in the warm autumn sunshine. In the trees the birds twittered. From a pond nearby came the occasional croak of a bullfrog. The cornfield buzzed with the hum of innumerable insects. It would have been hard to conceive of a more tranquil scene. Standing there waiting, I tried to think of the German garrison and tank crews, and not of the population of small farmers, shopkeepers and railway workers, of the old people, the women and children, who at this moment would be going about their everyday business in the streets.

Eleven-twenty came, and eleven-twenty-five. Still there was nothing. The peasants grew tired of waiting and started to drift away. At eleven-thirty the Chief of Staff consulted the immense turnip of a watch which he wore strapped to his wrist and looked at me inquiringly. I began to wonder whether there had not perhaps been a technical hitch.

Then, almost before we could take it in, it had happened. There was a noise of engines, at first barely audible, then rapidly growing to a roar, and looking up we saw at a great height row upon row of bombers steadfastly following their appointed course, their polished wings gleaming in the sunlight. The peasants started counting them: six, ten, twenty, thirty—they had never seen so many. Already the Fortresses were over their target—were past it—when, as we watched, the whole of Leskovac seemed to rise bodily into the air in a tornado of dust and smoke and debris, and a great rending noise fell on our ears. When we looked at the sky again, the Forts, still relentlessly following their course, were mere silvery dots in the distance. In a few seconds the noise of their engines had faded and everything round us was quiet again, the silence only broken by the wailing of one of the women; she had, they said, relations in the town. What was left of Leskovac lay enveloped in a pall of smoke; several buildings seemed to be burning fiercely. Even the Partisans seemed subdued.

The rest of that day passed in making a general reconnaissance in preparation for the night's activities. Nothing was stirring in the valley, and John and I walked down to a village just outside the town. We found it in an uproar, full of people who had just come out of Leskovac. The civilian casualties had been heavy; but the raid, it seemed, had achieved its object, for there had been direct hits on several buildings occupied by Germans, they had lost much of their transport and armour, and the morale of the garrison had reached a low ebb, particularly as far as the non-German portion of it was concerned. Many of the Četniks, employed on guard duties, were already on their way out to join the Partisans.

This augured well for the evening's operations and we now set out, while it was still light, to visit the Partisan positions nearest the railway, from which the main attack north of Leskovac would be launched.

We approached the line by a circuitous route, which brought us to the back of a little ridge immediately overlooking the railway. There we left our horses and climbed upwards through a field of Indian corn, which reached well above our heads and provided excellent cover. On top of the ridge we found Partisan outposts established. Crouching beside them, we looked down on the railway a few hundred yards away. An officer gave us some idea of the enemy defences. These consisted of concrete pill boxes and occasional patrols up and down the line. Suddenly, a machine-gun from one of the pill boxes opened up at an unseen target, and there was an answering chatter of automatic weapons all along the line. It looked as though the enemy were expecting trouble. As we mounted our horses and rode off, first one sniper's bullet and then another went pinging and whining past our heads.

It was to a nearby point low down on the face of the ridge and quite close to the railway that we returned that night after dark. A mile or two away to the south, the sky was lit up by the fires that were still burning in Leskovac. Every now and then a great tongue of flame would go leaping up into the night sky as the blaze got a firmer hold on the little town.

Round us, it was dark and quiet. We took up our position at the foot of the ridge and waited. The flat ground below the ridge was marshy and a mist was rising from it. It was cold waiting. I watched the flames leaping and flickering over the burning town and the thin white swirls of mist drifting up from the marshy ground. As I stood there, it occurred to me that all over Yugoslavia other little parties were at this time attacking or waiting to attack.

Then, suddenly, firing broke out at several places along the line, and soon on both sides of us bright fountains of tracer bullets were spurting from a dozen different points, while answering fire flew back to meet them. Here and there, the flash and thud of a mortar, breaking in on the chatter of the machine-guns, showed where the Partisans were bestowing special attention on a pill box. The attack had begun.

Under cover of it, the Partisans carrying the loads of explosive now made their way down to the line and laid their charges. Presently they touched them off, and, for a moment, the roar of one explosion after another drowned the lesser sounds of battle. The charges had been laid under a number of small bridges and culverts at intervals along the line. Now, to round off their task, the Partisans set to work tearing up long stretches of the permanent way. Stacked in heaps, the sleepers were set alight and blazed merrily. Someone had found a freight car in a siding, and this too was set on fire and sent flaming down the track towards Leskovac.

From some of the pill boxes there still came an intermittent trickle of tracer, but several had already been silenced and it was clear that the defence was losing heart. Looking over my shoulder as we made our way back up the ridge before dawn, the last thing I saw was a ring of triumphant Partisans who, with linked hands, were dancing a Serbian *kolo* round one of the fires that was blazing near the line, their black figures outlined against the flames like demons in hell.

It would be some time before that particular stretch of the Belgrade-Salonika railway was again open to traffic. The enemy forces in Greece, if they were to get out at all, would have to get out by road or by sea, a hazardous proceeding in either event. If everywhere else the Partisans had done their job as thoroughly as here, 'Ratweek' would have got off to a good start.

For the next day or two we remained in the region of Leskovac, collecting information and passing it back to Balkan Air Force. The Partisan attack on the line south of Leskovac had also been successful and so had our air attacks on a couple of bridges. From Bari and from my officers all over Yugoslavia reports kept coming in of operations successfully carried out both by the Allied air forces and by the Partisans. From Slovenia came news of another important viaduct demolished: the Litija bridge on the Ljubljana-Zagreb railway, a key point on the enemy's line of retreat. Here the Americans had given invaluable help. United States Army Air Force Mustangs had 'softened up' the target while Jimmy Goodwin, a hefty young American engineer officer who had been attached to us, had played a leading part in the Partisans' final assault on the ancient castle guarding the bridge—a part for which he was later awarded the Military Cross.

At first the enemy seemed stunned by the suddenness and violence of the onslaught. Then came the inevitable reaction. There was a counter-attack and for some days we were kept more or less constantly on the move.

In the skirmishing which ensued the neighbouring town of Lebane fell into the hands of the Partisans and we attended an impromptu political meeting held on the occasion of its liberation.

We did not stay long in Lebane. Soon we were on the move again, travelling northwards in the direction of the Toplica Valley where I hoped to join up again with Koča. The reports of 'Ratweek' which I had received hitherto were so encouraging that I was thinking of suggesting that operations should be continued for a second week, and I wanted to discuss with him future plans for Serbia.

Under cover of their counter-attack the Germans were already making frantic efforts to repair the railway, but they had reckoned without the Balkan Air Force. Every time we received reports of a breakdown gang at work, we signalled its location to Bari, and within a few hours our fighters were on to it.

Each evening towards sunset would come the cry of '*Avioni!*' and, looking up, we would see the familiar shapes of two or three Junkers 52 transport planes winging their way ponderously northward, like geese against the evening sky. The evacuation of Greece and Macedonia had already begun and these, no doubt, were senior staff officers and others, who preferred not to attempt the journey by train and were getting out by air while the going was good. Here was a loophole which needed blocking up. A signal to Bill Elliot, giving the time and approximate route of these flights, did the trick. Somewhere or other our fighters must have swooped down on them for after that we did not see them again.

But still we got no rest. The Partisans, it appeared, were advancing in the wake of the retreating Germans. What was more, the Bulgars had capitulated. This meant that the Partisans might be able to gain possession of the towns of Niš and Prokuplje. Then came confirmation over the wireless that Bulgar representatives were in Cairo, negotiating armistice terms with the British and Americans. Then the news that the Soviet Government, in order not to be left out of the peace negotiations, had somewhat belatedly declared war on the Bulgars with whom they had up to then maintained normal diplomatic relations. Our jokes about this somewhat transparent manœuvre on the part of our Soviet allies were not very well received. Then almost immediately we heard that the Bulgars had entered the war on our side. There was a tendency to refer to them as Slav Brothers. But this went against the grain with a good many people, for the atrocities committed by the Bulgars were still fresh in their minds. The Bulgars, for their part, did not seem to care very much which side they were on. Having hitherto fought for the Germans with efficiency and brutality, they now fought against them in exactly the same fashion, still wearing their German-type helmets and uniforms.

Prokuplje was liberated, and we entered it in triumph, a typical Serbian market town, at the end of a branch line of the railway, consisting of a single wide straggling sun-baked street of low houses, which at one point widened out into a market square. A group of statuary in the centre celebrated a previous liberation from some earlier oppressor. Outside the municipal building a notice had been posted proclaiming an amnesty for certain categories of collaborators provided that they joined the Partisans before a certain date. A little crowd of citizens were looking at it dubiously.

A Liberation dinner followed a Liberation luncheon. Photographs were taken, speeches made, songs sung and healths drunk. I was presented with a bouquet by a schoolgirl. In the intervals we went shopping. It was the first time we had been in a town of this size since we arrived in Yugoslavia and it rather went to our heads. The shops were full of German-made goods and local produce and we bought all kinds of things we did not really want. Just as we were leaving I caught sight of a full-sized enamel bath outside a junk shop and bought it for a pound.

There was talk of establishing our headquarters in Prokuplje itself, but for the moment we continued to camp outside. I myself slept in a barn which I shared with an owl and some largish animal which I heard but never quite saw—a stoat, possibly, or a polecat. My bath arrived on an ox-cart and we decided to have a hot bath— the first for weeks. The bath was erected in an orchard and a cauldron of water put on to boil. The Partisans and the local peasants watched the whole proceeding from a distance, now convinced that we must be quite mad.

But at this moment a messenger galloped up on a horse, shouting, '*Pokret!*' The Germans, it appeared, had counter-attacked, not unsuccessfully, and we were on the move once more. Reluctantly abandoning our bath, we stuffed our few belongings into our rucksacks, or, as we had come to call them, *pokret*-bags, and set out.

From Prokuplje we headed for the Radan, always a relatively safe refuge in case of trouble. On the way Koča and I, keeping in touch with the Balkan Air Force, planned further operations in continuation of 'Ratweek'. The enemy's counter-attack might temporarily relieve their situation, but, once it had spent itself, they would still be faced with the problem of getting the bulk of their troops out by one or two main routes which were open to attack for the whole of their length. The 'Ratweek' operations undertaken up to now had already sufficiently demonstrated what could be done in this way.

For the next two or three days we kept on the move. It was the same agreeable existence which I had led ever since my arrival in Serbia. The long early morning marches through the green, sunlit countryside; the halt at midday on the grass under the fruit-laden trees of some wayside orchard; the search, as night approached, for a good place to camp and the arrival of extravagantly hospitable villagers with grapes and peaches, bottles of wine and suckling pigs, fresh eggs and butter; the evening meal and the brief period of tranquillity in the half-light before it grew quite dark. Then either a night of alarms and excursions, of attacks and counter-attacks, of marches and counter-marches, of rumours and counter-rumours; or else, all the more peaceful by contrast, a long sleep under the stars with the wind on one's face and the trees rustling overhead, until the sun rose and it was time to start. And, bubbling again up within one all the time, a feeling of elation which came from the knowledge that victory, complete and overwhelming, was at last at hand.

IN THE CLOSING DAYS *of 'Ratweek', General Wilson radioed Maclean that Tito had disappeared from Vis. The young brigadier searched without success. A month later Stalin told Churchill that Tito had been to the Kremlin. When asked why he had kept his trip a secret, Tito answered, 'Mr. Churchill went to Quebec to see President Roosevelt and I only heard of this after he returned. And I was not angry.' It was apparent that the Partisan chief had not only become the head of a nation but that he was an independent man.*

SONS OF THE EAGLE

BY JULIAN AMERY

DURING THE LAST WAR *the world conflicts of our time ran their course in the microcosm of Albania. The great powers and the small struggled in this diminutive country.*

Italy invaded Albania in 1939 and King Zog fled. Briefly stymied at Durazzo by the defence of tribal chief Abas Kupi, who was more impassioned than brilliant, Italy finally conquered. Faced with Italy's failure in Greece, Germany moved into the Balkans and took over Albania along with the rest of that bloody peninsula. Then a struggle began that was to find its counterpart across the world.

The feudal tribal chiefs were driven by a love of freedom and king, while the illiterate peasants and workers possessed in addition to their love of freedom, a sense of social justice. Their mutual desire for a free Albania brought both groups into the field against the Germans. A mutual social distrust brought them into conflict with each other. The same conflict took place in Yugoslavia, Greece, and China—the Reds and non-Reds against a common enemy and each other for the post-war control of their countries.

Britain offered to supply arms to whoever was already fighting the Germans. The Communist Partisans, receiving supplies as well as technical advice from Russia, easily met this requirement. The non-Communists, poorly equipped and fighting among themselves, hesitated and talked. For many reasons the fear of German reprisals meant more to them.

Julian Amery, a British officer in Albania assigned to the tribal chiefs, tells this story of his attempt to bring them into the fight. He negotiated with Abas Kupi for months and then returned to his base for a final conference.

WE had next to consider what form of warfare they might be capable of waging. This called for some inquiry into the fundamental principles of revolt—a branch of the military art on which the textbooks of the Staff College offered but little guidance. Our masters had been Lawrence and Wingate: from Wingate we had learned the theory of the 'striking force'; from Lawrence much about example and the use of gold. Neither, however, had encountered the curious dichotomy of revolt which faced us in Albania and which was the cause of so much confusion at Headquarters. Lawrence, indeed, had written that 'revolt was more like peace than like war', but this had only been to state the problem. War and revolt were both extensions of politics; but it seemed to us that revolt was really war in reverse—the process whereby the vertical relationship between conqueror and conquered was changed into the horizontal juxtaposition of rival belligerents.

In war the contending parties faced each other across a more or less clearly demarcated front line. Behind the front the writ of each government ran much as in time of peace; the state continued to protect the essential interests of the public; and the resources of society were harnessed to each nation's war effort. The fortunes of battle might lead to the loss of large tracts of territory, but the government concerned would continue to administer the remainder, where its subjects might safely retire with their families and at least their movable property. The development of total war had increased the dangers and responsibilities of the home front, but the heaviest burden still fell on the armed forces who were called on to defend, if necessary with their lives, the land, the property, and the noncombatants of the nation. War was thus a process in which a whole community was organized for offence or defence under its natural leaders; in which those with the greatest stake in the community had most interest in the result; and in which the combatants bore the heaviest burden. Victory was only complete when the front line had ceased to exist.

Revolt began where war ended; for in revolt there was no front line; and the insurgents and their enemies lived cheek by jowl in the same towns, and even in the same streets. Revolt was, by definition, irregular and became war, in fact if not in law, as soon as the insurgents could defend and administer wide, inhabited regions; as soon, that is, as they passed from guerrilla to positional warfare. Until then the state powers of protection and coercion remained the monopoly of their opponents, and the insurgents could do little to defend the relatives or the property of their supporters. This was their weakness and at the same time their strength: it prevented them from defending fixed positions, but it left them free to fight only on ground of their own choosing and to disperse rather than face unequal odds. Their conditions of life might be harsh, but they were less dangerous than a soldier's in battle; a guerrilla had only his own life to defend; and to escape from foreign soldiers was no great problem for an able-bodied man fighting in his own country. This

elusiveness of the guerrillas drove their opponents to indirect retaliation; they imprisoned their families and confiscated their property,
and even proceeded against the harmless villagers who had failed to
denounce or to prevent their operations. Thus, in revolt, the
heaviest burden fell not on the combatants, as in war, but on the
wives and children, the cattle and the homes which remained as
hostages in the hands of the enemy.

It followed from this that the elements most naturally inclined to
revolt were the young who had no family responsibilities and the
'have-nots', who had no property to lose. To them revolt offered
faith, discipline, and a way of life; and the strength which they
acquired collectively in battle afforded hopes of wealth and power in
the event of victory. They started from nothing; their organization
was moulded in the forge of war; its growth was slow. Prolonged
guerrilla warfare was thus their natural military expression. By the
same token, those with a stake in the country were at a disadvantage
in guerrilla war; for their families and possessions were so many
hostages in the hands of the enemy. Heroes among them might
sacrifice their all to fight for freedom; the braver sort would run
great risks for great gains; but the majority would only take the field
if they knew that their families and homes were safe from enemy
reprisals. Without such protection, indeed, either they would withdraw their support from the revolt or else the social order itself
would be transformed by the destruction through reprisals of the
property relationships on which it was based. The leaders of an
established society would therefore tend to postpone revolt until
their hopes of victory outweighed their fears of reprisals. At the
same time—and this was their great advantage over the other sort
of revolutionaries—if they once decided to fight, they would not
have to create a new organization but would go into action with the
full force of an organized community behind them.

Applied to the situation in Albania, this theory explained the
difference between the Partisans and the Gheg tribal confederacies,
and showed that their military efforts must naturally develop along
different lines. The Partisans had started as a small Communist cell,
destitute of resources, and had slowly recruited their forces from
among the landless peasants and the youth of the towns. By joining
an avowedly social-revolutionary movement these recruits had
become outlaws; there could be no turning back; and, since they
lacked personal wealth or the backing of a tribe, they were easily
subjected to the discipline of a movement on which they depended
for their daily bread. With no resources of their own, the Partisans

had to fight if they would eat, and thus were driven from one raid to another by sheer necessity. Nor was their zeal for war and plunder restrained by fear of reprisals against property; for they were, by definition, of the dispossessed. Indeed they might even welcome reprisals; for, by adding to the number of the dispossessed, reprisals added to the number of their potential supporters, while the destruction of property which they involved weakened the economic foundations of a hostile social order. The operations of the Partisans, therefore, took the form of sustained guerrilla raids; and their movement fed on the devastation which it caused and grew, Phœnix-like, from the ashes of its own defeats. Sometimes they attacked the Germans; more often they plundered their richer compatriots; but whether they advanced the cause of national liberation or of social revolution, the bitterness of their enemies convinced them that they could never lay aside their arms with impunity, except as masters of Albania. Thus discipline was seconded by experience of battle, and morale was fortified by the knowledge that their only hope of safety lay in victory.

The conditions of a Gheg were altogether different, for the Gheg leaders were the representatives of the existing social order; and their strength was rooted in the tribal system. Gheg armies were nothing but the tribes on a war footing; and each contingent marched under the orders of its own tribal chief. In the simple conditions of highland life considerable forces might thus be mustered at little more than a day's notice; and each tribesman in them would be a natural guerrilla and an accurate marksman. Discipline, however, was rare; the habit of teamwork unknown; and at every stage in a campaign protracted negotiations supplied the place of concise orders. But, besides being invertebrate, Gheg armies were also short-winded; for they depended for their food supplies on the bounty of the clans, and no region could long support the expense of a campaign. The tribesmen, moreover, were shepherds and farmers, and, as such, were continually distracted by domestic cares and especially sensitive to the threat of reprisals against property. To obtain their support, therefore, the revolt must be a paying proposition; and it was essential to show that the prospects of plunder or subsidies would exceed the probable costs of fighting and outweigh the expectation of losses through reprisals.

This fundamental consideration lent certain distinctive features to the warfare of the Ghegs. They required a sufficient extent of territory as a 'safe harbour' into which the non-combatants might withdraw with their flocks and movable property beyond the reach of enemy punitive expeditions. They sought to raise the strongest possible fighting force, not only for its weight in the attack, but also to deter the enemy from lightly sending out troops to devastate their homes. Above all, they aimed at achieving a decisive victory in the shortest possible time, so as to win the spoils of war without incurring expenses or reprisals. The Gheg tribes were thus wholly unsuited to sustained guerrilla raids which involved living on the country and might lead to heavy reprisals. Instead, their natural form of offensive war was a general revolt, based on the full extent of their territory, supported by the strongest available forces and directed to attaining their objective in the shortest possible time.

We had seen for ourselves that no single Gheg leader swayed a broad enough region or a sufficient following to challenge the Germans alone. But if the five great chieftains, Abas Kupi, Gani Kryeziu, Muharrem Bairaktar, Jon Marko Joni, and Fikri Dine, were to rise up together they would encounter the German army on more equal terms. Their combined territories would provide an impenetrable 'safe harbour' where the non-combatants could withdraw with their flocks and where the tribesmen might await military supplies from Italy without fear of enemy interception. Their combined forces, moreover, would amount to somewhere between fifteen and twenty-five thousand rifles, which would be rapidly reinforced with mortars and machine-guns from the Allied arsenals. Such an army would be comparable in numbers, if not in equipment, and superior in valour, if inferior in discipline, to that of the L.N.C. (Partisan); nor was it by any means certain that the Germans still possessed the energy or could spare the troops for its suppression. We concluded, therefore, that Gheg resistance against the Germans must take the form of a general revolt.

This conception of a general revolt had for some weeks been shaping in our minds; and we had already prepared the ground for its fulfilment in our preliminary negotiations with the Gheg leaders. Gani Kryeziu was already fighting the Germans; agreement with Abas Kupi seemed to hang on instructions from King Zog; Muharrem Bairaktar had announced his readiness to take the field if armed; and Jon Marko Joni and Fikri Dine had sounded Abas Kupi to learn on what terms they might now change sides. Starting from this foundation the next step was to reach final agreement with Abas Kupi. Once this had been done we would summon a congress of all the Gheg leaders and their satellite chiefs and invite them to proclaim a general revolt of North Albania.

Our chances of success, however, were threatened by the danger of a conflict between the Zogists and the Partisans; and this it was our duty to prevent for weighty reasons, military and political: military, because civil war must consume the energies of both resistance movements at the expense of their operations against the Germans; political, because the probable event of a Partisan victory would lead to the establishment of a Russian-dominated dictatorship; a result which would be in keeping neither with our advocacy of democratic government, nor indeed with our more permanent interests. We were soldiers and in our minds the importance of 'War Aims' was naturally overshadowed by the purely military problem of how to beat the Germans. Nevertheless we could not altogether escape political responsibility; for we were the only British representatives in North Albania, and we knew that British policy in that country must in part at least be informed by our reports.

At this time the only Partisan forces in North Albania were the 'Kosmet' group, about a hundred strong, and two small bands, each of some thirty men, which were tolerated in their regions by Abas Kupi and Muharrem Bairaktar to please our Mission. There was thus no Partisan problem among the Ghegs; but the main forces of the L.N.C. were moving northwards towards the Shkumbi; and it could not be long before they came up against the Zogist outposts. No one could say with certainty whether civil war might then be averted; but we knew that the Zogists would resist any attempt by the Partisans to enter their territories.

We realized that civil war must disappoint our hopes of a Gheg revolt; for it was too much to expect that Abas Kupi or any of the tribal leaders should fight against the Germans and the Partisans at the same time. We feared besides that the Zogists might be reduced to such straits by the Partisans that they would accept help from the 'collaborationists', or even from the Germans. The natural right of self-defence might justify such action; but, if the Zogists once became involved with the Germans, from whatever motive, it might become impossible for us to continue to support them. Such a situation had just arisen in Yugoslavia and had led, for reasons not unconnected with the Conferences of Cairo and Teheran, to the withdrawal of the British Missions from General Mihailović. We had often reminded Abas Kupi of this example; and he had offered in return to meet the Partisan leaders and seek agreement with them. Enver Hoja, however, had contemptuously rejected these proposals and already stigmatized the passivity of the Zogists as 'collaboration' with the enemy. It was difficult, indeed, to see how interests so diametrically opposed might yet be reconciled. Abas Kupi represented the ancient supremacy of the Ghegs, the oligarchy of the tribal chiefs and a Nationalist tradition which looked to Great Britain as the Power most interested in assuring Albanian independence. Enver Hoja represented the self-assertion of the Tosks, the Communist will to power, and an exclusively Russian orientation in foreign policy. The decline of German fortunes had dissolved their short-lived community of interests; and events had now come to a pass where each rightly discerned in the other's attitude towards the invaders nothing but a manœuvre in their domestic struggle for power. Now only Abas Kupi stood between Enver Hoja and his goal; for, if Central Albania was once reduced, the other Gheg chiefs would be in no position to offer effective resistance to the L.N.C. Our information indeed suggested that Enver was already planning to attack the Zogists with the deliberate intention of driving them into the arms of the Germans and so discrediting them before the Allies. To identify rivals with enemies was part of Communist stock-in-trade; and it was by similar tactics that the Balli Kombeter had been destroyed.

The prospects of settlement were bleak, but we knew that some of the Partisan leaders disagreed with Enver Hoja's policy. It still seemed possible, moreover, that, if Abas Kupi took the field with the chief men among the Ghegs, Albanian public opinion might cause the Partisans to hesitate before attacking so popular and strong a leader. Besides, once Abas Kupi was at war, our Headquarters would be justified in bringing the strongest pressure to bear on the Partisans in favour of a reconciliation with the Zogists.

These conclusions were duly embodied into telegrams with a strong recommendation in favour of relaxing our insistence on the policy of 'No arms before action'. Our inability to give political assurances only seemed to increase the importance of providing the chiefs with some alternative encouragement. Besides, surprise was of the essence of a general revolt, and the success of the initial uprising would require some previous accumulation of arms. Beyond this it only remained for us to consider how strongly we should urge our plan upon Headquarters. Many factors in the situation remained imponderable; many obstacles still stood in the way of its fulfilment. Nevertheless we expressed our conviction that a general revolt offered the best, perhaps the only, means of bringing the Ghegs to fight the Germans and of averting civil war.

The day of our return to base had thus been devoted to the study of accumulated telegrams and to the discussion of plans. Abas Kupi had meanwhile withdrawn with his following to a nearby village, but returned to our camp next day to resume negotiations. Besides the Zogist chiefs of Central Albania he was now accompanied by Nik Sokol and Father Lek Luli. Nik Sokol was a tall, square-headed adventurer, who defended the Zogist interest in the lands beyond the Drin. His counsels swayed the *Bairaktars* of Nikai and Mertur, and he had for some time afforded hospitality in those regions to Neel and his Mission. Father Lek was a dark and turbulent young monk from Scutari, who preached the Gospel of Christ and the cause of King Zog with equal zeal to the Catholic tribes of the north. He wore the brown cowl and sandals of the Franciscan order; and the pistol and sub-machine-gun which he carried bore witness to his militant conception of the priesthood.

The sun shone and the numerous retinues of the Zogist chiefs milled around the camp, especially about the kitchens, or spread themselves on the broad, grassy slopes of the clearing. They were armed to the teeth and made a brave show in their ragged, but striking, costumes, whose varied style and colours proclaimed their several native districts. A few played cards with thumbed and grimy packs, but the greater part sat and smoked in silence, or gravely discussed the politics of their tribes. Sometimes one of them would seek to buy another's weapons, perhaps yielding his own in part exchange. Such commerce involved prolonged bargaining; for arms were the chief interest of the mountaineers, and regarded by them as their most valuable possessions. The younger guerrillas, however, exchanged their weapons freely in token of comradeship; and among Petrit Kupi's personal following sub-machine-guns and revolvers were continually changing hands.

Such gatherings were a severe drain on our resources, for the laws of hospitality and the prestige of our Mission required that we should entertain the guerrillas on a lavish scale. They afforded, however, a most welcome opportunity for discussions with the minor chieftains and allowed us, in the performance of our duties as hosts, to sound the feelings of the rank and file. On this occasion we entertained the chiefs and provided liberally for their bodyguards. Then, when all had eaten, we led Abas Kupi and Said Kryeziu apart to a sheltered ledge just beyond the ridge which rose above our camp. There we might talk undisturbed, looking out over the Shupal valley and away to the Qaf Tuyanit, the gap in the mountain wall which guards the northern approaches to Tirana. Sentries were posted out of earshot to restrain the curiosity of the tribesmen, and now that

Said was with us we had no need of the never-too-accurate, or too discreet, interpreters. In Said we had complete confidence, for his brother, Gani, was already fighting; and every consideration of personal honour, family interest, and political opinion engaged him to do his best to bring Abas Kupi back into the war.

Three weeks had passed since we had conferred with Abas Kupi at Shupal, but our Headquarters had not yet approved or rejected any of our proposals. The Foreign Office had not decided whether to seek private instructions for Abas Kupi from King Zog, and had advised us meanwhile to 'keep the pot boiling'; an operation which —as I ruefully reflected—leads in politics, as in physics, to the eventual evaporation of the contents. Nor had our colleagues with the Partisans succeeded in persuading Enver Hoja to accept Abas Kupi's proposal for a meeting between delegates of their two parties. Meanwhile the telegrams from Bari suggested that opinion there remained unyielding in its attachment to the formula of 'No arms before action' and might already be inclining to unilateral support of the Partisans.

With no word from Headquarters which might have strengthened our hand in negotiations, we could only draw on events for new arguments with which to urge Abas Kupi to take the field. Maclean accordingly gave an impressive exposition of the military situation in Europe, pointing out how closely developments were conforming to the forecast of events which we had made to the Agha at our first meeting. He spoke of the significance of the British landing in France, drew particular attention to the progress of our troops along the western shores of the Adriatic, and stressed ambiguously the importance of the Russian victories in Poland and Romania. The Allies were now making the supreme bid for victory; and the time had come for all who were our friends, or who wished to share in our triumph, to play their part. Then, turning to the local situation, he dwelt on the northward advance of the Partisans, whose forces were already reported across the river Shkumbi. The danger of civil war was grave; if it broke out before Abas Kupi had attacked the Germans we should be in no position to restrain the Partisans; and then he would be left alone. The sands were running out: it was high time to take the field. Gani Kryeziu was already fighting and might even then be receiving supplies; the Zogists had only to follow his example and arms would be dropped to them at once. All North Albania was waiting on Abas Kupi, and if he gave the lead the Ghegs would rise together in revolt.

Abas Kupi listened without a word and remained deep in thought for some moments after Maclean had done. Then in a single sentence he registered his disappointment at our failure to obtain instructions from King Zog or to arrange a meeting with the Partisan leaders. These were points which he might well have laboured, but with great delicacy he forebore from dwelling on a weakness of which we were only too painfully aware. We saw, however, that he was reluctant to expose his whole organization to the risks of war against a mere promise of supplies, backed by no assurances, or even signs, of political support. As a cornered chess player tests every possible move, so he probed each of our arguments in turn. To attack the L.N.C. was to break off relations with the British. To remain neutral was to expose himself to a Partisan offensive without hope of British support. To attack the Germans might seem to be the only course left open, but, if he chose it, would the tribesmen follow? And if they did, had they enough rifles and cartridges to hold the field until supplies were sent?

At length, after nearly five hours' discussion, Abas Kupi suggested that we should adjourn to allow him to return to his camp before dark. There he would consult with the Zogist chiefs and in the morning would bring us their reply. He left us, therefore, and that evening held a council of war with the chiefs; he told them the result of our talks; and each then spoke in turn for revolt or for neutrality. The younger men, hungry for adventure and untrammelled by the cares of property, were eager for a fight in which they might win their spurs. The older chiefs, however, declared that they could not make war without initial supplies of arms. The attempt would only lead to the destruction of their movement and to the absorption of its remnants by the Partisans. If the British really wanted their support they would send them arms; if not, then it were better to husband their forces against the dangers of civil war. The discussion was prolonged; and Said, with Father Lek, pleaded for immediate action. No formal vote was taken, but it was clear at the end that Abas Kupi must incline to the view of the older men; for, without their support, he could neither raise the clans nor keep them fed.

Next morning broke grey and cold; and, when we resumed our talks with Abas Kupi, we saw at once that the chiefs had pronounced against us. The Agha explained quietly that he was ready to attack the Germans as soon as we sent him supplies of arms, but that, without supplies, he could not and would not fight. He was ready to discuss the quantities of arms that would be required, but if we insisted on the formula of 'No arms before action' he could only offer to escort us to the coast for evacuation. We racked our brains for some saving formula; but there was nothing more to be said: we stood at the parting of the ways. The deadlock seemed absolute when suddenly a messenger was passed through the guards with an urgent letter for Abas Kupi. The Agha broke the seals and, since he could not read, handed the letter to Said. It was from the Zogist commander in Shiyak, the region to the south-west of Tirana, and reported that his forces had just been attacked by a body of Partisans. The Zogists had held their own; and the Partisans appeared to have withdrawn.

Abas Kupi turned grey and became suddenly very still, as men sometimes do when in great pain. There in his hand was the proof of all our argument. We sat without speaking for fully five minutes; and then Said suggested that we should adjourn for the midday meal. We ate together in silence; and as soon as he had finished Abas Kupi went off and sat down on the hillside, calling three of the principal chiefs to his side. Presently it came on to rain; and it was in a mood of deep despondency that we gathered in Smiley's hut to hear what the Agha might say. He began by suggesting that we should refer our problems to the proposed congress of Gheg chiefs. We answered firmly that we could not agree to calling such a congress until we had first come to terms with him. Then, seeing at last that there was no other way out, he said:

'Very well; you shall have action. Let Major Smiley come to me to-morrow and I will choose him a bridge. If he will bring the dynamite I will provide the men. Then you can tell your Head-quarters that Abas Kupi is fighting again.'

We embraced in token of agreement and Smiley produced a bottle of cherry brandy from under his bed. He had been bored and depressed by 'all this politics', but now brightened suddenly and was anxious to celebrate the prospect of 'blowing something up'.

SMILEY *blew up his bridge and the British dropped their first supplies to Abas Kupi and his fellow chiefs. In September they planned a raid on a German base and decided they needed additional help. Amery believed he could get this help from a very strange group of men who had once been part of the German army. He tells about these men and the raid.*

The Agha returned from Preza on the afternoon of September 3, and we held a council of war to determine our plan of campaign. There it was agreed that Abas Kupi with the main body of the

Zogists, assisted by Maclean, Smiley, and Sergeant Jenkins, should establish himself on the plateau of Mount Kruya and thence operate against the Tirana-Scutari road. Merret, with Sergeant Jones, was to remain at Vorre to await a suitable opportunity of attacking the German petrol and ammunition dumps in concert with Zogist forces from Preza. Meanwhile I was to take Petrit and a small bodyguard to try to win over the Turkoman garrisons in the region of Cape Rodonit.

A thunderstorm interposed between the making and the execution of these plans; and, while we still sheltered from the rain, a Zogist patrol brought in two Turkoman deserters. From them we learned that at least one company had already taken to the woods and that their whole battalion was on the verge of mutiny. We now reversed our plans once more and decided to march together towards the coast to organize the deserters and make ourselves masters of Cape Rodonit. The Agha readily agreed, for, with a strong Turkoman force, it might still be possible to take and hold Durazzo. That same night, therefore, we struck camp and, crossing the plain under cover of darkness, climbed into the low range of hills which follows the line of the coast southwards from Cape Rodonit.

The rain ceased as we marched, and the moon had already come out from behind the clouds when, towards midnight, we topped the escarpment that rises on the west of the plain of Kruya. There we divided our forces the better to round up the Turkoman deserters; Maclean and Smiley went with Abas Kupi to the village of Mazjhe; and Petrit and I made our way towards Ishm, where it was believed that we should find the ringleaders of the mutiny. We reached Ishm before dawn and took up our quarters in the house of a venerable *haji*—the only one I met in Albania—who had decorated his living-room with scrolls and crude lithographs brought back from the Pilgrimage. The Turkoman deserters were said to be hiding in the forest some distance away; and it was past six o'clock, when our scouts returned with four of their spokesmen. They were still dressed in German uniform, but had torn off their regimental badges and now demonstrated their hatred of the Germans in a fearsome pantomime. One of them was a lance-corporal and was referred to as *Marechal* by the others, who were ordinary troopers. They were darker skinned than most Europeans, but there was little of the Mongolian about their features. One of them indeed, a boy called Achmet, might have stepped out of a Persian oilpainting, with his ruddy cheeks and thick, arched brows meeting over black, almond-shaped eyes.

10*

Language was our first difficulty, and their knowledge of Russian was almost as slender as my own. By dint, however, of patience, sign language, and the free interpolation of Albanian, Italian, Serbian, and German words, we succeeded in the end in making each other understood. The four were Tajiks from a Turkoman battalion consisting of one Tajik and three Kazak companies. They had been in touch with one of our Turkish-speaking agents, and the night before had killed their German officers and taken to the woods. As yet only the Tajik company had mutinied, but their spokesmen were convinced that the Kazaks were also ripe for revolt. That same morning, therefore, we dressed up Achmet in Albanian clothes and sent him to stir up the nearest Kazak company to kill their officers and join the Tajiks. Achmet fulfilled his mission with conspicuous success, and a few days later I was awakened by the arrival in our camp of a group of small Mongolian men in German uniform. Their leader knelt down before me and untied a big, green handkerchief which he spread out on the ground. In it were six ears.

'Germans,' he said, and smiling, drew a finger across his throat.

After the mutiny of the Kazaks the Germans disarmed the remaining Turkoman companies and rounded up a number of the deserters. In the course of a week, however, we succeeded in organizing a striking force about a hundred strong, of whom some thirty were Tajiks and the rest Kazaks. They came to us fully armed and equipped, and the Tajiks brought with them two light machine-guns. Our Tajiks and Kazaks had served in the Red Army and had variously deserted to, or been captured by, the Germans. For a time they had endured the hardships of imprisonment, but then, seduced by the offer of military privileges, had volunteered for garrison duties in the German army. They had thus been formed into a Turkoman battalion and had already seen service in France and in Yugoslavia.

Soon after the Tajiks had joined us two of their spokesmen formed up to us one morning and complained that their *Marechal*, or N.C.O., had used them badly when they were in the German Army. We were just about to hold a council of war with Abas Kupi, and sent them away, saying that we would hear their complaint in the afternoon. They saluted and marched off, but an hour or so later, while we were still discussing plans, a shot rang out, and we heard the sound of rhythmic hand-clapping and of a song of triumph. An Albanian guard ran up shouting: '*Ka Vdek, Ka Vdek*' (literally 'He has death'); and, hurrying to the camp, we found the Tajiks standing in a ring, singing and clapping their hands while the handsome

Achmet danced a dance of victory round the corpse of the murdered *Marechal*. As a ballet it was splendid, but as discipline . . . and here I saw Sergeant Jones look meaningly at Sergeant Jenkins; for N.C.O.s are also an international fraternity.

We suspected that the Tajiks had murdered their Russian officers to desert to the Germans, and we knew that they had murdered their German officers to desert to us. It was now borne in upon us that we were become their officers; and, as we stood looking at the corpse of their *Marechal*, I ruefully reflected that from repetition to habit is but a step. The Tajiks were friendly and respectful, but so, no doubt, had been the Janissaries in their time. We therefore determined that, since the cheerful fellows must presently compare us with our Russian and German predecessors, the comparison should be favourable enough.

We ordered the burial of the *Marechal*, and, since we could not judge his guilt or innocence, thought his liquidation best forgotten. We declined, however, the invidious task of selecting his successor and left the choice to the chances of a democratic election. For a time all went well, but when the Kazaks began to murmur against the new *Marechal* we hastily deposed him while he yet lived. By this time we had brought the force under control, and the N.C.O. whom we then appointed retained our confidence and the obedience of the men until the end.

We presently organized the Turkomans into three squadrons, one of Tajiks and two of Kazaks. Each squadron had its own leader, who was responsible to the *Marechal*, or N.C.O. The *Marechal*, in his turn, was supervised by Ivan and Mishka I. The two Russians were fair but rather rough with the Turkomans, whom they openly despised as 'natives'. We had indeed already seen traces of this Blimpish attitude in their relations with the Albanians, but we did not discourage it, for it ensured that their allegiance was to us rather than to their Asiatic compatriots. Meanwhile the experience of fighting against the Germans under our leadership brought us the personal loyalty of the Turkomans; and we soon won their affection by our natural interest in their ways.

Since schooldays I have felt the lure of Central Asia, pored over the exploits of Genghis Khan and Tamerlane, and dreamed of the glories of Samarkand and Bokhara. Maclean shared this romanticism; and now, by a freak of war, the daydreams of boyhood came true and we rode at the head of a Turkoman horde. Our Tajiks were horsemen from the steppe and highlanders from the Pamir—a gay, fiery, and volatile people. They spoke a dialect of Persian, and, though their blood was mixed, the Indo-Aryan strain prevailed over the Mongolian. Tajikistan had never been wholly pacified by the Tsars and was the last of the Russian lands to submit to the Soviets. Collectivization only came in the late thirties, and had been fiercely resisted. Our men told us that there were still guerrillas in the Pamir, and some of them claimed to have relations who had fled from the Russians to settle in Persia or Afghanistan. Resentment against Russia still smouldered among them, and they had not forgotten the destruction of their great herds of horses which had followed the Kremlin's decision to check their nomad wanderings and force them to till the soil. Their physique was good, and most of them could read and write, but, though Soviet rule had brought them great benefits, they spoke with regret of the Emirates they had never known.

The Tajiks were friendly from the start; the Kazaks smiling, but more reserved. They were Turki-speaking and of Mongolian stock; a dour people, slow to action and slow to complaint. They had known both Tsarist and Soviet rule, and, unlike the Tajiks, sometimes spoke of themselves as Russians. Collectivization had come to them early, and, while they enjoyed its fruit, they had already forgotten the hardships of its early days. They seemed to have accepted Russia and might be counted good Soviet citizens.

Sometimes at night, when they gathered round their fires to roast or boil their evening sheep, the Turkomans would sing and dance for us. At first they sang shyly and only Red Army marching songs; later, when they came to trust us, they threw off the mask and sang their own songs and danced their own dances. The Kazaks made the best choir, with sad laments of the steppe which sounded both of Asia and of Europe. There was also an Uzbeg among them; an ugly fellow, but perhaps the best singer of them all. Uzbeg songs were like Turkish, but simpler, with the crystal purity of a mountain stream. Tajik songs had a wild gaiety; and the Tajik highlanders from the Pamir were the best dancers of all, with their whirling reels and triumphant sword-dances. It was Prince Igor with the Kruya mountains for a backcloth, and lit only by the camp fires and the moon.

On September 4, while we were dispersed over the coastal range, rounding up the Turkoman deserters, the Partisans crossed the Kruya mountains, and, raiding down towards the plain, burnt the Zogist headquarters at Luz. The Agha would have marched off at once to engage them, but he had given us his word to attack the

Germans; and Maclean could not release him from this promise. Our Headquarters were already growing impatient; and indeed the morning brought a message from Bari urging us to 'do utmost get Kupi fight'. Torn between the need to defend and the duty to attack, the Agha adopted a strategy of compromise: he sent Billal Kola with a small force to resist the Partisans, and assigned some hundred men to Maclean for operations against the Germans. Meanwhile he remained at Mazjhe, holding the bulk of his troops in reserve.

I was at this time some five hours' march from Mazjhe, in the village of Kurat, with twenty-eight Tajiks and some forty Albanians under Petrit. There, on the afternoon of September 5, I was joined by Maclean and Smiley with a force of a hundred and fifty Zogists commanded by Ndue Palli, a Catholic chieftain and former Captain of Gendarmerie, who had fought with Abas Kupi at Durazzo. Ndue was tall and lean, with a sorrowful yet questing look, and a way of walking which reminded us irresistibly of a bloodhound on the scent. He proved, however, a pleasant and resourceful companion and a loyal ally.

Petrit and I had already planned to attack a German post that night, but now that Maclean had come with reinforcements we decided to wait until the following day, when our combined forces might attempt a more serious operation. In the evening, therefore, we held a council of war and chose for our target a German Battery Headquarters which was commended by its lonely situation and the belief that it contained large supplies of ammunition.

We slept perhaps four hours, and then, with a small bodyguard, set out into the night to reconnoitre the German positions. After an hour's march through the woods our guide turned aside from the path and led us uphill to a rounded summit tufted with a clump of trees. As the night faded out of the sky we saw that we were standing on a range of barren hills, running roughly north and south. Beyond us to the west, and perhaps two thousand yards away, ran another range parallel to our own, but lower and thickly wooded. The fold of ground between lay under a blanket of mist, through which gleamed a single light—the duty officer of the enemy's camp. Taking advantage of the obscurity we now crawled some five hundred yards downhill to a projecting knoll, where we crouched in the bracken and waited, chilled and cramped, to watch the Germans awake.

After what seemed an age the sun rose behind us, and, as the mists parted, we saw that a road ran along the bottom between the two ranges. Beside the road, and perhaps four hundred feet below us, stood a wooden hut, where the solitary light still burned. Beyond, in the side of the wooded range opposite, we presently made out three or four barracks or store-houses. As yet no one stirred, but towards six o'clock a German soldier emerged from the lighted hut and stamped up and down on the road, blowing on his hands. Presently he turned into the wood, and a few minutes later a bugle sounded the *réveillé*. This was the moment for which we had waited, for we hoped that the movements of the men would reveal the positions of the camp. We therefore searched the wood closely through our glasses, and, as the soldiers woke up and set about their several routines, we became aware of a number of camouflaged tents and dug-outs which had thus far escaped our notice.

At seven o'clock six lorries drove up from the south and were loaded up from what we guessed to be a store-house by a working party of Italians, supervised by a German N.C.O. The drivers manœuvred clumsily on the narrow road, and once one of them backed his lorry into the ditch. His angry shouts were wafted up to us on the hillside, but, with the help of the Italians, his machine was presently righted; and by eight o'clock the whole convoy had driven away. Each of us drew a rough sketch of all that he saw, and tried, besides, to count the number of the enemy. This proved a harder task, for the soldiers were continually disappearing and reappearing among the trees; but we finally computed the strength of the garrison at some thirty men. Towards nine o'clock the activity of the camp subsided; and, feeling that we had seen enough, we crawled back infinitely slowly to the shelter of the clump of trees on the ridge above. There, with the enemy positions still in full view, we sat down to concert our plan of attack.

We decided to assemble our forces behind the eastern range two hours before dark, and, dividing them into three parts, to develop a pincer movement against the Battery Headquarters. Maclean, with Petrit, Ndue Palli, and a hundred Zogists would cross the bottom to the right of the German positions and approach them from the north. At the same time I would take our twenty-eight Tajiks as the other arm of the pincer and carry out a similar manœuvre, but from the south. Maclean would launch the attack with the Albanians; and, once the Germans were fully engaged, I was to fall on them from behind with the Tajiks. Smiley, meanwhile would remain on the eastern range with a reserve of some forty Albanians and three machine-guns. With these he would keep the road covered and might complete the discomfiture of the enemy should they try to escape eastwards. Finally, a small group of Albanians were to burn down a wooden bridge on the road, three kilometres from the camp, to prevent the enemy from receiving early reinforcements.

Back at Kurat the day passed slowly, though not without incident. This was the morning when the Tajiks murdered their N.C.O.; a deed which convinced us that, after the excitement of mutiny, their temper urgently required the discipline of battle and the cold douche of danger. Abas Kupi came also to discuss plans; and towards midday we received the first report from the young German officer in the Corps Headquarters in Tirana. This gave us, among a mass of other information, the identifications of the post we were going to attack. It was the headquarters of the Third Battery of the 297th Artillery Regiment. With so much business, there was no time to rest before the action; and, almost as soon as we had eaten, we set out to join our forces, already concentrating behind the eastern range. We reached the assembly point at five o'clock, and climbed to the crest of the range for a further brief reconnaissance. All was quiet in the German camp; we wished each other good luck, and departed each to his allotted task.

In the morning I had agreed with a light heart to take command of the Tajiks, but, as we marched off to the attack, I was oppressed by sombre reflections. I knew nothing of their training or their ways, and spoke besides so little of their language that I could not hope to make them understand my orders in the heat of battle. This ignorance might jeopardize the whole operation; but, as I anxiously considered how to impose my will on these wild Asiatics, there suddenly came back to me a fragment from a long-forgotten conversation with a friend who had once commanded an Indian brigade:

'It doesn't matter what you say to native troops,' he had told me, 'because they won't understand you. What matters is what you do. March in front of them and they'll do whatever you do; and, if you don't run away, they'll be as good as the Guards.'

I had been in Cairo at the time, ill from jaundice, and had forgotten his words with the next glass of medicine. Now, by some strange freak of memory, the sick-bed talk was become a counsel of action; and I remembered that Ivan and Mishka at least considered the Tajiks as 'native troops'. I went, therefore, to the head of the column, though not without some apprehension; the danger from the Germans in front might be part of the day's work; but only that morning the Tajiks had murdered their N.C.O., and I had to steel myself not to look back too often over my shoulder.

We crossed the low ground, where a tongue of woodland

stretched out from the western range, and, hurrying over the road, climbed on to the crest of the range itself. There we turned northwards, and, devoutly hoping that the Germans were off their guard, moved silently towards them through the trees. Presently we came to a low thorn fence, broken only by a stile, on the far side of which lay a clearing perhaps fifty yards wide. Beyond, the woods sloped steeply down to the enemy positions. I decided that we should cross the clearing and lie up in the fringes of the wood beyond, to wait until Maclean should begin the attack. I led the way, therefore, over the stile, and had gone perhaps ten yards when a machine-gun opened up savagely from a clump of trees some forty yards away. I looked round to see how many of the Tajiks were already across the fence, and, as I turned my head, somehow lost my balance and fell to the ground. I thought at first that I had only slipped, and it was some time before I realized that a bullet had caught me under the chin. The wound indeed was little worse than a deep shaving cut, and caused me neither pain nor serious loss of blood. The Tajiks, however, ran back, seeing me fall; and I lay in the clearing alone. The machine-gun was silent, the gunner taking me perhaps for dead. I waited for a moment, then sprang up and ran for the fence. The German opened up at once, and his bullets hissed round me like furious insects as I vaulted the stile and made for the shelter of the trees. The Tajiks rallied when they saw me safe, and, gathering round me, opened a blind and ragged fire in the direction of the machine-gun.

I checked them as soon as I had recovered my breath and my wits, and, more by instinct than by reasoning, worked my way round the flank of the machine-gun post. When I judged we were well past it I lay down, and, while the Tajiks got into position, tried to decide what to do next. It is sometimes a weakness to see things from the other man's point of view, but, as I imagined myself among the German defenders, I knew that they were beaten. After months of inactivity they had been startled from rest, perhaps from sleep, by our approach. Their machine-gunners had seen a few Turkoman deserters, but, in the darkness of the wood, they could not tell how many were their assailants, or where the attack would come from next. Their nerves must be strained by the uncertainty; and, while they would soon recover confidence, they might collapse altogether if I acted at once. The alarm had been given, and I therefore decided not to wait for Maclean's signal but to go in to the attack.

For a few seconds I vainly racked my brain for orders which the men would understand. Then on a sudden inspiration I stood up, and, hoisting my astrakhan cap on the muzzle of my sub-machine-gun, ran forward shouting 'Hurrah'. The Tajiks did not mis-understand, and, spreading out on either side, charged through the trees, shoulders hunched and eyes glinting. The machine-gunners fled; we dropped over the crest of the ridge, and saw the huts and dugouts of the enemy less than fifty feet below. I shouted 'Hurrah' again, and the Tajiks bounded down the hill like wolves, letting out blood-curdling yells and pouring a withering fire into the camp. As we carried the first buildings I saw a German standing twenty yards from me, stripped to the waist, with a *Schmeizer* pistol in his hand. For a moment we looked at each other without moving, then he crumpled to the ground, pressing his hands to his naked stomach. I had not heard the shot, but looked round to see Achmet grinning from ear to ear. We pressed forward, and, as I passed the dying German, I noticed that he was still a boy, with straight, fair hair and blue, staring eyes. His hands were clasped over his wound as if in prayer, and the blood was oozing quietly away through his fingers. Looking back a moment later I saw a Turkoman stripping him of his Wellington boots.

The enemy now returned a ragged fire, but we had taken them by surprise and they could not see us clearly for the trees. Several of them were shot down; and, as we came to close quarters, the rest broke and fled towards the road. There they ran into Smiley's machine-guns and were driven back, leaving one of their number dead. We were already masters of their camp; and they, too weak to counter-attack, fell back towards the south, sniping us from the cover of the wood.

Maclean and the Albanians had arrived on the scene just as we had gone in to the assault and had at once advanced to the attack. The first dead German, indeed, had fallen to Petrit Kupi's rifle; but, for some mysterious reason, the main body of the Albanians had failed to follow; and when we took the camp only Maclean, Petrit, and three of their bodyguards were there to join us. The rest of the Zogist forces now surrounded us, and, unaware that the Germans had fled, discharged volley after volley into the camp to our anger and alarm. Nothing could stop them; and the victorious Tajiks were forced to take cover from their Albanian allies in the German slit trenches and dugouts. Unable to make ourselves heard, Maclean and I sat behind a clump of trees and despondently surveyed the battlefield. A few yards away a Tajik was dying in the arms of one of his comrades. Several dead Germans lay outside the tents and huts; and a group of Italian prisoners huddled behind a heap of rubble under Mishka I's watchful eye. Spent shots whined around us, and it was beginning to grow dark. I felt suddenly tired and intolerably thirsty.

More than half an hour must have passed before Petrit managed to persuade the Zogists to cease fire. Night had already fallen, and it was now too dark to plunder the camp systematically. We told the men, therefore, to carry off such supplies as were easily portable, and, retiring across the road, climbed towards the eastern range. There we found Smiley and Ndue Palli, who produced a most welcome flask of *raki*. We sat down to enjoy it, and were discussing the next move when suddenly a flare burst in the sky above us, casting a lurid, metallic light over the hillside. A moment later two mortar bombs fell quite close, followed by a burst of tracer bullets fired at long range. German reinforcements had arrived; and, withdrawing slowly beyond the range, we trekked back to Kurat.

WHILE ABAS KUPI *had taken the field and the Germans felt the force of these guerrillas, the story of Albanian guerrilla warfare was taking a different turn. The Communist Partisans, spurred on by their Russian advisers, moved against the bases of the tribal chiefs. One at a time they captured their countrymen and eliminated them from the fight. Finally, the Partisans turned towards Abas Kupi, the strongest of the chiefs and the moral leader of the non-Communist groups. The British did not want to see Albania embroiled further in a civil war and brought every pressure to bear on Abas Kupi. He accepted their decision and did not fight. Enver Hoja, the Communist leader, took over the country, and Abas Kupi became a fugitive. At the insistence of Amery and his companions, the British saved the old man and withdrew him to Italy.*

Albania became a Communist country, and in the years since the war Hoja is rumoured to have eliminated all opposition by killing almost one-half of that country's population of a million and a quarter.

ISLAND AMBUSH

BY W. STANLEY MOSS

IN HISTORY'S *first parachute invasion, Crete fell to the Germans in May, 1941. The Cretan and British defenders upset the German timetable of a two-day invasion, but when the battle was over and the evacuation completed, twenty-eight thousand English and Greek troops were lost. The native defenders of the small, rocky island in the Mediterranean then returned to their villages and mountains, leaving the roads and ports to the invaders.*

The Germans lined up the women, bared their shoulders in search of rifle-recoil bruises, and shot five hundred persons out of hand for defending their homes. This proved to be a grave mistake. On the island which cradled one of the world's oldest civilizations, freedom has a long tradition and brigandry and tribal warfare a longer one. It is only a short step from brigandry against the laws of one's own government to guerrilla warfare against an invader. The weapons and techniques are the same, and the Cretans had little to learn. The Turks had found this out when they tried without success to control the little island for two centuries.

By late 1941, guerrilla warfare had broken out sporadically across Crete, and German reprisals became more vicious with each attack. Finally, in early 1944, British Headquarters in Cairo ordered Captain W. Stanley Moss, a twenty-two-year-old member of the Coldstream Guards, to infiltrate by submarine, contact the Andarte bands, and complete a spectacular mission. A month later, Moss and his companions kidnapped the German commander, General Kreipe, and exfiltrated back to Cairo.

In June, Moss, aided by his Cretan friend Deerslayer, tried the same trick again and missed. Then he and his Andarte companions resorted to guerrilla warfare's oldest tactic—ambush. Moss tells the story himself.

SIX escaped Russian prisoners had come over from the Lasithi area to join my band.

We equipped the Russians with battledresses and Sten guns, and listened to their stories of captivity and escape. They were a strong, healthy-looking lot, averaging about twenty-five years of age, and, strangely enough, without exception blond-haired. The Germans, they said, had recently announced that no Russian prisoner, whatever the course of the war, would be permitted to leave the island alive; and this, not unnaturally, had led to a series of attempted escapes from every POW cage. These six men were the survivors of a party of seventeen which had broken away from a labour gang on the Kastelli-Heraklion road. The remainder had been either killed or recaptured. I told the men that I hoped we would soon find an opportunity to revenge ourselves—little thinking, as I spoke, that that opportunity would present itself within the next forty-eight hours.

It was at noon on August 7, the following day, that a large number of refugees started to arrive at our headquarters. It was an entire village on the move: men, women, children, their chattels on their backs and a stream of sheep, goats, and mules following in their wake. They all had the same tale to tell: that morning a party of ten Germans had come to Anoyia—the largest village in Crete—in order to collect able-bodied men for enforced labour. The selected men had refused to go, and so, in retaliation, the Germans had taken fifty hostages from the village. No sooner had they left, however, than they had found themselves surrounded by *Andartes*, and in the brief fight which had ensued the entire German party had been annihilated and the hostages released. As a result, nearly everyone in the village had taken to the mountains for fear that the Germans would arrive in force on the morrow to effect reprisals.

All through the afternoon stragglers continued to arrive, and our small headquarters took upon itself the aspect of some vast, sprawling encampment. But there was a unique thing about these refugees: there was no gloom about them, none of the pathetic, heartbreaking sights that commonly attend a similar scene. Instead, there was laughter in the air, and brave words were spoken. The men had dressed themselves for battle, albeit with weapons as ancient as the hills about us, and even some of the womenfolk were seen to be adorned with ammunition belts and daggers.

The stage was patently set for action; and we found little difficulty in deciding what form that action should take. The Germans, bent on razing Anoyia to the ground, would in all likelihood arrive upon the scene in the early morning. They would certainly travel to the village along the Heraklion-Retimo road; and thus, if they could be waylaid before leaving their transport and deploying, Anoyia might be saved. With George and Deerslayer, I chose six of Mihale Xilouris's men to accompany us and the Russians. We would have liked to have taken more, but our supply of automatics was now exhausted, so we were obliged to limit the total number of our force to fifteen men. In addition, we asked for a couple of Anoyians to act as guides for us, at which a score immediately volunteered, and we compromised by taking four.

In the late afternoon we set off northwards, walking fast and feeling that now, at last, our luck must change. All the way to Anoyia we kept meeting more refugees, some of them leading mules piled high with impedimenta, others travelling with only their *sakulis* slung across their backs. They greeted us in passing, waving and calling and wishing us well.

It was dark when we reached the village. The streets were deserted, and no lights burned in the windows. There was a vast stillness in the air, which our imaginations charged with an electric expectancy. We hurried onwards until, at midnight, we stopped at a deserted garden to feed ourselves on a dinner of grapes and watermelons. After a short rest, we continued on our way; and at three o'clock in the morning we arrived at the main road. It did not take us long to discover the sort of position ideally suited for an ambush: a sharp curve in the road, bounded on three sides by high ground, with a little bridge in the centre of it.

Straightaway we busied ourselves with laying twin rows of Hawkins grenades across the bridge. Fortunately, the tarmac was in an ill state of repair, so the task of concealing the mines proved no great problem; and by dawn, at five o'clock, we were all lying in readiness at our posts.

It was an hour later that, for the first time, we heard a warning whistle from our scout on the high ground above us. Every man fingered his trigger, intently watching the bend in the road; but it was no German transport that we were soon to see approaching us: it was a flock of sheep, a shepherd, two small boys, and a dog. Hurriedly we scrambled down to the road and waylaid the man, telling him that he would have to spend the next few hours in our care. We did not dare risk allowing him to proceed on his journey, lest he should speak of having seen us, so we placed him and his entourage under the charge of one of our Anoyian guides, who led them, protesting only slightly, to a small valley which was situated about a quarter of a mile behind our position.

But this was only a beginning. During the next hour over eighty civilians, several flocks of sheep, donkeys, goats, and mules came stumbling in all innocence upon our emplacement. It transpired that there was a market day being held at a nearby village; but, by the time we had finished hustling each successive batch of arrivals off the road, it was rather we who appeared to be holding most of the market, for the little valley behind us, crammed to the full with bleating, braying livestock, looked like a corral after the most successful of round-ups.

By seven o'clock, however, the stream of market-bound peasants had thinned to a minimum, and the atmosphere reverted from that of the farmyard to one of waiting and expectancy. The sky was of the palest blue; and the young sun, with no warmth to cheer us, fumbled about the rocks where we lay concealed. Nobody spoke.

Then suddenly the look-out's whistle blew again; and in a moment we heard the rumble of a lorry engine, growing louder and louder until, swinging into view around the bend, a three-ton utility van bore down towards us. We could see two Germans sitting in the front seat, and half a dozen labourers perched upon the open side of the back.

Just before the truck ran on to the mines, some of the Cretans, unable to contain their eagerness any further, opened fire. Then the truck blew up. Momentarily the whole scene vanished in a cloud, while falling pieces of metal clattered on to the rocks about us; but, when the smoke cleared, we were able to see the buckled frame of the truck, and a dead German huddled behind the shattered windscreen, and his companion lying with his skull smashed to pulp on the roadway. The six labourers had been thrown clear by the explosion, and now they were scrambling down the embankment to shelter under the bridge. Straightaway Deerslayer was after them, leaping like a cat from his vantage point at the roadside; but just as he was about to overtake them, one of them turned and hurled a rock into his face.

Spitting blood from his mouth, Deerslayer rushed at the man, smiting him on the jaw with the butt of his automatic and sending him tumbling among the boulders.

The remainder straightaway put up their hands, and cowered in the shadow of the bridge like cornered rabbits. The man who had thrown the rock tried to scramble to his feet, only to receive a kick in the teeth which again sent him sprawling. Then Deerslayer called to one of the Anoyians and told him to escort the six captives back to the valley.

Once they had gone, we resumed our ambush positions, and scarcely had we got back to our posts when we heard a cry from the look-out.

The echo of his voice was still alive among the reverberate rocks when another three-tonner, pulling a large trailer, hove into sight around the bend; but the driver, on seeing the battered hulk of the first truck on the bridge, immediately jammed on his brakes, and the vehicle stopped dead. It was well out of range of our Sten guns, but this did not deter the Cretans, who each emptied a magazine of bullets vaguely in its direction. The driver, meanwhile, put the vehicle into reverse and tried to turn round, but he succeeded only in ditching the trailer.

We left our positions and started to make our way from rock to rock towards the truck; then, as the range narrowed, we paused at every few paces to fire at it. We could see a German N.C.O. in the front seat, and several Italians in the back. After a moment's hesitation, they all jumped clear of the truck and started running for their lives back down the road, with George, Deerslayer, and myself in hot pursuit. Then the German, pulling a Luger out of his holster, started firing at us over his shoulder; but his shots were wildly inaccurate, and we could hear the bullets fizzling overhead and whining away into the mountainside.

The Italians, like sheep, were running in a close bunch; so, when we stopped for a moment to take proper aim and fire into their midst, we were not surprised to see three of them stagger and collapse on the roadway.

By the time we had overtaken the prostrate bodies and dragged them into the ditch, the distance between us and the remainder of the quarry had increased to about two hundred yards. Nevertheless, the German continued firing at us. He fired two shots over our heads, and a third smacked into the rocks at the roadside. We watched him as he turned again to fire a fourth shot; but no shot came, and in disgust he hurled his empty pistol into the ditch.

For nearly a mile we chased them, sometimes losing sight of them around a bend in the road, and at others finding them running, as it were, in the opposite direction to ourselves as they followed a hairpin curve. Then, abruptly, we lost them altogether.

We raced for the spot where we had last seen them, and there we came upon a mule track which branched at right angles to the road; so up the track we went, until, some five minutes later, we reached a tiny village. A small boy was standing in the cobbled lane, and he waved gleefully to us as we approached.

'Where are they?' George shouted.

Without hesitation, the boy pointed to an empty-looking house at the end of the lane.

I sent Deerslayer round the back of the house, then with George slowly approached its front entrance. When we were within ten yards of it, we shouted for the men to come out; but there was no reply, so I fired a burst through one of the windows, and scarcely had the sound of the last shot died away than the four men, hands high above their heads, came tumbling out of the doorway, closely followed by Deerslayer. He treated the German to a brisk kick in the pants, and cuffed the Italians over the ears. Then I told them to get moving. They did not appear to understand what was wanted of them, and turned towards us, their eyes brimful of terror and bewilderment; so George fired a couple of shots at their heels—and this they understood.

The small boy applauded us delightedly as we passed, while other villagers, attracted by the sound of the shooting, stood gaping in their doorways to watch our departure. Back to the road we went, our prisoners running before us with their hands clasped across the backs of their necks; and thus, with sporadic shots to remind them that we were at their heels, we brought them back at a brisk trot to the scene of the ambush.

In our absence, we discovered, a *Volkswagen* had driven into the trap, and its two German occupants had been swiftly dispatched. Unfortunately, however, the vehicle had been ditched on a corner in such a way as to give ample warning of danger to any further traffic, so we were obliged to relinquish our positions in favour of an adjacent curve in the road which did not so admirably suit our purpose.

Ten minutes must have passed before we again heard the look-out's warning, this time heralding the advent of a large utility truck which contained an Italian labour gang. At the first shot the vehicle pulled up, and the Italians, excitedly waving white handkerchiefs, jumped to the road and surrendered themselves with only verbal protest; but I believe their animated chatter betokened rather a fear for their lives than indignation at their capture. As they were hurried away, I drove the truck round the curve in the road and left it in the ditch.

We resumed our ambush positions. George, I noticed, was chalking up the number of our morning's catch on a rock, and he grinned happily at me, as though to convey his satisfaction at the way things were going for us. In actual fact, however, I was growing a trifle anxious at the non-appearance of any German fighting troops. The time was already half-past eight, and we all knew that whenever the enemy descended on a village they preferred to go into action at dawn; but there was nothing we could do but wait and hope for the best, so we settled ourselves among the rocks and listened impatiently for the look-out's whistle. One of the Russians, squatting behind a boulder just below me, started humming a harvesting song, and his voice found an incongruous accompaniment in the razor-strop croaking of a host of cicadas. The war seemed somehow to have deserted us for a while, and the feeling of tension which we all held in our hearts was unobtrusively absorbed by the sun-warmed peacefulness of the scene about us.

For nearly an hour we waited.

Then, like a knife, the shrill scream of the whistle shattered the placid mirror of the morning, and I saw the look-out, standing on a high rock, frantically waving his arms.

We heard the dull throb of a powerful engine growing louder and louder, insinuating itself into the gentle exhalations of the landscape. There was little doubting the identity of the vehicle now approaching us; and when, a moment later, it lumbered into view, I do not think a man among us was surprised at recognizing the familiar, ungainly shape of a troop transport. Its thirty-five steel-helmeted occupants were seated in the back like twin rows of tailor's dummies, and altogether one felt as though one were witnessing the clattering advent of some squat, multi-ringed armadillo. The sun flashed across the windscreen, and the steel of barrels and helmets glinted like revolving mirrors in the white heat.

All unsuspecting, the driver brought the vehicle slowly round the bend until it was directly below us. Then, with our fifteen Sten guns, we opened fire.

Most of the Germans died in their seats before they knew what was happening, but some, trying desperately to disentangle their weapons, managed to rise to their feet, and four of them survived to jump to the road. We saw them go scrambling down the slope on the other side and take refuge behind the low stone wall of a vineyard.

Then, quite suddenly, everything became strangely quiet. There came an occasional groan from a dying man in the lorry, and we could hear the water boiling over in the radiator; but, apart from these sounds and a few despairing shots from the Germans in the vineyard, there was scarcely anything to disturb the peace of that very lovely morning. We could see the dead men sitting in stuffed positions on the benches, and there was blood and oil dripping on to the tarmac. And we could smell the nauseating stench of burned rubber and cordite and petrol. And somewhere a nightingale was singing, because nightingales in Crete seem mostly to sing in the daytime. Nobody moved or spoke. It was like that moment at the end of a great play, when the curtain has descended and the audience is still too enthralled to applaud. But the moment is short and short indeed it was for us that morning. A cannon shell, smashing into the rocks in our midst, brought us violently to our senses.

In the excitement of the moment, nobody had noticed the arrival of an armoured car. And now it came towards us, very slowly, firing into the rocks where we were hidden, with an officer standing in the turret to direct its fire. He must have been a very brave man, because everybody started to shoot at him and still he would not put his head down, but pulled out a Luger instead and returned our fire, very calmly and with great accuracy. And all the time the armoured car kept on coming, nearer and nearer. The Cretans, in their ignorance, started hurling Mills bombs at it; but these missiles, far from making any impression upon the armour, served only to shower the rocks about us with ricocheting fragments of stone and metal.

It was at this moment that one of our Anoyian followers—an elderly man, dressed in ancient clothes and grasping a firing piece which looked as though it must have remained concealed in a chimney stack since the Turkish invasion—elected to perform an act of temerarial bravado. With a shout, he jumped to the road, placing himself directly in the path of the oncoming vehicle, and started firing at it. The age of his rifle was such that after each shot he had to reload; and, in this fashion, he had just time to fire three shots before a cannon shell struck him in the stomach and sent him spinning into the ditch. Indeed, I was amazed that he had survived as long as he had.

This incident, however, rather than allaying the bellicose instincts of my fellows, gave rise to a further act of reckless daring, the protagonist on this occasion being none other than Deerslayer. Upon seeing his wounded countryman lying in the ditch, he leaped out from behind the rock where he had sought shelter, scrambled down to the road, hoisted the unconscious man on to his shoulders, and started slowly to clamber back up the slope, attended the while by a hail of bullets, not only from the armoured car, but also from the group of Germans in the vineyard opposite.

By this time the remainder of the Cretans, with the exception of George, showed themselves more than ready to take their leave; nor did I make any move to restrain them. It seemed that only one thing remained to be done before raising the ambush, and that was to put the armoured car out of action. The vehicle was now so close upon us that the chance to attack it from the rear became a distinct possibility; so, calling for a volunteer from the Russian party, I told him of my intention. He was a pleasant-looking youth, with fair hair and blue eyes that gave him an almost Nordic appearance, and he was quick to understand what was wanted of him. By way of rocks and boulders, we would make our way to the rear of the armoured car, while the remainder of the party gave us covering fire from the flank; then, once we had reached the vehicle's blind spot, we would descend to the ditch, crawl along it until we came level with the car's rear wheels, and finally jump aboard and throw hand grenades down the turret. The Russian conveyed this information to his colleagues, while I explained the situation to George. As we spoke, cannon shells continued to burst among the rocks around us, treating our urgent speech to the rudest of punctuation.

Now, all was in readiness, and with Vanya—for that was the Russian's name—I wriggled towards our starting point. Our greatest danger, we realized, lay in our initial effort to reach the rear of the car without drawing fire, and in doing this we would have to make a dash across a ten-yard gap of completely open ground before being able to find concealment behind a massively substantial rock formation. So off we went, one after the other, in a breakneck rush for our immediate objective.

Once there, grateful for the brief asylum with which the huge boulders provided me, I paused to review the position from this new standpoint; and happily I found that there would now be little difficulty in crawling down to the ditch and approaching the target from behind.

'Vanya,' I said in a whisper, and thrust out my arm behind me as if to grasp him.

'Vanya.'

There was no reply: only a shot from the car-commander's Luger.

Slowly I turned, suddenly apprehensive and frightened at what I might see. Nor did my presentiment deceive me. Face downward, his limbs spread-eagled as if in a primitive crucifixion, the Russian's body lay as it had fallen, midway between the two boulders that had been our havens. The blond hair was bright with blood—brighter because of the blondness—and the fingers, as if petrified, clutched at the parched grass in a way that no live fingers could.

I turned away, not horrified, but bewildered. One's thoughts race at moments such as these; and now, quite suddenly, I realized why the Germans had shot Vanya rather than me. The Russian had been wearing British battledress, while I was dressed from top to toe in Cretan black; and so, with a split-second choice of targets, the German had picked upon that man whom he had considered the more worthwhile victim. Could Fate ever have been more unjust . . . or more kind?

From now on, the task was simple. Maintaining a steady volume of fire from the rocks above, the covering party persisted in occupying the attentions of the enemy, while I, completely sheltered from sight and bullet, was able to clamber into the ditch without obstruction. Only twenty yards separated me from the target. I could see the car-commander, oblivious of my approach, continuing his courageous, almost foolhardy, retaliation; and thus he continued, firing from time to time, until I had drawn level with him. I had now only to watch for the moment when, as before, he would have to change the magazine of his pistol.

There was not long to wait. A shot was fired, the steel helmet bobbed down. To jump on to the back of the car and drop a grenade into the turret took a matter of seconds. The cannon did not fire again.

I scrambled back among the rocks to rejoin George and the Russians, calling to them to raise the ambush and start retreating.

Up the hillside we went, our hurried progress accompanied by stray shots from the Germans in the vineyard; but soon we were out of range and making our way along a gully which rambled southwards toward Anoyia.

Presently, when rounding an outcrop, we suddenly came upon Deerslayer. Somehow he had succeeded in commandeering a mule, and on it he had propped the unconscious figure of the wounded Anoyian. The beast's hair was smattered with blood—black where the sun had dried it, and glistening red, like a newly painted letter-box, wherever a fresh drop fell. Held half in, half out of the saddle by Deerslayer, the wounded man hung limply over the beast's neck. His eyes were closed, his limbs apparently lifeless.

'Is he alive?' I asked.

Deerslayer nodded.

George said: 'Is better leaving him here. No good to sit on horse.'

At first reluctant, Deerslayer was eventually persuaded that it would be best if we were to lay his compatriot beside a nearby stream, where he could rest until we had fetched a doctor from the village. So together we lifted the Anoyian off the mule and carried him to a sheltered spot at the water's edge. And there, having laid him on his back, we ripped off his shirt, soaked it in the stream, and with it bathed the hollow black wound in his belly. Then George strapped on a field dressing, and Deerslayer left a water-bottle on the grass beside the man's right hand.

The Russians were standing around us in a semi-circle, watching. I glanced at them, and in their expressions I saw that they were thinking exactly as I was: that the Anoyian would never regain consciousness, that he was as good as dead already. Their faces were masks, void of any emotion—just as they were when, a few moments later, we resumed our march and I told them: 'I'm terribly sorry about Vanya. It was bad luck. Perhaps we'll be able to bury him later.'

One of them shrugged his shoulders, another smiled, and a third said, '*Nichevo.*'

Within half an hour we had reached the outskirts of Anoyia, where, in the shade of a steep cliff, we came upon the remainder of our party. With a group of prisoners huddled in their midst, they were seated among the rocks, eating water-melons; but when they saw us, some of them looked rather sheepish, while others were quick to excuse themselves for having deserted us. I made no comment; but George, I noticed, had a few sharp words to say to them. Then he asked them if anyone was missing, to which they replied that one of their number, apparently remorseful at having left us, had returned to the scene of the ambush to see what had become of us.

Presently this man returned and, having embraced each of us in turn, informed us that the surviving Germans had retreated along the road, leaving their vehicles and a wealth of equipment behind them. Straightaway we sent six men to go and collect all the arms and ammunition they could recover, and told them to meet us at Mihale Xilouris's headquarters before nightfall. The remainder of the party was detailed to conduct our prisoners to the same destination; and then, with George and Deerslayer, I made my way to Anoyia. There, the scene of desolation persisted. It was the ghost of a village, where the empty lanes echoed our voices, and the cobblestones clattered like amplifiers beneath the trample of our boots.

We went first to the house of the village priest, thinking that there at least we might discover somebody; but the place was deserted, its rooms stripped of all but the heaviest furnishings. Deerslayer said he was going off to find a doctor. We were sceptical about his chances of success, but told him we would wait for him for an hour. When he had gone, we picked some bunches of grapes from the vine that grew over the porch, went into the parlour, sprawled on the floor, and waited.

Much to our surprise, he was quick to return, saying that he had found a doctor who was willing to accompany us. How he had discovered anyone, let alone a doctor, in that seemingly deserted cluster of houses, we could not guess; but, as we walked out of the front door, we saw a trim little man, carrying a battered leather bag, waiting for us in the street astride a mule.

With Deerslayer leading the way, we retraced our steps to the spot where we had left the unconscious Anoyian; and I must confess that with each pace we made I became more convinced that we were wasting our time and that the trail would end only in our discovery of a dead body. But I was wrong.

As we entered the clearing where we had laid him, the man stirred; and when we came and stood over him, his eyelids fluttered open, and he smiled at us. I felt ashamed at having so readily given up hope for him; and yet, when again I saw the enormous cavity that was his wound, I found myself once more persuaded that he would never live till the morrow. For a few minutes we remained there. Then, wishing him the best and telling him to get well quickly so that he could accompany us on our next skirmish, we left him in the doctor's care and set off at a brisk pace southwards.

NO FURTHER NEWS *was received of Anoyia, not even of German reprisals.*

Captain Moss was eventually withdrawn from Crete, sent to Macedonia and later to Siam. But the irregular war between the Germans and Cretans continued, and by the war's end, whole villages had been razed by the Germans. Among these villages was Boulgarelli, the site of a key battle in Greek history and a national shrine. Here again the Germans made a mistake. The Cretans remembered. Thousands joined the Andarte bands, and the entire population turned out to assist in the invasion which freed the island.

SPREAD OF ALARM

BY VLADIMIR PENIAKOFF

'THE UNIT I COMMAND *is very secret—most of you will never have heard of it before . . . a few of you may have heard rumours about us: before we go any further I want them to know that everything they may have heard is untrue. We do not go about the streets of Rome kidnapping German generals right and left, we have not been parachuted in our jeeps into a POW camp in Germany, I am not an eccentric Polish millionaire, we do not get treble pay, in fact the men who join us drop their rank and their pay suffers accordingly. . . .'*

Thus Lieutenant-Colonel Vladimir Peniakoff spoke of the P.P.A.— Popski's Private Army—to a group of potential recruits in 1942. He neglected to tell them, however, what the P.P.A. actually did—create alarm and despondency behind the enemy lines.

Peniakoff, or Popski, had had to go far and do much before he was permitted to form such an irregular raiding unit as the P.P.A. within the Armed Forces.

Born in Belgium of Russian parents, he was educated at Cambridge. He left the university in 1917 to join the French army. In 1924 he went to Egypt where he lived as a sugar refiner until World War II. He joined the Army as a second-lieutenant and was assigned to the Libyan Arab Force, a body of Senussi Arabs raised to serve as guerrillas. Early in the spring of 1942, Popski succeeded in getting himself appointed commander of an Arab commando unit.

After a series of brilliant operations behind the German lines in North Africa, he was called back to Cairo and given the command of a war establishment, M.E. W.E. 866 1, which someone humorously dubbed 'Popski's Private Army'. With the approval of the Director of Military Operations, this became the official name. Shoulder patches were designed with P.P.A., and Popski went out to recruit his authorized strength— twenty-three men including himself.

Popski himself tells of an incident which took place far behind the German lines in North Africa which earned him the right to form his private army.

O N THE FIRST DAY of my arrival I had sent word to all my Arab helpers asking them to find me large (if possible unguarded) petrol dumps, and the same instructions were given to every informant when he came into my camp with his piece of news. I dispatched such of my own men as I could spare to various parts of the Jebel on a similar quest. To prevent heart-searchings, which the prospect of reprisals might cause, I let everybody believe that the petrol dumps when found, would be bombed from the air. As soon as I could free myself of administrative duties I went and called on 'Abdel Jelil bu Tayeb, my spiritual adviser, and impressed on him the urgency of my quest. He thought he knew a man who would be able to help me and promised to send him along as soon as he could be found.

Two days later, at my headquarters, a short, lean, rather ragged Arab was brought up to me. He dispensed with any but the barest civilities and in a low and singularly deliberate voice he said that his name was Mohammed el Obeidi, that he had been sent by Sheik 'Abdel Jelil bu Tayeb, that he knew of an Italian petrol dump in the neighbourhood of a place called El Qubba (or as the Italians call it: Giovanni Berta), that his tent was not far from the dump and he knew the area well. Having said that much he stood silent, waiting.

His countenance was pensive, he seemed to be following an intricate pattern of inner thought. A grave, sombre man, of few words, when he was pleased, which was seldom, no more than a ghost of a smile lighted his features. An old soldier, he had spent a lifetime fighting the Italians, he knew equally the virtues of long patience and of swift action. I liked him from the first moment.

The interrogation followed its course:

'You know the dump?'

'Yes.'

'You have seen it yourself?'

'I have been in it.'

'How do you know it is petrol?'

'I have seen the black drums.'

'How many drums are there?'

'I don't know.'

'Are there a thousand?'

He made a mental calculation: 'More.'

'Are there two thousand?'

'I don't know.'

'When was the dump made?'

'In winter, soon after the Italians came back after the British troops left.'

'Has it been used since?'

'No.'

'Where is the dump?'

'Near the houses of El Qubba to the east. South of the road.'

'How far from the houses?'

'I don't know. Near.'

'Can you see the houses from the dump?'

'You can see the fort.'

'Is there a guard?'

'No. There is a wire fence on posts.'

'Are there any troops in the neighbourhood?'

'There is the camp of tents north of the road. In the village there are the workshops where the Italians repair the trucks, and the stores where they issue the rations. At night the trucks that travel on the road go into the car park.' (El Qubba at that time was a staging post on the main German line of communication.)

'Can the dump be seen from the air?'

'I don't know.'

'Are the drums covered?'

'No. But there are trees and the whole place is overgrown with thistles.'

'Can you take me to the dump?'

'I can take you inside the wire at night. There is no difficulty.'

'Even if I am in uniform?'

'Even in uniform.'

I liked Mohammed el Obeidi more and more. His information was accurate and to the point. I was sure he was not romancing. And if there were really more than a thousand forty-gallon drums of petrol in that dump and I succeeded in blowing it up at the right moment, there might be a small amount of 'alarm and despondency' in the enemy camp after all.

I told Chapman that I would be leaving for El Qubba the next afternoon, taking Chevalier with me, and one of my Arabs, and asked him to get a demolition party of three Arabs under Shorten to stand by till I sent instructions. Shorten was down at the dump in the Wadi Gherna but due back two days later.

That night a message came on the radio for me. It said: 'SPREAD ALARM AND DESPONDENCY.' So the time had come, I thought, Eighth Army was taking the offensive. The date was, I think, May 18, 1942. On the nineteenth in the late afternoon, with

Chevalier, Mohammed el Obeidi and one of my Arabs, I rode off from Er Rteim. The trip was timed to take us across the Martuba by-pass about two in the morning and to reach Sidi bu Halfaya before daylight. When we got there Mohammed el Obeidi took us to a huge, dry Roman water cistern hewn out of the rock on the top of a spur. The horses were put to graze and we made ourselves comfortable and drank tea in the three-roomed cistern which was to be our home for the next week.

At dawn I made my way cautiously to the western edge of the spur. A few yards from the opening of our cistern a vertical cliff fell three hundred feet to the wadi below. On my left, half a mile away on the opposite side of the wadi, I could see an Italian ammunition dump with trucks loading and, further to the left, a stretch of the Martuba by-pass on which the daily convoys were beginning to raise dust. To the right a wide panorama opened with, on the sky-line six miles away, the ambitious Italian monument that stands up on the hills beyond El Qubba. We took turns during the day, Chevalier and I, alternately to sleep and to watch through our glasses the Italian ammunition dump.

This dump might provide a useful alternative target, if the petrol dump at El Qubba could not, for some reason, be attempted, and I asked Chevalier to reconnoitre it at close quarters in the dark hours of the next night, taking with him our Libyan soldier, while I went to El Qubba with Mohammed el Obeidi.

I started immediately after dark—too early really—for we were much vexed with the barking of dogs and were compelled to make repeated detours to avoid Arab tents where the inhabitants were not yet asleep. I didn't care to be seen by anybody so close to an important enemy centre. Yet it could hardly be avoided and when a rider appeared coming directly toward us we had to stop and greet him, for any other course would have made us suspect. While Mohammed el Obeidi, quite changed from his ordinary taciturn demeanour, engaged the rider (an Arab returning to his tents after a day spent at El Qubba) in voluble talk, I grunted a few non-committal noises and drifted along out of sight in the dark.

I heard Mohammed el Obeidi explain away my churlish behaviour by saying that I was a rich merchant from Jalo Oasis travelling to Derna and very cross and hungry because Mohammed, my guide, had blundered and lost his way. I thought the story would not have taken in a mouse but the other man tactfully accepted it and commiserated with Mohammed el Obeidi on the troubles of a guide. He offered to take us both to his tent and give us a meal but my guide managed to disentangle himself politely and rejoined me, chuckling grimly. It must be realized that not *I* but *Mohammed el Obeidi* was the man who risked his life in this adventure: if the worst happened I would become an honourable prisoner-of-war, but my friend had a good chance of ending his life strung up by an iron hook through the jaw. For such was the kindly Italian method of dealing with disaffected Arabs.

A little later we alighted at the tent of Mohammed el Obeidi's brother, where we left our horses and ten minutes' walk took us to the dump.

Enclosed with a rustic three-wire fence it covered about ten acres of scrubby ground, dotted with trees and overgrown with tall dry thistles. The petrol was laid in lots of twenty-five to thirty drums lying close together on the ground. The lots were irregularly dispersed in the undergrowth but were not too difficult to discern, even on this moonless night. For two hours I walked up and down within the wire, counting the lots and making mental notes of landmarks. I found ninety-six lots: at an average of twenty-seven drums to the lot that dump held over one hundred thousand gallons of petrol. It seemed good—I wondered what snag there might be; with one or two exceptions all the drums I had lifted were heavy and apparently full. With a tool I had brought with me I unscrewed a few stoppers and verified that the contents were indeed petrol. Mohammed el Obeidi had served me well.

On one side the dump abutted on to a track leading to the main road, about five hundred yards away. Crossing the wire on my way out I saw a glow coming from the lights of El Qubba, but the little town itself was hidden by a low rise.

We arrived back in the cistern at Sidi bu Halfaya before daylight. Chevalier and his Libyan soldier were in: they had been unable to find the ammunition dump in the dark, and had returned having achieved nothing. I was annoyed because it was an easy task—the distance was no more than half a mile. Chevalier couldn't be blamed as he had no experience, but the Libyan, I knew, could have had no difficulty in reaching the dump and reconnoitring the approaches. He had had the whole day to map out a route of which every yard was visible from the top of our cliff. I said nothing but marked down our soldier as being a fool and faint of heart and resolved never to employ him any more on a job of this kind. His failure didn't matter much to me anyhow because, having decided to attempt the destruction of the petrol dump at El Qubba, I concentrated exclusively on this project.

I wrote a message to Chapman asking him to send up the demolition party with the explosives and gadgets required. I told him the size and the layout of the petrol dump and the manner in which I intended laying the charges. He would then have no difficulty in sending up the right stuff. We understood one another perfectly in these matters.

I had to wait till dark before dispatching the Libyan soldier with the message. I then told him that, in spite of the fact that he had been unable to find the ammunition dump half a mile away, I knew he was quite capable of riding in the dark sixteen miles to Er Rteim. If he got there safely before dawn, delivered the message and guided back to us the men that Chapman would eventually entrust to his care, no more would be said about the matter of his unsuccessful reconnaissance. He gathered my meaning, nodded (with relief I thought) and went off. I hoped I had made the best possible use of a very imperfect instrument.

From that moment till the arrival of the demolition party there was absolutely nothing for me to do and I fell into a delightful inactivity. I slept sixteen hours a day, ate and the remainder of the time I lay in the sun and watched the kite hawks wheel in the sky. Chevalier fretted and was bored and wanted to play paper games. I knew he was worrying, for he was cursed with a premonitory imagination; my duty was to soothe him and take his mind off the coming ordeal, but I couldn't do it, I was too lazy. I was out of the world of strife and wouldn't be recalled. If I failed him then I hope he has forgiven me.

On the second day of waiting Mohammed el Obeidi brought me back to our schemes. He came to me where I lay on a rock and asked permission to speak.

'When you asked to be taken to see the petrol,' he said, 'I thought you had in mind, after making sure of the target, to send on your radio a message to your aeroplanes, and they would come to bomb dump. I realize now that such is not the case. You have seen the dump, you have sent a letter with that simpleton to your friend the tall major, but yet you are still waiting here. I assume then that you intend blowing up the dump yourself and that you are waiting for your men to come up and help you to do it. I must tell you, Major, that I don't like it, because, if it is done in that way, the Italians will think that the *Arabs* set fire to the dump and there will be reprisals. My family, my friends, all have their tents around El Qubba. They may have to pay the penalty: some of them will be hanged, the others will be deported—their cattle will be taken from them, and they will starve. They are my people, Major: I don't like it.' He said these words in his deliberate way and paused as if listening to an inner voice. I knew only too well that the success of my scheme was in his hands. If his intention was to betray me and I couldn't talk him out of it, it seemed I would have to kill him. I had a pistol down in the cistern, but I liked the man. In a few minutes I would have to make up my mind.

Mohammed resumed:

'Why don't you trust me, Major? Why don't you open your mind to me? Tell me your plan. You are in command, you know best. If the aeroplanes can't do the destruction *you* know why and *you* know what has to be done. This is war and not the time to think of families. If you know that the petrol has to be burned and that it can't be done in any other way than by walking in and setting it on fire—so be it. I don't like it but I am a soldier, Major. What has to be, has to be. You must tell me your plan; I can help you.' He waited. I had to decide at once one way or the other, there was no middle course. I believed he was sincere. If he turned out to be a liar, I would be proved unable to judge men, unfit to command, unsuited for the tasks I had chosen for myself, bound anyhow to fail sooner or later. I was on test, not he. I made up my mind and I told him what arrangements I had made.

'When will your men arrive?' he asked.

'Late tomorrow night or the night after.'

'Mounted?'

'Yes.'

'How many will you be altogether?'

'Eleven.'

'How many men on the job?'

'Nine.'

'After you have been in the dump and laid your gadgets, how long will it be before the fire starts?'

'Three hours.'

He nodded, wrapped his jerd round him and walked away toward El Qubba. I had twenty-four hours—till his return the next evening—to wonder if I had been a fool.

He then came up briskly, sat down and spoke as follows:

'There is hurry. Soldiers have begun yesterday to load petrol from the dump. I hope your men arrive tonight. When they arrive they will be tired: they will rest here in the cistern till the next evening. Then, starting at ten, the nine of you and myself, we shall walk, carrying the explosives, to a dry cistern near my brother's tent at El Qubba, where we shall arrive before light. In the cistern there will be food and water. No one, under any excuse, will leave it during daylight—not even to relieve nature. On the slope outside there will be a little boy with his sheep and goats. If he sees anything alarming, such as armed soldiers making for the cistern, he will whistle in this way to warn you.

'At sunset more food will be brought. At eight-thirty you will be ready to go over to the dump, carrying only what is indispensable: explosives, one weapon I should say for every three men, and a few rounds of ammunition. The remainder of your kit will remain in the cistern. I will take you to the dump where you will arrive at nine. I will leave you there and you will do what you have to do. Not later than ten-forty-five you will make your own way back to the cistern, where I shall be waiting for you. You will collect your kit and we shall walk away to Kaf el Kefra.

'In the meantime your two surplus men will drive the mounts, carrying your rations and any kit left behind, to Kaf el Kefra where we shall find them when we arrive. There is water in a pool under some rocks and we can rest at the Kaf until the evening. We shall then ride back in the dark to Er Rteim.'

I said: 'It is good. We shall do as you say. I am grateful to you.' Mohammed el Obeidi grunted and went down into the cistern to boil himself some tea. He was my master in the art of war, and since that day every plan I have made has had his perfect 'operation order' as a model.

I couldn't find Kaf el Kefra on my map and the landmarks leading to it mentioned by Mohammed el Obeidi were all unknown to me; I had to be contented with the knowledge that it was 'not far to the west of El Qubba and south of the main road'.

I wanted to leave the enemy with the impression that the petrol dump had been raided by a motorized party and not by local Arabs. I remembered being told that after the unfortunate raid on Rommel's headquarters the parties waiting on the coast to be picked up by submarine had been lost because someone had carelessly dropped a map marked with the rendezvous. I wanted to do deliberately what had then been the result of an incredible folly, and I spent the next hours in marking a small-scale map with an imagined route, leading in to El Qubba from the west and leaving it toward the east, then curving down to the south in the direction of the open desert. The route I marked in yellow pencil, the halting points in green; a red circle surrounded the approximate position of the petrol dump, with a brown question mark. When I had drawn fasces in black for the Italian troops in El Qubba and a purple swastika for the Germans in Derna I thought that my map looked pretty convincing. I scribbled a few sums in the margins (petrol consumption for five vehicles doing eight miles to the gallon and suchlike calculations), then an address, Mademoiselle Laura Vanetti, 9 Rue Morpurgo, Alexandria. Next I folded the map backwards and forwards several times till the creases looked worn, then I spread it out and crumpled it up and spread it out again, laid it on a flat rock and wiped my shoes on it, smeared it with fat from a tin of bully beef, burned two cigarette holes in the right-hand edge and carefully tore it half down the middle. I then folded it up and put it in my pocket, ready for use.

Shorten with the demolition party arrived that night in high spirits. They rested, then they passed the time preparing the explosives. We used a device christened the daisy chain, made from guncotton primers threaded on a five-foot length of primacord, an instantaneous fuse that looks like a thick blind-cord. Guncotton primers, the explosive on which we relied to set the petrol on fire, are in the shape of a truncated cone, the size of a large pipe bowl and have a longitudinal hole through their centres. Five primers went to each daisy chain, spaced out and held in place by knots in the cord. At one end of the cord a detonator was fixed with adhesive tape: into the detonator we crimped a time-igniter, an automatic device that was meant to set off the detonator at a fixed time after the safety-pin had been withdrawn. On this occasion we used three-hour igniters. For our own safety daisy chains and detonators were carried separately and assembled at the last moment only, after the chains had been laid under the petrol drums.

We adhered strictly to Mohammed el Obeidi's schedule. About one in the morning, after three hours' stumbling walk, we arrived in the outskirts of El Qubba. Late as it was the little settlement still showed a few lights; a screeching radio played Italian jazz in the Army brothel on the hill, where I had once been billeted at a time when the place was ours. An electric welding plant in the workshops threw fitful flashes of cold, violet light. After our fearful march in the dark the mean lights and the thin noise coming from the well-known piddling Italian settlement of less than sixty houses were magnified by contrast and filled the landscape. I fell into a dreamlike fancy: the trees showing against the glow were a city park; beyond it were wide streets full of lights. Trams clanked, cars slid by, well-dressed people walked the pavements and sat in crowded cafés, where bands played soft music. Over the cinema neon lights flickered. I didn't click back into reality till long after we had slipped into our cave-like cistern.

The food provided by Mohammed el Obeidi's brother was good and plentiful. Our bellies well filled we all slept late into the next day. Our little watchman outside had no occasion to whistle. I was told later that two Italian soldiers had crossed the foot of our slope, but the child seeing them unarmed and their purpose but an idle wandering had wisely refrained from giving the alarm. The last hours of waiting wore heavily on my two British companions; Chevalier was gloomy and irritable, Shorten, excited, talkative and restless, laid down the law about the fine points of the art of demolition, and I had to interfere tactfully to prevent a quarrel. The Arabs, fortunately, were self-possessed and chatted drowsily together.

At seven-thirty that evening a small boy slipped in, carrying on his head a tray with a hot meal. At eight-thirty we hung our daisy chains round our necks, put the detonators and time-igniters in our pockets, and walked over to the petrol dump. We crossed the wire, and collected round a small, white rock, where I gave my instructions: I had divided my force into three parties of one British officer and two Arabs each. To each party I allotted a sector of the dump which I described to them as well as I could by the landmarks—trees, rocks and bushes—that I had noted on my previous visit. Starting from where we stood they were to work their diverging ways into the dump, laying one daisy chain under each of the clusters of drums they could find in the dark. Each party had twenty daisy chains and they were to lay as many of them as they could, bearing in mind that we were all to collect again at the white rock at ten-fifteen. On no account were they to be late at the rendezvous for, I said, I wouldn't wait one minute beyond the appointed time. Unused daisy chains were to be brought back. I repeated my discourse in Arabic, asked each man if he had perfectly understood where he was to go, what he had to do and where and at what time was the rendezvous. Our watches had been synchronized beforehand and off we went.

There was no moon but the sky was clear and, though the stars gave us enough light to work by, the darkness was sufficiently thick to make us feel safely invisible. Across the dump, in the distance, shone the headlights of three Italian trucks which were being loaded with petrol drums. I welcomed this activity for, I thought with pleasure, the enemy would find his dump gone up in flames at the precise time when he had planned to use it. It seemed unlikely that he would be able to replace this large amount of petrol so quickly that the course of the battle would not be affected.

We worked methodically and unhurriedly. My two Arabs lifted a drum and I laid a daisy chain underneath—then, while I fitted detonator and igniter (which has to be done with some care), one of them kept watch by me; the other walked ahead and prospected for the next lot of drums. In this way, and helped of course by my previous knowledge of the topography of the dump, we wasted no time.

It was too easy—I felt like a sneak, trespassing in the dark and, what is more, plotting to damage somebody's property. Wasn't I taking unfair advantage of the good-natured confidence of the owners of the dump who hadn't even thought it necessary to put a guard on it? Soon, however, the pleasure induced by our smooth teamwork dispelled my initial distaste, for I was no more a cowardly burglar but an honest workman doing efficiently a good job of work.

From lot to lot our broken way took us closer to the Italian trucks. Their lights were a comfort to me, they dispelled the anxiety I often feel in the dark, and anyway, by day or by night, the sight of the enemy is always exhilarating. Soon I could hear the men talking in Italian, as they handled the heavy drums. With many blasphemous repetitions, they cursed the officer who had caused them to be detailed for this unwelcome nightwork. We worked up as close to them as I thought reasonable, then made our way back. We were well ahead of time and we disposed of our three remaining daisy chains on lots we had skipped on our way up.

At eight minutes to ten with twenty-three minutes to go, we squatted near the white rock. Two minutes later Chevalier and his two men loomed out of the darkness and joined us. They had used all but two of their daisy chains. We waited in self-satisfied peace. At ten-past ten I posted one of the Arabs two hundred yards ahead in Shorten's sector to guide him in, in case he had trouble in finding the white rock. At twenty-five past the Arab returned, having neither seen nor heard anybody. I waited till a quarter to eleven: Shorten's party was then half an hour overdue. They must have come to grief in some unexplained silent manner, for they couldn't have lost their way; I took the decision (awful to me) to abandon them and withdraw the remainder of my men. We walked away in single file, and had gone perhaps thirty paces when the man behind me touched my arm and dropped to the ground. I did the same, and looking back toward the rock I discerned shadowy shapes moving. Our last man got up and made carefully back toward them. A moment later he brought up Shorten and his two men. I whispered weakly: 'You are late.' I was so shaken with relief that for a few seconds I couldn't think. He started talking and brought me back to my senses. 'We shall talk presently,' I said. 'Follow Chevalier.'

Back in the cistern, while the others gathered their kit, I had him up; he stood to attention, with a foolish grin of satisfaction on his pink face, and started his report.

'Sir. I laid sixteen daisy chains in sixteen different lots of petrol drums——' I cut him short.

'Why were you half an hour late?'

'Was I, sir? I didn't think I was that late. Surely?'

'Why were you late?'

'Well, sir, after we had laid our sixteen daisy chains I noticed that the primers were immobilized by a single knot on the cord. Now, sir, on the demolition course, we were advised to tie a double knot to make sure of the explosive wave propagating itself from the cord to the primer. So I went back to all the lots and tied a second knot in the sixteen daisy chains. Ahmed and Sayed have been most helpful, sir.'

'Christ Almighty,' I whispered. 'What do you think we are doing here? Running a bloody demolition course? I'll propagate an explosive wave up your f—— arse. You are sacked. Dismiss.'

I felt better—Shorten grinned in the light of my torch—he appreciated my language and was too pleased with himself even to feel guilty. I looked round:

'All set? Out we go,' and, Mohammed el Obeidi leading, out we went.

Time was running short. The first charges had been laid shortly after nine, two hours ago. If the delayed igniters worked properly the dump would start blowing up in an hour—or less—illuminating the countryside. We had to get away before this happened and the alarm was given—and I had still a job to do. I had arranged with Mohammed el Obeidi that he would take us along the side of the dump on to the main road. When we reached it I got everybody across, took the marked map out of my pocket and fixed it in a bush by the roadside, hoping it would look as if it had blown out of the back of a truck. The six remaining daisy chains and a few igniters I laid neatly in the ditch, together with a packet of cigarettes and a field dressing, as if they had been forgotten and left behind in a hasty departure. I then rejoined the rest of my party across the road. We skirted tents—a reinforcement camp that held up to two thousand troops—dispersed on the north side of the road. There were dim lights in some of the tents but we saw nobody about. When we had cleared the last tents I called to Mohammed el Obeidi to slacken the pace a little. With the camp and the road between us and the dump I thought we were safe for the time being; it was unlikely, if the alarm were given, that the enemy would search for us at first in his own territory, he would rather assume that we had escaped to the south, toward the desert or to the east, towards our own lines —not to the north-west where there was no cover and every village held troops and Italian settlers. We had, however, to get out of this area before dawn and we were taken by Mohammed el Obeidi in a wide curve to avoid El Qubba, then across the road once more and on to the mysterious Kaf el Kefra.

We had hardly dipped into a gully beyond the camp when a dull boom came from the dump, a dark red flame rose in the sky and fell again, leaving a glow behind it. Chevalier, who was walking with me, turned round without stopping and muttered softly: 'Oh Lord!' With a timid disposition he was a man of courage and persistently involved himself in improbable adventures. Pigheadedly he fought his natural inclination to take things easy; hardly out of one breath-taking scrape and still panting, he searched for some new way of getting himself scared. He was generally successful in his enterprises and, surprisingly, survived the war to return to cotton-broking in Alexandria.

We stumbled on in the dark led by Mohammed el Obeidi at the swift, tireless Arab pace. The glow in the dump behind us had died out. I was worried about it: that first explosion had been premature and had probably been caused by one only of our charges, but I thought it would have been sufficient to keep the fire going till the others went off.

We walked on. By one o'clock nothing had happened though all the charges should already have gone up if the time-igniters had functioned properly. With a sinking heart I felt the despair of failure overcome me. Weary and dispirited I walked on, suddenly so tired that, had I been alone, I would have lain down to sleep. Time dragged on; in my mind I kept going over the sequence of charge-laying: primers, fuses, detonators, igniters. How could they *all* have failed? We had laid fifty-four daisy chains and one only had exploded—without much effect apparently. I decided to keep up hoping till one-thirty. The half-hour came and nothing happened. Cursing the makers of our gadgets I admitted failure. As nothing could be done about it my spirits immediately began to revive and I started working out in my mind a plan to blow up a bridge on the railway line between Benghazi and Barce. I looked at my watch; my despair had lasted half an hour.

At five minutes to two the skyline behind us exploded. A broad curtain of yellow flames lifted to the sky and stayed there, lighting the bare landscape around us. Rumbling thunderous explosions followed one another throwing up more flames. Drums of petrol, projected upwards, burst in mid-air, blazing globes of fire that floated slowly down. A moment later a rolling wall of heavy, billowing smoke, lit to a fierce red by the fires burning on the ground, had taken possession of half the horizon and reached to the sky. It seemed incredible that the petty manipulations we had done so quietly in the dark could result in such a glorious catastrophe. It was more than we expected; our reward was ten times what had been promised, such a munificence made us wonder; we felt slightly awed and very powerful.

For a whole hour the blaze increased in intensity. Our men kept falling out to gaze back at the wonder and then caught up again at a trot. The glare of the burning dump lit our way and made the going easier. Then, as we increased our distance and intervening hills threw longer shadows, I found myself once more stumbling in the dark and hard put to it to keep up with our indefatigable guide. On we walked. Overcome with exhaustion, I renounced my self-respect and asked Mohammed el Obeidi how far we were now from Kaf el Kefra. 'Not far,' he replied laconically and we plodded on.

The first light of dawn came. The fire behind us shone with undiminished fierceness. We plodded on. The sun rose; we were in a barren wilderness of sandy hills and scrub. My head swam with fatigue; to keep awake I tried working out a sum: *The Germans have two hundred tanks—they do five miles to the gallon—in battle they run fifty miles a day. How many days' supply are one hundred thousand gallons of petrol?* I kept losing the threads of my argument and starting again from the beginning—then I got a surprising answer: *sixty-two days.* This was too good, it couldn't be correct. Patiently I began again. This time the answer came: *a third of a day, eight hours.* As a period as short as that was rather disappointing back I went to my premises. Mohammed el Obeidi came up to me and said: 'Kaf el Kefra is now near.' We were all well tired out by now but we went on under the warmer sun. I worked once more on my problem and got as an answer: *twelve days.* It seemed satisfactory and I lost interest. We walked. . . . Our guide said: 'Beyond that hill is

Kaf el Kefra.' I laughed out loud because of a joke of ours: When you start on a trip the guide says the objective is *far*—after four hours' walk he says it is *not far*—four hours later he says it is *near*—four hours' walk again and he says it is *beyond that hill*—then you walk another four hours before getting there. With dragging feet and an aching body I tramped along for another eternity, then I looked up again; the sun was hardly higher in the sky, which was surprising. Someone said in Arabic: 'There comes Musa riding a camel.' And indeed I saw a rider approaching across the yellow plain—one of our men, mounted on one of our camels. We had arrived. Musa slid off his camel and shook my hand with fervour—he patted me on the shoulder and pointed to the eastern horizon where a solid black cloud of smoke stretched from north to south.

We scrambled down into a semi-circle of low cliffs below the level of the plateau, dotted with caves: Kaf el Kefra. It was only half-past seven.

Musa and Yunes, the two men who had brought our kit and the animals from Sidi bu Halfaya, boiled tea for us and cooked breakfast. Squatting in the soft sand, quite revived, I looked at Mohammed el Obeidi; to my amazement his usual dark composure had gone; he was grinning and chuckling to himself.

'What is it, Mohammed?'

'Those Italian soldiers who were working last night in the dump. They are now under close arrest. The charge is "Smoking while handling petrol and thus causing grievous damage to Mussolini's property",' and, for the only time in my experience, he burst out laughing. We all laughed, we shook with uncontrolled mirth, we rolled in the sand, sobered down and then spluttered out again. We thought his remark infinitely funny, it summed up beautifully for us the events of the last week.

I took guard duty for the first hour, before turning in to sleep. I climbed up to the plateau and looked down; our men were all invisible, asleep in the caves—the campfire had been carefully covered with sand, and empty food tins buried. Our camels and horses were out of sight, grazing up and down the wadi. It was well. On the horizon the black wall of smoke billowed lazily.

The Arabs around El Qubba, including Mohammed el Obeidi's brother and his family, were all rounded up by the Italians and closely interrogated. They were released after a few days. Eventually a copy of the official Italian report on the incident came into my hands. It attributed the fire to the action of a *British motorized Commando*. I couldn't say whether this was the result of my attempts at deception or should be attributed to the desire of the local Italian commander to put the blame on a mysterious raiding party entirely beyond his control. After all he *might* have put a guard on the dump!

Tactfully no mention was made in the report of the amount of petrol destroyed but I was amused to learn that a dump of small arms ammunition which, entirely unknown to me, lay on the far side of the petrol dump, had been caught in the conflagration and had also blown up. Apparently the thistles and the dry under-growth had spread the fire and even several of the tents in the camp on the far side of the road had been burned.

A few days after our return to Er Rteim one of our amateur spies came in bursting with important news: British planes had bombed El Qubba and completely destroyed an immense dump.

The P.P.A. was formed in October, 1942, moved out from Cairo and fought alongside the Special Air Services Brigade and the Long Range Desert Group until Rommel's defeat. Then, with the size of his army almost trebled, Popski set off for Italy where he continued to 'spread alarm' behind the German lines.

The farmer's friends soon came down in droves. They were very excited and all thought they had vital information to give me. I interviewed them in turn and spent hours listening to fatuous gossip. I heard the story of the occupation of Poggio Orsini ten times over, and what the grandfather had said, and what the sister-in-law had seen. My difficulty was that these farmers didn't know their area. Apart from their own farms, and the towns of Gravina and Irsina where they went to market, they knew less than I did with my map. They couldn't tell me who lived over the next ridge but one, and none of them had ever been to Genzano, five miles away. I got the most fantastic accounts of the troops in Gravina: two hundred tanks, guns larger than a railway train, seven generals and so many soldiers that they couldn't be counted. 'Two thousand or thirty thousand, perhaps a hundred thousand!' Patiently I asked questions and listened: too often the talk digressed on to family matters and genealogies: these people were all related.

Still, a bit here and a bit there, I increased my knowledge—but by mid-afternoon I had a very poor showing for nine hours' work. I called to a little man who had been standing by for a long time waiting for his turn to speak, shy but less dim-witted than those other boobies. The first thing he said was:

'I know the quartermaster officer in Gravina, Major Schulz, the one who buys the supplies for the officers' mess. His office is in the piazza, the third house to the left of the trattoria, the one with the double brown door. My name is Alfonso.'

His words gave new life to my poor brain, dazed by so many hours of fruitless gossip with the natives.

'Alfonso,' I said, 'please tell those people who are still waiting that I shall talk to them tomorrow.' I took him by the arm and we sat down side by side on a stone. Alfonso had sold cheese, eggs and wine from his farm to Major Schulz; he had been in Gravina the day before and had noticed many things; he offered to go again and try and find out what I needed. Eventually we evolved another plan. First Bob Yunnie with four jeeps set off to watch the Potenza-Gravina road. He found a suitable hide-out on a height opposite the small mountain-top town of Irsina, close enough to the road to read the number plates of the passing vehicles. He organized the familiar routine of road watching, and I pulled back three miles to a deserted railway station on the Potenza-Gravina line. From the station telephone I called up Major Schulz. I had a long struggle to get through but eventually I got him. Speaking Italian mixed with a few words of German I told him, with a great show of secrecy, that I was the quartermaster sergeant of an Italian headquarters in a town which had recently been evacuated by the Germans. I had, I said, the disposal of eight cases of cognac which I would like to sell if he would offer me a good price. We haggled a good deal about the sum. When we had finally come to an agreement I said that for obvious reasons I didn't care to deliver the goods by daylight. If he would wait for me in his office that night at eleven o'clock I would drive up with the drink in a small captured American car. Would he give the word to the control post on the Spinazzola road to let me through without asking questions?

Major Schulz was a simple soul: he may have had scruples about buying stolen goods, but he wanted the cognac badly for the general's mess, and I had made free use of the name of his predecessor, Hauptmann Giessing, with whom, I said, I had in the past made several similar deals. (The relevant information came of course from Alfonso, a good schemer with an observant mind.) He agreed to my dubious request and promised to wait for me that night.

With Cameron we stripped our jeep and loaded in the back some

compo-ration boxes, weighted with stones. At ten to eleven the
guard on the road block lifted the barrier for us and waved us
through, and at eleven exactly we pulled up on the piazza opposite
Major Schulz's office. Cameron and I grabbed each end of one of
our cases, went past the sentry, up the stairs straight into the office,
where Major Schulz dozed at his desk. Wakened by the thump of
the case on the floor, he opened bleary, drunken eyes and gazed at
us uncertainly. Cameron didn't give him time to wonder at the
nature of our uniforms, but hit him smartly on the head with a
rubber truncheon. Schulz passed out and slumped in his chair.
Cameron went down the stairs for another case—while I went
through the papers in the room. By an amazing stroke of luck,
open on the desk lay the ration strength of the units of the First
Parachute Division and attached troops which were supplied by the
distributing centre in Gravina, dated September 12, 1943. While
Cameron brought up the remaining cases I collected more documents out of the files. We placed a quarter-full bottle of whisky,
uncorked, on Schulz's desk (the poor man deserved a reward), and
walked out into the street. The German sentry was idly examining
our jeep. Moved by an impish gust of Scots humour, Cameron,
the sedate, shook him by the hand, pressed on him a packet of 'V'
cigarettes, said:

'Good night, good German,' and we drove off.

Two hours later, from a fold in the hills, our radioman tapped out:

POPSKI TO AIRBORNE STOP TOTAL STRENGTH ENEMY FORMATIONS OUT-
SIDE TARANTO 12 SEP ALL RANKS 3504 RPT THREE FIVE ZERO FOUR
MESSAGE ENDS

On the 0900 call I received:

AIRBORNE TO POPSKI PLEASE CONFIRM TOTAL STRENGTH ENEMY
FORMATIONS TARANTO PERIMETER NOT MORE 3504

I knew that Intelligence had put the figure much higher. Slightly
piqued, I fell to the temptation of showing off and having by now
sorted out the papers I had stolen from the unfortunate Schulz, I
composed a lengthy signal which ran to four or five messages and
took the rest of the day to encipher and to transmit. It went something like this:

POPSKI TO AIRBORNE STOP CONFIRM TOTAL STRENGTH ENEMY 12 SEP-

TEMBER ALL RANKS 3504 RPT THREE FIVE ZERO FOUR INCLUSIVE OFFICERS
441 STOP LOCATIONS FOLLOW GINOSA OFFICERS 61 ORS 500 MATERA OFF
72 ORS 570 ALTAMURA OFF 83 ORS 629 SANTERAMO OFF 58 ORS 469
GIOIA OFF 92 ORS 755 GRAVINA OFF 75 ORS 140 STOP ORDER OF BATTLE
FOLLOWS ONE PARACHUTE DIV 19 RGT D COY O.C. LT. WEISS INITIAL
W.G. GINOSA B COY LESS ONE PLATOON O.C. HAUPTMANN SCHWARTZ
INITIAL ILLEGIBLE GINOSA . . .

and so on. Major Schulz had filed his strength returns with care.

With this flourish I considered that my first mission was completed, and I turned my mind to investigations much further afield.

Very early one morning we started winding up the narrow road that leads to Castel Vétera in Val Fortore and stops at this small town, two thousand feet up the mountainside. To the north of this road the map showed a patch of green, a wood, off the beaten track, in which I hoped we could shelter for a few days, make inquiries and lay plans for the future. The forest ran up a steep mountain and we could enter it nowhere, till we found a broad patch of fairly level ground. Here we plunged into the undergrowth and concealed our jeeps in a dark thicket between the hillside and a large boulder four or five hundred yards from the road. Day came, Sanders reconnoitred the neighbourhood and found a mule track which climbed down six hundred feet to the valley bottom. I interviewed a few peasants, dull-witted boobies who helped me little with a confused (but alarming) story of German vehicles going up to Castel Vétera and back on the previous day.

We were all in our bower eating our midday meal when we heard in the distance tanks coming up. We put out our fire and waited. There was nothing else we could do: our fortress had no back door and we were trapped. Two German scout cars showed on the road and pushed on towards Castel Vétera. Ten minutes later they returned and stopped opposite our level patch of woods; one remained while the other drove down. Meanwhile the tanks had stopped out of sight; half an hour later we heard them grinding up. Time dragged on; a first tank came into view and was waved off the road into the wood by the men in the scout car; others followed clanking, to be dispersed to cover under the trees. By nightfall we had a squadron camped, somewhat uphill from our position, between us and the road. Just after dark more tanks arrived and these stopped below us.

These elements of the Sixteenth Panzer Division moving over

from Salerno to the Eighth Army front, had, with motives similar apparently to our own, chosen this remote spot, well covered from the air, to camp in peace while the rest of their division moved to its concentration area.

The whole of that endless afternoon we kept ready to bolt up the mountainside, our weapons and emergency packs at hand, an incendiary bomb laid out on the seat of each jeep, but when darkness fell not one of the enemy had troubled to poke his nose behind our boulder. Hours of waiting in our trap, coming after all those days of snooping and hiding, had put us in a savage mood: we longed senselessly to hear loud noises and to feel our machine-guns rattle in our hands—unfortunately, though our half-inch bullets might knock chips off the armour of Mark IV tanks they couldn't penetrate it. We should have to use our wits and lay in turn a trap for the enemy who had so stupidly failed to catch us when he had us in his hand.

The position of the German tanks in two camps—one on each side of our way to the road—made me think of a possible deception; I conferred with Sanders, then called the men together, and we laid our plans. We divided all the explosives we had—about sixty pounds—into four lots and fixed to each one a long fuse. At one in the morning we crept out and placed two charges about fifty yards apart toward A Squadron on our left and similarly two charges near B Squadron on our right. At one-thirty the fuses had been brought back to our camp and five minutes later we detonated charge one. When the report went up and reverberated from the hills we started our engines and drove out between the trees towards the road, leaving one jeep behind to detonate the other charges at twenty-second intervals. I intended thus to cover the noise of our trucks and to distract attention from us altogether. Charge two went off, and as it had been laid at the foot of a tall, slender tree, brought it down crashing near the foremost tank of B Squadron. Charge three, on the other side, projected a clattering load of stones over a tank of A Squadron, then number four went off and brought down another tree.

We had now reached a position midway between the two squadrons, and while we waited for our last jeep to catch up we fired our only bazooka in the direction of A Squadron. The small rocket-propelled shell described a lovely parabola of fire and landed in a bush.

Now, at last, the enemy on both sides began to wake up: we heard shouts and the noise of a tank engine starting; but, puzzled as they must have been, they were not going to rush into action before they found out what was happening. We staggered our jeeps and fired a broadside of our ten guns towards A Squadron, then we moved on fifty yards and served B Squadron, moved again and sent streams of tracer towards A and B simultaneously. Most of our rounds hit the trees, a few reached their objectives, a lucky burst of incendiary hit a petrol can and lit a dim glare in the lines of A. Then at last coming from my left I heard what I had been hoping for, the short, deep report of a seventy-five millimetre. Somebody in A had lost his temper. We concentrated our pinpricks on B till they also let off, and after that all we had to do was to poke the fire. After ten minutes A and B were at one another good and proper and we edged off towards the road, splinters and branches showering down on us as shells—which were not meant for us—hit the trees overhead.

I fired a German signal cartridge which I had carried with me many months. It generated a lovely shower of purple and silver stars, and was followed immediately—which rather startled me—by the deafening report of a seventy-five fired, it seemed, at point-blank range from an unnoticed tank. I thought it was time to say good-bye, and I led my little company down the road, leaving the battle behind.

JUST AFTER FIGHTING *a last violent action outside of Venice one of Popski's men came to him. 'I've lost an arm. I've lost an arm,' the soldier said, clutching a bullet-pierced shoulder. 'So have I,' Popski comforted him as he pulled out of his shirt a dangling arm just smashed by a hand grenade.*

Popski's hand was amputated, but he remained on active duty with the British Army until his death in 1952.

NIGHT ATTACK

BY DOUGLAS M. SMITH AND CECIL CARNES

THE SPECIAL AIR SERVICE BRIGADE *formed in November, 1942, at Tabrit in the Suez Canal Zone was not an air unit and was not a brigade. It was more like a platoon. When Lieutenant David Stirling conceived the idea of an irregular unit to harass Rommel's troops behind their lines, he envisioned a small group of men dropped by plane into the desert. In the months that followed the formation of the S.A.S., the men took parachute and commando training. However, it became increasingly apparent to Stirling, who had become one of the youngest colonels in the Army, that the parachute is only a means of transportation, and was not always the best one for his purposes. As operations continued, the S.A.S. began to rely more and more upon the Long Range Desert Group—that strange collection of professors, archæologists, geologists, etc., who furnished transportation into the deep desert cutting far behind Rommel's lines. The wedding between the operations of the L.R.D.G. and the S.A.S. served Stirling's purposes well. In the months that the S.A.S. operated, Stirling's men raided the port towns of the Germans along the entire North African Coast. They sabotaged Rommel's airfields and harried his troops. As time went on, Rommel withdrew more and more men and planes to cover his rear.*

Eventually such men as Fitzroy Maclean, who rose to brigadier and Britain's liaison officer with Tito, and Randolph Churchill joined the S.A.S. These men accompanied Stirling on the bluff raid which forced the Germans to withdraw their air support to the rear and permitted Field-Marshal Montgomery to launch his major offensive from Egypt. The S.A.S. was ripped to pieces in this sacrifice manœuvre, but Montgomery's offensive was successful.

The story that follows is typical of Stirling's operations. It is told by Douglas Smith, an American who served with the S.A.S.

DAWN was just breaking as a commissioned officer, a sergeant, and ten privates clambered aboard an open light truck. Eight of the party, facing inward, settled themselves on narrow seats running lengthwise at each side; the officer jumped up beside the driver;

the sergeant and the remaining man perched on the floor of the truck, in the rear, their legs dangling over the lowered tailboard.

The officer twisted his head for a last minute check, scanning the faces of his squad. He scrutinized the orderly pile of supplies, ammunition, and equipment which filled the centre of the truck, making sure for the tenth time that the precious containers of water were aboard and securely lashed. Satisfied, he nodded to the men and turned to the driver.

'All set, Connolly,' he said crisply. 'Let's go.'

The engine roared, the truck started slowly, then gathered speed. In a few minutes it had left Kabrit behind and was heading into the trackless desert on the first lap of a five-hundred-mile run that would take the party almost to Nazi-held Tobruk.

By the standard of desert travel they fairly breezed along the whole first day, following a course which roughly paralleled the coast road, but which was a good hundred miles inland from it. Their chief danger—if not their only one—was of being sighted from the air. The officer in front and the sergeant in the rear were both equipped with glasses through which they continuously studied the skies, but not an enemy plane put in an appearance.

They halted at dusk for a quick meal. Supper over, and the men stretched out in the warm sand for a few minutes while they smoked, chatted, and relaxed, he told them more definitely the nature of their assignment. Their immediate goal was a curve in the coast road some thirty miles east of Tobruk—the coast road which was Rommel's main line of communication.

'Somewhere in the desert between here and Tobruk,' he explained, 'Jerry has established an outpost, complete with airfield, location of which we have not been able to determine. One of our secret agents in Tobruk, however, has discovered that a fleet of ten trucks, loaded with supplies for this outpost, leaves Tobruk every Saturday at dusk. The trucks drive east—how far, nobody knows. Some time during the night they turn off the road—somewhere— and head into the desert for the outpost. You fellows get the picture this far?'

A grunted chorus of 'Yes, sir's' reassured him.

'It's our job to find that camp and blast it. Somebody had the bright idea that we might waylay the Jerries somewhere en route and slip our truck into the parade. It'll be dark, you see, and they're using different kinds and shapes of trucks themselves, so we shouldn't be noticed. We lollop along, like one of the family, till Jerry gets where he's going. Then we'll—er—meet any situation that may arise. We have grenades, time bombs, one machine-gun, and a special gadget Captain Crumper made just for us.' He ended, buried the cigarette whose lighted butt had been carefully cupped in his palm, and stood up. 'Well—what d'you think of it?'

There was only silence from the shadowy figures until the sergeant answered.

'I think, sir,' he observed critically, 'it promises to be a—very—good—show!'

The men thought so, too, from the alacrity with which they hopped back into the truck. With a fresh man in the driver's seat, the wheels rolled again. They stopped at dawn, finding a convenient wadi.

It was the beginning of a calamity-ridden, nerve-racking day. The fierce July sun drew out a man's juice, then boiled him in it. The heavily laden truck was stuck twice in patches of soft sand; the second time the churning wheels dug themselves in hub deep, requiring an hour of frantic shovelling to set them rolling again. A lone Nazi patrol plane hunting for just such ground activity as theirs, caught them in an open, carpet-flat expanse; they spent a hideous hour beneath their burlap mats, tormented by heat and thirst and flies till the enemy pilot wearied of describing aimless circles above a seemingly deserted area and droned away to the north-west.

Yet they made fair progress between delays, and did particularly well that night, thanks to blundering on a camel road from which the larger boulders had been removed. The succeeding day, too, was kind, so that the Captain grunted with satisfaction as he checked their position that evening on his large-scale map.

At dusk on Saturday evening the truck was parked discreetly in a small deep ravine, out of sight of the coastal road but not twenty yards from it. A sharp-eyed sentinel with the field glasses established himself on a bluff overlooking a long curve in the road from Tobruk; an hour later he came slithering down to announce he had spotted twelve sets of dimmed driving lights approaching in the distance.

'Every man to his place in the truck,' said the officer, and waited till the order had been swiftly and silently obeyed. 'Now I'll let you in on the rest of the programme. These trucks we're waiting for will be driving as usual about a hundred yards apart. We let eleven go by. Before number twelve comes in sight around the bend, we cut into the road and fall in line. When we——'

'If you'll excuse me, sir?'

'Certainly, Sergeant. What is it?'

'Mightn't it be better, sir, to let all twelve go by and then fall in at the rear?'

'No,' said the Captain decisively. 'The men on the twelfth truck will know they're the last in line. They'd probably be suspicious of another car turning up suddenly behind them. As it is, number eleven will think we're number twelve, and number twelve will think we're number eleven. When we reach the Jerry camp, there are bound to be sentries to pass at the entrance. We can't risk one of them noticing thirteen trucks, instead of the expected dozen. So, when we find ourselves getting close to the camp—we're bound to see or hear some sign ahead—we break down in the middle of the road, blocking it. Jerry number twelve comes up, stops, and we get rid of him. We park our truck beside the road, where it will be our rallying point after the show. Privates Brewster and Guffey will stay with the car, ready to use the machine-gun, if necessary, to cover our escape. Private Jones will take Captain Crumper's gadget and proceed according to orders already given him.'

'I think they're comin', sir,' said the driver softly, sticking out his head in the direction of the road and turning it sideways to listen. 'I can hear somethin' that sounds like 'em.'

'Right. Get your engine going—quietly. The noise they're making themselves will drown out ours. Be ready to start when I give the word. You eight men in the middle, back there—get down in the truck and pull the camouflage net over you. Everybody check his equipment—canteen, iron ration, knife, revolver, bombs and two grenades. That's Etienne Latour beside you, Sergeant? Good. Better start chinning in German you two—be in practice if you need it later. And if anything goes wrong—*use your knives*! One shot would give the show away.'

'Here they are, sir!' whispered the driver. The dimmed driving lights of a truck swept into view around the curve, followed by another and another. Leaning forward to peer through the dark, the driver was studying the intervals between the units of the convoy as they flashed past the mouth of the wadi at an easy thirty-mile gait. He reported his findings with satisfaction. 'Keepin' a bit better than a hundred yards between 'em, sir.'

The Captain began counting aloud in a tense whisper. 'Eight—nine—ten—here comes eleven—*now!*'

The truck shot forward as if the word had cut some invisible leash. A lurch or two, a few stiff jolts, and it took the highway smoothly, pointing east, some forty yards behind the Jerry ahead and comfortably in advance of the one yet to round the curve.

'They're using no tail lights!' exclaimed the Captain swiftly. 'Douse ours, Barrett—quick!'

He crossed his fingers for the next two or three minutes, blushing inwardly for the childish superstition. He kept his head turned, staring back at Jerry number twelve, which had come out of the curve and was tailing them at the distance of a scant fifty yards. The Captain held his breath, hearing the beat of his heart over the sound of the truck's engine. What was the driver of number twelve thinking? What had he thought when he straightened out from the curve and discovered himself so close to the truck ahead? Would he think number eleven had fallen off the pace? Would he think he had been driving too fast himself? Would he speed up to investigate?

Now he could see number twelve more clearly. It was dropping back! Definitely, it was dropping back! Its speed was checked perceptibly till it was the required hundred yards to the rear. The Captain's pent-up breath escaped in a long sigh of relief. He uncrossed his fingers and rubbed the palms of his hands on his trousers. He swallowed hard and was himself again.

'Sergeant!' he called back softly. 'Could you make anything out of that fellow in back?'

'No, sir. Too dark, sir.'

'We'll be meeting Tobruk-bound trucks, I expect. Maybe their driving lights will show him up. Keep your eyes peeled, eh?'

'Very good, sir.'

They did presently meet a string of six empty lorries presumably returning to their base from the German front for further supplies of men or material. They rattled past, with a genial blinking of lights that Sam Barrett politely acknowledged with blinks of his own, and then the Sergeant threw his voice over his shoulder anxiously.

'Got a look at him then, sir! Small open truck—not much of a load, I'd say—bit of canvas pulled over it. Two men on the front seat.'

'We should handle them without difficulty when the time comes. Thank you, Sergeant.'

There was no further talking for a while. Ten minutes went by— twenty—a half hour. The evenly spaced line of vehicles, each keeping its position as carefully as a ship in a convoy, rumbled on through the luminous, starlit night.

Twenty minutes later there came an alarm that turned him colder than the night itself. It was three short blasts from the horn of number twelve, the car behind. The sergeant's voice was anxious as he reported a change in the situation.

'Number twelve put on speed a moment ago, sir. He's overhauling us fast, sir. I think he meant that horn as a signal for us to stop!'

Sanguine a minute before, the young officer was suddenly sick with apprehension. Any disturbance now would ruin everything—force them to ignominious flight into the desert. Just when things were going so nicely.

Another short blast from the German truck. It sounded querulous. The Captain forced himself to speak coolly.

'We'd best pull up, Sergeant. Let Latour do the talking. If a situation arises, meet it according to your best judgment. No more noise than necessary.'

'We'll manage, sir,' said the sergeant calmly.

Their truck drew over to the side of the road and stopped. Twenty yards to the rear, the German did the same. The man seated beside the driver jumped to the ground and came forward afoot. Outlined in the faint gleam of the driving lights behind him, his figure showed bulky, powerful—menacing. He walked with the slow, heavy tread of a beefy German.

The Nazi was within a yard of the truck. The sergeant and Etienne Latour were motionless, their legs hanging over the tailboard, their hands gripping their deadly knives. The German halted. He spoke. The British officer, who did not speak German but could understand it fairly well, strained his ears to catch the guttural words.

'Please, has anybody here got a match?'

A match! *A match!*

It seemed to the officer his stomach turned upside down. Relief was almost worse than the suspense. His taut nerves and muscles loosened with painful suddenness . . . . They snapped tight again as quickly. What started to be a hysterical laugh came out as a stifled groan. A hideous thought had come to him—one he felt every man in the truck was thinking. Sam Barrett, the driver, put it in stricken words.

'Oh, Gawd, sir, there isn't a bleedin' match in th' bunch except *English!*'

There it was. The officer's mouth went dry.

Everything was happening with the speed of light. Only an imperceptible pause followed the Nazi's request before Etienne Latour, born and raised in Alsace, was replying in fluent German.

'I am sorry, my friend, but neither my comrade nor I has a match. However, here is a lighter which I will gladly lend you.'

A lighter! The bloody fool! A French lighter! Bad as an English match! The Captain moaned inwardly.

Latour's voice went on serenely.

'Please, you must be careful of it and give it back to me, *hein*? I treasure it highly. It is a French lighter that I took from the body of a French major at Bir Hacheim.' He hesitated, then added a detail with the delicate care of an artist. 'I bayoneted him myself,' he said.

The Nazi vented a grunt of appreciation so deep it seemed to come from his bowels.

'Thank you, comrade, I will return your war trophy without fail.' An impatient toot from truck number twelve sped his departure. He called back gruffly: '*Auf Wiedersehen!*'

'*Auf Wiedersehen!*' said Etienne Latour. It was a promise, a deadly promise; not a man in the truck but felt ague at the tone in which it was uttered.

'Get going, Sam,' said the Captain rather weakly. 'Bear down on it, lad!' He was silent a minute or two while Barrett stepped on the gas, anxious to regain their ordained position before somebody came back to see where they were.

The driver braked abruptly, slowing their progress. 'Somethin' doin' up ahead, sir!'

'Control post, maybe. Dust off your German, Sam, and have it ready just in case; mine's rotten.' He leaned sideways over the edge of the seat to see why the column of trucks had checked its pace. He exclaimed excitedly, 'No, b'gad! They've slowed up to make a right turn off the road. We're leaving the coast road!'

The going was rougher here, yet not too bad. It was obvious to the Captain that the Germans had done a spot of roadwork; when they came to a steep wadi, the way down was cleared of rocks and the way up on the other side was surfaced with cord matting to afford traction.

He raised his glasses, and every time the truck mounted a rise he peered hopefully into the black distance. He didn't believe the Jerries would go too far into the desert just to establish a casual camp and airport. He was right. At the end of an hour, the invisible track they were following topped a height and showed a cluster of pin-point lights making a pale yellow circle in the blackness.

He announced the news quietly, without lowering his glasses.

'That's it, Barrett. Half-mile ahead.'

'Yes, sir.' Mindful of his officer, whose attention was distracted from the road, he added: 'Watch out, sir; we're just dippin' into a wadi.'

'A wadi!' The leader put down his glasses swiftly and braced himself as the truck dipped sharply forward. 'A wadi is just what we want. The crowd ahead can't possibly look back and see what we're up to. Stop when you get to the bottom and park us across the road—as if we'd lost control and skidded.'

'That'll be easy, sir.'

'Sergeant!'

'Sir?'

'Coming to the end of the line, Sergeant. You men stay in the truck till I give you the word; then jump out and get aboard the German truck and crawl under its canvas cover. Sergeant, I expect you and Private Latour can take care of those two on number twelve.'

'Yes, indeed, sir.'

The truck stopped with a stiff jolt. It was not quite the bottom of the wadi, but Sam Barrett had spotted a point where there was a huge boulder at each side of the narrow road. A twist of his steel wrists set the truck diagonally across the route with one of the great rocks at each end.

The Captain jumped to the ground. Sam Barrett took with him to the rear a big electric flashlight that he had routed out of a dashboard compartment. He planted himself in the middle of the road just as the yellow lamps of the Nazi truck appeared at the top of the slope. He watched them swoop forward and down as the truck took the declivity. The sergeant and Latour had slipped from their tailboard perch the instant they received their orders; Barrett could see or hear no sign of either, but he guessed they were hiding in the shadows by the roadside.

Bumping and clattering, number twelve came charging on. Barrett flashed his light an instant on the stalled truck; he wanted no chance of a collision that might disable their one unit of transportation. Then he swung the powerful beam straight into the eyes of the two men on number twelve, thereby accomplishing three desirable results. It deepened the darkness in which the sergeant and Latour were lurking; it blinded the two Germans, so that their truck stopped with a squealing of brakes; it startled and infuriated them—and angry men lose caution. They shouted guttural imprecations.

'Engine trouble,' called Barrett in passable German. 'Please, will you be so good as to descend and see if you can help us find the cause?'

'Are we not late enough already?' shouted the big man who had wanted a match.

Rumbling and grumbling, they jumped to the ground, one from each side of the cab. For luck, Sam Barrett gave them both another blinding flash from his torch.

They died quietly. There was only one deep grunt from the driver of number twelve; the big man went out with a wheezing whistle like a bicycle tyre deflating. The sergeant and Etienne Latour wiped and sheathed their knives, then hurriedly lugged their victims out of the roadway.

'All clear, sir!'

'Nice work, Sergeant! Tumble out, everybody! Into the other truck! Barrett, get our truck parked fifty yards up the wadi; that will be our rallying point after the raid.'

The guerrillas were in motion while he was still speaking. The one truck was emptied, the other filled. Latour eagerly announced his long familiarity with German cars of every kind. He jumped into the driver's seat, followed by the Captain. 'We must try to catch up with the rest of the trucks before they reach the camp.'

'Captain, sir! Captain!' It was a muffled hail from beneath the canvas in back. 'It's ammunition and explosives!'

'Oh, lovely! One of you fellows be sure to put a bomb in the middle of it just before you tumble out. That'll be when I yell "Jump!" After that, you know your mission. Scatter—keep in the darkest areas as much as possible—set your fuses for thirty minutes—plant your bombs where you think they'll do the most damage. Bateson, Connolly and I will locate the airfield and fix the planes. Jones—you're ready back there with the gadget? We'll drop you off just before we reach the camp—couple of minutes, now.'

Apparently quite untroubled by thoughts of the lethal cargo behind him, Etienne Latour was driving with the skill and inspired madness of a French chauffeur in a hurry. Number twelve swayed and swerved, missing some rocks, bouncing off others, but kept going at a rate which brought it up presently to its proper distance from number eleven. Trucks in the van of the convoy had already disappeared through a gap in what seemed a fence.

'Jones! On your way, and good luck.'

'Yes, sir. Good huntin', sir!' A thump, and a metallic *clunk* from the tin container he was carrying, announced Private Jones's contact

with the desert. Since Brewster and Guffey were back in the truck
with the machine-gun, acting as rearguard and reserve, the party
was now reduced to nine. The Captain was satisfied. He brought
his night glasses into effective play, reporting back for the benefit of
those in the body of the truck.

'We'll be passing through an entrance in a minute. A sentry each
side, but they aren't challenging. I can see a hell of a lot of barbed-
wire fencing; we'd better figure on coming out the way we go in.
Remember, everyone, a revolver shot is the danger signal for all
hands to run like hell for the truck. Now—quiet, men; make sure
you're out of sight. *Here we are!*'

Number twelve lumbered through a broad gap in a triple fence of
barbed wire. The sentries at each side were leaning idly on their
rifles, looking at the vehicle incuriously.

'Not too fast!' whispered the officer.

Latour checked their pace as they rumbled in the direction taken
by the other trucks. By the time they came into the parking space,
the men of number eleven were walking away from the dark bulk of
their charge—heading straight for tobacco and coffee and beer,
reflected the Captain. He spied a suitable niche smack in the centre
of the grouped trucks and pointed it out to Latour.

'Just the right berth for a truckload of explosives!' he explained
happily. A moment later the driver shut off the engine, put out his
headlights; the outer darkness leaped upon them, folding them in its
safe embrace. The officer spoke over his shoulder, a low-voiced,
clear command: 'Jump!'

Latour and five others hit the dirt, to vanish instantly in different
directions. The Captain dropped to the ground, where he was
promptly joined by Bateson and Connolly. The three stood for a
long minute in the shadow of number twelve, looking about them,
getting the feel of the sleeping camp.

'What are you doing, Bateson? If you're saying a prayer, put in a
bit for me,' the Captain whispered.

'I did that before we left the truck, sir,' said Bateson, a serious
youth. He came erect from his kneeling position. 'I think I've
spotted the airfield, sir,' he whispered. 'Got a glimpse against the
sky of a pole with what looks like a wind sleeve on it.'

'Lead the way, lad—slowly, and watch your step.'

They slid through the night. Cautiously they made a wide detour
around the one building that showed signs of life. A hum of voices
came from it, and a paper-thin strip of light from an otherwise
closely shuttered window.

'Cookhouse, I expect,' muttered the Captain.

They reached their immediate goal without incident. They halted for a brief survey of the airfield lying before them, a broad expanse of levelled ground with nothing showing on its surface.

'Planes dispersed around the edges, of course,' murmured the guerrilla officer. 'Connolly, you circle the field to the left. I'll go this way. Bateson, there's a group of buildings down at that end— see 'em? When you've used up all your bombs, you two, don't hang around waiting for me. Leg it back to our truck in the wadi and hop aboard.'

Left to himself, the Captain swung to the right for his tour of the field. Calm and unconcerned, he moved at a smart pace, only taking the precaution of doubling over so there would be less chance of his moving body being sighted against the sky. This might be the first raid he had led, but he had been on many like it and knew all the angles; it would be very bad luck indeed if anything went wrong before the last guerrilla was safely out of camp.

Presently he found what he was looking for—a wall of rubble and logs and rocks. Tucked behind it were planes, bombers and fighters both. 'Nine!' he exulted. He grinned delightedly as he noted the disposition of the ships; with typical attention to symmetry and neatness, the Germans had lined them up in threes, their wing tips almost touching. Knowing well the high explosive qualities of his bombs, he troubled only to place one in the centre plane of each trio.

He found two more revetments, but to his disappointment there were only three planes in the first and just one in the second. That brought his total up to thirteen; if Connolly did as well. . . .

He was reduced now to two bombs. He tucked one into the vitals of a small tractor, probably used for odd jobs around the field. He came to a small structure, well built and with a solid door secured by a heavy padlock. He thought it might be a tool shed—they'd keep that locked against light-fingered Arabs—and was satisfied. Tools in the desert were worth their weight in gold. He flattened his last bomb between his hands, armed it, and thrust it under a sill of the building as far as he could reach. If all went well, the one thing the Nazis would need on the morrow was tools; these would not be available.

His bombs gone, he proceeded like a good soldier to obey his own orders. He turned and went back over the path he had come, moving in the same swift and stealthy fashion. The camp was as peaceful as the night itself; not a ripple revealed the movements of nine dangerous men beneath the surface calm.

The officer rounded the field. He was abreast of the still lighted cookhouse when—it happened.

Out of the darkness near the building came a loud, harsh challenge in German. It was a shout of anger and suspicion.

'Halt, there! Who are you? Hands up! Quick, somebody—a light here! I've got——'

The shout ended on a choking gasp. But the alarm had been given. The cookhouse door flung open and a dozen men boiled out. An arc light flashed on, illuminating the whole area with its sudden blinding brilliance. It showed a thickset man on the ground, and another just yanking a dagger from the huddled body. The man with the knife headed for the nearest darkness, running like a frantic deer. Six or seven of the cookhouse contingent pelted after him at their best speed.

Just beyond the circle of light the Captain whipped out his revolver and fired at the leading pursuer. It was a snap shot, but snap shooting at night was something he had practised for months. The Nazi fell headlong, rolling over and over. The men at his heels took their cue; they dropped sprawling in their tracks, pancaking their bodies on the ground before more bullets should streak from the darkness.

Lights were springing out everywhere. The post was a bedlam of shouting and tumult. No other confusion can compare with the confusion of an armed camp jerked from its slumbers by the crack of a gun. Sprinting for the entrance before the whole place should be a blaze of light, the guerrilla officer could distinguish and interpret a few of the startled shouts. Who fired that shot? Where was he? What was going on—and *where*?

What appeared to be the answer to the last question came with amazing promptness. From a point in the desert just beyond the southern boundary of the camp came an earsplitting racket suggestive of a baulky truck engine being coaxed into life. The staccato explosions rose and fell convincingly, settled to a steady roar, then died away. No more than thirty seconds—just long enough for Private Jones to race away—had elapsed between the revolver shot and the moment when Captain Crumper's gadget went into action.

The effect was all the young officer had hoped. He grinned happily as he ran, for a stentorian voice was bellowing orders in a tone of authority.

'It's a raid! It's the damned English! They're over there! Get men! Get rifles! Get cars! Pursue them! You fools at the searchlight—swing it *south*!'

For the priceless minutes that the Germans were giving tongue to the south, and possibly discovering how they had been hoaxed, the raiders would be making their swift escape to the east. Meanwhile the camp was still in a turmoil; as if to stress it, there came a sharp burst of machine-gun fire from somewhere off to the British Captain's right. He wondered what on earth they could be shooting at there; certainly there weren't any guerrillas in that direction.

His thoughts snapped back to a consideration of his own situation. He had no idea whether he was ahead or behind the rest of the crowd, nor did it matter at this instant when everybody was strictly on his own to escape or perish.

He was about thirty yards from the gap in the barbed wire by which they had driven in. He remembered the two guards, and a lamp at one side which lighted the vicinity. He ceased running, while he was still in the shadows, and went slowly forward, revolver in hand.

He stood still when the gap was in clear view. The light was still burning. That meant a twenty-yard sprint in full view of anyone around; the alternative was a try at breaking through or climbing the fences. Hardly practicable, with every passing second cutting into his margin of safety. The truck would not wait long, even for the party leader.

He must make a dash for it. He had caught his second wind by this time. Where the devil were those guards? His roving glance picked up one, then the other. Two sentries whose tour of duty was ended. The first was stretched full length on the ground in the straight shadow of a fence post. Across the gap, the second man was doubled over the top strand of barbed wire, a monstrous human clothespeg, his arms and legs dangling grotesquely. Guerrillas had passed that way.

The Captain waited no longer. He put his head down and sprinted. With the guards out of the way, he crossed the danger zone without a challenge or a shot. The desert swallowed him

He went up the road at a brisk trot. The noise of the camp grew fainter behind him. He listened as he ran, but could hear nothing that sounded like organized pursuit except a mild hullabaloo in the far distance. He surmised the Nazis were still looking for that baulky truck.

The wadi at last. He half ran, half slithered down the steep incline. It was pitch-black just here; a few yards from the bottom, a mis-step started a small avalanche of pebbles rattling the rest of the way. The truck should be fifty yards to his right and a bit farther on.

Rashly, he left the road and tried for a short cut. In half a minute he was lost, trapped in the desert's favourite mental pitfall. He stood still, panting, a little more nervous than he cared to admit even to himself. He looked about and saw only darkness; he listened, and heard nothing. He drew in his breath sharply; could the truck have *gone*?

Ears as keen as his own were listening, too. Perhaps they had heard his stumbling step. Through the darkness, not at all from the direction he expected, came the softly whistled refrain of a barrack-room ditty then popular. He whistled it back. In a minute he was with his men.

'You're all right, sir?'

'Right as rain, Sergeant. You've called the roll?'

'Three missing, sir. No use going back to look for them, sir. They copped it—fair. I saw it. The four of us got twisted and came up against the wire. I found a hole and turned to call them. Then a light went on somewhere. There was a burst of machine-gun fire. That's——' the sergeant cleared his throat—'that's all, sir.'

'Oh. Oh—damn. We'd better get on with it, Sergeant. The rest aboard? Send Barrett to take the wheel.'

'He was one of the three, sir.'

'Hell!' The bitter irony of it hit the officer. He shook off the momentary mood. 'Very well, Sergeant. Send Connolly, if he's left to us.'

'Which way, sorr?' asked Connolly, touching the starter.

'The way we came. The last place they'll expect us will be on their private road.' He looked at his watch and did some figuring. 'When we're over the top of the wadi, pull up.' They were there in a minute. The officer jumped out when the big car was safely over the sky line. He called his men and led the way back to the crest. 'May as well see some of the show. After all—we paid our admission.'

They crouched, looking back in the direction of the Nazi camp. They were barely settled before the night split open like a ripe melon in a crimson burst of flame that streamed to the heavens. A crashing report almost deafened them; a concussion shivered the air and even at that distance shook the ground beneath them.

'That's number twelve, the bus we rode in,' muttered the sergeant. 'The first half-hour bomb was planted in her.'

With number twelve still hurling destruction in every direction as lot after lot of ammunition exploded, a minor sheet of flame shot up to the left.

A few succeeding eruptions of smoke and flame were claimed. Then the show really hit its stride and pyrotechnical effects came too fast and close together to be identified. There were two more major upheavals. One appeared to be a second truck of explosives possibly fired by burning debris from number twelve. The other, a thunderous fiery cataclysm, the Sergeant believed was an ammunition dump he had mined at the last.

A big stack of petrol tins sent a great curtain of flame to the sky. By its light the officer was able to get a clear view of the scene through his glasses. He saw few signs of human activity. He could imagine the helpless men, overwhelmed by the holocaust, taking refuge in bombproof shelters or rushing out to the bleak desert for safety.

He ran over the score in his mind—twenty planes, an ammunition dump, two truckloads of ammunition and explosives, storehouses of food and miscellaneous supplies, a tractor, the petrol dump, officers' quarters, a big barracks—he didn't try to estimate the number of smaller buildings and tents demolished. Against it, he set the loss of three brave men, killed in action—and the balance did not please him.

STIRLING'S MEN *knew their opponent well. Two weeks later they returned to the same field to even the score, and the Germans were no more secure than the first time. This time the raiders mounted a machine-gun on their truck and placed the truck on a height overlooking the camp. In the few minutes of confusion which followed the explosion of the first bombs, the S.A.S. poured machine-gun fire into every concentration of Germans tumbling from the buildings. The score was even.*

With the capture of Colonel Stirling and the change in the North African campaign, the S.A.S. was abandoned. But the men who survived its operations went on to serve in similar groups across the world.

BEHIND THE LINES

GIDEON FORCE

BY W. E. D. ALLEN

EARLY IN 1941 *the irregular unit known as the Gideon Force gathered on the Sudan border north of Ethiopia. And to the far south-east of that country, General Cunningham's African troops were preparing to drive north. Between these two forces lay Addis Ababa and Italy's East African Empire.*

The Gideon Force, led by Major Orde Wingate, was to 'smite the enemy hip and thigh'. The slight English major envisioned something new in military warfare—an invasion using guerrilla tactics. With fewer than one hundred Englishmen as the spearhead and a couple of thousand native partisans comprising the rest of his force, he planned to harass, harry, frighten and confuse the Italians. He had to shake them from their well-supplied fortifications on to the roads where he could rip at their heels and tear at their flanks.

On January 20, 1941, the Gideon Force moved into Ethiopia. After marching for seventeen days under a fevered sun, the column could be oriented by the stink of dead camels. Eighteen thousand of them were carrying equipment.

In early February, Wingate made contact with the enemy, and by March the Italian rout was under way. Thousands of demoralized Italian troops fled south to avoid the diminutive Gideon Force, and the fleeing troops increased in number as more and more units abandoned their positions and went on to the roads. Wingate's men ambushed the confused columns by day and machine-gunned the disorganized camps by night. Meanwhile, the natives fought to strip the Italians of their clothes and equipment.

The South African and Kenyan troops moved relentlessly northward closing the trap, and in early May Addis Ababa fell. One of the last remaining Italian strongholds lay north of the capital at Agibar. Captain W. E. D. Allen of the Gideon Force tells about the final chapter of this colourful campaign.

AFTER the Motal expedition we rested a day in Debra Marcos, then moved out on the two hundred-mile march to Addis Ababa. It took us three days to cover the fifty-odd miles to the

341

crossing of the Blue Nile opposite Safartak. On the way the Italian prisoners from Mota passed us in trucks. They waved in good-humoured derision. They were on their way to spend the rest of the war in comfortable camps in Kenya.

The great canyon of the Blue Nile is one of the wonders of the natural world. We made a two days' march of it. Over a distance of fifteen miles, the Escarpment falls six thousand feet in successive bluffs to the bed of the river—where the water, still low at the end of the dry season, poured down from Lake Tana through gorges of pink granitic rock. After the thin cold air of the plateau, the heat came down like a shroud, and we rode sweltering into a tropic land. I saw wild goats on the heights and flights of pigeon and guinea-fowl that were almost tame. In the depth of the gorge, great trees sheltered beaches which were a terrestrial paradise after the sleet-swept flanks of Chokey. We bathed—although some said that there were crocodiles about; killed a meal of perch with Mills bombs; and drank the last of the Debra Marcos champagne. Only with sundown, swarms of mosquitoes came out to trouble us; the canyon of the Blue Nile is a hotbed of malaria, as those learned who were working on the repair of the bridge blown up by the Italians in their retreat.

All next afternoon and the following morning we were climbing the eastern side of the Escarpment—one of the best defensive positions in the world—which some eight thousand Italians had abandoned after a show of fighting to Johnson's company of Sudanese and a few hundred guerrillas. Six of the camels failed to make the grade; they were the first deaths among many.

We camped on the evening of the 2nd of May on the bare up-land of Salale; we were now in Ras Kassa's country—a part of the Emperor's own kingdom of Shoa, the heart of the dominion of the House of Solomon.

Trucks from Addis Ababa came in the morning to pick up the 2nd company, with Maxwell, Barlow, and Creedon. They were to constitute the Sudanese contingent which was to take part in the triumphal entry of the Emperor into Addis Ababa on May 5—the fifth anniversary of the entry of the Italian armies into the Ethiopian capital. It was, in its way, a significant event.

As Animal Transport Officer I remained with about a hundred men—disgruntled enough at being left behind—to bring on the baggage and the animals. I was the recipient of some expressions of sympathy from my companions who would be dining that night in Addis Ababa, but I was in the pleasant state of psychic coma of the wanderer and I was happy enough to contemplate the continuance of the daily round of shidding up and morning march, the grazing hours, the second march, and then the night's camp.

We camped for the grazing of the middle day by a village where an old lady in a big straw sun hat and of a wondrous medieval grace, leading her pretty granddaughter by the hand, came out to offer a gift of *tedj*, chickens, and eggs. Henceforth, the daily friendliness of the Shoan countryside was to provide us with an excellent pot at night.

It was the last of the fine days. The 'Little Rains' were on us. On the morning of the 4th of May I received an order from H.Q. at Fiche to leave the main road—which was clearly more suitable for camels in view of the approaching rains—and take a short cut through the mountains lying to the north of the road. We had a descent through beautiful but difficult country and a stiff climb on the rise. For the middle of the day we camped on an upland arm where the scenery was perhaps grander than I have seen in any country. Half a mile away was a church surrounded by very ancient trees: I think that the cult of sacred trees survives often enough in the Christianity of the Ethiopian highlands. The local Gerazmach, with the delightful manners of the Shoans, came to greet us and provided us with a day's feed for the animals: Italian barley which had been stored in the native wicker containers raised off the ground to protect them from the damp and grouped inside a fenced enclosure.

In the afternoon torrential rain caught us, and the convoy began to stretch out over four or five miles with the wretched camels slithering through the mud. I rode on my mule, Prester John, to find a camp site before night came down; grass for the mules and ponies was excellent everywhere, but the thorn—essential in the diet of camels—was becoming scarce. I struck the main road and camped beside it. The last of the camels did not come in until after 2300 hours. They had suffered badly in the slippery 'black cotton' mud and many had been crippled doing 'the splits': fourteen had been left to die in their tracks. The men, weary from changing loads in the dark and rain, were wet and exhausted. The damp and cold was bringing out the malaria endemic in many Sudanese.

We slept all night—and woke next morning—in the pouring rain. Staggering about in the water-logged ground, we kicked the poor beasts up and rode for dreary hours over the uplands towards Fiche. It was the day of the Emperor's triumphal entry into Addis Ababa. Coming to Fiche after noon, I put up my tent and started writing letters. For the camels there was some bad thorn grazing round the outskirts of the town; and I knew that it would warm the men up and cure their fevers to go drinking in the *suk*.

Most of the morning of the 6th passed in collecting the drunken troopers from the arms of the fuzzy-haired *houris* in the grass huts of Fiche. We rode on through some very weird country—curiously recalling Japanese landscape paintings: great isolated rocks rose out of the plain, with fine old umbrella trees grouped up their flanks and small thatched cottages sited in interstices of the rock. Camels continued to slump and die lugubriously. The thin air, the frequent rain, and the cold of the nights, with the lack of good thorn grazing, was proving fatal to them. Rest did them little good as the cold winds cut round them.

On midday of the 7th we halted at the side of a small escarpment where much thorn was growing. I decided to stay the rest of the day and give the camels good time for grazing. But through the afternoon and evening driving rain and wind hurried round the camp. Even Sergeant Shawish Said was faltering and shivering with fever. The men made a shelter of camel saddles and rigged a big Italian tarpaulin over it. They huddled together, shuddering and miserable, while I doled out my last pills of quinine. Having lived for ten years in the dampest house in Northern Ireland and frequented the half-tide rocks of Strangford Lough for winter flights of duck, I had no need to complain as I crouched in my forty-pound tent; but I could see that the Sudanis, bred in the hot Nilotic plains, had had enough. After a frigid night, I found sixteen camels dead on the lines; and the men were groaning with misery. I decided to abandon any further effort to conserve the animals and to get the men to Addis Ababa as quickly as possible.

The whole of the 8th we rode on in pouring rain and sleet, descending into and climbing out of two minor scarps. In the evening we struck the main road again and camped alongside it.

On the 9th—our twelfth day out from Debra Marcos—we made two more long shidds. The morning was fine, but heavy clouds overhung the afternoon and a penetrating drizzle soaked the ragged men, as they sat humped in their blankets on their mules. By luck, I was able to stop a truck and send on the sickest men into Addis Ababa. Towards evening I saw another truck standing by the road, and Wingate by it. He was on his way to Fiche to take over command of the force still operating against the Italians in the mountains between Fiche and Debra Tabor. Apparently his Palestinian clerk Akabia had been looking for me for the last two days along the main road, while we had been proceeding across country by the

shortest route—according to instruction. Wingate had intended the
animals to stay at Fiche so that Nott and Johnson could have the use
of the mules for the operations to the north. I suggested sending
the sick and the camels on to Addis Ababa—now only one day's
march away—and myself returning to Fiche with the fit men and
the mules (although the latter were in bad enough condition).

We camped the night of the 9th only ten miles from Entoto—the
mountain to the south of which lies Addis Ababa. But it was 2200
hours of the following night before I finally landed the men up at
the Italian Parco di Quadrupedi—where there were dry barrack
accommodations and where the animals could graze and rest.

Of the luckless camels only fifty-three reached Entoto Hill out of
the hundred and twenty which had left Debra Marcos a fortnight
before. Four others which straggled in with Wingate's H.Q. *hamlia*
saw Addis Ababa out of the 18,000-odd which had been gathered in
the Sudan. Apart from the climate, Addis Ababa was unsuitable for
camels owing to the lack of thorn grazing; and I had orders to shoot
the gallant fifty-three on the slopes of Entoto before coming down
into the town. Slinging his rifle, Shawish Said led them off to carry
out the gruesome duty.

Meanwhile the Nigerians were fighting a tough little war of their
own across the Omo River and up towards Jimma. And at the end
of May, in the mountains north of Fiche, less than 200 Sudanese and
a couple of thousand of Ras Kassa's men had cornered near Agibar
the last 8,000 troops of the former Italian army of the Gojjam.

The Italians had been making, originally, for Dessie—two
hundred miles to the north-east. Unimpeded, they should have
made the march in a fortnight. At the forts of Addis Derra and
Agibar they had strong points to cover their main force in retreat
and ample reserves of ammunition and supplies. And even when
Dessie fell to the South Africans at the beginning of May, the
enemy still retained the possibility of making for Debra Tabor with
the object of uniting with the still formidable army of General Nasi
in the Gondar area.

Snapping at their heels like a terrier worrying an elephant was a
small guerrilla force which numbered a few hundred Ethiopians and
140 Sudanese. Their leader was Bimbashi Johnson—a short, wiry,
rather shy fellow who until a few months ago had been an em-
ployee of the Sudan Cotton Syndicate. Johnson had been in all the
fighting round Burye and Debra Marcos, and he had won the
D.S.O. in the ambush on the Safartak road. His second-in-command
was Riley, Bathgate's partner on the march up through the Shank-

alla wilderness. Riley was a Regular; he, too, had that peculiar shyness which gave almost an impression of lassitude—and which seems to characterize guerrilla leaders and prize fighters. The third of a shy trio was the long, willowy Thesiger who was acting as Political Officer to the force. The son of a diplomat formerly stationed at Addis Ababa, he spoke Amharic and Arabic equally well. He combined the intellectual face and the vague, delicate mannerisms of a Dons' Common Room with a taste for hard living which outdid even Wingate. Two Centre subalterns, Rowe and Naylor, were with the force; and later Donald Nott appeared to take over the command and add a D.S.O. to his M.C.

After abandoning Safartak and all attempt to cover their retreat by leaving a strong rearguard to hold the ravine of the Blue Nile, the Italians took to the mountains north of the Fiche-Addis Ababa road. Day after day they climbed the wet tracks over the steep hillsides and struggled up and down the deep ravines: 1,100 white and 7,000 native troops—burdened, as it transpired later, with 2,000 native women—the accumulation of five years of Italian soldiering in Debra Marcos. It was a 'retreat from Moscow' in miniature, and, like Denis Davydov and his Cossacks, Johnson hung on the fringes of the unhappy fugitives, giving them rest neither day nor night. His own condition was desperate enough: the expected co-operation of a South African unit from Fiche and of Nigerians east from the Dessie road failed to mature. Johnson was short of food and running low on ammunition; his ragged men lacked greatcoats and blankets in the drenching rain; and the wet was bringing out the malaria in the plainsmen; others were racked with rheumatism and falling out with pleurisy.

On the 21st of April Johnson attacked at dusk an enemy defensive position with only sixteen men and three light automatics. The Italians were taken by surprise, nervous and hysterical; and in the dark Johnson was able to draw off his party, leaving two groups of the enemy firing all night at each other. When morning came he found that they had abandoned camp, leaving all their equipment. On another occasion, Riley, attacking through the mist with only twelve men, hustled the Italians out of a position which they had intended to hold on to for some days more.

On the 25th of April, a fortnight after Johnson had crossed the Blue Nile, old Ras Kassa arrived with his surviving son. He was the hereditary lord of all this country and, four years before, his two elder sons had been shot by the Italians in Fiche after they had come in under a flag of truce. Kassa was bringing 2,000 of his Shoans—

better fighting material than the impoverished Gojjamis worn by five years' war—and he now unleashed the first five hundred of them on the tail of the retreat.

On the 23rd of May, covering their fortified position at Addis Derra, the enemy showed a last gleam of spirit. Supported by the concentrated fire of many heavy and light machine-guns and two pack guns, two battalions attacked the Frontier Battalion camp; the battle was fiercely maintained and lasted four hours. The Sudanese Bash Shawish (Sergeant-Major) who was present in the front of the position when the attack started, ordered the men to hold their fire until the enemy were within 300 yards and then let go everything. The Italians suffered heavily before they could take cover. The Sudanese had to conserve their ammunition and only 6,000 rounds were fired from eight light automatics during the whole of the action. One Sudanese corporal was killed, while the enemy—as was later ascertained—lost sixty killed and a very large number wounded.

On the 14th of May Wingate arrived. He brought with him only thirteen cases of Coptic bully beef, which the strict Moslem Sudanese would not touch. Two days later the enemy evacuated the Fort of Addis Derra. From the captured fort British officers watched the Italian column, nearly eighteen miles in length, disappear into a 5,000-feet-deep canyon and emerge on the farther side. The Italians were now making for the next fort of Agibar whence they could reach the road through to Debra Tabor and Gondar. They had ample animal transport and they were entering the Wollo country which remained not unfriendly to them. If they could make a successful retreat their numbers would still constitute an important reinforcement to General Nasi's undefeated army in Gondar.

The Wollo highlands consist of a series of tablelands separated from each other by deep canyons or ravines. Sometimes these are connected by narrow panhandles or necks of land constituting bridges between one tableland and another. Joining the massif which the enemy was now climbing to the neighbouring one on which Agibar lay was one of these high bridges or panhandles—not more than 1,000 yards across.

In order to reach Agibar the Italians had to march along this panhandle. Wingate saw his chance. He gave Thesiger one hundred Sudanese and several hundred patriots; his orders were to take two days' dry food only, and not one baggage animal, and to march the fifty miles across country to the panhandle, ignoring any sniping which might come from pro-Italian *bande* on the way. Thesiger

12*

was to seize and hold the panhandle while Wingate pressed the
enemy up against him from the other side.

While Ras Kassa's Shoans were pouring into Addis Derra to constitute a force which was now mounting into thousands, Thesiger,
on the night of May 18–19, moved off on his long march. By the
20th he had reached the panhandle. Meanwhile Wingate's forces
had climbed the escarpment north of Addis Derra and attacked the
rearguard of the retreating enemy. After resisting stubbornly
enough for two days the Italians began to withdraw. Wingate
sent after them a letter inviting surrender. They were attacking
Thesiger whom they now found barring their retreat across the panhandle to Agibar. But Thesiger, reinforced by a steady stream of
patriots and deserters from among the Colonial Battalions of the
enemy, held his ground. On the 23rd the enemy surrendered with
large quantities of arms and material.

The immediate situation was not without difficulty; for the
Italians were laying down their arms to a force of which Ras Kassa,
whose family they had treated with particular treachery and
brutality, was in fact the political master. Wingate himself con-
fessed that when the moment came to receive the vanquished army
he felt more alarm than at any time during the battle. Across a
level plain sloping to a hidden valley, the Italian commander and his
staff of thirty officers advanced on horseback. Behind them came a
battalion of 800 Blackshirts, and then column after column of
colonial troops—many of whom were known to be reluctant to
surrender. To receive this beaten army stood thirty-six Sudanese;
these were formed up to make five lanes through which the enemy
troops poured, laying down their arms in heaps; they then re-
formed in units and passed down into the valley where they
expected to find the army which had beaten them. Instead they
passed only small groups of patriots, and, standing grimly by, grey-
bearded old Ras Kassa and Wingate, lean and glaring in a shapeless wet toupe. But their arms already lay piled—covered by the
Sudanis' Brens.

Next day the long march over the soaked mountainsides to Fiche
and on to Addis Ababa began. The straggling columns of prisoners
covered over eighteen miles. They were protected by a leading
platoon of Sudanese under a British officer. Wingate brought up
the rear with another platoon. The Italians were marching over
two hundred miles of country which they had conquered only
five years before—by methods ruthless enough. The pillage and ill
treatment of the prisoners—if not a terrible massacre—might have

been anticipated. Wingate appealed to the Christian tradition of the Ethiopians. The grizzled old Ras, erect in his heavy black cloak, stood in silence as the long files shuffled by. He was responsible for the safety of the same men who had driven him into poverty and exile and slaughtered his sons and tribesfolk. But not a prisoner failed to reach the main road. Some Italian officers afterwards complained that their wrist-watches had been taken from them.

IMMEDIATELY AFTER *the fall of Agibar, Major Wingate drove to the nearest airport and flew back to British headquarters. His mission was completed. He was transferred almost immediately to Burma where other plans were already under way. But before Wingate left the Middle East, he let it be known that he had no designs on the mantle of T. E. Lawrence of Arabia and that he felt too many men of World War II would claim it. In time he became known in his own right as Wingate of Burma.*

OPERATION PONGO

BY FITZROY MACLEAN

KINGCOL *rolled east from Palestine in the spring of 1941—seven hundred and fifty men bound across the desert to tangle with the Iraqi Army of forty thousand. Two months later Brigadier Joseph Kingston's column occupied Baghdad, and German attempts to disrupt the Middle East behind the British forces desperately trying to hold on to North Africa were temporarily suspended.*

But by September, 1942, the Germans appeared to have won the war. They were only one hundred miles from Cairo in the west, and they were reaching down through the Caucasus into Persia. Stalingrad seemed ready to fall, and in a single sweep the Middle East would take its place as part of the Greater Germany. Persia could tip the scale for victory either way. Persia meant oil, the gateway to India, and the Anglo-American supply line to Russia.

Eager to be on the winning side, many of the Persian tribesmen were willing to deal with the Nazis.

The British General Staff in Cairo, looking to the future, called in Captain Fitzroy Maclean, sometime-officer in Colonel David Stirling's North African S.A.S. Maclean was directed to reconnoitre the area for future guerrilla operations in the event of the Germans picking up Persia along with the other chips.

However, after a few weeks of comfortable sight-seeing, Maclean was called to Teheran. An emergency had arisen. He tells the story himself.

I FOUND General Baillon at the British Legation in conference with the Minister, Sir Reader Bullard. They told me that they had a job for me. For some time past, they said, there had been signs that some kind of trouble was brewing in south Persia. The tribes, the Qashgai and the Bakhtiari, had German agents living among them and seemed likely to rise at any moment, just as they had risen in 1916, when their rebellion had caused us a disproportionate amount of trouble. Were this to happen, our supply route to the Persian Gulf might be cut. There was also discontent in Isfahan and other towns, largely caused by the hoarding of grain by speculators, which we were unable to prevent. This discontent might at any moment flare up into open rebellion. Worse still, if there were trouble, the Persian troops in south Persia were likely to take the side of the rioters.

A sinister part was being played in all this by a certain General Zahidi, who was in command of the Persian forces in the Isfahan area. Zahidi was known to be one of the worst grain hoarders in the country. But there was also good reason to believe that he was acting in co-operation with the tribal leaders and, finally, that he was in touch with the German agents who were living in the hills and, through them, with the German High Command in the Caucasus. Indeed, reports from secret sources showed that he was planning a general rising against the Allied occupation force, in which his troops and those of the Persian general in the Soviet-occupied northern zone would take part and which would coincide with a German airborne attack on the Tenth Army, followed by a general German offensive on the Caucasus front. In short, General Zahidi appeared to be behind most of the trouble in south Persia.

The situation was a delicate one. The Allied forces of occupation in northern Persia had been reduced to a minimum, in order to meet demands from the fighting fronts; there were practically no Allied troops in south Persia at all. The nearest British troops to the seat of the trouble were at Qum, two hundred miles north of Isfahan. There was very real danger that any sudden movement of British troops in a southward direction might provoke a general rising which we should have serious difficulty in containing with the small forces at our disposal. On the other hand, if we allowed events to take their course, the results would be equally disastrous.

In short it was essential to nip the trouble in the bud, while avoiding a full-scale showdown. General Baillon and Sir Reader Bullard had decided that this could best be achieved by the removal of General Zahidi and it was this task that they had decided to entrust to me. How it was to be done they left me to work out for myself. Only two conditions were made: I was to take him alive and I was to do so without creating a disturbance.

My first step was to go to Isfahan and see for myself how the land lay. That city's mosques and palaces, unrivalled in the whole of Asia, provided an excellent pretext for visiting it. I let it be known in Teheran that I was going to spend a few days' leave sight-seeing in the south, and set out.

I reached Isfahan the same night after driving all day across a bleak plateau fringed with distant snow-capped mountains. The flickering lights of a *chai-khana* shone out of the darkness, showing two or three dim figures squatting in the doorway, drinking their tea and smoking their long pipes; then a group of houses; then some shops; and then we were in the main street in a seething stream of carts, donkeys and camels, whose owners turned round to stare at the first jeep and the first British uniforms to make their appearance in Isfahan.

I drove to the British Consulate, where I was welcomed by the Consul, John Gault. Soon Sergeant Duncan and I, in the time-honoured phrase of the British soldier, had 'our knees under the table', and were making good progress with a brace of the local brand of partridge, washed down by delicious wine from the town of Shiraz, which, according to some, disputes with Xeres the honour of being the birthplace of sherry.

Over dinner I disclosed to my host, a robust young man who gave the impression of being equally alert both mentally and physically, the true purpose of my visit. He was delighted. General Zahidi, he said, though pleasant to meet, was a really bad lot: a bitter enemy of the Allies, a man of unpleasant personal habits, and, by virtue of his grain-hoarding activities, a source of popular discontent and an obstacle to the efficient administration of south Persia. He, too, had heard that he was plotting with the Germans and with the tribal leaders. Indeed, according to information which had reached him, one of the opening moves in General Zahidi's plot was to be the liquidation of the British Consul in Isfahan, a piece of news which completely outweighed all the General's personal charm, as far as he was concerned.

I asked Gault where Zahidi lived. He said he would show me, and after dinner we strolled out of the Consulate, across a narrow many-arched bridge, and along a broad avenue of plane trees, until we came to a massive pair of gates, set in a high stone wall and flanked by a sentry box and guardroom. Outside, a Persian infantryman was marching up and down while others, all well armed, slouched at the door of the guardroom. We took a turn round the back premises, where the surrounding wall was pierced by another gate, guarded by another sentry. This was the General's residence. Then we continued our stroll along the avenue under the trees. A few hundred yards further along we came to a large modern barracks, which according to Gault contained the greater part of the garrison of Isfahan, ready to rush to the assistance of their commander in case of trouble. It did not look as though a frontal attack by a small raiding party would have much chance of succeeding.

If Zahidi could not conveniently be winkled out of his place of residence, the obvious alternative was to ambush him when he was away from home, travelling from one point to another. I ascertained from Gault that at the same time every morning he crossed the bridge on his way to his headquarters. Would it not be possible to take advantage of the narrow bottleneck formed by this ancient monument to hold up his car, drag him out of it, and make off with him?

I gave this plan careful consideration, but there were two serious objections to it. In the first place Zahidi was reputed to go nowhere without a heavily armed bodyguard, whom it would be necessary to overcome by force. Secondly, even assuming that we managed to avoid a pitched battle with the bodyguard, we were unlikely to succeed in kidnapping a general in broad daylight in the middle of so populous a town as Isfahan without attracting a good deal of attention. The two of us driving peaceably along in the jeep had been a sufficiently novel spectacle to hold up the traffic in the main street of Isfahan; the same party with the addition of a struggling general and his bereaved bodyguard could scarcely fail to introduce into the proceedings that very element of uproar which my superiors were so anxious to avoid. I went to sleep that night with the feeling that the problem before me was not as simple as it had at first sight appeared.

Next day, after further thought and another talk with Gault, I came to the conclusion that, unless I was prepared to risk a serious incident which might have unforeseeable repercussions, I should have to rely primarily on some kind of a ruse in order to get my man. In short, what was needed was a Trojan horse.

Once I had started thinking on these lines, it was not long before there began to shape in my mind a plan which seemed to offer a better chance of neatly and successfully eliminating the source of the trouble without setting light to the powder magazine of south Persia. That afternoon I sent off a cipher telegram to Teheran giving my proposals for Operation 'Pongo', which was the code name I had chosen for the abduction of the General.

The first thing was to find a pretext for introducing myself into Zahidi's house. I suggested that I should be given authority to assume for the occasion a brigadier's badges of rank; that I should then ring up the house and announce myself as a senior staff officer from Baghdad who wished to pay his respects to the General. If the latter agreed, I would drive up in a staff car, accompanied by Duncan and one or two other resourceful characters, hold him up at the

point of the pistol, hustle him into the car, and drive away with him
out of Isfahan before the alarm could be given. I also asked for a
platoon of infantry to lend a hand in case anything went wrong.
I undertook to work out some means of introducing these into
Isfahan in such a way as to attract as little attention as possible.

Having sent off my telegram, I spent two agreeable days making a
detailed reconnaissance of the city, with special attention to the best
line of withdrawal in case of an emergency, and at the same time
enjoying its peerless beauty.

The arrival of an urgent message from G.H.Q. in reply to my
telegram, submitting my proposals and requesting instructions,
brought me back to the realities of the Second World War. My
plan was approved in principle and I was instructed to go ahead
with my preparations. Only one item of my highly unorthodox
programme stuck in the throats of the well-trained staff officers at
the other end. It was not (repeat: not) possible, they said, to
authorize an officer of my age and seniority (I was a captain) to
masquerade, even for a day, as a brigadier. Rather than allow this,
they would place at my disposal, for a limited period of time, a
genuine brigadier, for use as bait or for any other purpose within
reason. Moreover this officer, for the purposes of the operation,
would receive his instructions from me. For administrative purposes I was directed to report to General Anderson, the corps commander at Qum, some two hundred miles from Isfahan, who had
been asked to furnish the brigadier and also such troops, equipment
and transport as I might require.

I lost no time in reporting to Corps Headquarters, where I was
provided with a platoon of Seaforth Highlanders, who were told
that they had been specially selected for training in commando
tactics. As surprise was clearly essential to the success of our enterprise, secrecy was of the utmost importance, and at this stage
practically no one except the corps commander and I was aware of
our real objective. The Seaforths were equipped with tommy-guns
and hand grenades and we repaired to a secluded part of the desert
near Qum to rehearse our act.

I had decided that the Seaforths should only be used in case of an
emergency. My plan was that on the appointed day they should
arrive in Isfahan in two covered trucks, disguised as far as possible
to look like civilian vehicles, shortly before I set out for the General's
house. One would draw up under the plane trees on the far side of
the avenue, opposite the main entrance to the house, and stay there.
The other would take up a position covering the back entrance.

The men, clutching their tommy-guns and hand grenades, would remain in the back of the trucks, out of sight. Only if they heard firing or a prearranged signal of three blasts on the whistle would they emerge from their hiding place, overpower the guard and force an entrance, after which their task would be to cover the withdrawal of the party in the staff car, which it was hoped would include Zahidi whatever happened. If, on the other hand, all went well, the two trucks would simply wait until the staff car drove out with Zahidi in it, and then fall in behind and escort us out of Isfahan to a point in the desert where an aircraft would be waiting, ready to fly our prisoner out of the country.

For our rehearsals I chose a ruined fort in the desert. Again and again the two trucks took up their positions outside; the staff car drove in; the whistle sounded; the Seaforths poured out of the trucks and into the fort; an imaginary victim was bundled unceremoniously into the car, and all three vehicles drove off in triumph, the occupants tossing dummy hand grenades out of the back at imaginary pursuers, as they went. The Seaforths gave a splendidly realistic performance. Indeed their enthusiasm was such that my only anxiety was lest on the day itself they would emerge from their place of concealment, whether things went well or badly, and massacre a number of harmless Persians out of sheer ebullience.

It now only remained to fix the day. This was done after a further exchange of signals with G.H.Q. Baghdad and with the Foreign Office via Teheran. I also extracted from the authorities, not without difficulty, permission to shoot General Zahidi, should he be armed and resist capture.

Our D Day was fixed, and on D minus one we set out from Qum. I had decided that the Seaforths should spend the night well out of sight in the desert about ten miles from Isfahan. Next day, while the main party entered the town in the two trucks, smaller parties were detailed to cut the telegraph wires connecting Isfahan with the neighbouring Persian garrisons. Meanwhile I collected the Brigadier, a distinguished officer whose well-developed sense of humour caused him to enter completely into the spirit of the somewhat equivocal role that had been allotted to him, and set out for the British Consulate.

On our arrival a telephone call was put through to the General's house and an appointment made for the same afternoon. After a copious lunch we took our places in the staff car, which was flying a large Union Jack. A reliable N.C.O., armed to the teeth, occupied the seat next to the driver, while Guardsman Duncan and a Seaforth

Highlander, both carrying tommy-guns, crouched in the luggage compartment at the back, under a tarpaulin. Gault followed in his own car. As we approached Zahidi's house I was relieved to see our two trucks, their tarpaulin covers concealing the battle-hungry Seaforths, drawn up in their appointed places. At the gate the Persian sentry was deep in conversation with Laurence Lockhart, a Persian linguist from R.A.F. Intelligence, whose services I had enlisted for the occasion. So far everything had gone according to plan.

On our appearance, the sentry at the gate reluctantly put out the cigarette which Lockhart had given him, broke off his conversation, and presented arms. We drove on up the drive and drew up in front of the house immediately outside a large pair of open french windows. A servant ushered us in and went off to fetch the General.

When, a couple of minutes later, General Zahidi, a dapper figure in a tight-fitting grey uniform and highly polished boots, entered the room, he found himself looking down the barrel of my Colt automatic. There was no advantage in prolonging a scene which might easily become embarrassing. Without further ado, I invited the General to put his hands up and informed him that I had instructions to arrest him and that, if he made any noise or attempt at resistance, he would be shot. Then I took away his pistol and hustled him through the window into the car which was waiting outside with the engine running. To my relief there was no sign of the much-advertised bodyguard. As we passed the guardroom, the sentry once again interrupted his conversation to present arms, and the General, sitting bolt upright, with my pistol pressed against his ribs and Duncan breathing menacingly down his neck, duly returned the salute. The two 'plain vans', with their occupants now bitterly disappointed, fell in behind; and the whole convoy swept at a brisk pace over the bridge and into the main avenue leading out of Isfahan.

Some miles outside the town we passed a large barracks, full of General Zahidi's troops, but the telephone wire from the town had duly been cut by the wire-cutting party, and there was no sign that the alarm had been given. Meanwhile Zahidi continued to sit bolt upright and to assure me that there was a very good explanation of any aspects of his conduct which might at first sight have seemed at all suspicious. Soon we reached the point in the desert where we had spent the night and here I handed over my captive to an officer and six men who were standing by to take him by car to the nearest landing ground where an aeroplane was waiting to fly him to Palestine. This was the last I saw of General Zahidi.

THAT NIGHT *Maclean sat down to examine Zahidi's papers. In addition to an illustrated register of the prostitutes of Isfahan, the kidnapped general had correspondence from an agent in the hills who signed himself 'German Consul General for south Persia'. It appeared that the English had acted just in time. But the Germans were not finished in Persia. A year later German commandos unsuccessfully supported an uprising of the tribes. After Operation Pongo Maclean went to Yugoslavia to serve as a brigadier and the senior liaison officer to Tito.*

After the war General Zahidi was reappointed military commander of south Persia. In 1953 he placed the King back on the throne and became Prime Minister of Iran.

CROSSING THE SHWELI

BY BERNARD FERGUSSON

'COME YOU BACK, you British soldier, come you back to Mandalay. . . .'
In 1942 Kipling's poem must have rankled the men who planned the
strategy of the Allies in Delhi, India. Beyond the Chindwin River,
Mandalay and Burma lay in Japanese hands.

While the refugees streamed into India, somewhere in central Burma
Colonel Wingate was trying to find out all he could about that exotic
jungle country. Wingate had nurtured a theory for years. The enemy is
weakest far behind the lines, where if he has troops, they are his poorest.
Here a small unit could do damage beyond all proportion to its numbers.
He proposed to disrupt all enemy lines of communication and destroy his
supplies. As far back as April, 1934, from a platform in the Royal
Geographical Society in London, Wingate had lectured on this very
theory. Since then he had led the Gideon Force which had beaten the
Italians in Ethiopia.

However, few people were willing to listen to the bearded, Bible-
quoting colonel when he came back to the general staff section at Delhi.
This latter-day Joshua quarrelled with everyone and proposed grandiose
schemes for the reconquest of Burma. Almost no one listened except Field-
Marshal Wavell, who had been his commander in the Middle East.

By January, 1943, Wingate had his brigade—eight columns marching
towards the Chindwin and beyond. They were bound back towards
Mandalay. But they had no sooner crossed into Japanese-held territory
than an air-drop containing mail fell into enemy hands. Within three days
the Japanese knew the names of the men and could guess their intentions.
However, the raiders pushed eastward through the jungle, creating confusion as they went. Finally, after almost three months of jungle marching
and counter-marching, they found they could go no farther. The men and
mules were tired. Supply drops had gone astray, and the alerted Japs were
pressing them hard. On the 26th of March Wingate ordered his columns
to split up and make their separate ways back to Burma as best they
could.

Major (later Brigadier) Bernard Fergusson, who led Column 5 out of
central Burma, writes of the exodus himself.

BRIGADE led, and I resumed my old position as tail column except for the Burrif headquarters, to whom had been allotted the difficult task of obliterating our trail. Brigade left at 1 a.m., and it was close on 3 a.m. before I saw the last man in front of me move off, and gave the word to march. We had all had a good rest; and had it not been for hunger (for we had to husband our scanty ration) we should have been in very good form.

Everything depended on our reaching Inywa without our turn-about being suspected; and our route therefore avoided all tracks. Wingate's uncanny instinct for cross-country marching—his sense of watersheds, good gradients, thinner jungle and so forth—was apparent even from my place far down the long procession. But it was a slow business, with frequent halts; and, with the knowledge of the Irrawaddy stretched like a barrier between ourselves and the free country beyond, the march was anything but exhilarating. Wingate had said himself that, once over the 'Waddy, we were seven-eighths out of the wood. Meanwhile, one was aware of its sinister breadth ahead of us, a malevolent ally, however passive, of the Japanese.

But the most depressing aspect of that miserable march was the slaughter of the mules. Were this to become known to the Japanese, our intention would be clear to them. Wingate had directed that they should be led off the track and slaughtered as opportunities occurred. They could not be shot on the hill-tops, for fear of the sound carrying; but every time we descended into a *chaung* half a dozen would be led away from the track we were making, their loads and saddlery concealed in the undergrowth, and six shots would ring out. Poor Bill Smyly, who had looked after them so wisely and well all the way from the banks of the Narain Nullah in the Central Provinces, to whom they were the light of his life, who had quarrelled with half the officers in the column on their behalf, who had not lost a single beast from avoidable causes—poor Bill Smyly marched that day with a white face, slipping away every now and then to dispatch a few more, and rejoining the column with tears on his cheeks.

Soon a message came back down the line that no more were to be shot; even although the places were chosen with some care, the sound was carrying up to the head of the procession, where the Brigadier was marching. The message said that they were to be slaughtered noiselessly. We had been using pistols instead of a rifle, in the hope that the noise would be lessened. Now we tried

the ghastly experiment of cutting their throats; but the first operation sickened us all so much that I said we should try it no more.
We had already disposed of sixteen animals since leaving the
bivouac.

The Brigadier's orders, at the conference the previous afternoon,
had been as follows. We were making for Inywa, where the
Shweli enters the Irrawaddy. Leaving the Hehtin Chaung at 1 a.m.
on March 27, we hoped to make Inywa at 6 p.m. on the 28th, and
to begin the crossing that night. The proposed bivouac area for
the night 27th–28th was the marshes of Chaungmido, where one
of the other columns had reported finding water on the southward
journey. If by chance the march was interrupted, the rendezvous
was to be in the jungle one mile south of the village of Pyinlebin.

Once arrived at Inywa, there were to be tasks for each column.
Burrif H.Q. were to help 8 Column collect boats from the lower
reaches of the Shweli: 7 Column was to cross first and make a
bridgehead on the west bank: Brigade Headquarters were to cross
next: and 5 Column was to throw a screen all round the crossing
area, to protect it while the rest of the brigade crossed. We were to
be the rearguard, the place of honour; and to be the last over.

There was a very real possibility that, with the Japs lining both
the Irrawaddy and the Shweli, we were already in the bag. All
columns had reported their awareness of reinforcements moving up;
we in No. 5 Column had learned of it in the neighbourhood of
Mogok and Myitson, and other people had similar tales. There was
little one could do in the way of insurance; but two things I had
already arranged. I had asked Gim Anderson and the Brigadier to
make a note, in case I failed to reach India, that I recommended both
Duncan and John for decoration for their sterling services; I had
witnessed Gim write down their names, along with those of various
N.C.O.s and men, in his notebook. Secondly, I enjoined on both
Duncan and John that, in the event of their getting out alive and
my failing to do so, they were to seek an audience with General
Wavell in Delhi, on my behalf; and to give him my views on the
feasibility of this form of warfare. I made them repeat several
times over the arguments which, even should the expedition finish
in disaster, seemed to me irrefutable proof that such enterprises were
worth while.

Mentally and physically, it was a horrid march. At one o'clock,
soon after crossing a track running north and south, the first we had
seen, Hosegood, the brigade intelligence officer, came back to meet
me, and to say that we were going into a midday bivouac, moving

off at about three. The spot chosen was the junction between the Hintha Chaung and one of its tributaries; there was a little water in pools. Hosegood settled me down half a mile short of brigade and a little later the Burrifs came in behind me. I ordered tea to be brewed up, and told John Fraser to have his men kill a mule, and distribute it for meat. Leaving Duncan to settle in the column, I went forward to see the Brigadier.

I found him eating some rice and raisins, and had ten minutes' talk with him; he was in good form and cheerful. I returned to the column, and had been back ten minutes when I heard some shooting on the hill above and behind me. I immediately sent out Philippe and Tommy Blow with their platoons and sent a runner to the Brigadier to say that I had done so. Colonel Wheeler came along, and said that one of his riflemen had been fired on while relieving nature a couple of hundred yards from the bivouac; he also had sent a party under Macpherson to investigate. It seemed to us that the patrol, or whatever it was, must have come along the north and south track which we had crossed shortly before we halted and either seen the smoke of our fires, or followed up our track, although a party of Burrifs had been systematically obliterating it, so far as possible.

A mounted officer came along the *chaung* from brigade with orders. Columns were to get on the move at once; brigade was already moving off. No. 5 Column was to lay an ambush, and deal with any attempt to follow up. I asked for more details: I wasn't clear how to lay an ambush in an area which it was by no means certain the enemy would come through; but all he could say was that I was to lay an ambush: he had been given no details.

I went back to the column. Philippe and Tommy were both back, but had nothing to report; Tommy was short of one section, under Corporal McGhie, which never turned up again. Wheeler came along, and said that Macpherson was also back, having seen nothing. Since the first exchange of shots, all had been silent. He agreed that the patrol had probably done its job in locating us, and had gone off to report; somebody claimed to have heard a motor-bicycle starting up, but this was by no means certain.

At about half-past four, I started laying my false trail.

We marched down that *chaung* in the most disgraceful fashion. Moving six abreast, and chucking down litter on the scale of a paperchase, we fairly plastered the sand with footprints; Robinson Crusoe would have had three fits and a spasm if he had seen them. We had once again the old precarious feeling of the Pinlebu Road and the approach to Tigyaing: but, as Duncan said, it was rather fun being so deliberately naughty. According to the map, the hills closed in on the *chaung* till it became a dangerous defile, about a mile and a half south of Hintha village; then they opened out for good, and the *chaung* ran away north into the flat jungle plains stretching to the Shweli. Until we were through the jaws of the defile I was thoroughly apprehensive; but we got past them without incident about six o'clock.

I had resolved, and Duncan enthusiastically approved, to make a false bivouac just before dark; and this we did on the *chaung* a mile from the village. We lit enormous fires, which felt as though they could be seen from twenty miles away; and on these we brewed our tea. The meat from a mule which the Burrifs had been slaughtering when the scare occurred had unfortunately not been distributed: we had all had to go to action stations, and except for some eager and provident Burrifs nobody had picked up any meat at all. So the food problem was acute, and I allowed only a couple of biscuits to be eaten. We certainly shouldn't be able to have a supply drop until well beyond the Irrawaddy, and whatever success attended the crossing there were obviously lean days ahead.

As soon as it was dark, we stoked up the fires in the bivouac till they looked like Jubilee Night; we tied some mules to trees well away from each other, in the hopes that they would feel lonely and bray; we used our last few explosives in setting booby traps; and in addition we pulled the pins out of grenades and weighted them down with tempting articles of kit. Then, very quietly and cautiously, in contrast to our disgraceful behaviour heretofore, we stole away five or six hundred yards down the chaung and, crowded together as never before, slept an uneasy sleep until three in the morning.

Hintha village was shown on the map as being about a mile away. It seemed to me probable that it was occupied. If the enemy had us under observation at all, Hintha would be a likely place to have a post. It lay on a track junction where one track ran east and west, and another north and south—the one we had crossed just before the unlucky bivouac; and the fact that there were few tracks or villages in the area enhanced its importance. My plan was to send the column straight on down the *chaung*, while I myself took two platoons into the village to see if there were Japs there, and, if there were, to hit them. This should attract to the neighbourhood any other Japs there might be about, and distract them from following up and harassing the main body.

The plan broke down because the *chaung* proved to be blocked with prickly bamboo, and reconnaissance disclosed no alternative route to the main track into the village.. This was the north and south track already mentioned, which dropped down from the hills into the *chaung* just about where we had laid the false bivouac; from this point to the village it was wide enough to take a bullock-cart. I had no alternative but to take the whole column with me so far, until the bamboo gave place to decent jungle; there I would send off the column, and go on into the village with the two platoons.

I halted more than once to probe for a gap in the bamboo, but drew a blank every time. According to the map I still had half a mile to play with before reaching the village; but the time factor was worrying me, for it was now nearing four o'clock, and by six that night we had to be at Inywa, a distance of twenty miles. I went on a little farther down the track, and suddenly saw, a hundred yards ahead of me, the sloping roofs of houses, half a mile too soon.

They say that the mind plays curious tricks in moments of crisis, and I remember distinctly that the sloping roofs at that moment reminded me of the medieval roofs of the old town of Chinon, as I saw them one moonlight night from the terrace of the ruined castle, fifteen years before. I had stumbled right into the outskirts of the village. The path forked at my feet; one branch, the less used of the two, ran along the edge of the bamboo; the other ran straight on towards the houses. Between the two was low undergrowth over which it was just possible to see: I fancy it must have been *bizat*, a thick thornless bush six or seven feet high, very common on the site of deserted villages, or on cultivation which has been allowed to fall into disuse.

The moon was still low, and where the track was flanked with trees it had been very dark: but here, where it was open, one could get a good view of the sleeping houses, moonlit on the east but with deep shadows on the west side of each. It all seemed still and peaceful; no sentries were guarding the approach; and I began to think that we had been playing our bivouac drama to an empty house. I was worried at the column being jammed together on the track behind me, with no means of getting off it should the village prove to be held. The men were very silent, fully realizing how much depended on the next few minutes; the only noise came from the mules, as they shifted their feet and creaked their saddlery. I told Duncan to organize a resumed search for a way into the jungle from the track, while I went forward with Philippe Stibbé's platoon to investigate; I passed the word also for a couple of Karens to act as interpreters.

Without waiting for Philippe to complete his orders, I moved cautiously forward with Po Po Tou and Jameson. As we went, we saw over the *bizat* the reflection of a fire against one of the houses on the left. Seventy yards or so from the fork in the track, we came to a T-junction, flanked by houses, and with a small track only, between two large houses, continuing the line of that on which we were: we had obviously come on to the main east and west track.

The fire was about forty yards along to the left, in the compound of the second house. With a grenade in my right hand I walked quietly towards it. Round it, symmetrically, one on each side, sat four men. They looked so peaceful and innocent that I immediately concluded that they were Burmese; and in that tongue (of which my knowledge was limited to a few sentences) I asked, 'What is the name of this village?'

The men on the far side looked up, and those on this side looked round: I was only three yards from them. They were Japs. Resisting a curious instinct which was prompting me to apologize for interrupting them, I pulled the pin out of my grenade, which had suddenly become sticky with sweat, and lobbed it—oh, so neatly—into the fire. I just caught the expression of absolute terror on their faces; they were making no attempt to move; and ran. It was a four-second grenade, and went off almost at once. I looked round when I heard it go, and they were all sprawling on the ground.

Back at the T-junction, Philippe had just arrived and was looking eager. I told him to get in at once with the bayonet and capture that end of the village. As I spoke, a man ran past me from the direction of the fire: I shot him in the side with my pistol, and he sprawled on the ground for a moment, but was up and away again in a flash.

Philippe lost no time, but as he reached the point on the track opposite the fire, light machine-guns opened up; he and his men had to go to ground, though not before they had spitted several men running out of the house beyond the fire. I called to Philippe to ask if he could get on, but he shouted back in a singularly calm voice: 'I don't think we can—it's pretty hot. I'm afraid I've been hit myself.'

I went back down to the fork tracks, and got hold of Jim Harman. I told him that Philippe's platoon would keep the Japs in play from where they were, and that he was to take his platoon up the little track and catch the Japs in flank. There was still no news from the rear about any signs of a route into the jungle. I went back to

Philippe and warned him what was going to happen, shouting across the same information to Sergeant Thornborrow over the way. Somewhere in the darkness we heard a motor-cyclist trying to start up his machine.

Philippe was hit in the shoulder; not badly, but he had lost a good deal of blood. I was talking to him and Corporal Litherland, who had also been hit: the two of them were at the foot of a tree on the right of the track up which we had come, just at the junction. Suddenly there was a rush of Japs up the track from the right, where Peter Dorans was, and two or three grenades came flaming through the air: the Japs have a glowing fuse on their grenades, very useful in a night action to those at whom they are thrown. One rolled to within a few yards of me, and I flung myself down behind a dark shadow which I took to be a fold in the ground; I realized only too clearly as soon as I was down that it was nothing more substantial than the shadow of a tree in the moonlight. The thing went off, and I felt a hot, sharp pain in the bone of my hip. At that moment there was a series of loud explosions: Peter, from the ditch where he was lying, had rolled half a dozen grenades among the Japs. Where I had seen them dimly in the moonlight and shadows, there was now a heap of writhing bodies, into which Peter was emptying his rifle. There was no further attack from that side.

I hopped to my feet and was overjoyed to find I was all right and able to walk. But poor Philippe had been hit again, this time in the small of the back; so had Corporal Litherland, and a third man who had been groaning and was now dead.

Philippe could still walk, and I told him to go back out of the way down the column. He walked a couple of yards, said, 'Blast, I've forgotten my pack,' picked it up and went off. This was the last time I saw him. Litherland also, with some help, was able to walk down the track.

There came a burst of shooting and some grenades from the little track where Jim and the commandos had gone.

There came another burst of fire from the little track, a mixture of light machine-guns, tommy-guns, and grenades. The commando platoon alone in the column had tommy-guns, which was one of the reasons I had selected them for the role. Their cheerful rattle, however, meant that the little track was no longer clear. I hurried back to the fork, and there found Denny Sharp.

'This is going to be no good,' I said. 'Denny, take all the animals you can find, go back to the *chaung* and see if you can get down it. We'll go on playing about here to keep their attention fixed; I'll try and join you farther down the *chaung*, but if I don't then you know the rendezvous. Keep away from Chaungmido, as we don't want to get brigade muddled up in this.'

Another casualty was Abdul the Damned. Somehow he had wandered up into the battle leading Duncan's horse. Abdul had a nasty wound in the shoulder and was weeping bitterly, howling like a child. The horse had also been hit in the shoulder, and could barely walk. Duncan shot it there and then.

The sound of shooting opened up where I had expected it; away back down the column, the flank attack was coming in. It was audibly beaten off, and I sent another message down the column warning them to look out for a repeat performance still farther down the line. Then a messenger arrived, and said:

'Captain Macdonald's killed, sir.'

'Nonsense,' I said. 'How do you know?'

'Mr. Harman's back, sir. And he's badly wounded.'

I went back to the fork. Jim was there, with blood streaming from a wound in his head, and his left arm held in his right hand. Alec had led the way down the track, with Jim following; then Sergeant Pester and then Private Fuller. They had met two light machine-guns, new ones, which had opened up. Alec had fallen instantly, calling out, 'Go on in, Jim!' Jim had been hit in the head and shoulder. Pester was unhurt, Fuller killed. Jim and Pester between them had knocked out both guns, and the track was again clear. They had had a look at Alec on the way back, and he was dead.

I reckoned we had killed a good many Japs, one way and another, but it was nearly six o'clock and would soon be light; and what I dreaded more than anything else was the possibility of being caught in daylight on the track, with the little, lithe Japs, unencumbered by packs or weariness, able to crawl under the bushes at ground level and snipe the guts out of us. There was no sign of any animals; Denny seemed to have got them back all right, but what, if any, luck he was having at the *chaung* I didn't know. At that moment somebody (I think John Fraser) came up with the news that a place had been found a couple of hundred yards back where you could squeeze through the bamboo into a stretch of disused paddy, beyond which there was open teak jungle. This decided me. At this moment came the noise of the 'repeat performance' on the tail of the column which we had been expecting. There was a couple of minutes of shooting, then it too stopped.

'Well, what do we do now?' I said vaguely to John and Duncan.

'Well, you'd better make your mind up, and bloody quick too!' said Duncan affably.

'Get everybody in sight into the paddy,' I said, 'and don't forget Thornborrow.'

The paddy was as it had been described, and in the growing light it was hard to see why we hadn't discovered it earlier. It was a stretch about a hundred yards long by forty wide, opening off the track to the westward, towards the *chaung*. And, greatest boon of all, beyond it, quite clearly in the dim daylight, one could discern that the jungle was teak—good, open teak, where you can move in any direction at any pace you like, and yet be swallowed up from view in less than a hundred yards.

'Now,' I said to Duncan, 'are we quite sure that everybody knows the rendezvous?'

'Absolutely,' he said. And with that assurance I told Brookes the bugler to blow on his 'instrument', as he always called it, the call known as 'Second Dispersal', on hearing which every group in the column was trained to break off from the main body and make its way independently to the rendezvous. I waited for a moment, to reassure myself that it was being acted on; and then joined my own group as it went off confidently into the jungle on a northerly bearing.

Soon we came to the east and west track, put out stops to prevent interruption, and crossed it rapidly in one wave. We travelled about a mile, and then halted to take stock. It was now about seven o'clock.

Duncan counted heads, and made us about sixty. We had two or three of Tommy Roberts's animals, which he had refrained from sending back with the others in case he was required to give mortar support. We also had one chestnut charger.

Abdul and I were the only two wounded, and Tommy Blow, who had been a member of the St. John Ambulance Brigade in civil life, was ordered by Duncan to have a look at us. There was a very small jagged hole just above my hip joint, bleeding mildly, on which he put a field dressing: it felt no worse than a kick in the football field. Abdul, on the other hand, had a really bad hole, and was in a good deal of pain. Tommy washed out the wound with sulphanilamide, of which he had a few tablets in his haversack, and put a dressing on: he also produced a sling, and made him put his arm in it. Then we pushed on: we had still nearly twenty miles to do, and eleven hours to do it in; there was no time to be lost.

We had a halt for tea sometime about midday; otherwise we

marched all day. Once or twice people suggested that I should get on the charger, but I was obsessed by the idea that if I did my leg would get stiff; and anyway with a stout stick I got along very well. During the morning we got rid of all the animals except the charger, and buried their loads, leaving the mules at a place where they had water to drink and bamboo leaves to eat. The charger we kept, partly in case somebody passed out and had to be carried (everybody was pretty weak for lack of food by now) and partly because it would do for meat later. Mules are better eating than horses, but none of the support mules would do for riding, and as we had to get rid of their loads, to get rid of them as well quickened our speed across country considerably.

Early in the afternoon we found a column's track. It came in from the south-west, and headed pretty well the same direction as that in which we were going. It was fresh—not more than an hour or two old, and definitely British; so we followed it until just before dusk, when I dug my toes in and said I couldn't manage another yard. The map had proved as inaccurate this side of Hintha as it had while we were approaching the village; but we had little doubt that we were pretty well at the rendezvous, one mile south of Pyinlebin; or at all events not more than a half-mile out. During the last half-hour of daylight, we had seen some animal droppings which were still warm, and we knew we must have been gaining on whoever was making the track; so Duncan shoved on a bit, and came back with the welcome news that he had found the head-quarters of the Burma Rifles, just going into bivouac, and had spoken to Colonel Wheeler. The Brigadier had ordered them to do just what we had been doing: to make misleading tracks off to the north-east.

I sent John Fraser to see them, to discuss what to do in the morning if there were still no signs of the brigade, and then tried to settle down for some sleep. Almost all the blankets had been lost. Duncan and I huddled together vainly for warmth, but tired as we were it was too cold for sleeping. We were anxious too, for John Fraser never came back: whether he had run into enemy or was just simply lost we could not tell, but when morning came, and brought no John, we were really anxious. We sent a patrol to the Burrif bivouac, but they had flitted.

Soon after seven there came the sound of firing over towards the Irrawaddy, and we girt up our loins and marched westward towards the sound of the guns. At nine o'clock we suddenly came to the edge of the jungle, and gazed out over a couple of miles of paddy to the river. Beyond it, the friendly hills of the Gangaw Range climbed steeply into the blue sky. The shooting had stopped, and the whole morning looked peaceful and Sabbatical. Two hundred yards out into the paddy was a small hovel, with one or two children playing outside it: Duncan and I went over and talked to the man and woman whom from time to time we saw moving about their morning tasks.

Duncan had a very good head for languages, and had picked up a little Burmese. He bought some rice and asked about Japs. The man seemed vaguely reassuring, but we couldn't follow all he said.

When I reached my bivouac, I was delighted to find Denny Sharp, Jim Harman and most of his commandos. They had had a longer march than we, having failed to get down the *chaung*, and having been compelled to go back up in the way we had come in, the previous evening. Once on the hill, they got away across country; but while climbing up it, two of the most precious mules of the whole string had tumbled over the cliff into the *chaung* below: one carried the wireless, and the other the ciphers. Lance-Corporal Lee had gone back down to recover the ciphers, and had not been seen since. They had heard, as they came away, the sound of explosions from the dummy bivouac, where some Nips presumably paid the price of their inquisitiveness. Otherwise they had not been interrupted. There had, however, been one more serious loss: while going through some elephant grass, their column had split in two, and the rear half had not caught them up again.

One piece of news they brought plunged us all into sorrow, and filled us at the same time with an admiration which will never diminish:

Philippe Stibbé had lost a great deal of blood by the time the dispersal was sounded, and had to be mounted on a pony. Bill Aird had had time to dress both his wounds; the second one looked as if it might be in the kidneys. To start with he had been with a party which had no other animals with it, and which was in a bad bit of country. Realizing that he was slowing up the party, he had begged to be left behind. Those with him indignantly refused; but when, after another half-mile, his pony had been responsible for several more delays, he slipped from the saddle to the ground, and said, 'Now you've jolly well got to leave me.' Nor does the story end there; for a Burma rifleman, unwounded, cheerfully said he would stay with Philippe and look after him; and in spite of Philippe's vehement orders to the contrary, he did so. We believe that this was Rifleman Maung Tun. The Burrifs had always had a great affection for Philippe, and this noble story, with its double heroism, is the highest manifestation I have known of the comradeship between the British and Burman soldier.

At three o'clock John Fraser turned up. He and Macpherson had found brigade. Two platoons of 7 Column had got across before interruption occurred, and a fierce fire had opened on the near bank from the west side. Through glasses more Japanese had been seen along the bank, hurrying towards the crossing place; and the bridge-head was not considered strong enough to hold them off. Jacksie Pickering had had an unpleasant time rowing a rubber boat about in the middle of the river under heavy fire; Scotty had had a bullet through his map case as he stood on the near beach; the intelligence sergeant on brigade headquarters had been killed by a shot from the far side of the river. Reluctantly the Brigadier had called it off, and was now in bivouac near Pyinlebin, where he had not previously been: arriving late the night before, he had had to cut straight to Inywa, trusting to pick up the Burrifs and myself later.

John and Macpherson had both talked to the Brigadier, who had told them that his orders now were to split the whole brigade into small parties to make their way to India independently. These parties should not exceed forty in strength, since that was the maximum number which could comfortably feed on the country. He was arranging a supply drop for brigade headquarters and the Burma Rifles; had he known that I was in the area and had lost my wireless, he would have included me also. As it was, he would put in an indent for me for any place or time that I might choose.

John had also seen Gim Anderson, the brigade major, who told him that most of the missing elements of my column had joined up with Ken Gilkes and 7 Column.

We had a little over an hour of daylight left, and we marched off towards the point in the woods where John had seen brigade. We failed to make it before dark by about a mile, so I halted for the night, impressing on the sentries that they must rouse us the very second they became aware of impending dawn. They did so, and we hastened to the brigade bivouac area. We found the place, with the depressions in the grass where they had been sleeping; but they had gone, and, with the usual standard of junglecraft which under the eye of the Brigadier they always attained, they had not left a vestige of a trail. Brigade had gone, and with them our chance of a supply drop. We were free to make for India.

We marched east, along the northern edge of the jungle. Open land, pasture, with coarse grass on which water-buffalo were grazing, stretched on our left hand towards the Shweli. A couple of miles brought us to a marshy patch, marked on the map as a *chaung*. Here we watered our one remaining animal, the chestnut charger.

At about eleven o'clock, we came to the village of Thetkegyin. We had to approach it across open paddy, with the usual feeling of nakedness; and when we got there we found one woman, two or three men, but no boats. They suggested we might find boats the next village along. This was Seikngu. Seikngu, a mile along the bank, we found deserted except for one man with goitre—sinister, unsmiling, malevolent. No, he had no boats. No, he had no rice. Yes, a party of Burman soldiers with four European officers had come through the village at four o'clock in the morning, and stolen all the rice he had.

As we talked to him, a post which I had established on the outskirts of the village brought in two young men, obviously superior and intelligent, but sullen and sour. One wore European clothes. We questioned them. No, there were no boats. No, there were no Japs. Very well, then, where were there boats? The Japs had taken them all.

At that moment, 'Donnelly', who had retained the field-glasses which he had had as an officer, said:

'Excuse me, sir, but I can see at least half a dozen boats at that village opposite.'

I borrowed his glasses, and sure enough, moored close under the bank were boats. I told John Fraser to tell the men to go and get them. Very reluctantly they stripped to a loincloth, and taking some bamboo poles which were lying on the bank, they began riding across the river on them in that fascinating fashion which I have so often tried and failed. At the same moment, two of my men came up and said they had found a perfectly good boat under one of the houses. Goitre was lying. If he had lied about the boats, perhaps he had lied about the rice: I ordered a search to be made. It revealed almost at once two bags of rice under one house alone. Meanwhile I watched the bamboo riders making their way across the river. They arrived at the sandbank in the middle, walked upstream, and then started across the second half. 'Donnelly' watched them through his glasses. I was attending to something else when I heard him exclaim:

'Where are they going? . . . That's not the way to the boats. . . . Japs!'

Instead of walking along the bank to the place where the boats were lying, they had run nimbly up the bank, and into a large house opposite where they had come ashore. Almost immediately, fifteen or twenty Japs emerged from the doorway, and looked across the river at us. Peter Dorans lay down on the ground, and brought his sniper's rifle to his shoulder, but I stopped him. At that moment, as if summoned by telepathy, three large lorries rolled up to the village opposite and disgorged another thirty or forty Japanese soldiers. I reckoned that, as a potential crossing place, Seikngu had slumped, and I wasn't taking any shares.

But I was all for taking Goitre, and we kidnapped him, together with the two bags of rice and two more men who entered the village just as we were leaving it. We entered the jungle, and found some stagnant water in a marsh: it wasn't more than three hundred yards from a point on the bank from which we could keep the Japs under observation. We cooked some rice and tea, and even gave Goitre some. We finished our meal at about the same time as our post reported the Japs bringing the boats round to the house where we had seen them appear from first; and then we moved.

The next few miles of jungle were exceedingly thick, and although we left the stagnant water at four in the afternoon, it was eleven next morning before we had covered the eight miles which I considered would bring us to the next point in the Shweli which I wanted to try. (Admittedly, we spent the hours of darkness sleeping: the moon didn't rise until about 3 a.m., and we were sadly in need of sleep.) At about ten, I reckoned we were within striking distance of the river, and I sent out two patrols to find it. The first, under Gerry Roberts, I sent along a track which we had stumbled on half an hour before, and which looked as if it led somewhere; the second, under Sergeant Pester, I sent on a north-easterly bearing.

Gerry was back about noon. He brought with him two frightened Burmese, whom he wanted to shoot. He had found the river by following the track, but on his way back he found these two lighting a fire on the path; and, mindful of the signal fires at Tigyaing, he had assumed that they were intended to disclose our position. Questioned, the two Burmese not only ceased to look frightened: they even laughed, and explained that there were so many wild elephants about that they were in the habit of lighting fires on the tracks to keep them away from the villages: elephants dislike the smell of burning, even when the fire has been two or three days extinct. It was such a tall story, and their manner in telling it so obviously spontaneous, that we felt it to be genuine, and acquitted them of the charge brought against them.

There was no sign of Pester's party, and I began to get anxious. Meanwhile, John was talking to the two latest prisoners, whom we had been at pains to keep separate from Goitre. He came to me with an idea which they had put forward. They each owned a boat, capable of carrying four men each. We wanted the best boats, they had them. There were no Japs in their village, but there were some in both villages on the other side. Just opposite where the track by which we were bivouacked came out on the river, there was an island which could be reached by wading. If we liked to be there soon after dark, they would meet us with their boats, and would land us on the far bank of the Shweli midway between the two Jap-held villages, one mile from each. They realized we might not trust them; and they therefore suggested that one should be held as a hostage, while the other went off and brought the two boats.

To me, the thing stank; but I couldn't see why. Even if it was fishy that they themselves should suggest the hostage business, where was the catch? We would have the hostage all right. I felt strongly that every day we delayed crossing the Shweli, the harder it would be; and I resolved to close with the offer. Soon after I had made up my mind Pester and his party returned. They had found the river, but had nothing else to report.

We waited for the rest of the afternoon, feeling very apprehensive. I could not dismiss from my mind the risks I was taking with my column. I pored for hours over the map, staring at the Irrawaddy and the Shweli, and racking my brain for a better plan. We had failed to cross at Inywa, we had failed at Thetkegyin and at Seikngu; and at the latter place we had seen with our own eyes the building up of the wall around the moat. There were motor roads, by which troops could be brought from the large reserves round Mandalay: we had seen that process at Myitson ten days before, and one of those motor roads ran from Myitson down the Shweli along the very bank to which we were about to cross. I tried to make up by mind whether my impatience to get the crossing done with was the impetuosity of foolishness, or the wisdom of resolution. It was while I bit on this problem that there came into my mind the lines of Montrose, which went far to crystallize the decision I had taken:

> He either fears his fate too much
> Or his deserts are small,
> That dares not put it to the touch,
> To gain or lose it all.

At five o'clock, we dispatched the man entrusted with the task of collecting the boats; to send an escort with him would have been impossible, without news reaching the Japs when they arrived in the village; while to escort him only as far as the outskirts of the village would have done no good, and would merely have shown the man that we did not trust him. Before he left, he talked to his colleague, with John Fraser as chaperon, and arranged that we should leave our present location as soon as it got dark, and meet him at the head of the island.

At half-past six we released Goitre, paying him for the rice we had taken, and which had been enough to allow of a distribution to each man of the equivalent of two teacups full. My total strength at this moment was a hundred and twenty, including nine officers.

At seven we started to move. The relief was tremendous; the waiting had been intolerable. Silently we marched for half a mile along the track, and tiptoed down the bank on to the sand: I was leading with Tommy Roberts, Duncan and John bringing up the rear. I had not realized how far we would have to march up the island, and I had ordered a rear position to be manned and held on the river bank opposite the island, in case we were caught out in the middle of the river. John was the only interpreter we had, since Maung Kyan could not speak English; so that I could not ask my guide how much farther we had to go. After half a mile I told Tommy to lead on, and I turned back myself to bring on John, Duncan and the rearguard.

When I got back to the head of the column again, I found that the crossing had already begun. The boats were there, all right, but they were much smaller than we had hoped—mere dugout canoes. Two men with their packs were the most that could be carried, and even that freight was precarious. The night was pitch black, and the water swirled most horribly past: I had had no idea the current was so strong. The sand bank on which we were, at the extreme north end of the island, was steep too, and the scour of the water close under it very powerful.

Tommy Roberts and several of his support men had already crossed; Denny Sharp had constituted himself the embarkation officer, and was directing the men how to sit in the bottom of the boat, with their packs on the floor in front of them. It was a nervous business, for the boat rolled with the slightest movement, and the freeboard was negligible. The boatmen handled them superbly, but the moment when the bow was allowed to pay out from the bank, by letting the stream flow inshore of it, was a moment of terror every time; for the boat heeled, water sometimes came over the gunwale, and unless the passengers sat still, the worst would happen. I watched the process several times: the whispered instructions by Denny, the men settling into the boat, the hands anxiously gripping the gunwale, the rifle between the legs, the gingerly paying out of the bow, the swirl of the black water between the bow and the bank, the immediate heavy list, the sudden jerky roll as the men tried to compensate it, and then the disappearance of the boat downstream into the dark before the boatman's frenzied paddling took effect.

Each trip took ten minutes, each boat two men. I worked out the sum, and reckoned that we should all be across by 3 a.m. barring accidents. I took Peter Dorans, and went across on the next boat, enjoying it not at all. The worst of the stream was at the embarking point; the boatman paddled furiously across the river, allowing the current to help him all it would by keeping the canoe at an angle; and soon we were in slack water. He had asked John in Burmese to explain to the troops that they should get out and wade once they were in shallow water; and we still appeared to be in mid-river when he anchored the boat with his paddle, and motioned us over the side. However, it proved to be not more than two feet deep, and we soon found ourselves on dry sand, among fifteen or twenty wet and waiting soldiers.

'Why the hell are you hanging about here?' I asked.

'Captain Roberts is trying to find a way off the sand,' someone answered, also in a whisper. 'This isn't the far bank at all, it's another sandbank.'

I went up the bank to look for Tommy, and found him with disturbing news. He had been nearly half a mile up the sandbank, to find a place where one could wade ashore, but there was none. It was desperately deep, and the current as bad here as where we had embarked. He was certain of treachery, and so was I. These boatmen had marooned us on an island in the middle of the river. I went back to the northern end, where I had come ashore, and sent a man across with an urgent message for John Fraser to come and interpret.

When John had learned what was wrong, he got hold of the next boatman returning, and asked him to show us the way across. He stripped and plunged off the northern end of the sandbank, followed by Tommy and another man. We waited for ten minutes, and then the boatman came back. Somewhere out there in the blackness, presumably Tommy had got ashore.

'All right,' I said. 'Let him go on with the ferrying. I'll go over.'

I took with me Denny Sharp, who had handed over his embarkation duties to Duncan, Peter Dorans and two more men; it was not until I reached the other side that I found that Abdul—wounded, weak, weeping Abdul—had attached himself to me and crossed as well.

There is no word for it but 'nightmare'. The roaring of the waters, the blackness of the night, the occasional sucking of a quicksand were bad enough, but the current was devilish. At its deepest, I suppose it was about four feet six or a little more: I am over six foot one, and it was more than breast high on me. The current must have been four to five knots. It sought to scoop the feet from under you and at the same time thrust powerfully at your chest. The only method of progress was to lean against the current, to attempt to keep an intermittent footing, to maintain your angle against the stream, and kick off the ground whenever your feet touched it. If once you lost your vertical position, you knew as a black certainty that you would disappear down the stream for ever. It was not until almost within reach of the bank that the river shallowed to a couple of feet; and even then it was all one could do to make one's way upstream against it. Although the crossing cannot have been more than seventy or eighty yards, one finished at least forty yards further downstream than the point of the sandbank.

Tommy's voice hailed me from the bank as I arrived, breathless and exhausted, bidding me work my way upstream. Five yards brought one to a place where one could clamber up the bank with the help of a branch of a tree which hung low over the river. The bank itself was about ten feet high. I scrambled up, and found myself on the road.

When I got my breath back, I began making calculations. The crossing was feasible, but some of the smaller men would find it difficult. The boats would not finish ferrying on to the sandbank until 3 a.m. and it would be light before six. It might be possible to divert the boats after that hour to bringing over the smaller men, but the vast majority must wade it. I told Denny Sharp that, as soon as he felt strong enough to do so, he must go back over, and order everybody to start, bar the very small men, whom we would bring over in the boats later. He went; and a few minutes later a long line of men began to arrive. We directed them upstream, as Tommy had done for me, and hauled the weaker ones up the bank at the one place where it was possible. As they arrived, we sorted them out into platoons, and posted them on the road two or three hundred yards either side of the crossing place, in case of interruption by enemy patrols.

Several times one heard cries for help, as some unlucky chap lost his footing and went off helplessly downstream; I fear that it happened to four or five in all. In the inky blackness there was nothing one could do to help. Some parties tried to hold hands all the way over, but it was impossible to maintain one's grip. Once during the night, the solitary charger arrived under the bank; how it had got there heaven knows, and I never found out; we tried desperately to get it up the bank, but failed; and at last with a sort of whimper it gave up the struggle, lay down in the water and in an instant had disappeared downstream.

About half the column was across when a mile or so to the northward, we saw the headlights of three lorries approaching. It seemed as though they were coming along the river bank. I sent a runner to Tommy, but Tommy had already seen them; so had the people on the sandbank, and the crossing ceased. The stops on the road were ready to engage them, and some men had the pins out of their grenades, when we saw the lorries halt, and their lights illumine the shrubs by the roadside, while they backed and went forward again in the act of turning round. Then to our boundless relief we saw them going off again the way they had come.

Somebody came across about three in the morning with the catastrophic news that the boats had gone; the accident we had been dreading all night had happened, and a nervous man had capsized the boat, which had gone off downstream. He himself had managed to reach the sandbank, but of the boat and boatman there was no sign. The other boatman had to be forcibly restrained from going off to look for him, of which the effect was to reduce the number of passengers each trip, since he had to be escorted on the return journey. When at last he had delivered the ultimate man on to the sandbank, he gave us the slip; and now at four in the morning we were left without boats. Big men and little men alike must cross to the bank, or stay where they were.

Some willingly, if not happily, came across at once, and joined us; but some turned back and some would not start at all. Several officers went back again to persuade them to try, but what with hunger and cold and several hours of waiting on that grim sandbank, and hearing the cries of the occasional lost man, their nerve had been undermined. Everybody was weak from lack of food, and morale depends more on food than on anything else. I sent across a message to say that I could give them only fifteen minutes more, and then I was setting out due east. John Fraser made a last attempt to rally them, and got them all started, but unfortunately he himself lost his footing, and was swept away downstream, choking and helpless. Luckily for him, the moon was now up, and it was possible to see him; and he was rescued, though not without much difficulty. But for the others, this was the last straw, and they turned back to the sandbank.

I had to make the decision. Another hour and a quarter remained till dawn, when the Japanese patrols would renew their vigilance. I could stay and wait till dawn, take a chance on being interrupted, and search up and downstream, for more boats. There was no bamboo, or other material suitable for the quick manufacture of a raft. There was no rope. The likelihood of being able to do anything more at dawn than I could do now was remote. If I stayed, I would fling away the chances of those who had put their trust in Providence and come out safely, for the sake of those who had not had the faith to do so. The wounded were all across, and some of the Gurkhas, the smallest men of all. The salvation of those who remained on the sandbank was in their own hands.

I made the decision to come away. I have it on my conscience for as long as I live; but I stand by that decision and believe it to have been the correct one. Those who may think otherwise may well be right. Some of my officers volunteered to stay, but I refused them permission to do so.

We marched for an hour, and then, in a bamboo thicket high on the hill, we risked a fire. We were paralysed with cold, and had nothing dry but our weapons, ammunition and such other articles as we had been able to hold above our heads. We brewed some tea, and had an hour's sleep; during which time two men from the sandbank joined us. They had screwed up their courage, and done it, but they had failed to induce any one else to share their venture. They had had some difficulty in finding our track, but had eventually done so.

Before pushing on, we counted heads. Our strength was reduced to nine officers and sixty-five men; in other words, forty-six men had either been drowned or left on the sandbank. Of these the latter were certainly the vast majority.

It is a matter of fact that those who had crossed and were with the column included all the best men, and the men whose behaviour throughout the expedition had been the most praiseworthy. It does not absolve me from my responsibility for the others to say so, but it was and is a comfort to me that among those whom I thus abandoned were few to whom our debt, and the debt of their nation, was outstanding. There were two or three whom I particularly regretted, and of these one was almost certainly drowned, and two were especially small in stature. There were two more who, had they got out, would have had to face charges at a court martial.

Nevertheless, the crossing of the Shweli River will haunt me all my life; and to my mind the decision which fell to me there was as cruel as any which could fall on the shoulders of a junior commander.

OF THE 318 MEN *of Column 5 who had entered Burma in January, 95 returned to India. Back in Burma a year later Fergusson found a Gurkha near the Shweli—one of the men who had remained on the sandbank. He told the major that the morning after his departure, the Japanese captured those who had remained behind. In 1945 twenty-eight of these men were found in a Rangoon prison.*

CHINDIT 76

BY WILLIAM DRURY

AFTER THE WITHDRAWAL, *Wingate left Burma more convinced than ever that his concept of long-range penetration could be successful. He returned to London and convinced Winston Churchill, who took him to the Quebec Conference to convince the Americans. There it was decided to give Wingate his way. Colonel Cochran of the American Air Force was assigned to direct the air support, and new raiding columns were trained.*

Wingate named his new unit the Chindits *after the stone dragon that guards the figure of Buddha in the Burmese Temple. In March, 1944, the Chindit columns entered Burma, and less than a month later Wingate was killed in an air crash. But the columns moved on towards Mandalay. Merrill's Marauders, entering Burma from the east, moved in to meet them.*

Though the Chindit columns were completely successful, they had no easy time of it. As isolated small units deep in Japanese-controlled territory, they were vulnerable to attack at any time the enemy could locate them. A Flight-Lieutenant who went into Burma as an air-liaison officer tells the story of one of these attacks.

I AWOKE and rubbed my eyes. It was a dull grey dawn. Ford was standing outside in the thin drizzle of rain; his green shirt was silvered with the morning moisture. I could just see his back through the narrow entrance of the shelter, and I noticed that he held his Sten-gun at the ready. I glanced at my wrist watch—it was 5.15. I called to him, softly, and he ducked his head through the leafy aperture.

'Is it Stand To?' I asked.

'Yes, sir—nearly over. I didn't wake you because you had a restless night.'

I reached for my boots, put them on and stood up. The pain in my leg made me gasp. I reached for the water bottle; it was empty. I threw it down and Ford handed me a half-filled chagul. I sipped a mouthful and said: 'We must have some more water.'

Ford rubbed his stubbly chin. He said:

'Wish we could have a wash. I feel lousy.'

The silence was oppressive. Not a man moved or spoke outside, and the sound of a rifle shot when it came stung the nerves like a knife jab so that we jumped at the suddenness of it.

'What was that?'

We listened intently. It came again; another shot, two, three! I said:

'That's no accidental firing.'

I went to the entrance and looked out. The Chindits were lying in the grass at the top of the bowl-shaped hollow. A man, doubled low, was coming past the door of the shelter and I stopped him.

'What is it?'

'Attack, sir! Some Japs are coming up the north side.'

I ducked inside and picked up my carbine. It was loaded. A babble of voices broke out from the north slope, followed by a high-pitched order in Japanese, and then silence. There was no sound from the crouching Chindits and I went past them to where the Colonel stood. His face was tense; he held a Colt .45 in his hand. Tony Firth and the Doctor were with him. I asked:

'How many are there, sir?'

'About sixty or more.'

He cocked his head and listened. There was a faint hum of voices on the north slope. He said:

'Now what are they up to?'

A thunderous volley of shots echoed his words and the whine of slugs sang in our ears. We instinctively crouched lower. The volley ceased but for a few spasmodic shots. Now and again a Sten would chatter or the sharp crack of .303 answered the enemy. Around the perimeter a man stood in each narrow slit-trench, his eyes watching the thick curtain of trees. I looked at the men around me and saw on the face of each a mask of grim determination and hatred, and I realized that, outnumbered as they were, they would fight to the last bullet rather than be captured and subjected to the inhuman torture meted out to the Essex men at Cheswema.

The weapons were silent again and I left the Colonel and went back to my trench. I slithered into the trench and fumbled for a cigarette but found none. Ford was leaning over the parapet, his cheek on the breech of his gun. I said:

'Have you a cigarette?'

He passed over a squashed packet and resumed the nursing of his gun. Neither of us spoke for a while. I watched his youthful, emaciated face. He was barely twenty. I said to him:

'This is your first campaign, isn't it?'

He turned his head sharply and stared, then his face relaxed in a half smile. He nodded.

'Worried?'

'A little,' he admitted. He seemed glad to have somebody to whom he could tell it. I lit him a cigarette and passed it over. He drew a couple of puffs and asked:

'How many are there?'

'The Colonel thinks about sixty.'

We chain-smoked his cigarettes for a while. He nodded to the trees on the north slope and said:

'Wonder what they are doing now.'

There was no sound from the enemy positions. It was maddening to know they were there and not be able to see them. We watched and waited. The sun was higher now and the rain had ceased. A butterfly fluttered over our heads. I looked at the time; nearly two hours had passed since the first attack. It seemed like two minutes. We were cramped in the narrow space and I dragged myself on to the parapet and stood upright to stretch my legs. Still no sound. . . . I wondered if the enemy had gone. But as I wondered the shrill voice of the Jap commander came again—this time from behind us. The voice was harsh and commanding. It was echoed by other voices; garbled chattering voices; voices to our right, left, front, rear—we were surrounded. The very trees seemed alive and unfriendly. The final command rapped out and another volley opened up. I ducked my head as the lead flew past, and dropped into the trench. A sharper and much louder explosion joined in the uproar and a heavy object screamed through the air above us. Ford hissed:

'Mortar! They've got a bloody mortar on us somewhere!'

The noise was terrific. The crack, crack of rifles and the vicious buzz of the missiles like a swarm of angry bees was punctuated with the heavier thud of a mortar. It lasted nearly fifteen minutes in this fashion and then died in intensity, rising and falling again; shot and reply and sometimes the clatter of a Bren-gun when a khaki-clad shape showed for a fleeting moment through the trees. They were nearer now! The Jap officer's voice screamed again from the north side and then bedlam broke loose. The trees disgorged a howling pack of Japanese and they came at a run towards our thin green line of Chindits, firing wildly into our midst.

'Ch-a-a-arge!' they yelled in English as they broke the cover, and the air was hideous with their hysterical screams. We shivered as we watched the mad bayonet-charge hurl itself on us across the clearing.

My ears were pounding with the clamour and I hoped that our line would not falter before the terrifying spectacle. But I had no need to worry. A blast of fire smote the attackers and carved down the leaders almost on top of our trenches, so that the charge was broken and the enemy turned and fled to the shelter of the trees.

We were sweating and we mopped our faces clean, watching the flying dust spots as the bullets tore the grass. There were five or six dead that the Japs had left behind, but none would cross the clearing in an attempt to bring them in. Our guns were hot and smoking. We fired every time a figure moved in the dark behind the trees. Sometimes the Jap mortar would join in and the metal fragments would whistle past and strike with a dull thud in and around the bivouac. The Jap officer could be heard calling out his commands from one side and then the other, and each high-pitched order was followed by a fusillade of shots into the camp.

We wondered what was the fate of Bill Fazackerley's Commando platoon, which had been left in the village below Ponce Fort. Had they been surprised and overwhelmed? Or had they managed to escape into the nullah?

'Whoomph!' went the mortar and the fragments hissed viciously in our ears. A hefty, dark figure slid into our narrow trench and said in a broad Yorkshire accent:

'Make room for a big 'un.'

It was Private Wertley, batman to Major Simmonds. His accent was guaranteed to make you look twice at Private Wertley, who was a broadly built young English Negro, with a crop of short woolly hair and a wide white smile. Wertley never got ruffled and his slow Yorkshire speech was as unconcerned and genial as a farmer 'up for the day' at Stokesley Show. He opened the bolt of his rifle and slipped in a fresh clip of cartridges. He said:

'Did you see the size of those bastards, sir? Proper big sods. Ah thought all Japs was supposed to be little.'

I said:

'Not these boys. They look like Imperial Guard types.'

'Ah'll Imperial Guard 'em,' said Wertley, ignoring the bullets that suddenly showered over the trench.

The Jap commander screeched from the west side.

'Yap, yap, yap!' mimicked Wertley, 'here the bastards come agen.'

The volley burst out afresh and once more the shrieks rose to a deafening crescendo as the Japs charged. The noise was unearthly. They came, slipping from tree to tree, sunlight flashing on the bare steel bayonets, howling like a savage pack of wolves. They were a little more cautious this time and took cover from the forest as they came. Every time a khaki body showed against the foliage, a score of rifles cracked simultaneously. The cornered Chindits were fighting furiously.

A hysterical wail started up behind us and our south side defenders fired into the attack which started on that side. The Brens rippled out short staccato bursts into the frenzied mobs as they came in at the front and rear of our camp. It hardly seemed possible that our morale could face up to the double attack and as the Japanese broke cover and fell on the trenches with bayonet and grenade, I must have thought that this was the end. But the men stood without a flinch and met the steel with bullet and calm courage, and again the enemy was cut down as he reached the trenches. We were swearing and sweating and the weapons were hot in our hands. Steel for steel and bullet for bullet, the bloody contest was fought and won. As the enemy fell back, the Chindits fired until there was nothing left to shoot at and the jungle was quiet once again.

We had lost only two men in that mad fight but the enemy had lost more. His dead could be seen around the trenches and behind the trees, awkward, motionless figures that looked grotesque in the attitude of death.

The time passed and we sat and stared into the belt of trees. Less than forty, sick in health, emaciated, none knowing the outcome. To evacuate the position seemed hopeless. We were outnumbered and surrounded. Our only chance appeared to be to wait for night-fall and make a break-through in the dark—if we could keep the enemy at bay until then and provided our ammunition did not run out.

There was always the possibility, too, that the enemy would bring up reinforcements and this seemed very probable.

I climbed from the trench and walked to my shelter. I wanted my cigarettes. It was now mid-afternoon. The sun was hot; there was little cloud about. A deathly stillness clung to the clearing and only the trees whispered of the danger that lurked there. Slanted eyes were watching us, we knew, and all we could do was sit tight and wait . . . and wonder.

I chose a cigarette and lit it. I was thirsty and I picked up a half-filled chagul to drink but, remembering that this was our only water, I contented myself with wetting my lips. The pain was throbbing in my leg so I lay down on the damp parachute-bed. A huge bug made room for me. I watched my cigarette smoke drift and curl to the cloth ceiling. All the time I was wondering of the lost Commando platoon. There was no sound from the village. I hoped to high heaven Bill had got his men away safely.

Voices broke out on the west side, about thirty yards away. A shot was fired and then another, and a man cried out:

'Don't shoot! It's us—Commandos!"

Commandos! I got to my feet and looked out. Five of our men stood quietly behind the trees, their rifles aimed at the underbush. A sergeant waved down their arms and called out:

'Okay! Come on in.'

Eight men led by a corporal broke down the bushes and almost staggered into the camp. They were exhausted and in a pitiful condition. Eight men and a corporal! A section! What had happened to the others? The Colonel walked up.

He said: 'Where is Captain Fazackerley?'

'Don't know, sir,' panted the corporal. 'We were out on a patrol and some Nagas met us just before we got to the village and told us Mister Fazackerley had left and that the Japs were there.'

'Captain Fazackerley has left the village?'

The corporal nodded; he looked very weak. He said:

'Yes, sir. The Nagas say he was surprised by the Japs and had to pull out. I thought mebbe he had come here so I came up as well.'

The Colonel said: 'Didn't you see the enemy, then?'

'Yessir; we saw 'em in the trees just as we got to the top here. One of them shot at us and we dodged behind the trees and then one of our chaps fired at us.'

I turned back into the basha. So Bill Fazackerley had got his platoon away; all but this one section. That was good news. Tojo bawled an order again and the shooting recommenced. I went out to the Colonel and sat down with my carbine on my knees. The Colonel's face relaxed and he pointed to the leather belt on which hung my revolver. He said:

'Don't let them catch you with that, or they'll have your scalp.'

The belt had belonged to the Jap the Chechama Nagas had killed.

The Doctor started to speak: 'These devils——'

He broke off as a man came through the trees and ran down the short slope.

'It's L., sir! He's been hit with a grenade and he's bleeding bad!'

Donald got to his feet immediately. He snapped to his batman: 'Quickly! A blanket!'

He snatched the proffered blanket and followed the messenger up the slope. His thin face, pale with illness, showed no sign of fear as he went out to where the enemy lurked. The M.O.'s batman calmly picked up his Sten gun and went after him. The C.O. stared stonily at the jungle that swallowed them up, and we listened to the bark of rifles and the sharp stuttering of machine guns. Our thoughts were out with Donald on his errand of mercy.

A grenade thudded and the fragments flew. Another one, and another . . . the pace was getting hot. The Colonel's face was impassive. He gave no hint of what was in his mind; his .45 twirled slowly in his fingers as he sat. The big Irishman, Simmonds, picked up two grenades and got to his feet, rather unsteadily. He did not say a word; simply walked into the forest in the direction taken by the Doctor. We followed him with our eyes.

Tony said: 'Denis is ill.'

No one answered. The time ticked by; seconds seemed like hours. Then the bushes parted. It was the Doctor.

Somebody breathed: 'Thank Christ!'

The Doctor came down the slope with the limp figure in the blanket borne by the batman and another man. Donald's stubbled face looked tired. He said:

'He's in a bad way. I may have to amputate his legs.'

The Colonel's lips moved but he did not speak. He nodded.

The buzz of a light plane sounded above the din of battle. It came nearer and I stood up, the better to see. An L.5 was heading for our position, flying low.

The C.O. said: 'Is he coming here?'

I said: 'Looks like it, sir. I'll warn him off if he orbits.'

I picked up the Very gun and slipped in a red cartridge. The plane banked and commenced to circle overhead at about 200 feet. I fired the red and it arc-ed skyward. I ejected the empty case, inserted another red, picked up the Walkie-Talkie and spoke into it.

'Ground to aircraft, ground to aircraft—are you receiving me?'

No reply; the receiver crackled in my ear. I tried again—still no reply. The pilot had evidently not seen my Very. I fired the second cartridge; it was my last. The plane turned steeply and came in just over the tree-tops. I yelled:

'Judas! He's going to drop!'

Whee! screamed the mortar and the dust-spots flew. The L.5

waggled its wings as it purred overhead, and I breathed relief when nothing dropped from the open cockpit door. It was a dummy run. I *had* to contact him this time—he *must not* drop!

'Ground to aircraft—are you receiving me?'

No answer. He turned in for the approach. The bullets sang a tenor chorus.

'Ground to aircraft! Ground to aircraft! Do not drop! Do you understand? Do not drop! Return to Base immediately. We are being attacked!'

I was fairly screaming into the transmitter. A voice sounded faint above the crackle in the receiver.

'Aircraft to ground. I am coming in now——'

The rest was unintelligible. God damn it! He couldn't hear me! He planed down to the treetops and I yelled over and over again:

'Do—not—drop! We—are—being—attacked!'

For Pete's sake, I moaned, could he not see?

Two canisters left the plane, hung in space for a brief moment, and drifted down on their parachutes—right into the Jap lines. The L.5 continued over our heads and we were horrified to see another object leave the cockpit and parachute down. It was a short length of bamboo. Orders from Brigade. The documents were always dropped in a stick of hollow bamboo. The chute dropped into the wood where the Japs were attacking in our rear, and the Colonel swore and leaped from his mule-box seat. He took the slope at a run and disappeared into the trees where the Japs hid.

I sat on the box, feeling limp, and watched the now fast-disappearing aeroplane.

The Colonel reappeared in a short while. He brushed aside the spidery arms of a thorn bush and dropped into the camp. He held the bamboo tube in his left hand; his right grasped his .45 Colt automatic; blood trickled from thorn scratches on both arms; a rent in his trousers disclosed his knee. He raised the bamboo in triumph and smiled. When he smiled you knew why they called him 'Boy'.

The forest was quiet again. The sky, which had been bright all day, was now overcast and rain threatened. It was still very sultry and we were thirsty but the Colonel had given orders that no one must drink unless the Doctor deemed it advisable. Water was something of a problem. We were unable to replenish empty bottles and this state of affairs might go on for God knows how long. The men stayed at their posts. They were just remembering they had eaten nothing all day and it was now five-thirty. Parched lips sucked at pebbles, grass, buttons, anything. Beard-stubble, hollows, grime and sweat made Frankensteins of our faces.

The M.O. was fighting for the life of the wounded Chindit. Blood plasma flowed through a tube into the tortured body. Donald Gunn worked quickly and efficiently, without rest.

It was interesting to see the faces around me. There was Denis Simmonds, big-built, pale, stubble-cheeked. He sat on a mound watching the Doctor, saying nothing, simply staring. His large hands played with a grenade, rolling it round and round in his fingers. The Colonel sat on his mule-box. He was burning his papers. His fingers were steady as he held the flaming match and his face betrayed no emotion as he watched the fire eat its way up the sheaf of documents. Baxter, the youthful intelligence clerk, was looking fixedly into space. His eyes, red-rimmed, were unseeing. He fumbled with a stone and his hands shook with the illness that racked his body. No one spoke. Each was concerned with his own thoughts. The man with the Bren gun on the bank above the big Irish Major took his eyes from the green wall for an instant and looked in his shirt for a cigarette. He found one and put it between his lips. It was crumpled. His gaze strayed back to the trees and he absently struck a match and lit the cigarette. The blue smoke curled and streamed on a slight breeze that stirred the branches and made the leaves rustle so that we looked up for a brief moment before eyes wandered back and rested again on emptiness.

There was something damnable about the silence, I thought. It was a quietness that was *too* quiet. It pounded on the ears like a roaring of high winds and struck deep into the nerves because we expected *something* but it seemed as though it would never happen. Yet it had to happen. It was annoying; like a dog with no tail. Sometimes a man would get up and walk across the camp and you followed him with your eyes and wondered why he did not drop with a bullet in him. He walked three steps, four, five, and you waited for the shot which you knew must come but never did. That seemed awful, somehow. He should have died but he remained alive. It was not that you wanted him to die, but if he had you would have felt that nothing was out of the ordinary. The silence would have been smashed and you would feel mad at his death; fighting mad; a roaring, seething, don't-give-a-damn kind of madness that would pull you out of this dull, frightening, sinister mood. But, no! The trees just whispered and you knew their greenness hid a black heart. And when a bee buzzed about your head you suddenly hated it because it was a part of the nature which was hiding your enemy. You brushed your hand at it spitefully because it looked peaceful and you hated peace, wanting the noise of battle so that you knew where you stood in the pattern of the enemy's plans.

These were my own thoughts, jumbled, uneasy, nervous. Men feel this way in such circumstances. I don't think it was the fear of death; we had lost that. How can I explain it? It was inward excitement without means of outward expression. Like a mute, his heart bursting with patriotism, trying to shout 'God Save the King'. The restless chafing against inactivity. The feeling of wanting to do something—anything—to break the monotony. It affects men in many ways. Some whistle, some laugh—at almost anything, some chain-smoke, a few pray. Some make designs on the ground with the heel of their boot, toss pebbles, chew grass. I chew matches. This time I had only one match; I chewed that to pulp.

The Doctor raised his head. He spoke softly.

'He's gone, sir.'

The Colonel nodded. His face looked troubled for a moment. He said:

'Get some rest, Don.'

Donald walked away and lit a cigarette. I saw his hands. Small and efficient, the pale skin was streaked with blood. His broad shoulders were bent. The vitality was sapped from his weary body. He hated defeat when he struggled with fate for the life of a man, but he never gave in.

Somebody started to whistle quietly. His neighbour snarled: 'Shut up! Blast you! You get on my nerves!'

The whistling ceased abruptly and the solitude closed in again. The sun was losing its heat. A breeze stirred the trees and cleaved the humid air with its cool draught. The little, thin man next to me spoke in a hoarse whisper.

He said: 'Damn them! Why don't they start something?'

The trees alone rustled a reply. The thin man's eyes never left the green wall. They darted left to right along the rows of upright trunks, as if striving to see beyond them into the unknown blackness. They were restless eyes, small, black and troubled. His thoughts were obvious. They are many and we are few. They have us trapped. Why don't they shoot? Shoot, you lousy bastards! Shoot! Shoot, and be damned to you! He was puzzled. He could not understand the meaning of the long silence. He was a soldier and understood action but this was something beyond his comprehension. Something mysterious and hateful. God in merciful heaven! Give us noise and bullets and a cold-steel charge and the screams of the wounded, but in the name of mercy stop this silence! My watch ticked away the seconds and each small quick tick was the throb of a drum that impinged on the brain and scarcely died before the next pulse came.

Then it happened—a sharp *clop*! and the vicious whine that followed it—and the suspense was over. The enemy's diabolical screams of hate came from the north slope and relief showed on the grimy faces of the Chindits as they hugged their rifles and waited for the charge. The climax came with all its sound and fury when the shrieking mob burst from the foliage in an all-out attempt to smother the little camp. Our guns chattered frantically; Stens, rifles, revolvers and the two Bren-guns, spitting into the Japanese. The enemy mortar raised its voice and the fragments flew with sickening frightfulness. Grenades joined in with their thudding and whining and the awful peace was forgotten in the awful bedlam. Now we knew where we stood. There was no mystery about this give-and-take battle for our existence. The jungle fighters slammed cartridge after cartridge into the breech and wherever a khaki figure showed for a moment a round sped to its mark. God help us if the ammunition runs out. How long will it last? A snarling Japanese giant of the Imperial Guard leaped into a slit-trench and bayoneted the occupant, stabbing savagely again and again into the fallen body. The hate on his face turned to stupid surprise as a bullet drilled him clean, and he fell on his victim in the bottom of the trench. Two more broke through, screaming English book-learned phrases— 'Drop your gun!'—'Surrender!'—'Charge!'—and dropped dead in the hail that greeted them.

Peter Goatley stared at the bloody mess of his hand a bare second after the grenade had burst in front of him. A man of his platoon lay at his feet, lifeless. The Doctor raced up and hustled Peter away to the comparative safety of a mound.

As quickly as it had begun the battle ended as the enemy withdrew for the third time into the forest. They were still unable to take us.

The shooting now was infrequent. We were loth to spend a single round unless it bought death for a Japanese soldier. Our ammunition was running low. The Colonel called the officers around him. He said: 'We shall evacuate the position after dusk, if it's possible. That will mean destroying the radio and anything else we cannot carry.' He looked at the Doctor, who was bandaging Peter's mangled hand, and said:

'I'm afraid your medical panniers will have to go, Donald.'

Donald Gunn said, simply: 'I'll carry what I can, sir.'

'Right. Norman——!' The C.O. spoke to Captain Wright. 'Divide the money among the men, and bury any we cannot carry. I'll give the word when we will leave.'

Dusk settled and deepened into night. Sometimes a shot rang out but we could see nothing in the blackness beyond our perimeter. There was no moon. Quickly and silently, the wireless-set was destroyed and thrown into a slit-trench. Our dead were lowered on top of the wrecked equipment and the earth was heaped into the trench. The grave was hidden beneath a carpet of dead leaves and rotting vegetation so that when the work was finished none could tell of its presence.

Sergeant-Major Woods approached me from the darkness. He whispered: 'I'm afraid I've got to ask you for your batman, sir. We need the batman to stay behind whilst we slip out.' I bit my lip. Poor Ford. He was just a kid; new to all this.

I said: 'I'll tell him, Sergeant-Major.'

He limped off. I told Ford. He was upset at first. I took his arm, and said: 'It's got to be done. Don't worry—you'll get out.'

It sounded so futile and meaningless, but I hardly knew what else to say. He just stood without saying a word.

'I'll see you soon. You'd better go now.'

It seemed so heartless. He might never get out. He was expendable. But, then, none of us might escape. We were still surrounded and the enemy would be expecting us to attempt a get-away under cover of darkness.

I turned away and hurriedly packed. Out of the corner of my eye I saw Ford go to his trench. I wondered if I would see him again.

I put my harness on. God-damn! That hurt! The rough webbing side-pack and water-bottle chafed the sores on my hips. When I strapped the back-pack to my shoulders I found it less painful to bear than the side-equipment, since there were no sores on my back. The *kukri* knife, which I usually carried at my side, I strapped to the back-pack. The knife slipped from the scabbard and fell to the ground. Only much later did I notice the loss.

The Chindits lined up to depart. Forgotten Men? No. England has not forgotten them. You cannot forget men of whom you have never heard; whose exploits are delegated to the insignificance of a single-column paragraph between the obituaries and the cross-word puzzle on the back page of the Sunday paper.

Silently, soberly, they filed out into the forest to God knows what! The Colonel was leading, walking on a compass bearing through the blackness that swallowed him up so that the man behind him had need to hurry lest he be lost. Progress was slow. Trees loomed out and struck us, unseen by our straining eyes until they almost touched our faces. The man I was following stopped abruptly and I collided with his heavy pack. He stood for a moment, listening. I whispered: 'What is wrong?' He put his mouth close to my ear and breathed:

'I can't find the man in front of me. Can you hear them?'

There was no sound, nothing but the wind soughing in the branches. I fumbled for my pocket compass, snapped it open and read our bearing. We were ten degrees off course. I said in a low voice: 'Follow me, and for Christ's sake keep quiet.'

Down the side of the hill we went, not daring to make a sound, inwardly cursing the dead-wood which crackled under our feet and which our taut nerves magnified to the proportion of thunder. We expected every minute to walk into the enemy. We expected the splutter of rifle fire and a volley in our backs. We expected any-thing, everything, and hoped for nothing. Curse the blackness! We cannot see! The ground would drop where there was an invisible pit and down we would go, one by one. Each heard the man in front drop but he had to go on himself because he could see no way round and it was fatal to lose sight of the man ahead.

I fell rather than stepped on to the track. The ground which had been sloping beneath my feet suddenly dropped and my toes found air and then a jolt which shook my spine. I could just make out the grey ribbon left and right of me that told me of the track. It was the road through Phezachedama, and the enemy were five hundred feet above us now. The man behind me dropped with a thud and cursed. I motioned him to silence. We waited for the others; they came one at a time, each unsuspecting the drop before him. When the last man appeared I counted them. They were ten. I whispered: 'Any more?'

'No, sir—we're all here.'

'Good. Don't make a sound. Two of you walk along the track that way and see if you can find the Colonel's party. I'll look this way.'

I turned right, toward Phezachedama. I walked quietly, hugging the side of the track where the gloom was deepest. I had only gone about two hundred yards when I saw shadowy figures a few feet away. A voice said: 'Who goes there?'

'R.A.F. officer. Where's the Colonel?'

'He's here.'

I said: 'All right, I'm coming back again with ten men, so don't shoot.'

I returned to the waiting men and brought them back to the Colonel's group.

They were leaving the track, descending into the nullah. I joined in the wake of the last man and the other ten followed me.

The ground was worse now, steeper and pitted with holes that dropped a man with an alarming jerk. The trees seemed more numerous and the undergrowth tore at the clothes and flesh with invisible fingers, renting garments and leaving angry red scratches on the skin. Ahead of me Peter Goatley stumbled and tripped, impeded by his right arm which was bound in a sling so that he could not use it to clutch at vines and branches to help his progress.

A fusillade of shots from above shattered the silence. It sounded like another attack on the camp. I thought of Ford and inwardly prayed for his safety. They should be leaving by now. Suppose they had been trapped as they sneaked out? It was a horrible thought.

The shooting continued in short sharp bursts for a few minutes and then stopped.

We were hot with exertion. A yawning crevice appeared at Peter's feet, and he slithered down. The pain from his hand wrung a moan from his lips. I looked down into the dark abyss but could not see him. His voice came up low and gasping.

'Slide—down! It's too—steep to walk.'

I whispered it back to the others and lowered myself gingerly to the earth, then, easing forward, foot by foot, I found the drop and slid down on my haunches. But it was steeper than I thought and my slide increased in momentum, the rough ground scraping at my sores until I almost shouted with pain. The others followed with a rush and one man gave an involuntary cry as his ankle twisted beneath him. Another savagely snarled at him to shut his mouth and it looked like the makings of a first-class fight.

I hissed: 'Be quiet!'

They subsided, muttering. Their nerves and tempers were frayed. My own ire was roused. I struck fiercely and resentfully at a creeper which lashed at my face. Christ! If only we could see where we were going! Down and down, we stumbled and fell, slithered and tripped. Downwards to the nullah bed which lay five thousand feet below, somewhere in the dark beyond. Sometimes a man's temper got the better of him and he swore at some obstacle in his path; the others would urge him to silence. We came to what appeared to be a tunnel caused by undergrowth hanging over a cleft in the rock. It sloped dangerously and we had to feel our way down every foot of the way. A man incautiously struck a match the better to see. It was struck from his hand. He said viciously: 'What the hell did you do that for? I can't see!'

The other answered:

'You bloody fool! Do you want us all to get caught?'

'I'll knock your effing head off, you——!'

'Shut up for Christ's sake!'

Others hissed at them. Their voices came to me out of the dark; I couldn't see a thing in front of me. There was silence again save for the laboured breathing and the crackle of the undergrowth. Another fell and twisted his ankle; his rifle clattered to the ground. We struggled along like this for over two hours. My watch showed thirty-five minutes past midnight. God knows what distance we had travelled; it could not have been far. The Colonel halted and said:

'We can't go any further like this. Take off your packs and try to get some rest. Each man find a tree to put his feet on.'

To find a tree was necessary for lying down. It prevented a man from sliding down the steep hillside in his sleep. But none of us slept, though we were thoroughly exhausted. Despite the tree we found ourselves sliding until our legs bent double against the tree trunk. A soldier indiscreetly lit a cigarette and it was snatched away. Some were losing all sense of caution due to frayed nerves and sickness. To cap it all the rains came and we pulled out our groundsheets and cowered under them in the damp, smelly mould.

At the first sign of dawn we rose and set off again. As the light increased we began to see where we were going. Trees took shape and pot-holes became visible; our progress was much easier. In time we emerged from the forest and found ourselves in the valley. We decided to make for the shelter of the trees at the end of the ravine on the opposite bank of the stream. On both sides and in front of us towered the wood-covered sides of the valley. Looking back, I was amazed at the steepness of the mountain we had descended in the all-obscuring gloom. Down here, in this deep cleft in the earth, there were no foot paths. The ground was strewn with boulders and the stream splashed along at a brisk flow between the rocks, making waterfalls where it hurtled over stone ledges. The air was filled with the roar of rushing waters. Masses of rich green vegetation spread everywhere in loose profusion. It was like a lost world. Nothing moved in its depths save the flowing stream and the thirty-odd men who filed along the river bank. Even the

birds and brightly-coloured butterflies seemed to have forgotten
this valley. It would have seemed peaceful but for the Japanese who
camped on the road that circumnavigated the ravine; the convoy-
road to Kohima which lay on the hilltops above us. We edged
across a water fall and the strong current whipped at our ankles.
The spray stung our faces. We forded the river and arrived at the
end of the valley where we toiled the hill-slopes and buried ourselves
in the forest.

'And here,' said the Colonel, 'we stay all day—until dusk at least.
Every man will fill his bottle and chagul and get a wash, but no one
must stay by the river more than a few minutes. The Japanese are
above and can see into the valley, so when you have washed get back
here under the trees and remain here. Get as much rest as you can.'

MAD FORTNIGHT

BY F. SPENCER CHAPMAN

WAR CAME THROUGH THE JUNGLES *to a fat, complacent Malaya in 1942. The British High Command, sitting behind the world's most expensive bastion at Singapore, looked smugly towards Japan across the sea and was completely unprepared for the blow which was struck from behind. Only the year before the High Command had rejected stay-behind and guerrilla training as 'an extravagant and impractical notion'. And even though the 101 Special Training School was set up by September, 1941, the British ambassador at Bangkok, Siam, did everything within his power to prevent this group from operating 'on the ground that such preparations were unnecessary and would merely upset the people'. In October a detailed plan for guerrilla operations was turned down by the Governor and Commander-in-Chief in Malaya. The Chinese, who comprised almost a third of the population, were Communists and could not be armed.*

With the surprise Japanese landings up the peninsula and the quick surrender at Singapore, the picture changed. Guerrilla warfare was the only means available to fight the invader. Everything that could be done to prevent the Japanese from capitalizing on this rich conquest in tin and rubber had to be done.

The Malayan Communist Party, linked directly to Mao Tse-tung's Chinese Communists, took the field. It was wholly Chinese. The Malayans, once a fierce and war-like people, were now passive and indifferent. Very few concerned themselves with the war being fought across their peninsula.

With only the Chinese as allies, a few British officers and men crossed through the jungles deep into the rear of the Japanese and began to fight. Lieutenant-Colonel F. Spencer Chapman tells this story of his early activities as a guerrilla.

O N the night of February 1, 1942, we went into action and for the next fortnight operated almost every night. Although, as I write, it is four and a half years ago, every detail of that mad fortnight remains in my mind with far more clarity than many events that have happened since. Our routine was to leave the hideout at about 5 p.m., with our faces and hands darkened and wearing battle-dress carefully camouflaged with patches of mud. Each of us carried a tommy-gun, a pistol, and two grenades, as well as army packs filled with explosive and the various requisites for making up charges.

In order to protect the people in the valley, as well as for the security of our hideout, we made it a definite rule at first never to operate within five miles of our base, except in Tanjong Malim itself, which was just under four miles away. Normally we tried to return to the edge of the jungle well before dawn and then to find our way back to the hideout with a torch, which Leu Kim had given us. To follow a jungle path, even on a moonlit night, it was necessary to use a light of some sort, so we put a green leaf inside the glass, not only to make the torch less bright, but to accustom our eyes to a dim light. Outside the jungle we made a point of never using a torch at all, and it was remarkable how quickly our eyes got used to the dark. When our only battery ran out, we discovered that a few fireflies or luminous centipedes in the reflector of a torch gave quite enough light to read a map, lay a charge, or even follow a path. We all gave up smoking, as our lives depended on our senses working at full efficiency, and the use of tobacco certainly affects one's sense of smell.

I was now to learn that navigation in thick mountainous jungle is the most difficult in the world—and I had always rather fancied myself at map reading and finding my way in all types of country from Greenland to Australia. In the first place, it is quite impossible to find out where you are on the map. The limit of your visibility is fifty to a hundred yards, and even if you are on some steep hill-side, where a small landslide has opened up a window through which you can catch a glimpse of another steep blue tree-clad hillside, you are none the wiser, as one hill is exactly like another. There *are* no landmarks—and if there were, you could not see them. Another difficulty is that there is no way of judging distance: it took us more than a week to realize we were taking eight hours to travel one mile on the map instead of the three or four miles we imagined, judging by the amount of energy we were expending.

Perhaps the greatest impediment to navigation is that, having decided to move in a certain direction, you are quite unable to do so owing to the difficulties of the terrain. We were continually forced off our course by swamps, thickets, precipices, outcrops of rock, and rivers. It was impossible even to follow a ridge unless it was very steep and clearly marked.

As I was responsible for the navigation, and because my eyesight seemed to be much better than that of the others, I always went in front, followed by Sartin and then Harvey, whose cheerful bulk gave me great confidence as rearguard. We invariably walked in single file within touching distance if it were dark and further apart out in the open or in moonlight. We evolved a special system of signals, so that it was rarely necessary to talk. We made a clicking noise between the upper teeth and side of the tongue—the sound used to encourage a horse. This is an excellent signal, as it can be made very softly and on a still night it will carry a great distance. It is a sound that does not unduly attract attention, as it might well be a bird, an insect, or a rubber nut falling. A single click meant *Stop* or *Danger*, and two clicks indicated *Go on* or *O.K.* The only other signal we needed—for such signals must be as few as possible and absolutely unmistakable—was a rallying cry, which I alone made, to call the party together again if one of us were lost or if we had scattered in a sudden emergency. The signal used was the hunting cry of the British Tawny Owl. This piercing cry carries for a great distance even in thick woodland, cannot be confused with any other cry heard in the Malayan jungle, yet to the uninitiated—and we included the Japs in this class—it passes without notice in the variety of weird nocturnal voices.

Before setting out we practised walking and running past each other to make sure that no bit of metal caught the light and nothing such as a half-empty box of matches could betray us by its rattle. We even wrapped our tommy-guns in adhesive tape to stop them shining in the moonlight. With a little practice we learned to walk heel first on hard ground and toe first on soft ground, so that we passed absolutely silently, and with our camouflaged clothes and darkened faces were virtually invisible. To walk in this way requires much practice and, as it calls into use muscles not normally used, is extraordinarily exhausting at first. It was certainly very effective, for time and time again we passed within a few yards of natives, and unless they happened to be looking straight at us they would be unaware of our presence. Often, seeing us moving silently in the darkness, superstitious Malays and more particularly Tamils would frighten us in turn by uttering a scream and rushing away.

If we were operating far from our base or ran into trouble, we did not take risks in order to hurry home, but returned in broad daylight in our disguise as Tamils. As soon as we saw the dawn approaching we would make for the jungle, go in some distance (later always walking up the course of a stream because the Japs brought two Alsatian police dogs to Tanjong Malim to track us), eat some food, and sleep for a few hours. If the water in the streams looked unhealthy, we could always be sure of finding uninfected water in the cups attached to the rubber trees to catch the latex—though it was often thick with the wriggling larvæ of mosquitoes. Sometimes, if we were far enough away from a path, we would even light a fire as in the jungle smoke disperses long before it reaches the treetops. Then we would take our tommy-guns to pieces and pack them, our battle-dress, army packs, and anything else suspicious, into innocent-looking gunny-bags that we had brought for the purpose, make up our faces, arms, and legs, and put on our Tamil clothes. We always kept a pistol and a grenade tucked into the tops of our *sarongs* in case of emergency.

Here Harvey came into his own, as he was a born buffoon and not only spoke Tamil fluently but had all the right gestures of arm and head, and really looked like a Tamil—indeed, he even smelled like a Tamil, for the *kampong* dogs, which at once saw through Sartin's and my disguise, never barked at him. Often we came upon people too suddenly to turn aside, and Harvey usually made a point of talking to them. I do not know what the genuine Tamils thought about it, but I am convinced that the Chinese and Malays, and certainly the Japs, were taken in by our disguise. Quite often we saw in the distance patrols of Japanese cyclists, presumably looking for us, and once we had to stop and speak to them. I was terrified, but Harvey rose to the occasion admirably and whined to them in abject Tamil.

In spite of the equality of all races in their much-vaunted brotherhood of New East Asia, if you met a Japanese—whether you were a Chinese, Malay, or Tamil—you had to cover your face with both hands and bow down low before him. If you were afraid that you were rather tall for a Tamil, that your features were rather European, and that some of the stain had run off your face with the sweat, you were only too glad to cover your face with your hands and bow down before anybody. I consoled myself with noticing that the Japs did not have their weapons ready, and as I bowed low I pressed my elbow reassuringly against the butt of my .38, which I could have drawn at the least sign of danger.

We would walk home through the rubber and jungle, avoiding as far as possible the *kampongs* and roads. When we reached our hide-out, we would bathe in the stream which ran only fifty yards away, eat the enormous meal that Leu Kim always left for us, tell the old

man all about our last raid if he were there, then sleep solidly until
it was time to get ready to go out again.

As we were far too small a party and far too tired to be able to
maintain a sentry during the day, we had to rely on booby traps
which only Leu Kim and Abang knew how to pass in safety. Also
we prepared a getaway through the back of the hideout into a
ravine which led across the tin-tailing towards the pipe line. Our
only scare was when some passing Malays, probably the men who
guarded the pipe line, saw us bathing in the stream; but nothing
happened and probably they had the sense to hold their tongues.
During our fortnight's operations—except on this occasion—we
were never once, as far as I know, recognized as Europeans, though
we must have been seen by hundreds of Japs, Indians, Malays, and
Chinese.

Our first raid was carried out immediately to the south of
Tanjong Malim. We crossed the Bernam river into Escot Estate
as soon as it was really dark, then followed the wide estate road past
the coolie lines to the railway and underneath it to the road. As
this area was only three hours' walk from our camp, we had at
least six hours in which to operate. Our objective was the bridge a
mile south of the railway station, but when we reached it we found
that it was a much more formidable target than I had remembered.
It was of the heavier type of those used on the Malayan railways,
in which the bridge is suspended from semi-circular girders. It was
far too solid to demolish with the small amount of explosive that
the three of us were able to carry—always our limiting factor—so
we buried a charge of about thirty pounds of plastic explosives
(P.E.) in the middle of the line against the abutment of the north
side of the bridge. This charge was connected to a pressure switch
placed beneath the rail, so that it would be set off by the weight of
the engine. We hoped that the next train to pass would thus be
derailed and, with any luck, would fall against one side of the bridge
and overturn the whole structure, so that both train and bridge
would crash into the river and road below.

Having hidden every sign of our handiwork, we walked up the
line to our next objective—a heavy masonry bridge by which the
road crosses the railway. This again was quite beyond our means,
so we contented ourselves with walking back up the line, setting a
number of five-pound charges, each of which was to be detonated
by a simple delayed-action device called a time pencil. In this type
of device, the operator, when all is ready, squeezes a copper tube

and thus breaks a phial of acid which gradually eats through a fine wire. When this wire is dissolved, a spring is liberated which forces a striker against a percussion cap, thus igniting an instantaneous fuse. The length of the delay (denoted by coloured bands on the outside of the pencil) is regulated by the thickness of the wire and varies from half an hour to twenty-four hours.

The advantage of both the pressure switch and time pencil is that the operator has time to get well clear of the scene before things start to happen; but the time pencil is not so effective as the pressure switch, which will not only demolish the line but will derail, and possibly wreck and overturn, the train that sets it off. A fog signal placed on top of the line is as effective as a pressure switch, but as it is clearly visible it should only be used if it is quite certain that the train will arrive before daylight. Time pencils, however, were very useful to detonate small charges set up and down the line on either side of a derailing charge—as long as none of them went off before the arrival of the train. The point of this is that once a train has been derailed, the line keeps blowing up on either side of the wreckage for another twenty-four hours so that breakdown gangs are distinctly discouraged, if not actually prevented, from reaching the scene of the original demolition. It will be seen that demolishing a railway line gives plenty of scope for ingenuity. It has been said that the dynamiter's dream is to cause the head-on collision of two trains, both full of troops, in the middle of a tunnel. Though we never achieved this, we did our best to keep the Japs from getting stale.

By now we had used up our night's ration of explosive—one hundred pounds was the most the three of us could carry in addition to our weapons and other gear—but before we started for home I swarmed up the telegraph posts in several places and cut the lines with pliers. There were about thirty wires, and I dared not cut all of them in any one span lest the resulting tension on only one side of the post should pull it down—and me with it. As we were on our way through the rubber, we heard to our unspeakable delight a train leaving Tanjong Malim station half a mile away and starting very laboriously down the line. Our excitement was so great that we could scarcely breathe.

The train came on down the line so slowly that it seemed hardly to be moving. We gripped each others' hands to control our agitation. The train drew nearer and nearer, yard by yard, clanking and chugging and wheezing. Surely it must have reached the charge! Had something gone wrong? Suddenly there was a most blinding flash followed by a crash that shattered the night and reverberated across the valley. Fragments of metal whizzed into the air and fell with a loud thud some seconds afterwards, hundreds of yards from the scene of demolition. The train clanked to a standstill and there was a loud noise of escaping steam and shouting.

We longed to go and look at it, but there was now a brilliant moon and we thought it wiser to get home and ask Leu Kim next day to find out how much damage we had done. On our way home we heard two more explosions and the Chinese reported several others next day. We discovered to our disappointment that the train had merely left the line after being derailed and had neither turned over nor done much harm to the bridge, but the locomotive was completely wrecked.

As we heard that the Japs had sent armed patrols round the *kampongs* to the south of Tanjong Malim and had arrested several Chinese, we decided on the following night to go in the other direction. Our first attempt to reach this target area was abortive. We set off with Abang as guide to take a short cut which was supposed to follow the Sungei Salak to the main road, from where we intended to walk the four-odd miles down a side road to Kampong Behrang station. Abang found he did not know the way, and after we had disturbed the occupants of several isolated huts and had been shot at by a Chinese, who probably thought we were after his ducks, we became discouraged and returned.

On the following night we tried to cut straight across to the railway, our objective being a group of iron bridges just south of Kampong Behrang and about seven miles up the line from the scene of our last raid. We planned to go to the end of the pipe line and then down the lane to the main road, but as we did not know the way across the intervening two miles of rubber to the railway line, we asked Leu Kim to provide a guide. Much to our surprise, not a single one of his Chinese dared to accompany us, and old Leu Kim was so disgusted with them that he volunteered to come himself. He insisted on walking in front, carrying the tommy-gun, in comic exaggeration of the correct crouch that we had shown him and ready to shoot up the first Jap he should meet! On this raid we were also accompanied by a strange Chinese, vouched for by Leu Kim, who said he was an anti-Japanese soldier. As this man's Malay was poor, Harvey had some difficulty in conversing with him, but at last it was agreed he should act as a porter, which meant that we could take another forty pounds of explosive.

It took us more than three hours to cover the two miles of

Behrang Estate between the end of the Sungei Salak lane and the railway. The ground was a maze of small hillocks, streams, isolated strips of jungle, and patches of seedling rubber. Once there was a burst of firing about a mile behind us in the outskirts of Tanjong Malim. Leu Kim said it was a band of Chinese gangsters who were molesting the Malays, and cursed them loudly. When we reached the railway, the old man left us, saying that he would sleep at his rubber estate near by and return home next day.

Soon after we had started walking north up the railway line, we saw what we thought was a Japanese patrol approaching us. The moon was behind us and seeing them some distance away, we hid in the long grass beside the line. Some wore wide-brimmed hats, and they walked very noisily and seemed exhausted. As they passed there was a peculiar odour of sour sweat and tobacco which was strangely familiar. It was not till some time after that we realized they were probably British soldiers, but I decided not to go after them. We might be wrong, and in any case they would only be an embarrassment to us (and to Leu Kim), and we could have done little to help them.

As we passed some Tamil coolie lines, some huge dogs set up a fiendish barking and the Tamils ran out with sticks. Our Chinese was very frightened and insisted on rushing into a thicket where he thrashed about like an elephant. This drew the hunt away from us, but it was some time before we could collect him again.

Soon after this incident we started putting charges on the line. Sartin used to supervise this work, while I helped him and Harvey kept guard. We had found an ideal place for a derailment, where there was a curve above an embankment, and had just finished laying the charge when Sartin suddenly gasped and said, 'Christmas! You're lucky men!' It seems that we certainly were! Ten pounds of guncotton had been carefully placed beneath the outer rail and connected by detonating fuse to the pressure switch, which then had to be packed up carefully with stones so that it just touched the lower surface of the rail. While doing this, Sartin had pushed it up too hard and the spring had gone off—but, by the grace of God, the cap was a dud and had failed to detonate the charge.

Dawn was not far distant, so we decided to put all the rest of our explosive, about twenty-five pounds of P.E., on a small girder bridge just south of Kampong Behrang station, and to detonate it with a pressure switch. A job like this used to take us about half an hour, as separate charges had to be placed against every rail and girder, each one connected by detonating or instantaneous fuse so

14

that, as the pressure of the train fired the switch, all the charges would detonate simultaneously. Then each lump of P.E. had to be carefully lashed or jammed in position so that it would not be shaken off by the vibration of the approaching train. As far as possible we prepared the charges before we left camp, but there was always a good deal of work to be done at the last moment, usually against time and in darkness.

On this occasion we had almost finished the job when I thought I heard a train far away to the north. The others listened, but as they could hear nothing I came to the conclusion I was mistaken. Soon afterwards, however, we heard a definite whistle. There was no doubt that a train was approaching fast. We had intended to detonate the charges with a pressure switch placed at some distance from the charges so that the bridge would be demolished in front of the train and—with any luck—it would be unable to get across the gap and be thrown down the embankment in a glorious tangle. But now, hearing the train so near, we simply put a fog signal on top of the line and hastily connected it with the main fuse leading from the charges.

Suddenly the train whistled again as it came through the station less than a mile distant. In a minute it would be upon us. We hastily finished off the job and, collecting our bits and pieces, pushed them into our packs. It took us some time to find the precious pliers, and then Sartin remembered he had put his box of detonators in a safe place on the bridge. By now the train was in sight, just up the line. With one accord we started to race down the footpath beside the track, having no desire to be run over as well as blown up. The Chinese took off like a sprinter and ran so fast that we soon lost sight of him. Over our shoulders we could see the dark mass of the train bearing down on to the bridge with sparks spouting from its funnel. On one side of the line there was a hill covered with thick jungle, so we turned aside and dashed down the banking, only to find ourselves up to our waists in a foul swamp. At this moment there was a blinding white flash, which gave me a glimpse of the other two, open-mouthed and holding their tommy-guns up out of the water.

Almost at the same moment came a shattering explosion, which nearly burst our eardrums and shook even the soft mud in which we were stuck, followed by a frightful grinding and rending of metal. A shower of missiles roared and whistled above us to crash into the jungle or splash into the wide swamp on the other side of the line. To our horror the train did not stop, but dragged itself slowly on over the bridge, clanking hideously. We were momentarily floodlit as the cab, bristling with Japs, passed less than ten yards in front of us and came to a standstill a little further on. Above the loud hiss of escaping steam we heard some altercation. Then two chattering Tamil drivers with an escort of Jap soldiers armed with tommy-guns and flashing their torches walked back between us and the goods wagons to examine the wrecked bridge. We covered them with our tommy-guns as they passed, but they did not see us, and after a few minutes they returned accompanied by three more Japs, presumably from the brake-van at the back of the train. As the locomotive was quite useless, they abandoned it and set off down the line towards Tanjong Malim.

As soon as they were out of sight, we extricated ourselves from the bog and went to have a look at the engine. We dared not approach too near, as water and steam were gushing out on to the line and we expected it to blow up at any moment. Harvey insisted on lobbing a grenade into the open door of the furnace, and we took cover as it exploded. We found that both the twelve-inch steel girders of the bridge and one rail were cut through, but the charge on the other rail had apparently been displaced by the vibration of the train. Both brick abutments had crumbled, and the rails, especially the severed one, sagged right down, yet the train had been able to drag itself over the gap and remain on the rails on the other side. We wanted to finish off the job, but we found that our Chinese friend, who had vanished when the train 'chased' us, had disappeared into the jungle with all the rest of our fuse in his pack. He eventually returned to our hideout, without his pack, having been lost for two days.

By this time it was already beginning to get light, and as we were afraid some Japs might appear from Behrang station, we made our way through the rubber, being careful to avoid being seen by the Chinese and Malays who were already abroad, having been woken up by the explosion. At last we reached a patch of thick jungle, and here we knew we were safe.

When we undressed to bathe in the river, we found many bloated leeches stuck to various parts of our bodies. I had been bitten round the waist and neck, since the foul creatures, being unable to get at my legs, had worked their way up my clothes until they could find an opening. I had pulled off scores and did not know any had crawled through until I felt the blood running down my chest. Harvey was very badly bitten about the ankles and hands. He had been using a stick and the leeches had crawled up it to reach their

14*

favourite of all places—the web-like flesh between the bases of the fingers. Sartin had also been bitten all over the legs, as they had crawled through the eyeholes of his boots and through the folds of his puttees. As we removed the surfeited leeches, Harvey regaled us with charming stories of people who had died from leeches—or the swelling resulting from their bites—blocking the more intimate orifices of the body. The theory is that leeches should not be pulled off, as their teeth stay in and fester. They should be removed by touching them with salt, tobacco, a solution of areca nut, or a cigarette end. My experience is that the wounds bleed just as much and are just as likely to become infected, however they are removed.

After a few more expeditions against the railway we came to the conclusion that we needed a change. A single line, the nearest point of which was three and a half miles away from our base, did not give us much scope without returning too often to the same spot, unless we could somehow procure bicycles. Since we were now beginning to meet Jap patrols on the line, it became obvious that the railway was no longer a healthy place for us. Also we were not quite certain how effective our demolitions had been, since we dared not return to the scene of our operations. True, we used to hear our charges exploding at all hours of the day and night, and Leu Kim used to bring up encouraging reports of trains wrecked and lying on their sides, but we were afraid that several of the charges had not gone off—presumably owing to dud caps—and that even when they had detonated, the damage was not as great as it should have been.

Where we had been able to examine results, our demolitions had not been entirely successful, and Sartin even began to wonder if the explosive had deteriorated from damp in the jungle. Another cause of mistrust of the efficiency of our methods was the extraordinary speed with which the Jap breakdown gangs managed to get the line in running order again; and I came to the conclusion—though Sartin would never agree to this—that a train, at any rate a Malayan train, can jump a six-foot gap in one rail. To make quite certain of the job at least ten feet should be cut, preferably of both rails. Yet another worry was that on the railway we were getting through our explosive at the rate of a hundred pounds a day. Leu Kim had averted a crisis by securing a tin of five hundred detonators, a roll of safety fuse, and several hundred pounds of blasting gelignite from a tin-mining friend, but even so we were finishing the explosive too fast and not making use of any of our large supply of tommy-gun ammunition or grenades. My conclusion was that we should turn our attention to the main road.

On our visits to the railway line south of Tanjong Malim, which for several miles is only separated from the main road by a narrow strip of rubber, we had had plenty of opportunity of observing the road traffic at night, and while returning by daylight from more distant raids on the line north of the town, we had spent many hours making careful traffic counts. In the daytime practically all motor transport, including a few armoured vehicles, innumerable lorries and staff cars, and a good many motor-cycles, moved southward, and there seemed to be little attempt to drive in convoys. There were also large patrols of cycle troops going south and a few civilian cyclists and pedestrians moving in either direction. At night civilians seemed to avoid the road entirely and we saw no cyclists, but large convoys of trucks and staff cars moved southward at any hour of the night, driving very fast with headlights full on and with no proper interval between vehicles. In other words, they were just asking to be ambushed.

One night, when returning home from the railway, we noticed a pile of glowing embers at the roadside, and on investigating we found that six one-ton trucks were parked almost touching each other in the grass beside the road. There were no sidelights burning and no sign of the drivers or any sentries, though we dared not go too close in case they were being really clever and watching from a distance. Unfortunately we had no explosive left, but Sartin remembered that we had hidden about twenty pounds of P.E., which we had left over one night, in the roots of a rubber tree less than a mile away. While Harvey stayed to watch the trucks, Sartin and I collected the explosive as fast as we could. When we returned—after giving and receiving the double click of recognition—Harvey said that judging from the snoring he had heard coming from the trucks, they were full of troops, though it might have come from the sentries or the drivers. While Harvey, with his tommy-gun ready, continued to keep watch, Sartin and I crawled underneath the lorries and jammed two pounds of P.E. on each one just between the crankcase and the clutch. As we worked our way along the line of trucks, we connected the charges together with detonating fuse—a job which took over an hour to complete. As we wanted to see what would happen, we set off the charge with a copper-tube igniter and four feet of safety fuse, thus giving us two whole minutes to crawl away and hurry to a safe distance down the road. When the charges exploded, we were most disappointed that not one of the trucks caught fire—though neither they nor their drivers were much further use to the Japanese war effort. After this we usually took with us a few clams—small magnetic bombs which adhere to metal and can be set off with a time pencil—to use against vehicles parked by the roadside. Once we were able to attach three of these while their drivers were sitting round a fire a short distance away.

Our first road ambush was quite fortuitous, as it resulted from our desire to try out a new bomb we had invented. We had several hundred pounds of gelignite which had suffered so much from the climate that all the nitro-glycerine was running out of it. The textbooks say that such gelignite is very dangerous and should be thrown away, but in our circumstances we were very reluctant to waste good explosive. As the stuff was very sticky, Sartin had stored it inside a section of bamboo—and this had given me an idea. We had often discussed the possibility of setting mines in the roadway, but had given up the idea as we had no apparatus for boring holes through the metal of the road. We had, indeed, suggested scooping out a hole in the soft side of the embankment to set a crater charge beneath the middle of the road, but, though this would crater the road and cause a certain amount of annoyance, it would use up a great deal of explosive, it would not damage any vehicles, and the Japs would soon fill up the crater again. But it struck me that a bomb on the surface, concealed in a section of bamboo—which, on a Malayan road, would not attract attention—would be very effective and would be easy to prepare.

The bomb would be detonated by a pull switch, a device similar in principle to a pressure switch. This switch is buried in the explosive or connected to it by instantaneous fuse. Then, at the required moment, the operator from a safe distance pulls a length of fine piano wire which is quite invisible at night, and detonates the charge. A great advantage of detonating a mine by this means is that it gives much more control. Not only can you choose the exact moment for detonating the charge, but, if an unsuitable target appears, you can let it pass harmlessly over the danger spot and wait for better game. If it is unwise to wait, a trip wire can be laid across the road so that whatever runs into it is automatically blown up.

Our first trial of the bomb was carried out early one morning on the way back from an expedition to Kalumpang railway station, three miles south of Tanjon Malim. Along this section of the line we had left about fifty separate charges to be detonated with time pencils. Each one consisted of two-pound slabs of guncotton placed just beneath the junction of two rails so that both of them would be damaged and would have to be replaced. We had discovered that the Jap repair gangs were very quick at filling up large craters and replacing damaged bridges, but we thought a fusillade of small explosions at odd intervals of time up and down a mile or two of line might keep them away and render the railway unusable for at least twenty-four hours.

We had already prepared a bomb consisting of a section of bamboo about eighteen inches long, filled with five pounds of gelignite and a pull switch. On the way down the line earlier in the night we had crossed over from the railway to the road and found an excellent place for our ambush just by the fiftieth milestone (from Kuala Lumpur). Indeed, our bomb, which was oozing nitro-glycerine, seemed to be in such a dangerous state that we hated carrying it further than was necessary and we hid it behind the milestone and collected it again on our way back.

The rubber came up to the edge of the road and ended in a low bank which gave sufficient cover from the explosion, while a little path back to the railway provided an excellent getaway. We scattered several other bits of bamboo on the road, so that if any driver was suspicious he could satisfy himself that they were quite innocent. We then put the bomb in the middle of the road, anchored it to the milestone, and took up our position behind the bank.

Success in an operation of this sort depends very largely on careful planning, and before we had left our hideout each of us knew exactly what he had to do. Sartin was to have the honour of pulling the line if I hit him on the back, which I would do if I decided that the target was worthy—but not too worthy—of our attention. In this ambush, as we were such a small party and not in a very good defensive position, I decided that I would only stop a single Jap car or a very small convoy. Sartin was to pull the line just as the nose of the first car passed over the bomb, then we would all take cover and hope for the best. The moment after the explosion, Harvey and I, from behind the bank, would each throw two grenades. As soon as these had gone off, we would each empty a tommy-gun magazine into any target that we could see, then race like hell back to the railway line, on the far side of which we would rendezvous to make sure all was well, cross the Sungei Inki by a footbridge that we had placed there some time before, and go home straight across Escot Estate.

Unfortunately this ambush, like many more important battles in history, did not go exactly as planned, because we had gone into it far too lightheartedly at the end of a heavy night's work. It was a brilliant moonlit night and we lay behind the bank in a state of intense excitement. There was a sharp explosion to the south—this was one of the shorter delays we had put on the line. Then we heard a train coming down from the north and we wondered if it would be able to get over the gap cut by the explosion that had just occurred; but the train stopped at Tanjong Malim—probably a night watchman had heard the explosion and they were holding up all traffic until they had examined the line. Suddenly we saw head-lights approaching down the road.

The great moment had come. I counted the lights of six cars, but I could not tell what sort of vehicles they were. As this might be our last chance that night, I hit Sartin on the shoulder and we all pressed our bodies down into the soft soil. Harvey and I pulled the pins out of our grenades. As far as we could make out on reconstructing the scene later, the bomb must have exploded beneath the petrol tank and ignited that too, for not only was there the usual flash and explosion, which almost threw us upright, but the flash was followed by a steady and brilliant blaze which lit up the whole scene like a stage setting. As I threw my grenades, I caught a glimpse of another large closed truck crashing into the burning wreckage and the third one turning broadside on with a scream of brakes. After the explosion there was a harsh stutter as Harvey emptied his tommy-gun in one burst up the road. I did the same and then found myself racing down the path, flood-lit by the funeral pyre of the Jap lorries.

It was not until we had reached the railway line that the Japs opened fire, at first sporadically and then at an increasing tempo. Apparently they were not expecting trouble and none of them had his weapons ready. As we dashed across the line, we saw in the clear moonlight a party of men with lanterns a hundred yards up the track. They opened fire too and started shouting—though for all they could see we might easily be Japs escaping from the blazing convoy. This must have been a patrol sent down the line from Tanjong Malim on hearing the earlier explosion down to the south. As we plunged through the rubber and then raced along a footpath to gain the estate road, on which we could run even faster, the night was hideous with the noise of rifle, machine-gun, and even mortar fire. Our whole action had taken only half a minute, yet the Japs kept up their firing practice—for they could not possibly have seen anything to shoot at—for over an hour. It was really most frightening, though none of the bullets or bombs came very near us. Having safely passed the estate coolie lines, we lay down to rest and recover our breath, congratulating ourselves on a very successful, though very terrifying, ambush.

This experience taught us a great deal, and as the Japs would probably be prepared in future, we determined from now on only to carry out an ambush in cuttings, so that we should have adequate protection from enemy fire and the bursting of our own grenades as well as the possible explosion of the vehicles. We remembered having noticed several suitable places where there were small cuttings on the west side of the lonely four miles of road between the end of the Sungei Salak lane and the turning off to Behrang station. There was rubber on the upper side of this road and virgin jungle on the other. Although this section of the road was rather nearer to our hideout than we had intended to operate, it was the only suitable stretch within reach of our camp. But as most of our operations hitherto had been to the south of Tanjong Malim, the Japs would, we hoped, conclude that we were based on that side of the town and leave the northern side in peace.

We now improved our ambush technique. In order to cover a greater number of vehicles, the three of us took up positions about thirty yards apart, depending on the nature of the cutting. As our supply of grenades was limited and they were rather heavy to carry so far, we made our own bombs by putting a stick of gelignite, with detonator and fuse attached, inside a tin or a section of bamboo, then filling it up with several pounds of road metal. The fuse was lit by pressing a small igniter in a copper tube, thus obviating the use of matches. One great advantage of making our own bombs was that we could vary the length of the fuses, so that the explosions would continue for some time after we had left the scene and would discourage the Japs from answering our fire till we were well back in the rubber. We continued to stop the leading vehicle with a bomb operated with a pull switch, then emptied our tommy-guns in a few short bursts, threw several grenades, changed the magazines of the guns while waiting for the bombs to explode, fired another magazine, then threw as many home-made bombs as we had had time to make, and ran back along prearranged routes to a R.V. at my signal. All through the action, we shouted and yodelled at the tops of our voices not only to encourage ourselves, but to make the enemy think we were a considerable force.

Sometimes the vehicles contained stores only and then there was little opposition, but more than once we attacked convoys of troops, and this always started a scrap which lasted until we were far out of range. After we had carried out three full-scale ambushes along this section of road, in a different place each time, and one more to the south, the Japs defeated us by the simple expedient of not using the road at all at night. We soon got very tired indeed of waiting hour after hour for convoys that did not appear, and we considered ourselves too small a force to attack them in daytime.

Our second ambush on the road to the south was very nearly disastrous. As the country there was fairly level, there were no real cuttings, and Sartin's first grenade bounced back off the canvas cover of a lorry and exploded within a few feet of where he lay behind a low bank, stunning him and covering him with earth. When we retired, he failed to appear at my usual rallying cry and we had already given him up for dead when he joined us, having had to wait until the Japs ceased fire before crawling back. He reported that on this occasion the Japs were firing into the rubber on both sides of the road. He also saw at least thirty casualties.

After we had been operating for about a fortnight we came to the conclusion that we should have to move. Now that we had been forced to operate so near home that our battles were plainly audible from Leu Kim's *kongsi*-house, the old man was getting more and more embarrassed by our presence. He said that his wives gave him no peace and insisted that we should go, and that he was afraid some of his coolies would soon betray us. Wholesale massacres had been carried out in several *kampongs* south of Tanjong Malim, and Jap patrols had already come half-way up the Sungei Salak side road, and Leu Kim was afraid that somebody had given some information against him. He could not sleep at night for fear of what would happen to him and his people if the Japs found out anything further.

By now we were completely and absolutely exhausted and our muscles and nerves could stand no more. On each raid, carrying loads of forty or fifty pounds, we had covered an average of ten or twelve miles and been away from our base for as many hours. The greatest risk inherent in living dangerously—whether it is rock-climbing, driving a motor-car fast, or shooting tiger or Japs—is that through overconfidence or overexhaustion one begins to relax the vigilance and the taking of every little precaution on which one's life depends. I had noticed that this was already happening to us: we had begun to forget the taste of fear. Hecate's words in *Macbeth*, 'Security is mortals' chiefest enemy', are an excellent motto for guerrillas. We all agreed that the last fortnight had been the most marvellous time of our lives—far more exciting and satisfactory than hunting or big-game shooting. But when we had started

operations, we had hardly recovered from our crossing of the Main
Range and since then we had all steadily lost weight with the strain
of going out night after night and of being systematically hunted
by the enemy. Even back in our hideout we never felt really safe.

While Harvey and I thoroughly enjoyed dressing up and pretending to ourselves that we did not care a damn for the Japs, we all
found difficulty in sleeping at night, and Sartin, who showed the
strain more than any of us, had begun to have such nightmares
that we were getting really worried about him. Already we were
very short of explosive and fuse, and had run out of some vital
demolition devices and would have to visit our dump at Sungei
Sempan to obtain any more. The Japs seemed to have stopped using
the road and railway at night altogether, so there was not much we
could do here until we had given the area a good rest and allowed
the Japs to regain confidence.

CHAPMAN MOVED ON *and fought through most of the war as a guerrilla.
Afterwards he learned that in his activities during this two-week period
he had been so destructive that the Japanese had assigned two thousand
soldiers to the task of running down what they believed to be a force of
two hundred Australians. The destruction totalled about eight trains,
fifteen bridges, sixty cuts in the railway line, forty motor vehicles, and an
undetermined number of Japanese killed or wounded.*

AMERICAN GUERRILLA

BY IRA WOLFERT

WHEN THE AMERICANS *surrendered on Corregidor, those soldiers who were isolated throughout the three thousand islands which make up the Philippines had three choices. They could escape to Australia: some of them tried it in broken-down launches and native boats. Few of them got there. They could surrender, but few did. Or they could fall back into the hills and the isolated villages. A number did this. For months they sat and licked their wounds, got to know the natives, and dreamed of home. Finally, they started killing Japs.*

Guerrilla bands formed all over the islands. At first they were led by native desperadoes and adventurers who lived off the natives and shunned the Japs. Eventually, General MacArthur gave Colonel Wendell Fertig, a one-time mining engineer, and Commander 'Chick' Parsons of the Navy the job of organizing the guerrillas. Parsons, via submarine, served as liaison between the islands and MacArthur's South-west Pacific Command.

Fertig organized Mindanao, eliminated the bandits, and appointed Colonel Ruperto Kangleon his representative on Leyte. Kangleon had served in the Philippine Army for twenty-seven years and was the first native divisional commander appointed by MacArthur. The Filipino Colonel named Navy Lieutenant Iliff Richardson his chief of staff, and they set out to do two jobs: furnish intelligence to MacArthur and kill Japs.

The story of Long Baxter, one of the American guerrillas, shows how the men gathered and how they killed Japs. It was told by Richardson to Ira Wolfert.

TAKE a fellow like Tom Baxter. His story is a fair sample of what the guerrilla was like for the non-technician type—the fighting man type. I think Baxter's first name is Tom. We always called him 'Long'. He wasn't very tall, about five feet nine, but he was taller than the Filipinos and they gave him the nickname Long. I think he came from somewhere in the East. He's a boy in his early twenties.

Long had been an enlisted man in the Air Corps stationed at Del

Monte. He cut loose and started hiking across the hills. The hills there are empty of all people except Manobos and Minandayans. Except that the Manobos live in lean-tos built against trees and the Minandayans live on platforms in the trees, they are six of one and half a dozen of another. Maybe they know there is a war going on, but they've got their own wars to worry about. Their tribal feuds have been going on for thousands of years.

When Baxter piled all his supplies in a dugout canoe and the canoe hit a log and he lost everything and he had to depend on the hill people, his health started to go down fast.

He finally made Hinatuan on the coast, but he was in bad shape. The mayor and the chief of police invited him to dinner. They gave him a pretty fancy chow to make it last until late at night. Then the mayor took him over to show him something in a corner and the chief of police put a gun in his back and marched him off to jail. They wanted to do that late at night so none of the population would interfere. Their idea was to ingratiate themselves with the Japs, who had already been in Hinatuan twice on patrol.

They kept Long in jail for about a month, waiting for another Jap patrol to arrive. Several people offered to break him out of there, but Long was too tired and too sick and too discouraged. An orchestra came and stood outside his bars to play for him because he liked swing. They didn't play so good, but their hearts were in it. They offered to spring him, too. But he said no. What the hell was the use, he thought, of living in a tree and eating stinking meat. He'd take the prison chow.

The Japs finally arrived and brought him in slow stages to the municipal jail at Surigao. They treated him all right all the way up there. Long was parched for cigarettes. He swapped a Parker fountain pen with his guard for fifteen cigarettes and then he sat on his wooden bunk in his cell smoking up a storm. The cell was very dirty, but Long felt then it was going to be all right. (But for two weeks after that, the American was beaten and burned every day until unconscious by a pathological specimen named Captain Gidoka.)

Then on a Saturday afternoon, Long, looking out of his cell window, saw work begin on a gallows. There was a plaza back of the jail and Filipino labourers were putting it up there under the supervision of Japs. Sunday morning, Long found out the gallows was for him and another prisoner, a Filipino. The guard told him. He said the following Saturday was a day of fiesta and the Japs intended to celebrate it by hanging the two of them.

'Why?'

The guard shrugged. He did not know, but the execution was to be witnessed by the population and they were to draw a lesson from it.

Long waited all day for darkness. Those were as long hours as anybody ever has spent. His time for work was so limited. When darkness finally came, he went to work. He started in on the window bars with a beer can opener he had found in the cell.

The bars were very thick and were made out of the hardest wood there is in the world—Bayong wood, which is much harder and denser than teak, or mahogany, or oak. He found out he had to knock out two of them. With only one, the opening wouldn't be wide enough for his head. The first thing, he rubbed a groove about two inches long with the sharp point of the beer opener. Then he worked with the curved end, scraping and extracting, first on the right side of the groove, then on the left. But the curve, even from both sides, didn't cover the whole width of the bar. It left a middle part untouched. Long sharpened the handle end of the opener on the stone floor and attacked the middle part with that, chipping it out. His idea was to hollow the two bars out, top and bottom, to keep the Japs from finding out during the day what he was up to. Then, when both bars were hollowed out, he'd snap them off and go.

He couldn't work steady. Two guards walked by outside intermittently all night long. Long's cell was on the ground floor and they could easily see if anything unusual was going on. But Long always saw them coming in time. His hands got blistered up in the first two hours of work, he worked so desperately, but he kept on until first light. Then he mixed the sawdust with dirt to hide it. He made a mud of dust to stuff into the holes he had worn in the bars. At dawn he'd run his hands over the bars unostentatiously to make sure the holes didn't show.

By dawn Tuesday morning, he had hollowed out the bottom part of the two bars.

Thursday night, nine o'clock, a typhoon blew up. There was a lot of rain with the wind. Then by ten o'clock it was all over, but there had been a failure in the power plant and the street lights didn't go on again. Long waited two minutes after the guards had passed outside, counting the seconds in his mind. He figured that would give him thirteen minutes. Then he snapped the bars off. The first one came clean. The second one took tugging by both of them together, and then it didn't break off all the way at the top. There were twines of wood there still holding. When it broke, it broke with a crack like a pistol shot. Long nearly fainted, but the wind was still loud in the trees and that must have covered the sound, for no one came.

Then Long lit out for the beach. He didn't know what to do. Along came an old man, a fisherman who had been out fishing all night. He had part of his catch on a string in his hand. He gasped and nearly dropped his catch when he saw Long. He could not talk any English, but he took Long to his hut, fed him, and covered him all over with copra sacks, and Long went right to sleep.

The old man lived all alone. Late in the afternoon, Long woke up. The old man was standing over him with a pistol. There was a ten-year-old boy alongside him. Long thought he was finished.

'I am my father's son, sir,' the child said. The old man had brought him along because he spoke English. 'My brother, sir, in Army. Before he will surrender, he give my father a pistol, sir. Sir, now it is to you.'

It was a .32 and there were five rounds of ammunition with it. The old man took Long that night to a village down the coast. The whole village had buqweed except for one family.

Long stayed with this family about two weeks. The whole family worked in the fields all day except for one girl child, too young to work. She played around the house by herself and Long slept all day and all night. He hardly ever got out of bed, except for meals. (He was still weakened by his beatings.) But some fifth columnist found out he was there anyway and told the Japs, and the Jap-controlled Philippine Constabulary sent two men down to pick him up. They figured to cover the front and rear exits and holler for him to come out with his hands up. They knew his habits. They knew he had been beat up and slept all the time. So they just went at it easily and carelessly. They forgot about the little girl.

The little girl woke Long up. 'Two men,' she said. She was a wise child. She spoke in a very low tone. 'They come here, sir.'

'Go outside and play,' Long told her. 'Go quietly, but if they do not see you, run. Run as far away as you can, and play there and do not come back until it is time for supper.'

It was then about two o'clock in the afternoon.

Long had his gun with him. He had learned to sleep with it cocked by his side. In all the years I knew him, I have never known him to sleep otherwise than with his gun cocked by his side. He went quietly to the window and saw a man standing there looking at him with mouth open with surprise.

There is no glass in the window of a nipa hut. It is just an empty space. The window came about half-way up on Long. He was standing with his gun down by his side. The man reached into his back pocket for his own gun. The hammer caught on the lining. He tugged at it and Long brought his gun up past the police badge on the man's chest and shot him dead between the eyes. Then he saw the second man running for the trees. The second man had been out back answering a call of nature. He ran with his trousers around his ankles. In one hand he held his gun and with the other he was trying to pull up his trousers. He didn't want to shoot until he had cover. Long shot and hit him in the side.

'Oi God, murder,' the man screamed and spun all the way around and fell down. Long put another bullet into him. The man was still flopping. Long put a third bullet into him and waited. The man didn't flop any more. Long waited motionless for more than five minutes. He still had one bullet left. He did not want to waste it. After a while he climbed cautiously out of the window and went to the man and saw he was dead.

Long got two more guns out of the deal. The first cop had had a police positive .38 with six bullets. The second had had one of those bulldog revolvers, a .45 with six rounds in it and three more in his pocket. Now Long had three guns and sixteen bullets for them, and with these he started his own guerrilla army.

Bamboo telegraph usually brought word to one American of the existence of another. When they heard, they naturally started out for each other. In this way, Long Tom Baxter hooked up with Gordon Smith, who had been a cook in the Army Air Corps, and Dutch Geysen, a character not even Joseph Conrad would have dared invent. Dutch is dead now, I am pretty sure, but in his time he had done everything a man could do running in sail and steam between Chile and the Orient, had learned all the languages there are, pretty near, from Russian to Mandarin, French, Visayan, Portuguese, and had been in every trade from mining to running slaves for rich Chinese.

But this twenty-two or three-year-old American boy, Long Tom Baxter, was good enough to make himself the leader over even a man like that. They went up to the Mindanao mother lode mine and got a piece of iron Shelby tubing about eight inches long and grooved it with a file so that it would fragmentate when it exploded. They worked two sticks of dynamite into it, that they found in the mine, a cap and a fuse, and then plugged the tubing at each end with threaded iron stoppers. They left about two inches of fuse outside.

Then they went down to Malamono, where about twenty Japs were using the schoolhouse as a barracks. Geysen and Gordon Smith stayed on a hill there to give protective fire, and Baxter sneaked through tall grass there to an outhouse just behind the school building. They came at four o'clock, figuring to catch the Japs at chow.

The sweat from the excitement of working his way up to the outhouse had soaked through the scratch paper on Baxter's matchbox and for a long time he couldn't get a match to light. But he blew and fanned and finally a match lit and the fuse began to sputter. He held it in his hands a second or so, listening to the splutter and the Japs chattering inside the building, then heaved it straight-arm towards the window. It nearly missed. It went in just below the top.

'After that,' Baxter told me, 'nothing happened. I was running like hell. Then I looked back. The sides of the school building seemed to bulge a little. It bulged and snapped back and then things started flying through the clapboard walls.'

There were seven or eight Japs late for chow. They saw Baxter running up the hill. He couldn't run very well at the time because his legs were still sore from his prison beatings. They threw a blast at him. He was wearing a great big straw hat to keep the sun out of his eyes and give his eyes a chance to heal from the beating they had taken in prison. When he fell flat, the brim of the hat hit and turned sideways on his head. A Jap bullet took the hat right off his head, the rope tied around his chin to hold the hat on pulling out through the straw.

Dutch and Gordon Smith lit out without firing a shot to cover Long. He had to zigzag away all by himself. Maybe that was why he was leader.

After parting with old Dutch and Gordon Smith, he had fallen in with Captain Khahl Coder—the mighty Coder of the River, as he was called—and Captain Zapanta and they were sitting over some tuba with Mrs. Zapanta when a volunteer guard brought the news a Jap patrol was monkeying around in the neighbourhood. The place where they were was well hidden. It was the only good hiding place for miles. It was flat country there, mostly rice paddies. So nobody made a move except Mrs. Zapanta.

'We attack,' she said.

The men glanced at each other nervously. They knew her well.

'No, my sweet,' said her husband. 'To-day it is too warm. In the evening perhaps, if the moon is not too early.'

It was not country for a hit-and-run attack. It was very good for the hit, but for the run it was worthless.

'All right, you come in the evening, reinforce me.' Mrs. Zapanta took up her husband's gun. 'I attack now.'

'Sweet, my sweet, my very sweetest, you will kill us to force us this way.'

'I attack now.'

'But, my sweet!'

'There are Japs now. I attack now.'

Zapanta looked at the mighty Coder of the River. Then he looked at Long. He seemed very uncomfortable.

'Zapanta, my friend,' Long said, 'you certainly married a lulu.'

'What means that?'

'It means your missus is a lulu.'

'If I go where she forces,' Zapanta said, 'there is a chance I will be killed. If I do not, it is certain. She will attend to it.'

'It is clear, Zapanta, you will die of love.'

They decided finally to leave Mrs. Zapanta home. She could not run fast enough. The running would be very important in this attack. It was agreed that, to expedite the running, the soldiers with tommy-guns—'Thompson tommy-guns,' the Filipino officers called them, seeking to be formal—and with automatic rifles would throw them into a carabao wallow from which they could be retrieved later. A carabao is like a pig and cannot sweat. He needs to lie in mud twice a day. There was a good deep wallow hidden in a declivity along the line of retreat that would hide the heavy guns very well.

Long said he would cover the retreat past the wallow with his Garand.

The country did not permit ambush. There was only grass and rice paddies and an occasional tree. The guerrillas hit. They held their ground a few minutes while the Japs deployed. Then the mortars and machine-guns started and the guerrillas began to run. Long stood behind a tree. He fired at every Jap that showed his head. He fired wherever sounds of firing were coming from and between times he fired at the spaces in between.

There was one young guerrilla who ran too excitedly to think well. When he came to the wallow, instead of throwing only his gun in, he threw himself in as well. He climbed out swiftly. Then he ran swiftly. He had got about forty yards when he realized he was still carrying his gun. He ran all the way back into the bullets, threw in his gun, and turned and fled.

Long watched him admiringly. He has everything but brains, he thought.

After that, there were more little things for Long. He found a hand grenade and took up a position near a footbridge over a canyon. The canyon was almost one hundred feet deep. Jap patrols had by that time become very wary of bridges. The first Jap materialized suddenly. He had crawled on his belly to one end of the bridge. Then he had popped up and dashed across and flung himself down in the jungle on Long's side of the canyon.

Long had not intended to waste his grenade on the first. He knew if the first Jap made it, the others would become less wary. A grenade was a great rarity. It could not be employed merely on one. Long did not worry about the Jap on his side of the canyon. Since he had got his Garand one Jap anywhere did not worry him.

Then three Japs came towards the bridge. They did not crawl. They were merely crouched over. Long took the pin out of the grenade. He held it in his hand. A thousand and one, he counted, a thousand and two, a thousand and three, a thousand and four. Then he threw it as high into the air as he could over the bridge. He wanted an air burst that would kill all three Japs at once, or at least blow them off the bridge.

The grenade went in a high arc. It fell steeply. It passed the bridge without exploding and fell into the canyon and lay there silently. Long stood looking down at it disappointedly. Then boom, it went off, reverberating massively in the canyon. It must have had a ten-second fuse.

All the Japs ran frantically to the other side of the canyon, and the patrol withdrew.

Then the guerrillas all got together and decided on something big. They were going to take a town. They picked one that was fat with supplies yet did not have too much garrison, and they moved on it in three columns. Clyde Childress led one. Bill Knortz led the second, and Long led the third.

Knortz was one of the great men of the guerrillas. He had been a college and professional football player back home. Then he had joined the Air Corps. He studied judo at Hickam Field and won the black belt there. The black belt is as high as you can go in judo. The white belt is first, the brown belt is second, and then the black belt. The only way to win it is to take it off somebody who has it. I think there are only twenty of them in the world. Knortz was a big, immensely powerful, very friendly man. He always carried a BAR with two belts of ammunition—150 rounds—and two .45 calibre pistols. The guns were his undoing. Some months ago, when his banca overturned in a storm, he drowned trying to swim with them. He let go of them too late, when he was too exhausted to go much farther.

There was even a cannon for the attack on the town. It had been made by Captain Zapanta and his wife. The barrel was a piece of gas pipe, three inches in diameter. It was kept from blowing up by metal sleeves and rings. Metal wedges were hammered between the sleeves and the rings to reinforce the barrel further. The firing pin was a tapered marline-spike given tension by rubber bands made from an inner tube. The Zapantas had made three shells for their cannon from three-inch brass pipe filled with battery lead and babbitt, and junk they found around. On to the back of each they had welded a disc. The powder charge was in a case about four inches long. They filled it nearly to the brim with black powder. They wanted to make sure the shell would go. The primer was out of three shotgun shells. Mrs. Zapanta herself had done the ticklish job of forcing the three shotgun primers together and securing them into the back of the shell with sticks of wood so that the marline-spike would hit all three at once. The whole contraption was mounted on wooden wheels. The lanyard was about thirty feet long. They were pretty sure that, if the thing worked at all, there was going to be a recoil.

Where Long's column came into the town, there was an outpost and supply bodega. He started with about one hundred men. By the time he got within firing distance, there were only twenty left. The rest had faded back, getting a good head start on the retreat they expected to have to make. Long used a kind of roving-centre plan of attack. He split his twenty men into two groups of ten. They'd throw a concentrated fire into the outpost from one point, then run quickly to another point and throw concentrated fire from there. The Japs felt outnumbered and retreated into the town.

The supply bodega was full of shoes and maong—a kind of dungaree material. When Long started to empty it, he found his column had grown from twenty to three or four hundred. Not only had all his own soldiers returned, but the men of the neighbourhood were there, too, helping themselves. The civilians were hard to tell from soldier. Everybody everywhere was dressed in whatever he could find.

Long was trying to weed out the ringers when a commotion broke out near by. The Japs had left a sniper behind in a tree. Some men had surrounded the tree and ordered the sniper down. He came down quickly. He was a sturdy little boy about ten years old with long, thick, dry black hair that stood up wildly and seemed to be trying to fly from his head. The Japs had given him a rifle and ten pesos and had told him to shoot for the emperor, *banzai*. He had fired three or four times, but had not hit anything.

His twelve-year-old sister had been watching fearfully. They stood the boy with the back of his head against the tree. Then they knocked in his face with a rifle butt. When Long came up, they were holding a tin cup under his chin to catch the blood. The cup was nearly full.

'What in the name of God is going on here?' cried Long.

'We make her drink it.' The man who spoke pointed to the boy's sister who had been forced to stand there.

Long kicked the man in the stomach. 'You Jap-brained son of a bitch,' he said, 'I'll kill you.'

There was an angry growl from the crowd. The crowd moved on Long.

'It is an example for the people,' they said.

The little girl broke loose and ran. A man ran after her with the cup of blood.

'You stop!' screamed Long. He pointed his gun at the man. 'Stop, you bastard, or I'll shoot your guts out.'

The man threw the cup at the girl, hitting her and splattering her. She ran on wailing with terror and he turned sullenly to face Long.

'There are going to be courts martial out of this,' said Long. 'I'll see to that. I'll see that every one of you murderers is tried and convicted after the battle.'

'If we live that long.'

'You'll live. You bastards will live all right. I don't know why, for God sakes, but bastards like you always live through anything.'

Long took the boy to a doctor himself. He wanted to make sure the doctor would treat him, but the boy was already dead. Long listened to his heart himself to make sure.

All the Japs, a hundred and ten of them, fell back from the three columns into the town's schoolhouse, which had concrete walls six feet thick to keep the heat out. They took their mortars with them and machine-guns and a radio and four prostitutes. They used the radio to ask for reinforcements. Aeroplanes came and bombed and strafed. Aeroplanes came every day, but they couldn't do themselves much good. There was too much jungle around there for them.

At two-thirty every morning one of the guerrillas would sneak into the church and set the church bell ringing while everybody else fired one shot. That was to make the Japs think it was a signal for an attack and use up their ammunition shooting all over the place. The Japs bit every time. They shot wildly for hours at every ricochet of one of their own bullets. But they had plenty of ammunition.

On the evening of the second day, the Zapantas wheeled their cannon into place. They spent all night, a whole excited crowd of them with everybody giving advice, aiming the cannon. There were no sights or calibrations on the cannon. They had to aim it by raising the limber with flat rocks. They waited for dawn to make sure everything was just right. Then everybody fell back and Mrs. Zapanta took the lanyard and pulled it. There was the biggest explosion ever heard on earth. The cannon leaped high into the air from the recoil, turned a complete somersault, landed on its barrel, then flipped over and began to bounce. It bounced so far back, Mrs. Zapanta had to run, but the shell had gone right through the six feet of concrete wall, tearing a hole a foot in diameter and banging concrete fragments into the Japs behind it. The Japs could be heard moaning and whimpering all day, but every time anybody showed himself they fired.

The gun was out of commission for two days after that. In the meantime, the guerrillas were busy taking all the supplies they needed in town. The Japs had used many of the houses to billet their men, and there were bodegas scattered everywhere. Major Dongalio made a dash across a cleared space and got into the municipal building. He forced the safe in the treasurer's office and got ninety thousand pesos real money and one hundred thousand Jap pesos. Then he found cases of Jap cigarettes. He threw them out of the window across the cleared space to where his men were hiding. But by the time he made the dash back, most of the cigarettes had vanished.

After midnight on the fifth day, Long brought his men up close to the schoolhouse for a dawn assault to be synchronized with the second shell from the cannon. They hoped to get across the cleared space around the schoolhouse under cover of night, lie low until the shell passed over their heads, then dash into the schoolhouse on top of it. The Japs had turkeys staked out in the clearing to serve as watchdogs. Long's men shot the turkeys the afternoon of the fourth day and early in the evening Long crawled into the clearing and got them. Then they all had turkey dinner together.

At first light, with dawn only minutes away, Long gave the signal and started creeping for the clearing. Looking around, he found only a few men following him. The rest were hanging back. It was very hard to see there. It was still quite dark. Finally Long made out eight men standing in single file behind one palm tree. They were all trying to keep the one tree between them and the Japs. Long waded into them with his shoes and gun butt, and hammered them out towards the clearing.

Then he ran around looking for more, but before he could find any, wham! the cannon went off and the Japs started firing back. There was only one man in the clearing, a fourteen-year-old boy. The Japs hit him. Long ran out and dragged his dead body to safety. Then the attack was over.

There could not be another. The barrel of the Zapanta cannon had peeled back like a banana. One of the prostitutes in the schoolhouse told the guerrillas later that if they had fired one more shell, the Japs would have surrendered.

The guerrillas now started to burn the town. Japs needed towns to live off. Towns made good collecting points for food, and Jap garrisons were always based on towns. All the people had run away from the fighting and to keep them from returning the guerrillas burned down every building and house in town except the concrete ones. Those they dynamited.

On the seventh day, Jap reinforcements came and the guerrillas withdrew with two motor launches and a whole wagon train of supplies.

The battle taught an important lesson in guerrilla tactics: Never attack a town; firing on troops in entrenched positions wastes too much ammunition.

Long looked very well when I saw him. His face bore no marks from Gidoka, and the scars on his sunburned legs looked hardly more than deeper streaks of sunburn.

'I don't sleep so well when I have nothing to do,' he said. 'I think too much. When I have something to do, I don't think at all but just do it and then I sleep like a baby.'

He told me he had put together the best combat company of guerrillas in the Philippines. 'I have weeded out all the slow joes.

My boys are as good as the best in the United States Army.' They had been working in malaria country and their Atabrine had been short. 'I thought of something to save on Atabrine and tried it out on myself,' he said. 'I dissolved one Atabrine pill in 5 cc. of water and then put it in me with a needle. It knocked hell out of the fever, the one pill did, and saved me using all that regular dose.' He was very proud of that.

Long had come down to the submarine for supplies. His next mission was to hold a river. There were no jungle paths along there, and if he could deprive the Japs of the river they would have to go miles around to keep contact between their garrisons.

The last I saw of Long, he was slouching along with his men, so sunburned and wild-haired that he looked very nearly like one of them.

'So long, kid,' I called. He was younger than I.

'Keep punching.' He waved back at me with his Garand.

The mission was very dangerous. The only way he had to patrol the river was by baroto. There was place for ambush all up and down the whole length of that damned river, and I never heard of Long again. I don't know whether he's alive or dead. Long Tom Baxter, United States Army Air Force. I sure hope he's alive. He was living on borrowed time the last I saw him, but I sure hope his credit continues good for ever. He had a wonderful smile. It was the kind of smile that takes over your heart completely and at once.

BY THE TIME MACARTHUR *was ready to retake the Philippines, the guerrillas were operating as a regular military unit. They furnished the information needed for the naval battle of the Philippines, and they backed up the invasion of the islands by the regulars. When Richardson met MacArthur, he was stunned to discover that the busy General had read every one of the information reports sent from the islands during the long isolation and knew the contents of each.*

FERDINAND

BY ERIC A. FELDT

OPERATION FERDINAND *is the story of the coast-watchers who gathered information in lonely jungle camps and treetops in the Japanese-infested islands of the South Pacific.*

The men of Ferdinand picked their symbol well. Like the famous bull they sat and watched, and then reported on improvised radios the messages which warned the Allies of raids, of invasions, of enemy activities wherever the Japanese were located. The coast-watchers prepared the way for the return of the Allies through the South Pacific and the great naval victories.

By strange and devious ways, thousands of miles behind Jap lines, these men were also able to rescue Allied airmen, evacuate civilians, and maintain control and sympathetic support of the natives.

But intelligence came first. With the coast-watchers' radio breaking the silence under the very eyes of the Japanese fleet and occupying army, the irregulars of Ferdinand became the Allied eyes of the South Pacific.

The Australians had long been conscious of their undefended coast, and in 1919 *they first started to link up the outer fringes by weaving a radio net operated by missionaries, plantation operators, farmers, harbour masters, schoolteachers, etc. When the Japanese began to threaten the islands in* 1939, *Eric A. Feldt, a retired naval officer, was assigned the task of vitalizing this radio net designated Operation Ferdinand. He based his headquarters at Port Moresby and began to pull the threads together to tie in Papua, the Solomons, and New Guinea.*

Commander Feldt's account of Cornelius Lyons Page, the watcher on Tabar Island, east of New Ireland on the outer perimeter of the coast-watcher defence, in many ways epitomizes the frustration, the improvisation, and, in the light of what was happening, the almost unreasonable faith which were the themes of the coast-watchers' existence in the six months after January, 1942. *It is the story of a man among his enemies, defiant almost to the extreme. This story of magnificent and tragic courage is also a story of a strange and hauntingly beautiful loyalty.*

PAGE was only thirty years old when Japan entered the war, but he was already a confirmed and seasoned islander. Brought up in a Sydney suburb, he had come to the islands with his parents at the age of nineteen.

In Rabaul, 'metropolis' of the North-east Area, he was given a job behind a counter in a store. But his eyes ranged far away beyond the hills that fringed the harbour. He met men who lived untrammelled lives (or so it seemed to him)—recruiters, miners, planters. The glamour of far places in the islands called him insistently, whispering of white beaches and palms in moonlight and of hot, still jungle, but not of loneliness and melancholy.

So Page left his job in Rabaul and settled on Massau Island, north-west of Kavieng. He took up land and commenced to plant it with coconuts, trading with the natives to pay his way. Personal freedom, complete freedom was his. His dream was realized. Now he had only to live it, unspurred by further ambition.

Days, unmarked, drifted to months, and months to years. Having no European neighbours, Page talked to natives, growing from a stranger to a familiar with them. Their thoughts impinged upon his, slowly at first, but shaping his ideas as time went by, as two stones rubbing together shape themselves to each other. He came, imperceptibly, to regard Massau, Kavieng, and the nearby islands as his country, indeed as his world, to feel that other places were nebulous and far away.

Big and virile, he enjoyed his life. And yet, under the overlay of his contentment, his heritage of energy, will, and pride, unchannelled towards a goal, was at odds with his environment. Aimlessly goaded to further adventure, at length he sold his plantation on Massau and went to Tabar, where traces of gold had been found. He tried prospecting, then took jobs here and there in the New Ireland area, never staying long in any.

Familiarity had bred an acceptance of the natives in a higher status, a place closer to himself, than the European generally concedes, and on Tabar Page took a young native girl, Ansin Bulu, to live with him. This was more than an outlet for excess sexual vitality. Through companionship the relation between the two developed into something much deeper than is usual in such liaisons.

When war broke out with Germany, Page felt the urge to fight, but it all seemed far away and not of his world and, undecided and restless, he let the days drift by. Then, when copra became all but unsaleable, a planter who decided to go after ready money gave him a job as manager of his plantation, Pigibut, on Simberi, one of three small islands in the Tabar group. Earlier a tele-radio had been lent to this planter by the Navy, and so with his plantation duties Page also undertook the coast-watching duties of his predecessor.

The island group was a small world of its own, its only connexion with the outside world an unreliable twenty-mile canoe journey to the nearest point on the New Ireland shore, and the occasional visits of copra ships. It was a backwater, a little group of land specks of no importance whatever.

On Simberi, in addition to the plantation which Page managed, there was one other plantation, managed by 'Sailor' Herterich. On Tatau Island, three miles to the south, a plantation was owned and managed by Jack Talmage. Talmage was an elderly veteran of World War I, a quiet man, respected by his neighbours. Sailor Herterich was not. He had settled in New Guinea when it was a German colony, but when the war was lost to Germany he became not so much German as the husband of a native woman, and so escaped deportation. In the years since, he had managed plantations, a lazy, unreliable man, who drifted along with the tide of life.

The other four plantations in the island group were owned by a firm and run by a succession of managers, transients who came, stayed awhile, and left. The only other inhabitants were the natives, who had the reputation of being idle, quarrelsome, and lacking in character.

With the outbreak of war with Japan, the Tabar group was immediately jolted from its inconsequential position in the outer nebula of New Guinea. Those who navigate aircraft differ little in their methods from the navigators of ships. After a long trip over open ocean, the navigator likes to make a landfall to fix his position. For Japanese pilots, flying from Truk to bomb Rabaul, the usual landfall was Tabar.

In the month that preceded the fall of Rabaul, Page kept watch for these planes, reporting them day and night. It is interesting to speculate on the possible difference this might have made in the course of the war, had there been a squadron of modern fighter aircraft at Rabaul instead of the antiquated Wirraways. Page's warnings would have given them time to reach altitude, intercept the unescorted bombers, and shoot them down like ducks. The enemy losses would have disorganized the Japanese capacity for long-range attack and reconnaissance. Perhaps Japan would have paused, given us time to move our forces to the area, and smash the enemy convoy when at last it moved, so that there would have been no campaign in the South-west and South Pacific. All a might-have-been, but if it had happened so, what fame would have been Page's!

While Page watched and signalled, Sailor Herterich considered his position. The Japanese would come, and then what would happen to Sailor? He had best be a German again, an ally of Japan. Busily he spread word among the natives that the Japanese would come and were to be treated as friends.

Page heard the whispers being passed around, and countered them. The Japanese would not come, he said, and if they did would soon be driven off. He, Page, was staying. The natives, hearing both opinions, uneasily reserved their decision.

Page's radio signals had not escaped the notice of the Japanese, and with the fall of Rabaul and Kavieng, he became a hunted man. Once they were established in the area, the Japanese promptly sent a warship to raid the plantation. Page had already moved his tele-radio to a hut in the jungle, however, and he was not discovered. When the ship had gone, he signalled over his tele-radio, reporting its departure.

At our headquarters in Townsville, Page's position appeared untenable. I signalled, 'You have done magnificent work. Your position is now dangerous if you continue reporting and under present circumstances your reports are of little value. You are to bury your tele-radio and may join either party on New Ireland or take other measures for safety. Good Luck.'

Page took no notice of the signal. He was on Simberi, a master who had told the natives he would stay. This was his world, his only frame of reference. He was fighting a war, but it was the Tabar War, his own war.

He continued to send signals concerning the extent of the Japanese occupation at Kavieng, the names of Europeans in the area who had been captured, enemy guns and defence positions.

In Townsville, we knew nothing of his local problems or his state of mind, but it was obvious that he had no intention of leaving. This being the case, the best course was to try to keep him quiet until a time came when his information would be of greatest use. A sudden complete silence might lead the Japanese to think he had gone. So we sent another signal: 'Your reports appreciated, but it is more important to keep yourself free. Do not transmit except in extreme emergency. You will be ordered to make reports when they will be of greatest value.'

Finally, as he still came on the air, we ordered him to cease transmission altogether, until ordered to recommence. Even this did little good. Such disobedience, inconceivable in any other war-time operation, was not too surprising in an islander. We had to accept it, interwoven as it was with other traits so valuable to us.

Meantime, extremely worried over the civilian status of men in Page's position, we were making recommendations that Page and others be given naval rank. Possibly rank would be no protection against a brutal enemy, but, even so, every aid was needed. Apart from its dubious advantages of personal safety, rank would permit us to pay the watchers and to provide for their dependants.

At long last, in March, 1942, the red tape was cut, and Page, unseen by authorities or doctors and without signing any forms, was commissioned a sub-lieutenant, Royal Australian Naval Volunteer Reserve, probably a happening without precedent.

On Tabar, as the natives watched events, they slowly began to lean towards Herterich and the Japanese, although Talmage supported Page to his utmost. Ironically, Page, the man who had been so close to native life and native thinking, was losing his influence and with it his control. In March, renegade natives from Kavieng, possibly encouraged by Herterich, looted the plantation and threatened to report Page's whereabouts to the Japanese.

Shortly after this event, Hans Pettersen, a half-caste, a fat, sly swine of a man who had been in disrepute since boyhood, came to live with Herterich. He too preached acceptance of the Japanese and gradually the natives' attitude towards Page drifted from uncertainty to positive opposition.

In view of these developments, it was problematical that Page's whereabouts could be kept secret even should we be able to impress upon him the need for discretion. We advised him to make for Buka, northernmost island of the Solomons, which was still clear of the enemy. Beset by an obstinacy which was aggravated by his dislike of Herterich and Pettersen, Page rejected the suggestion. His reply was to send a further list of captured Europeans and to warn that Namatani airfield on New Ireland was mined, information he had obtained by careful questioning of runaway natives.

Other radios were also on the air, and coast-watchers were listening to each other to glean any news they could. Page and a watcher on Bougainville were accustomed to chatter to each other in Kavieng dialect which both knew and which was as safe as any code.

Once tele-radio eavesdroppers heard two missionaries in Papua talking to each other when Page wanted to send an urgent signal. The missionaries were depressed as they discussed their prospects, and Page listened with growing impatience while one said, 'I will pray for you, Brother.'

The other replied, 'And I will pray for you, Brother.'

At this point, Page was heard to break in, 'Get off the ruddy air and I will pray for both of you.'

For his signals to headquarters, Page obtained new code key-words during communication with his mother in Australia, through names of persons and places woven into the conversation.

By the end of March, Page was a dot in a Japanese-held ocean. Every surrounding keypoint had been occupied and even thought of escape was futile, unless it could be managed by outside aid. Supply, too, was becoming impossible for him locally, with fewer and fewer natives supporting him. His plantation supplies were nearly consumed, and he had no arms whatever to defend himself. He moved into caves, and at one time only Ansin Bulu, his native wife, stood by him.

To drop supplies from an aircraft was the only solution, but our few aircraft were overworked and each trip threatened a loss that could ill be spared, while parachutes were as rare as diamonds.

So it was late in May before a drop could be made ready. Cap and badges of rank, food, a rifle, and ammunition were included in the supply packets. The pack containing the rifle jammed in the bomb-bay doors, during the drop, and had to be returned to Port Moresby in that position—just one of those things that happened. The other supplies, fortunately, were successfully dropped and found by Page.

Shortly afterwards his radio developed a fault in the voice trans-mission, and he had to send his signals laboriously by Morse, touch-ing two wires together in place of a key. The signals were hardly readable. Ken Frank, the Amalgamated Wireless man at Port Moresby, guessed the fault as a broken lead-in, and the whole part was dropped to Page by parachute, rectifying the fault—a fine feat of remote diagnosis.

The supplies, indicating outside support for Page, restored his prestige a little with the natives. But when he signalled that the Japanese were enrolling native police we knew that he could evade the enemy for very little longer. We decided to attempt to evacuate him.

Several United States submarines had recently arrived in Australia, and, with the help of the U.S. Naval Liaison Officer, a rescue trip and a rendezvous were arranged. Page at last agreed to take our advice and to make his escape on the vessel.

For three nights, Page kept the rendezvous, flashing the agreed signals from a torch in a small boat. Every flash must have seemed an invitation to unseen enemies. Every ripple of the water must have made his heart leap with hope of friend or fear of foe. Those three nights must have been a fairly complete catalogue of hope, desperation, and triumph over panic.

But no submarine came. Later we learned the vessel had developed a serious mechanical defect and had been hard put to limp back to port. These were old submarines, which had already taken a beating in the Philippines and were not to be compared with the models of efficiency which later operated in the South and South-western Pacific.

We made distracted attempts to get another submarine to undertake the mission, but there were other tasks of urgent strategical value and the Navy regretfully decided it could do no more.

In the meantime, Page signalled that a ship with Japanese, natives, and dogs was due on a certain day to hunt him. One of our aircraft, searching for the ship, could not find it, but during its hurried run bombed an old wreck to impress the natives with the fact that Page still had support.

When next we called Page on the radio, no answer came. The Air Force, in spite of the risk entailed, then sent a Catalina with a crew of nine on a last rescue attempt. The pilot, flying low around the island and searching carefully, saw only natives sitting stolidly on the beach, unmoving and giving no sign.

In 1944 an Australian Naval Officer put in at Tabar on a PT boat. A native told him how on June 16, 1942, the Japanese had captured Page and his planter friend, Talmage, while they slept. The two were taken with Ansin Bulu to Kavieng jail. After a few weeks Ansin Bulu was released, Page and Talmage executed. As the Australian Officer was leaving the island, an emaciated and aged-looking native woman came forward to meet him. Simply, she handed him a piece of toilet paper, dirty and crumpled. In faint pencil it read,

To C. O. Allied Forces
for Lieut.-Com. E. A. Feldt, R.A.N.
from Sub-Lieut. C. L. Page, R.A.N.V.R.
        9th July.
Re the female Ansin Bulu
        Nakapur Village
        Simberi Island, Tabar.

*This female has been in my service seven years. Has been of great value
to me since Jan. Japs looted all she owned value £50 put her in prison and
God knows what else. Her crime was she stuck. Sir, please do your best.*

Sub-Lieut. C. L. Page

SOURCES AND ACKNOWLEDGMENTS

The editor and publishers would like to record their gratitude to the authors, agents and publishers of the various books from which the stories in *Behind the Lines* have been taken, for their kindness in allowing this copyright material to be reproduced.

'Morgan's March on Panama' from *The History of the Buccaniers*, by John Esquemeling (Henry Smeeks).

'Partisans Against Napoleon' from *Journal of Partisan Warfare*, by Denis Davydov. Selected and translated from the Russian by F. E. Sommer.

'Ranger Mosby' from *Ranger Mosby*, by V. C. Jones. Oxford University Press.

'War Chief Victorio' from *Death in the Desert*, by Paul I. Wellman. Macmillan & Co., Ltd.

'Jagunço Rebellion' from *Revolt in the Backlands*, by Euclides da Cunha, tr. Samuel Putnam. Victor Gollancz Ltd.

'Caucasian Ferment' from *Unending Battle*, by H. C. Armstrong. By permission of the estate of the late H. C. Armstrong and the publishers. Longmans, Green & Co., Ltd.

'With Smuts on Commando' from *Commando*, by Deneys Reitz. Faber & Faber Ltd.

'Lawrence and the Arabs' from *Seven Pillars of Wisdom*, by T. E. Lawrence. Jonathan Cape Ltd. Also from *Secret Despatches from Arabia*, Golden Cockerel Press. By permission of A. W. Lawrence.

'Tunnel Warfare' from *Report from Red China*, by Harrison Forman. Robert Hale Ltd.

'Commandos at Vaagso' from *Commando*, by John Durnford-Slater. William Kimber & Co., Ltd.

'They Sought Out Rommel' from *The Green Beret: The Story of the Commandos, 1940–1945*, by Hillary St. George Saunders. Michael Joseph Ltd.

'Équipes Boulaya' from *Maquis*, by George Millar. William Heinemann Ltd.

'Maquis Notebook' from *Army of Shadows*, by Joseph Kessel, tr. H. Chevalier. Cresset Press Ltd.

'Mission for a Dictator' from *Skorzeny's Secret Missions*, by Otto Skorzeny, tr. J. Le Clerq. E. P. Dutton & Co., Inc.

'Secret Army' from *Secret Army*, by T. Bor-Komorowski. Victor Gollancz Ltd.

'Daniele—Četnik' from *Irregular Adventure*, by Christie Lawrence. Faber & Faber Ltd.

'Ratweek for Tito' and 'Operation Pongo' from *Eastern Approaches*, by Fitzroy Maclean. Jonathan Cape Ltd.

'Sons of the Eagle' from *Sons of the Eagle*, by Julian Amery. Macmillan & Co., Ltd.

'Island Ambush' from *A War of Shadows*, by W. Stanley Moss. T. V. Boardman & Co., Ltd.

'Spread of Alarm' from *Private Army*, by Vladimir Peniakoff. Jonathan Cape Ltd.

'Night Attack' from *American Guerrilla: Fighting Behind the Enemy Lines*, by Douglas M. Smith and Cecil Carnes. The Bobbs-Merrill Co., Inc.

'Gideon Force' from *Guerrilla War in Abyssinia*, by W. E. D. Allen. Penguin Books Ltd.

'Crossing the Shweli' from *Beyond the Chindwin*, by Bernard Fergusson. William Collins, Sons & Co. Ltd.

'Chindit 76' (William Drury) from *Chindit Column 76*, by W. A. Wilcox. Orient Longmans Ltd., Calcutta.

'Mad Fortnight' from *The Jungle is Neutral*, by F. Spencer Chapman. Chatto & Windus Ltd.

'American Guerrilla' from *American Guerrilla in the Philippines*, by Ira Wolfert. Victor Gollancz Ltd.

'Ferdinand' from *Coast Watchers*, by Eric A. Feldt. Oxford University Press.